T0314969

Praise for *Behavioral Science in the Wild*

"I loved reading *Behavioral Science in the Wild*. It's a great collection of essays on how to apply insights from behavioral science to interventions that will actually work. Mažar and Soman are the world experts on designing successful interventions, and they have assembled an impressive list of authors who explain the complexity of behavioral interventions in clear and simple terms. The result is a guide that is both practical and fun. If you design behavioral interventions, you need to read it. If you're curious about the behavioral science, you'll enjoy reading it. If, like me, you're both, it's a double win."

Ayelet Fishbach, Jeffrey B. Keller Professor of Behavioral Science and Marketing, University of Chicago Booth School of Business and author of *Get It Done: Surprising Lessons from the Science of Motivation*

"This book shines a wise and nuanced light on the study of behavioral insights. It helps us understand the questions of when interventions will work and how large of an effect we can expect. A great collection of case studies supplements important discussion of how to do interventions effectively. The field will be better and more effective because of this book."

Eric J. Johnson, Norman Eig Professor of Business, Columbia Business School, Columbia University and author of *The Elements of Choice*

"This is an absolute gold mine of practical wisdom from deep experts in real-world applications of behavioral science. It's brimming with examples that give precious guidance on what to expect when science makes the leap from laboratory to real life – leaving the reader feeling both informed and inspired to rise to the challenge. A precious resource for anyone serious about driving change in their company or community."

Caroline Webb, author *How to Have a Good Day: Harness the Power of Behavioral Science to Transform Your Working Life*

Behaviourally Informed
Organizations

BEHAVIOURALLY INFORMED ORGANIZATIONS

To date, there has been a lack of practical advice for organizations based on behavioral research. The Behaviourally Informed Organizations series fills this knowledge gap with a strategic perspective on how governments, businesses, and other organizations have embedded behavioral insights into their operations. The series is rooted in work by academics and practitioners co-creating knowledge via the Behaviourally Informed Organizations Partnership (www.biorgpartnership.com), and is written in a highly accessible style to highlight key ideas, pragmatic frameworks, and prescriptive outcomes based on illustrative case studies.

Also in the series:

The Behaviorally Informed Organization, edited by Dilip Soman and Catherine Yeung

Behavioral Science in the Wild

EDITED BY NINA MAŽAR AND DILIP SOMAN

UNIVERSITY OF TORONTO PRESS
Toronto Buffalo London

Rotman-UTP Publishing
An imprint of University of Toronto Press
Toronto Buffalo London
utorontopress.com

Library and Archives Canada Cataloguing in Publication

Title: Behavioral science in the wild / edited by Nina Mažar and Dilip
   Soman.
Names: Mažar, Nina, editor. | Soman, Dilip, editor.
Description: Series statement: Behaviourally informed organizations | Includes
   bibliographical references.
Identifiers: Canadiana (print) 20220162344 | Canadiana (ebook) 20220162352 | ISBN
   9781487527518 (cloth) | ISBN 9781487527532 (EPUB) | ISBN 9781487527525 (PDF)
Subjects: LCSH: Organizational behavior. | LCSH: Industrial management –
   Psychological aspects. | LCSH: Human behavior. | LCSH: Psychology, Industrial.
Classification: LCC HD58.7 .B423 2022 | DDC 302.3/5 – dc23

ISBN 978-1-4875-2751-8 (cloth)
ISBN 978-1-4875-2753-2 (EPUB)
ISBN 978-1-4875-2752-5 (PDF)

We wish to acknowledge the land on which the University of Toronto Press operates. This land is the traditional territory of the Wendat, the Anishnaabeg, the Haudenosaunee, the Métis, and the Mississaugas of the Credit First Nation.

University of Toronto Press acknowledges the financial support of the Government of Canada and the Ontario Arts Council, an agency of the Government of Ontario, for its publishing activities.

Canada Council   Conseil des Arts
for the Arts   du Canada

ONTARIO ARTS COUNCIL
CONSEIL DES ARTS DE L'ONTARIO
an Ontario government agency
un organisme du gouvernement de l'Ontario

Funded by the   Financé par le
Government   gouvernement
of Canada   du Canada

Canadä

Contents

Preface ix

Acknowledgments xvii

Part One: The Translation and Scaling Challenge

1 The Science of Translation and Scaling 5
   DILIP SOMAN AND NINA MAŽAR

2 When Governments Use Nudges: Measuring Impact "At Scale" 20
   ELIZABETH LINOS

3 Prescriptions for Successfully Scaling Behavioral Interventions 28
   LAURA GOODYEAR, TANJIM HOSSAIN, AND DILIP SOMAN

4 The Last Yard Problem: Tailoring of Behavioral Interventions for Scale 42
   PIYUSH TANTIA, SAUGATO DATTA, ALISSA FISHBANE, AND CASSIE TAYLOR

5 The Limited Importance of External Validity in Experimental Economics 52
   COLIN F. CAMERER

Part Two: Some Popular Behavioral Interventions

6 Why Many Behavioral Interventions Have Unpredictable Effects in the Wild: The Conflicting Consequences Problem 65

INDRANIL GOSWAMI AND OLEG URMINSKY

7 Norm Nudging: How to Measure What We Want to Implement 82

CRISTINA BICCHIERI

8 The Fresh-Start Effect: Motivational Boosts beyond New Year's Resolutions 108

JASON RIIS, HENGCHEN DAI, AND KATHERINE L. MILKMAN

9 Reminders: Their Value and Hidden Costs 120

CHRISTINA GRAVERT

Part Three: Domain-Specific Behavior Change Challenges

10 Applying Behavioral Insights to Cultivate Diversity and Inclusion 135

JOYCE C. HE, GRUSHA AGARWAL, AND SONIA K. KANG

11 Sustainable Nudges for the Wild: Recommendations from SHIFT 153

DAVID J. HARDISTY, KATHERINE WHITE, RISHAD HABIB, AND JIAYING ZHAO

12 START Communicating Effectively: Best Practices for Educational Communications 170

JESSICA LASKY-FINK AND CARLY D. ROBINSON

13 A Psychological "Vaccine" against Fake News: From the Lab to Worldwide Implementation 188

SANDER VAN DER LINDEN AND JON ROOZENBEEK

14 Developing Effective Healthy Eating Nudges   207
ROMAIN CADARIO AND PIERRE CHANDON

15 Wellness Rewarded: A "How To" on Designing Behavioral
Science–Informed Financial Incentives to Improving Health
(That Work)   219
MARC MITCHELL AND RENANTE RONDINA

16 Increasing Blood and Plasma Donations: Behavioral and
Ethical Scalability   230
NICOLA LACETERA AND MARIO MACIS

17 Evidence-Based Interventions for Financial
Well-Being   250
DANIEL FERNANDES

18 Financial Inclusion: Lab-Based Approaches for Consumer
Protection Policymaking in the Wild   263
RAFE MAZER

Part Four: Tools and Techniques

19 Implementing Behavioral Science Insights with Low-Income
Populations in the Global South   277
CHANING JANG, NEELA A. SALDANHA, ANISHA SINGH,
AND JENNIFER ADHIAMBO

20 If You Want People to Accept Your Intervention, Don't Be
Creepy   284
PATRICIA DE JONGE, PEETER VERLEGH,
AND MARCEL ZEELENBERG

21 Digital Nudging: Using Technology to Nudge for
Good   292
MICHAEL SOBOLEV

22 To Apply and Scale Behavioral Insights Effectively,
    Practitioners Must Be Scientific   300
    NATHANIEL BARR, MICHELLE C. HILSCHER, ADA LÊ,
    DAVID R. THOMSON, AND KELLY PETERS

23 It's All about the SOUL! Why Sort, Order, and Use Labeling
    Results in Smart Scorecards   309
    CLAIRE HEARD, ELENA REUTSKAJA, AND BARBARA FASOLO

24 Applying Behavioral Interventions in a New Context   316
    BARNABAS SZASZI, KRISZTIAN KOMANDI, NANDOR HAJDU,
    AND ELIZABETH TIPTON

Contributors   323

Preface

Nina Mažar and Dilip Soman

Over the past several years, governments, for-profit enterprises, welfare organizations, and other entities have increasingly started relying on findings from the behavioral sciences to develop more "human-compliant" products, processes, and experiences for their internal and external stakeholders. This growth was perhaps catalyzed by the 2008 book *Nudge* by Richard Thaler and Cass Sunstein, and the subsequent establishment of the first-ever behavioral insights team within the government in the United Kingdom in 2010.

A SCIENCE OF USING BEHAVIORAL SCIENCE

The two of us were part of a group of scholars at the University of Toronto who were instrumental in setting up a center called BEAR (Behavioural Economics in Action at Rotman) with a simple and clear objective. We had heard from several practitioners both in governments and in business that the ideas raised by books such as Richard H. Thaler and Cass Sunstein's *Nudge* and Dan Ariely's *Predictably Irrational* were tantalizing and appealing. However, practitioners lacked an understanding of the process that they could use to generate ideas like these, and to embed the science within their organization. Our goal at that stage was to create a platform for academics and practitioners to co-create knowledge that would help better embed the behavioral science in practice. We were hoping to create a science of how to use behavioral science.

More recently, an international partnership of academics and practitioners (www.biorgpartnership.com) housed at the BEAR research center contends that while behavioral science is growing, the benefits that it offers to organizations have not been harnessed anywhere close to their potential. In developing a science of using behavioral science, the partnership identified two major challenges. The first has to do with preparing organizations to use behavioral science most effectively. This preparation includes the development of appropriate resources like experimentation, expertise, and the agility to be able to respond to learnings from experiments, as well as an appreciation of the scientific method, and active efforts at pushing down the cost of experimentation. A previous book from this partnership (*The Behaviorally Informed Organization*, edited by Dilip Soman and Catherine Yeung) presented some of the partnership's work in this area. The second major challenge, as the field has grown and as practitioners have become more involved in the co-creation of interventions, has to do with *knowledge translation and scaling*. In an effort to simplify a seemingly complex science and to draw more people into the field, many organizations had started developing simple heuristics – frameworks or rules of thumb – for designers of intervention to follow as they tried to solve complex social problems. These rules of thumb did indeed play a big role in popularizing the science and communicating its key ideas.

However, one of the hallmarks of research in our field is the idea of context-dependence. An intervention based on successes in a particular context and with a particular type of target audience might not work well in a different context and substantive domain, or a with a different audience. As the imprint of behavioral science began to spread from simple laboratory and pilot demonstrations into a) more scaled-up versions and b) newer domains that had not been the topic of inquiry in the past, these context dependencies started to show up in starker form. These issues are precisely the focal topic of the present book.

FROM THE LAB TO THE FIELD

For the purposes of this book, we use the term "practitioner" to mean any entity that is conducting applied behavioral work outside the well-controlled environment of the laboratory. Thus, a practitioner could include employees of either the academic or non-academic sectors who are working to create behavior change to meet an organizational goal and not for the sake of creating knowledge alone.

Consider a behavioral practitioner who reads an academic paper showing a strong effect of a specific intervention on a particular behavior. This practitioner looks to use a similar intervention in their world, perhaps by taking the idea from the paper and embedding it into an existing touchpoint (say, by changing a form, or by updating a website), or by creating additional touchpoints (perhaps text message reminders, or mailings). After conducting a field trial, they conclude that the intervention was not nearly as effective as it was in the original demonstration that they read about. As we'll learn in this book, this is not an uncommon occurrence. Indeed, a recent paper (discussed in Chapter 2) showed that when published interventions were reproduced in applied settings, their effect sizes tended to be significantly smaller. This reduction in effect size in translating from the lab into the wild has been labeled as a voltage drop (for a detailed discussion, see Chapter 3).

There are a number of reasons why a voltage drop occurs. First, there is an academic publication bias whereby research with the highest effect sizes is the most likely to get published. Second, the wilderness of the real world presents additional challenges that are not immediately obvious in laboratory or RCT (randomized control trial) settings. Not only is "the wild" manifested in additional contextual variables that might change results, but there is also heterogeneity in terms of how recipients of interventions respond to these treatments. The effectiveness of the intervention might weaken in the wild, or might even backfire because the target audience reacts differently to the intervention or because the intervention creates additional psychological processes that might cancel and overpower the original effect.

More generally, it is important for an applied behavioral scientist to get a more nuanced understanding of effects from published research. When do the tested interventions work and when do they not? Under what conditions are they especially effective? For what kinds of populations are their effects the most pronounced and how might they interact with other variables? The goal of this volume is to develop a nuanced framework for how we should think about translating research and then scaling it from our labs and from pilot studies into the field. In particular, what prescriptive advice can we give to a practitioner who reads about a research finding in a published paper and is wondering about whether and how they should incorporate that finding into their own behavior change challenge?

BEHAVIORAL SCIENCE IN THE WILD

Our book is organized into four parts. The first part presents an overview of scaling and translation challenges, a framework for how to think about why these challenges occur, and a series of prescriptions for practitioners as they are looking to learn from the work of others and embed it into their own behavior change challenge. In Chapter 1, we present some factors that determine how knowledge from academic publications eventually makes its way into practice. We contend that a practitioner first needs to be aware of the behavioral science, then needs to make sure that the organization is adequately prepared to be able to use a behavioral approach, then identify evidence that is relevant to the behavior change challenge at hand and assess the relevance of that evidence. Finally, they need to implement learnings from published work, test, and then scale up. We believe that there might be obstacles at each of these stages. In Chapter 2, Linos illustrates one such obstacle – the idea of a publication bias whereby published research is significantly more likely to show larger effect sizes than unpublished work. This can often create overconfidence in the abilities of behavioral science. In Chapter 3, Goodyear, Hossain, and Soman make the case for a) developing a practice of relentlessly testing every intervention in the context (i.e., in-situ) where it will be deployed and b) embracing heterogeneity and developing the ability to customize interventions as a function of who the recipient is, a tailored approach. In Chapter 4, Datta and colleagues from ideas42 discuss a series of examples that illustrate some of these scaling challenges. And in Chapter 5, Camerer makes the provocative argument that not all research and all experiments need to have external validity (i.e., need to be immediately applicable to settings in the wild). In particular, he argues that the goal of basic science is not always to respect external validity and that, in many cases, research without external validity can also be of immense practical value.

Four chapters in Part Two of the book look at popular behavioral interventions and take a deeper dive into questions such as "When do they work?" "Do they always work?" and "What have we learned about how to best design these interventions?" In Chapter 6, Goswami and Urminsky present a general framework for thinking about why interventions don't always work across a diversity of settings and illustrate their framework using three specific case studies. In Chapter 7, Bicchieri looks at norm nudging – the practice of informing individuals about others' behaviors and beliefs – and discusses the conditions under which making norms salient increases compliance with those norms. In addition to the examples in the chapter, norm nudging has been widely used in a number of different domains recently, including World Bank projects on gender equity in the labor market and toilet use in India,[1] and behavioral interventions to tackle the water crisis in South Africa.[2] In Chapter 8, Riis, Dai, and Milkman discuss the fresh-start effect – the idea that there are some points of time at which people are more motivated to take action and change behavior, and that these moments should be harnessed in order to encourage behavior change. Finally, in Chapter 9, Gravert discusses the value of sending behaviorally informed reminders as well as their hidden costs. She makes the point that if reminders are mindlessly used, they may backfire for a multitude of reasons.

Nine chapters in Part Three of the book home in on specific domains of behavior changes, review what we know has (and has not) worked, and offer prescriptive solutions to practitioners in those relevant domain areas. These areas include diversity and inclusion (Chapter 10, by He, Agarwal, and Kang), sustainability (Chapter 11, by Hardisty and colleagues), education (Chapter 12, by Lasky-Fink and Robinson), misinformation (Chapter 13, by van der Linden and Roozenbeek), healthy eating (Chapter 14, by Cadario and Chandon), wellness and healthy behaviors (Chapter 15, by Mitchell and Rondina), blood and plasma donations (Chapter 16, by Lacetera and Macis), financial well-being (Chapter 17, by Fernandes), and financial inclusion with a focus on consumer financial protection particularly in the context of emerging markets and digital financial services (Chapter 18, by Mazer). These chapters not only highlight issues to watch out for in translating and scaling knowledge but also start to shed light on how to best translate extant knowledge into regulation as well as policy by both governments and businesses.

Six chapters in Part Four, the final part of the book, provide a series of succinct tools and frameworks to guide academics as well as practitioners. In Chapter 19, Jang and colleagues from the Busara Center outline prescriptions for implementing behavioral insights in low-income population countries in the Global South. In Chapter 20, de Jonge, Verlegh, and Zeelenberg make a case for helping the practitioner understand whether citizens and consumers will accept their interventions and what they can do to increase acceptance. In Chapter 21, Sobolev applies the concept of nudging in digital environments. In Chapter 22, Barr and colleagues from BEworks discuss how best to use behavioral insights to drive behavior in businesses in domains ranging from finance to energy and health. In Chapter 23, Heard, Reutskaja, and Fasolo make a case for why designers of scorecards (a common behavioral intervention) need to consider how to sort, order, and label in order to create more effective scorecards. Finally, in Chapter 24, Szaszi and colleagues discuss things to keep in mind when developing behavioral interventions in a completely new context.

As we continue on the journey of developing a science of using behavioral science, we believe that this volume represents an important step in ensuring that the science is used in a scientific manner when transferred and scaled into the wild. Along the way, authors in this volume have touched on a number of critical issues. Is the

organization ready to be scientific? Does the organization understand that the nature of evidence in the behavioral sciences is fundamentally different from evidence in other sciences that are not
as context-dependent? What are specific tips and guidelines that
applied behavioral scientists need to keep in mind as they embrace
the science and use it to develop interventions to influence stakeholder behavior appropriately? We are confident that the reader will
finish this book feeling that they have gained the ability to think
about the behavioral sciences differently, to be more critical of the
evidence that is presented to them, and to ask the right questions,
but also to develop the right tools (for example, quick testing) so
as to adapt the findings appropriately to help them solve their
problems.

Nina Mažar, Boston, USA
Dilip Soman, Toronto, Canada

NOTES

1 Project descriptions available at The World Bank Mind, Behavior, and Development.
   (n.d.). Retrieved from https://www.worldbank.org/en/programs/embed#1
   on June 23, 2021.
2 Martinus, A., & Naru, F. (2020, October 19). How Cape Town used behavioral science
   to beat its water crisis. Retrieved from https://behavioralscientist.org/how-cape
   -town-used-behavioral-science-to-beat-its-water-crisis/ on June 23, 2021.

Acknowledgments

The co-editors thank all the members of the Behaviourally Informed Organizations partnership (biorgpartnership.com) housed at the Behavioural Economics in Action at Rotman [BEAR] research center for their many comments and suggestions on the manuscript. Special thanks are due to Cindy Luo for managing the book project, to Bing Feng and Liz Kang for their tireless work on managing the partnership, and to Renante Rondina, Matthew Hilchey, and Karrie Chou for their contributions to the discussions and for feedback. We also thank members of the steering committee and the internal review board of the partnership – Abigail Dalton, Dale Griffin, Melanie Kim, Katy Milkman, Kyle Murray, Kelly Peters, Sasha Tregebov, Melaina Vinski, and Min Zhao. This book is made possible thanks to funding by BEAR, and through the partnership grant program of the Social Sciences and Humanities Research Council of Canada (SSHRC).

The material in Chapter 3 originated as a commentary in the journal *Behavioural Public Policy*, published by Cambridge University Press. The citation for the original article is Soman, D., & Hossain, T. (2021). Successfully scaled solutions need not be homogenous. *Behavioural Public Policy*, 5(1), 80–9. doi:10.1017/bpp.2020.24. Chapter 3 is an expanded and updated version of this article. We also acknowledge Iris Deng (Instagram: @deng.it) as the illustrator for Figure 3.1.

BEHAVIORAL SCIENCE IN THE WILD

PART ONE

The Translation and Scaling Challenge

CHAPTER ONE

The Science of Translation and Scaling

Dilip Soman and Nina Mažar

APPLIED BEHAVIORAL SCIENCE COMES OF AGE

Since the publication of *Nudge*[1] in 2008 and the subsequent introduction of the Behavioural Insights Team in the UK government (followed by similar units in many countries around the world), the use of behavioral insights to design interventions for changing citizens' behavior has been commonplace.[2] The field of applied behavioral insights has proliferated rapidly in the past few years. This proliferation has not only taken the form of organizations, departments, and units that specialize in behavioral interventions, but also of a large group of practitioners[3] interested in creating real-world behavior change and citizens with a general interest in the field. There have been active communities of practice, Twitter discussions, meetups, podcasts, and blogs in this area. Indeed, the growth of the applied behavioral science field over the past decade has wildly surpassed expectations.

In hindsight, it is easy to see why the field has become popular. Books like *Nudge, Thinking, Fast and Slow*,[4] *Predictably Irrational*,[5] and *Misbehaving*[6] offered the promise of seemingly simple, low-cost, and scalable interventions that organizations could adopt to create large changes in stakeholder behavior. And the claim that all organizations – governments, businesses, not-for-profits, policy units, startups, and even universities – are fundamentally in the business of behavior change rang true for practitioners.[7] If the fictitious cafeteria in *Nudge* could encourage people to eat healthy foods simply by changing the manner in which food was displayed, or a magazine could encourage consumers to purchase pricier subscriptions by using a decoy product, many felt they could use the same tactic to increase demand for their products. If changing defaults (Chapter 6), social norms (Chapter 7), the fresh-start effect (Chapter 8), or reminders (Chapter 9) are indeed general phenomena that work to change behavior, it is tempting to believe that they can be generalized from one particular context at a particular point in time to other contexts and other domains. And it is also true that we have seen a large number of successes in using behavioral science to solve social[8] and business problems[9] across a multitude of contexts.

THREE CAUTIONARY TALES

Despite the apparent ease of influencing human behavior and the seeming simplicity of many of the interventions, behavioral interventions haven't always been successful in making the jump from our laboratories and trials to the field in fully scaled formats. Consider the following examples.

Researchers in the Netherlands ran an experiment and a large-scale field trial in partnership with the retail bank ING to study the effect of social norms on increasing nest egg savings by Dutch households.[10] Their intervention was inspired by a great amount of research showing that informing people that their actions deviate from those of others can motivate them to change their behavior to become more consistent. In an often-quoted example, the Behavioural Insights Team showed that providing information on what percentage of people in one's local area paid taxes on time, and highlighting that someone is in the minority who deviates from that described social norm, increased the likelihood that one paid tax.[11]

Households in the treatment condition of the study in the Netherlands received an otherwise identical email to households in the control condition with one extra sentence that read: "You have a lower buffer with us than most other ING clients in your neighborhood."

Results showed that the intervention did indeed stimulate these households to display different behaviors; they clicked more on the link in the email bringing them to their automatic savings page. However, despite what one may describe as increased savings intentions, researchers did not find an effect of the social norm intervention on the number of automatic savings transactions, nor on the automatic savings amount or the buffer savings more generally. (For a review of interventions to increase financial well-being, see Chapter 17.)

Why did this happen? The authors explored various explanations, such as that the effects may have varied over time or across groups of customers. After all, it is reasonable to assume that the nudge only had an effect at the beginning when it was new, or only much later after households had a chance to adjust their spending patterns. Similarly, the nudge may have worked only on those with more favorable cash flows that allowed for more opportunities to increase savings, or only in more homogeneous neighborhoods, where a social norm nudge may be more relevant to a customer. Finally, the authors explored whether perhaps customers had found out about the different conditions from other customers, which may have contaminated the experiment. But none of these potential explanations seemed to play a role. Thus, we are left to speculate that perhaps the context needed for an effect to translate to the final outcome was far from ideal. While the intervention might clearly have increased interest and intention to save (click-through rate), the actual effort required to increase savings rates might have been complex, or perhaps there were additional unknown demands and constraints on households that acted as barriers to saving. This example illustrates a fundamental point – behavioral interventions might indeed point citizens towards the right behaviors, but there might be so much sludge[12] or complexity in the system that mere increases in intention do not translate to actual outcomes.

In another well-cited paper on organ donations,[13] the authors presented data on organ donation consent rates from several European countries and found a striking pattern; these data were highly bi-modal. In explaining the very-high-or-very-low consent rates, the authors correctly pointed out two differences in the process that citizens need to go through to be considered as organ donors. In some countries (the ones with low consent rates), citizens needed to actively complete paperwork to be organ donors. On the other hand, in countries with higher consent rates, all citizens were presumed to be donors unless they actively opted out. Unfortunately, this descriptive conclusion has often been misinterpreted as prescriptive advice. In particular, many commentators have suggested that a simple way for countries to increase organ donation rates is to shift from an opt-in to an opt-out system. Indeed, the government of Wales did so in 2015, as did the UK in 2020. Interestingly, though, research suggests that despite an increase in Welsh donor registrations, the new system has not really resulted in an increase in the supply of organs.[14] How do we reconcile this conclusion with the data presented by Johnson and Goldstein? (For a related review of interventions to increase blood and plasma donations, see Chapter 16.)

The use of defaults to influence behavior is common.[15] A computer manufacturer who sells online might discover that setting the default purchase to the high-end configuration (and allowing people to remove features that they don't want) versus the low-end configuration (and allowing consumers to add features) results in an increase in revenue. But there are two fundamental differences between the computer example and organ donation. First, the computer example involves a single-stage decision – changing the default changes of the configuration chosen (and hence revenue). For organ donation, changing the default may have an effect on consent rates, but not on whether an organ is actually donated. Actual donation requires the consent of next of kin after the donor's death. Therefore, the second difference is that the computer purchase decision is typically made by a single entity, the buyer, while the organ donation involves two entities – the donor and the next of kin.

It is now easy to see the challenges associated with using the simple default intervention to improve the supply of donated organs. Not only are people who have actively opted in to be organ donors more likely to express their wishes to their families but also, even if they do not, there is little ambiguity for the surviving family about the deceased's wishes, and therefore, their death is more likely to result in the harvesting and supply of a donated organ. People who are on the registry simply by virtue of failing to opt out will likely have no such discussions with their family, and thus there is a lot of ambiguity for the surviving family about the deceased's wishes.[16]

A third cautionary tale comes from researchers in Germany who developed a smartphone app that randomized a goal-setting nudge in an attempt to reduce electricity consumption.[17] The app prompted users to set energy consumption targets. Users in the treatment condition were informed about whether they had actually reached their goal and received either positive affirmation (a thumbs-up) if they succeeded or a negative (thumbs-down) if they failed. Previous research has also shown that goal setting increases the likelihood that the person setting the goal will comply with the target.[18] In contrast, this study found no significant effect of the goal-setting prompt on electricity consumption. While it might be tempting to dismiss these results by concluding that "goal setting does not work," there were important contextual differences that made this study different from other successful ones. Unlike earlier studies, participants in this study self-selected into it. The roll-out of the app was promoted by a mass-marketing campaign and financial incentives, but the demand for the energy app in the general customer population was low (the authors' most optimistic estimate was that only 2% of customers took up the app). What is more, their data suggests that the primary customers who took up the app were those already motivated to conserve energy with low consumption levels before the start of the study. In addition to this unfavorable selection bias, the study found that the nudge significantly reduced the probability of using the app over time. (For a review of interventions to increase sustainable behavior, see Chapter 11.)

Goal-setting interventions clearly worked in studies designed to motivate people to get their colonoscopies, or to pay off their credit card debt.[19] However, it's the factors that are oftentimes less discussed in an academic paper, such as characteristics of the target behavior (i.e., one-time versus repeated), the medium and timing that are used to deliver the intervention, the actual design of the user interface and feedback messages, and the way participants are selected and attention to the intervention is ensured, that matter at least as much as the actual message intervention. Transplanting a study from a carefully controlled environment (like a plant grown in a nursery) into the wild (a plantation) where additional factors play a role can result in failure. We also note that failures arising from transplantation are not exclusive to governments or to social and welfare initiatives – for-profit businesses are also susceptible to similar failures. Failures in the social welfare domain are simply more likely to be published.

A NUANCED PERSPECTIVE

To balance all of the successes, our three stories offer a cautionary tale. We find that successful results in the lab or in pilots might not translate and scale because of four (and possibly more) reasons.

1. **Additional Constraints.** The intervention might indeed be successful in getting people to change intention and be motivated to change behavior, but "the wild" might impose sludge, competing priorities and distractions.
2. **Indirect Measures of Success.** The practitioner takes an intervention that has an effect on one outcome measure (e.g., consent rates) and uses it to solve a problem on another outcome measure (e.g., organ supply).
3. **Limited Attention.** The noise "in the wild" might reduce attention to or salience of the intervention, and thus the intervention might not even be noticed by everyone.
4. **Heterogeneity.** There is considerably greater variance in both recipients, with their motivations and habits, and contexts.

These factors combine to produce an overall reduction in the effectiveness of interventions when they are transplanted from the lab to the field and then scaled up. This phenomenon has been called a "voltage drop."[20]

To better understand why these voltage drops occur, it is important to understand the process that a practitioner might follow when applying academic research insights. Based on a series of interviews

Figure 1.1. Six stages in the process of translating and scaling academic research

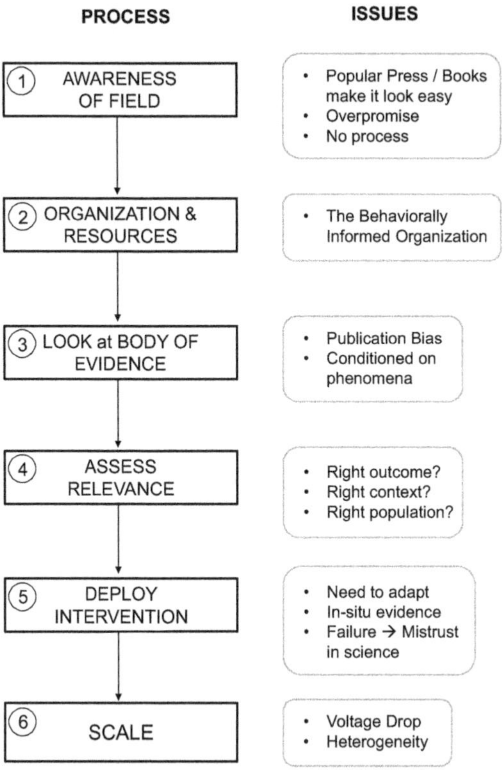

PROCESS   ISSUES

PROCESS	ISSUES
(1) AWARENESS OF FIELD	• Popular Press / Books make it look easy • Overpromise • No process
(2) ORGANIZATION & RESOURCES	• The Behaviorally Informed Organization
(3) LOOK at BODY OF EVIDENCE	• Publication Bias • Conditioned on phenomena
(4) ASSESS RELEVANCE	• Right outcome? • Right context? • Right population?
(5) DEPLOY INTERVENTION	• Need to adapt • In-situ evidence • Failure → Mistrust in science
(6) SCALE	• Voltage Drop • Heterogeneity

Note: While this figure depicts the process as a linear one, in reality there is a lot of iteration back and forth between stages. This simplified version is meant to highlight the six stages, and not to be an accurate representation of the true complexities of the process.

and conversations with a diverse set of practitioners, we identified six stages in the knowledge translation process. A simple, stylized, and seemingly linear version of a more comprehensive process is presented in Figure 1.1. Our goal in presenting this framework is simply to serve as a basis of discussion and not to accurately portray the complexities of this process. In reality, there is a lot of iteration and back-and-forth between the six stages on this process.

The process starts with developing an **awareness of the field**. This usually happens through the popular press and books like *Nudge*, *Predictably Irrational*, and *Thinking, Fast and Slow*. The authors of these books have done a tremendous service to the field of applied behavioral insights by awakening practitioners to its many possibilities. Yet the nature of the book publishing process creates some insidious messages. In an effort to highlight the promise of the field, books typically focus primarily on successes and not failures. In order to enhance readability, authors tend to leave out all of the concrete (boring) details underlying successful interventions, therefore inadvertently portraying the field as "easy to do." Consequently, readers might have unreasonable expectations about how easy it is to design and deploy interventions, and about the likelihood of these interventions being successful.

In order to harness the promise of behavioral insights, the practitioner needs to ensure that their **organization** has the right **resources**. The behaviorally informed organization needs to have an empirical mindset, the willingness to relentlessly experiment, iterate, and customize its products and processes, and the agility to be able to respond to the learnings from experimentation.[21] Many success stories are from organizations that have implemented these steps, and it is likely that not all organizations could replicate them.

The next stage in addressing a specific behavior change problem is to look at the **body of published evidence**. This usually takes the form of published academic papers, grey literature, and research reports. In reading through the extant literature, the practitioner will notice two things. First, the literature is replete with examples of successful interventions. It has only been in recent years that null effects have started appearing in the literature. As Chapter 2 discusses, there is a significant publication bias – studies with stronger results are more likely to be published, and therefore, a reading of the published literature is not representative of what might actually happen in the wild. Second, the literature is typically conditioned on theories or phenomena and not on practical problems.[22] For example, it is easier to find papers on behavioral phenomena such as framing effects, social comparisons, or fresh-start effects than it is to find papers on practical problems like improving health, educational outcomes, informativeness, diversity, and inclusion – something that we try to address in Part Three of this book. Academics are incentivized to become experts on theories and phenomena and not on applications. This makes it difficult for the practitioner to find examples of interventions that might fit their particular behavior change challenge.

Next, practitioners need to **assess the relevance of evidence**. This is perhaps the most important stage, yet many practitioners report that there is no systematic way of assessing whether the evidence from the published literature is relevant to the situation at hand. As our three cautionary tales suggest, it is important to ensure that contextual details from the experiment are perfectly aligned with the context in which the practitioner is looking to implement the intervention. Questions that need to be asked at this stage include (a) Does the experiment measure the same outcome as the one I'm looking to influence? (b) Are the institutional details of the current context similar to the one in the experiment? (e.g., will it be as easy for my respondents to change behavior as it was for respondents in the experiment, will they have the same levels of attention and focus on the behavior change task?), (c) Will my implementation details be identical to what was done in the original experiment? (e.g., will my intervention be delivered using the same medium and at the same time as the original experiment?), and (d) Is there a match between my population and the population that participated in the original experiment? (For example, might there be language, culture, age, or other social and demographic differences in respondents that could impact the underlying psychology that made the original experiment successful?)

The process of assessing relevance is not easy for two reasons.[23] First, there is no consensus on what dimensions of context are important. There is no well-established checklist or set of guidelines on how a practitioner might assess the similarity in context and populations. Second, a lot of the published literature does not provide much contextual detail. Context changes outcomes; hence, simply borrowing an intervention that worked well elsewhere is no guarantee that it will work well for the practitioner.[24] Therefore, putting important contextual details in a published paper or report is as critical to its successful translation and scaling as the results are. Also, the effects of context are difficult to gauge from a single paper (and hence a single context). It is critical for the field to produce empirical generalizations or meta-analyses to indicate when and where a particular effect works and when it does not.

Next the practitioner needs to adapt and **deploy that intervention**. A couple of issues might create problems at this stage. First, in situations where time is of the essence and the practitioner is under pressure to act (admittedly a very large percentage of most practical situations), they tend to simply borrow an intervention and deploy it as is. Second, rather than thinking of intervention design as a process in which the evidence from the literature serves as a good starting point or a hypothesis to test, learn from the test, and then adapt the intervention, practitioners might simply not have the experimental mindset and hence use the solution off the shelf. Success at this application stage is critical, because failure often results in a mistrust of the behavioral sciences within the organization more generally and disillusionment of the behavioral practitioner. One easy way of overcoming this tendency is to develop the discipline of conducting in-situ testing – testing of the intervention *in the context* in which it will be deployed.

Finally, interventions that have been successfully piloted are now **scaled** to broader populations. Scaling could be either horizontal (for instance, targeting the intervention to a similar segment across geographies) or vertical (for instance, targeting the intervention to all segments in all geographies). Because of some of the issues we raised earlier (changes in context, changes in population, heterogeneity of population, lack of adaptation of intervention), fully scaled up interventions tend to have weaker effects than the original pilot.

FIXING THE GAME: SIX PROPOSALS

It has now been over 12 years since the publication of *Nudge* and over 10 years since the first behavioral unit in government started functioning. While we have made a lot of progress as a field, we believe that the applied science is at a critical juncture. Our efforts at this stage will determine whether the field matures in a systematic and stable manner, or grows wildly and erratically. Unless we take stock of the science, the practice, and the mechanisms that we can put into place to align the two, we will run the danger of the promise of behavioral science being an illusion for many – not because the science itself was faulty, but because we did not successfully develop a science for using the science.[25] We offer six prescriptions for how the field of applied behavioral science can better align itself so that it grows in a systematic and not in a wild manner.

1. **Offer a balanced and nuanced view of the promise of behavioral science.** We believe that it is incumbent on leaders in both the academic and applied space to offer a balanced view of the promise of behavioral science. While we understand that the nature of the book publication process or of public lectures tends to skew on additives to highlight success, we also believe that it is perhaps more of a contribution for the field to highlight limitations and nuances. Rather than narratives along the lines of "A causes B," it would be helpful for our leaders to highlight narratives such as "A causes B in some conditions and C in others." Dissemination of this new narrative could take the form of traditional knowledge mobilization tools, such as books, popular press articles, interviews, podcasts, and essays. Indeed, this book is one attempt at communicating the nuance associated with the science of using behavioral science.

2. **Publish null and non-surprising results.** Academic incentives usually create a body of work that (a) is replete with positive results, (b) over-represents surprising results, (c) is not usually replicated, and (d) is focused on theory and phenomena and not on practical problems. As has been discussed elsewhere (Chapter 2), this occurs because of the academic incentive structure, which favors surprising and positive results. We call on our field to change this culture by creating platforms that allow and encourage authors to publish null results, as well as unsurprising results. We also would encourage academia to create opportunities and reward authors for publishing empirical generalizations, meta-analyses, and nuanced literature reviews that can push the science of using behavioral science further. Finally, we also encourage academics to conduct large-scale mega-experiments with organizational partners. In this approach

(pioneered by the Behavior Change for Good Initiative),[26] multiple behavioral science interventions could be tested simultaneously as part of a larger field experiment. This allows research teams to identify which strategies work best, under what conditions, and for whom.

3. **Prepare the organization.** We call on practitioners to develop their own framework for skills, resources, and structures that need to be put into place to create a behaviorally informed organization. A recent book, *The Behaviorally Informed Organization*, presents a series of essays and frameworks that practitioners could use to accomplish this. The essence is to create an organization in which the cost of experimentation is low, and an organizational structure that can adapt to quick evidence. Failure to do so might mean that even the best use of the existing evidence might not result in success because of the organization's inability to learn and adapt.[27]

4. **Publish contextual details.** Academic papers, unfortunately, do not provide enough details about the implementation of experiments or the context in which those data were collected to allow practitioners to assess relevance to their own context.

5. **Use in-situ evidence and avoid borrowing interventions.** Context changes the results of experiments. Because it is highly likely that the context of a published experiment is different from the context in which a practitioner is looking to change behavior, results will likely differ. Using language from Chapter 3, practitioners could simply borrow interventions from a metaphorical "nudge store," or iterate, test, and adapt an intervention that was published elsewhere in a tailored approach. As with apparel, the tailored approach takes more time, effort, and money, but results in a better product! It is critically important for practitioners to (a) use the published intervention as **a starting point** (a hypothesis) rather than as the final solution, and (b) create a culture and the ability for rapid testing **in-situ** (in the context in which the intervention would be deployed).[28] This can only be accomplished if the costs of experimentation are low. We also encourage practitioners not to simply read the results of a single study or a single set of

interventions, but rather also to read meta-analyses or structured literature reviews. Both could provide additional insights into when an intervention might work and when it might not, and perhaps also comment on different ways in which the same intervention was actually designed and delivered across different contexts. Indeed, the four chapters in Part Two of this volume do exactly this by providing a nuanced view of four often-used interventions in our field.

6. **Embrace heterogeneity.** Solutions need not always be homogeneous to successfully scale. The mental model of successful scaling seems to argue that scaling is only successful with a one-size-fits-all intervention. With diversity in how people think, act, feel, and consume information, as well as the greater diversity of contexts and media used to make choices, the likelihood that a one-size-fits-all intervention solves the problem is increasingly low. However, advances in data sciences and machine learning now provide us with better tools to identify heterogeneity. As a result, we believe that successful scaling might include a mosaic approach in which the researcher might have different variants of an intervention, and the practitioner deploys these different variants to different sub-segments in the population as a function of learning about heterogeneous responses.

In closing, we would like to emphasize that while this chapter might sound like a story of doom and gloom, our intentions are quite the opposite. We, as well as the other authors in this book, believe in the ability of behavioral science to tackle tough social and business problems. That said, our point is simple. As we increasingly transplant ideas from the laboratory or controlled pilot settings into the wild, it is simultaneously increasingly important for the field to pay attention to the nuances of the science of how to use behavioral science. Failure to do so might result in a wild and erratic, rather than a systematic, growth and impact of the field.

NOTES

1 Thaler, R.H., & Sunstein, C.R. (2008). *Nudge: Improving decisions about health, wealth and happiness*. Penguin Books.

2 See, for example, Halpern, D. (2015). *Inside the nudge unit: How small changes can make a big difference*. Ebury Publishing; and Soman, D., & Yeung, C. (2021). *The behaviorally informed organization*. University of Toronto Press.

3 We use the term "practitioner" to mean any entity that is conducting applied behavioral work outside the well-controlled environment of the laboratory. Thus, a practitioner could include employees of either the academic or non-academic sectors who are working to create behavior change to meet an organizational goal and not for the sake of creating knowledge alone.

4 Kahneman, D. (2011). *Thinking, fast and slow*. Farrar, Straus and Giroux.

5 Ariely, D. (2010). *Predictably irrational: The hidden forces that shape our decisions*. Harper.

6 Thaler, R.H. (2015). *Misbehaving: The story of behavioral economics*. W.W. Norton & Company.

7 Soman, D. (2015). *The last mile: Creating social and economic value from behavioral insights*. Rotman-UTP Publishing.

8 See, for example, OECD (2017). *Behavioural insights and public policy: Lessons from around the world*. OECD Publishing. https://doi.org/10.1787/9789264270480-en.

9 Sutherland, R. (2019). *Alchemy: The dark art and curious science of creating magic in brands, business, and life*. First William Morrow hardcover. William Morrow, an imprint of HarperCollins Publishers; and Chataway, R. (2020). *The behaviour business: How to apply behavioural science for business success*. Harriman House.

10 Dur, R., Fleming, D., Van Garderen, M., & Van Lent, M. (2019). A social norm nudge to save more: A field experiment at a retail bank. *SSRN Electronic Journal*. https://doi:10.2139/ssrn.3442797.

11 Larkin, C., Sanders, M., Andresen, I., & Algate, F. (2018). Testing local descriptive norms and salience of enforcement action: A field experiment to increase tax collection. *SSRN Electronic Journal*. https://doi:10.2139/ssrn.3167575.

12 Soman, D. (2020). *Sludge: A very short introduction* (pp. 1–7). Conference. Behavioural Economics in Action at Rotman.

13 Johnson, E.J., & Goldstein, D. (2003). Do defaults save lives? *Science, 302*(5649), 1338–9. https://doi:10.1126/science.1091721.

14 Hawkes, N. (2017). Welsh opt-out law fails to increase organ donations. *BMJ*. https://doi.org/10.1136/bmj.j5659.

15 Jachimowicz, J., Duncan, S., Weber, E., & Johnson, E. (2019). When and why defaults influence decisions: A meta-analysis of default effects. *Behavioural Public Policy, 3*(2), 159–86. https://doi.org/10.1017/bpp.2018.43.

16 Robitaille, N., Mazar, N., Tsai, C.I., Haviv, A., & Hardy, E. (2021). Increasing organ donor registrations with behavioral interventions: A large-scale field experiment. *Journal of Marketing*. https://doi.org/10.1177/0022242921990070.

17 Löschel, A., Rodemeier, M., & Werthschulte, M. (2020). When nudges fail to scale: Field experimental evidence from goal setting on mobile phones. *SSRN Electronic Journal*. https://doi.org/10.2139/ssrn.3693673.

18 Rogers, T., Milkman, K.L., John, L.K., & Norton, M.I. (2015). Beyond good intentions: Prompting people to make plans improves follow through on important tasks. *Behavioral Science & Policy, 1*(2), 33–41.

19 See Milkman, K.L., Beshears, J., Choi, J.J., Laibson, D., & Madrian, B.C. (2013). Planning prompts as a means of increasing preventive screening rates. *Preventive Medicine, 56*(1), 92–3. https://doi:10.1016/j.ypmed.2012.10.021; and Mazar, N., Mochon, D., & Ariely, D. (2018). If you are going to pay within the next 24 hours, press 1: Automatic planning prompt reduces credit card delinquency. *Journal of Consumer Psychology, 28*(3), 466–76. https://doi:10.1002/jcpy.1031.

20 Al-Ubaydli, O., Lee, M., List, J., Mackevicius, C., & Suskind, D. (2021). How can experiments play a greater role in public policy? Twelve proposals from an economic model of scaling. *Behavioural Public Policy, 5*(1), 2–49. https://doi:10.1017/bpp.2020.17.
21 Soman & Yeung (2021).
22 See also Soman (2021), Chapter 1 of ibid.
23 See also Yeung and Tham (2021), Chapter 16 of ibid.
24 See, for example, Gauri, V., Jamison, J.C., Mazar, N., & Ozier, O. (2019). Motivating bureaucrats through social recognition: External validity – A tale of two states. *Organizational Behavior and Human Decision Processes.* https://doi.org/10.1016/j.obhdp.2019.05.005. The same intervention in the same country did not replicate across two states because of differences in context.
25 See also Soman (2021), Chapter 1 of Soman & Yeung (2021).
26 See Behavior Change for Good Initiative (2021, February 12). Retrieved from https://bcfg.wharton.upenn.edu/.
27 Soman & Yeung (2021).
28 See Chapter 3 for further details. Also see Chapters 2 and 16 of Soman & Yeung (2021).

CHAPTER TWO

When Governments Use Nudges: Measuring Impact "At Scale"

Elizabeth Linos

In 2009, as the world was still reeling from a global financial meltdown, a book was published that said, and I paraphrase heavily here, that if we use insights from psychology and economics to design programs, low-cost tweaks can have a disproportionately large impact on people's behavior. The implication of *Nudge*[1] was music to any practitioner's ears. Finally, some credible evidence that you *can*, in fact, do more with less; that you don't *necessarily* need to spend a lot of money to move people's behavior. As David Halpern describes in his own book about presenting early results of the UK's Behavioural Insight Team (BIT) to senior politicians: "Britain, like many other countries, was in the grip of austerity. Most departments faced major cuts, ranging from 10 to 30 per cent ... Here in front of them was a tool they could use. And if the numbers were right, it was a tool that might actually work."[2]

Fast-forward a decade – approximately four minutes in government years – and there are now closer to 250 units across the world dedicated to using evidence from behavioral science in governments.[3] Governments are not just loosely interpreting an academic idea in their policy proposals. At any given moment, hundreds of teams across the world are designing, rigorously testing, and scaling nudges in any policy area you can think of, often with the help of trained behavioral scientists. This movement has quickly progressed beyond behaviors that were considered early successes, such as getting people to pay their taxes or encouraging lower energy use. In Peru, the Ministry of Education is using nudges to improve school test scores and teacher motivation.[4] In New South Wales, the government is designing interventions to reduce domestic violence.[5] In New York City, redesigned court summonses reduced over 30,000 unnecessary arrests.[6] Just in the US, I estimate that 40 million Americans have been nudged by their governments since 2015.

This is an evidence-based policymaker's dream. Unlike in so many other parts of policymaking where programs and services are implemented without much of an evidence base at all, government agencies are not just *consuming* rigorous academic evidence around nudges, they are *producing* it. Furthermore, many of the governments that have committed to using behavioral science in their program design have also committed to rigorous testing, often using randomized controlled trials (RCTs). This allows us now to ask a simple but very important question: how effective are nudges in government? Put differently, if I am a public manager and I'm thinking about using a nudge to improve my program or service, what impact can I reasonably expect?

Stefano DellaVigna and I collaborated with two of the largest "Nudge Units" operating in the US – the Office of Evaluation Sciences and BIT-North America – to answer this exact question: what is the average effect of a government nudge?[7] The Office of Evaluation Sciences (OES), based at the General Services Administration (GSA), supports and implements behavioral experiments in federal agencies across the US government. The Behavioural Insights Team (BIT) North America, based in New York, works primarily with state and local government agencies to do something similar: help local governments design and test nudges on key priority areas. Between them, these two teams have nudged over 34 million people in the US since launching in 2015. Their work spans many policy areas, such as helping veterans access programs for which they are eligible, encouraging homeowners to comply with code regulations, diversifying the government workforce, and encouraging people to get vaccinated. Importantly, they have kept excellent records of every single nudge trial they have conducted, allowing us to correctly measure what the average effect of a nudge is, without overweighting the success stories that get media attention, or get published, or are referenced in TED talks.

Here's the headline finding. The average effect of a government nudge is statistically significant and positive. Across all policy areas and types of nudges, a nudge improves the targeted behavior by about 8% (a 1.4 percentage point increase in take-up over a control group mean of 17%, which often represents the government's standard approach). Almost all nudge trials conducted by these teams in the US are either no-cost (e.g., changing the language on a mailer that is already being sent out) or low-cost (e.g., sending out new mailers or changing a website), and so the return on investment of government nudges is remarkably high. OES estimates that one in five nudges are delivered at no additional cost, while another 73% are delivered at low or very low cost. Indeed, the empirical evidence matches the 10-year-old promise of *Nudge*: when governments use insights from psychology and economics at scale, they *can* create disproportionately large impacts with low-cost tweaks.

Yet, when we took a step back and compared this finding to what researchers report in the broader academic literature, all of a sudden this large and significant finding looked smaller. We did a similar exercise and documented what the average effect of a nudge appears to be, if one were to look only at nudges published in scientific journals, using recent meta-analyses of the academic literature.[8] Using the same criteria we used for our own analysis, we find that in that published sample, the average effect of an "academic" nudge is 33.5% (or an 8.7 percentage point increase) compared to the average effect of a government nudge of 8% (or a 1.4 percentage point increase).

Why the gap? Although both are statistically significant and positive, the policy implications of expecting an 8% improvement are very different from the policy implications of expecting a 33.5% improvement. In our study, we consider many potential explanations, ranging from who spent more time designing an intervention all the way to which populations are more "nudgeable." I focus on two of the most critical questions here. First, are governments just implementing less effective nudges? Maybe governments face more institutional constraints than their academic counterparts, which lead some great ideas to be less feasible in government settings. For example, we know that interventions that nudge individuals to "stick it to the man" can be particularly effective.[9] But those types of interventions may be less politically palatable when considered by a government agency. Or maybe governments *try* to implement the same idea, but have less capacity to implement it according to the original design.[10] Alternatively, perhaps it is not that academics are implementing more effective nudges, but rather that they are focusing on more nudgeable populations. An interesting study by Hunt Allcott on nudges to reduce energy usage shows that the first few experiments conducted on this very important topic were much more successful than subsequent evaluations, partly because they targeted different populations.[11]

When we test these hypotheses in our data, we can explain part of the gap between Nudge Units and academic papers by considering the type of nudge implemented. In our samples, some modes of delivering nudges are less common in government than in the academic literature. First, the obvious: very few government nudges involve in-person nudging, even though it is relatively common in academic papers. This is a feature of going to scale, not a bug. Part of going to scale means reaching more people at the same time, and doing so with an in-person intervention would be prohibitively expensive. Second, the types of nudge tools used are different. For example, "active choice" nudges that ask people to choose between two options, rather than just emphasizing or defaulting people into one, seem to be particularly effective *and* more common in the academic literature. To be clear – this may not be causal. Not all nudge tools and modes of delivery are available in all settings, so if we see an active choice intervention being more successful, it could be because of the nudge itself or because of the context. Last, our sample misses changes that governments *can* implement quite readily but that are harder to measure using an RCT. Implementing a change in defaults, where residents are asked to opt out of a service instead of opting in, are rarely used by Nudge Units, even though there is reason to believe they would be very effective.[12] Ultimately, however, even when we account for all the differences in policy areas, nudge tools used, and modes of delivery, we can't fully explain the gap between the average effect of a government nudge and what we see in academically published papers.

So we turn to the second critical difference: is this just publication bias? Over the past decade, the fields of psychology and economics have been grappling with a "replication crisis." Some of the truths that we held to be self-evident are not in fact true when scholars try to rerun the original seminal study. Indicatively, Camerer and co-authors find that only in 62% of cases can they replicate an experimental study from the highly respected journals *Nature* and *Science*, and the effect size is on average half as large as the original effect size.[13] While many contextual and statistical factors may impact the likelihood of a successful replication, the most relevant factor here is a very clear problem in academia: statistically significant findings are more likely to be published. If all we see when we read the literature are the studies that made it to the top academic publications, we are missing a large volume of studies that are left in the proverbial "file drawer": studies that never see the light of day, either because the academics never wrote them up, or because they never got published. A slightly more nefarious explanation for the replication crisis is one that, until recently, was common practice in much of quantitative social science: if you torture the data enough, it confesses what you want it to say. For years, scientists would shift around control variables, or cut their data into various subgroups, running more and more analytical models until they could find something that crossed a completely arbitrary but career-changing threshold: a p-value of less than 0.05. Statistical significance. A growing commitment to transparency highlights two potential solutions. Scholars are now often asked to (1) pre-commit to which analyses they'll do, to avoid fiddling with data later on, and (2) publish findings, no matter what the results. In terms of transparency, then, some Nudge Units are years ahead of many academic shops. The OES, for example, not only publishes every study they've ever run but have also started to pre-register their analyses so any person can check their code. In our collaboration with both teams, we were able to see all the trials that have been conducted, and therefore eliminated the "file drawer" problem.

When we take a look at both data sets with an eye towards publication bias, we find very clear evidence that publication bias may be explaining the gap between what we observe in the academic literature and what we see in government nudging. In fact, we can close the gap between the two samples completely just by accounting for publication bias. A closer look at the meta-analyses of academic papers will reveal that almost no papers are published without a positive and statistically significant finding. In the very few papers where the primary outcome isn't positive and statistically significant, the write-up of the paper focuses on a secondary outcome that is. To be clear, this does not imply that the results we read about are not true. Sometimes when the sample size is small, a finding appears to be statistically significant but does not correctly describe an underlying true causal relationship. But what is most likely happening in parallel is that we're just not seeing all the studies, and therefore interpret the most successful nudges as the average. Imagine trying to get a sense of how an average basketball player shoots, but only ever being exposed to the highlight reel at an All-Star game. It's not that that incredible dunk didn't happen, it's just that the dunks do not capture the full story. In our analysis, we too see a distribution of success stories. Most government nudges will give you an average effect of less than 1 percentage point, which is still positive and statistically significant. But sometimes (in 13% of cases), a nudge has an average effect of more than 5 percentage points, which can translate to improving take-up by more than 18%. If policymakers only see those striking cases, then they will have a distorted view of how successful a nudge can be.

What does this mean for governments thinking about using nudges? The news is overwhelmingly good. Nudges can be very cost-effective, and in expectation, will lead to a positive and statistically significant improvement in service delivery. In fact, running iterative experiments to steadily and consistently improve programs and services is a no-brainer when nudge costs are as low as they are. Even if we add the cost of creating or collaborating with a Nudge Unit to the calculation, government nudging is still likely to be cost-effective. In fact, Nudge Units can do something that individual projects cannot – by running multiple projects at the same time, not only can Nudge Units help public managers learn what works quickly, they can also minimize the political risk of not having any success story to share with the public. And while any individual project may only offer a modest improvement, implementing the approach at scale means unlocking multiple hurdles or pain points in a process over time, leading to major impact.

At the same time, if we agree that the "true" effect of a nudge is closer to 8% than 30%, it becomes clear that nudges are only one tool in the policymaker's toolkit. Hunger and homelessness will not be solved with one nudge. Systemic inequality will not be solved with one nudge. Good behavioral scientists – especially those at top Nudge Units – know this and are pushing for a more realistic and nuanced view of what can and can't be done with low-cost tweaks. They view nudges as complementary to other larger and more systemic reforms that may still incorporate insights from behavioral science, but that wouldn't qualify as a "nudge."

Last, these results show that governments can lead the behavioral science community on questions of transparency and data credibility. It may seem strange to see governments pioneering a scientific approach, but the nature of governmental accountability and the relatively lower emphasis on academic publication means that governments have an opportunity to invite the public into their decision making in ways that make for better science *and* better policymaking. When governments use nudges and share their results transparently, we can all make better-informed decisions about when to use a nudge and when a nudge is simply not enough. Other government agencies, as well as academics, for-profits and non-profits, are all watching, excitedly.

NOTES

1 Thaler, R.H., & Sunstein, C.R. (2008). *Nudge: Improving decisions about health, wealth and happiness.* Penguin Books.
2 Halpern, D. (2015). *Inside the nudge unit: How small changes can make a big difference.* Ebury Publishing.
3 OECD. (2017). *Behavioural insights and public policy: Lessons from around the world.* OECD Publishing. https://doi.org/10.1787/9789264270480-en.
4 Afif, Z., Wade Islan, W., Calvo-Gonzalez, O., & Dalton, A. (2019). *Behavioral science around the world: Profiles of 10 countries.* World Bank.

5 New South Wales Government. Reducing domestic violence. https://www
   .dpc.nsw.gov.au/programs-and-services/behavioural-insights/projects
   /reducing-domestic-violence/.
6 Fishbane, A., Ouss, A., & Shah, A.K. (2020). Behavioral nudges reduce failure to
   appear for court. *Science, 370*(6517). https://doi:10.1126/science.abb6591.
7 Dellavigna, S., & Linos, E. (2020). RCTs to scale: Comprehensive evidence from two
   Nudge Units. https://doi:10.3386/w27594.
8 See Hummel, D., & Maedche, A. (2019). How effective is nudging? A quantitative
   review on the effect sizes and limits of empirical nudging studies. *Journal
   of Behavioral and Experimental Economics, 80*, 47–58. https://doi:10.1016/j
   .socec.2019.03.005; and Benartzi, S., Beshears, J., Milkman, K.L., Sunstein, C.R.,
   Thaler, R.H., Shankar, M., ... Galing, S. (2017). Should governments invest more in
   nudging? *SSRN Electronic Journal*. https://doi:10.2139/ssrn.2982109.
9 Bryan, C.J., Yeager, D.S., Hinojosa, C.P., Chabot, A., Bergen, H., Kawamura,
   M., & Steubing, F. (2016). Harnessing adolescent values to motivate healthier
   eating. *Proceedings of the National Academy of Sciences, 113*(39), 10830–5. https://
   doi:10.1073/pnas.1604586113.
10 Bird, K., Castleman, B., Denning, J., Goodman, J., Lamberton, C., & Rosinger,
   K.O. (2019). Nudging at scale: Experimental evidence from FAFSA completion
   campaigns. https://doi:10.3386/w26158.
11 Allcott, H. (2015). Site selection bias in program evaluation. *Quarterly Journal of
   Economics, 130*(3), 1117–65. https://doi:10.1093/qje/qjv015.
12 Choi, J.J., Laibson, D., Madrian, B.C., & Metrick, A. (2003). Optimal defaults.
   American Economic Review, 93(2), 180–5.
13 Camerer, C.F., Dreber, A., Holzmeister, F., Ho, T., Huber, J., Johannesson, M., &
   Wu, H. (2018). Evaluating the replicability of social science experiments in *Nature*
   and *Science* between 2010 and 2015. *Nature Human Behaviour, 2*(9), 637–44. https://
   doi:10.1038/s41562-018-0399-z.

CHAPTER THREE

Prescriptions for Successfully Scaling Behavioral Interventions

Laura Goodyear, Tanjim Hossain, and Dilip Soman

TRANSLATION AND SCALING ISN'T EASY

A human resources manager is tasked with improving the retirement contributions among the employees of their firm. They come across a paper that shows that pre-commitment to saving a portion of income after a pay raise improves savings rates, and they decide to implement the same strategy in their workplace.[1] A policymaker is troubled by the fact that many people in their country need an organ transplant and are unable to get one because of shortages. They read a paper suggesting that an opt-out system of organ donation outperforms an opt-in system,[2] and they lobby to change the system in their country. A sales manager tasked with improving the take-up of energy-efficient appliances reads that framing information as a potential loss can outperform framing the same information as a potential gain.[3] Therefore, they design communication that reads "If you fail to upgrade to the energy-efficient appliance, you will lose money on your monthly bills."

As it turned out, the interventions employed by our three protagonists were all met with mixed success. The human resources manager found that while the pre-commitment idea worked for a small number of employees who received frequent pay raises, it did not work for others. As discussed in Chapter 1, the policymaker realized that a shift to opt out increased the number of implied organ donors, but it did not result in any changes to the actual organs harvested. The seller of energy-efficient appliances learned that while the loss framing worked in situations where other competitors were not employing a similar tactic, it failed miserably when everyone in the marketplace was also adopting loss-framing messaging. These mixed results highlight two important issues: (1) published research does not always readily translate into results in the field, and (2) when scaling up the results of an intervention from an experiment or pilot to a larger population, there might be success for one subset of the population but not for others. Taking an intervention that has found success in an experiment or pilot to the broader field often results in much weaker effects overall. The drop in effectiveness of interventions as they are scaled has been referred to as a voltage drop.[4] Voltage drops occur because researchers are often motivated to make broader and more general inferences when they interpret their original experiment; the procedure or the context of the original experiment might not be representative of the real world, or the respondents in the original experiment might not be representative of the entire population.[5]

One of the key findings in the area of behavioral science is the notion of context-dependence.[6] This notion of context-dependence can be traced back to the late 1800s in the writing of American philosopher and psychologist William James. James maintained that human behavior is a function of an interaction between the organism (the human being) and their environment (the context in which they make decisions).[7] Put differently, the same organism might exhibit different behaviors as the environment they are acting within changes. The idea of context-dependence was further developed in the work of Hungarian psychologist Egon Brunswik. Among his many contributions to psychology, Brunswik was particularly known for his insistence on ecological validity – the idea that if we use our experiments to inform us about what would work in a given world, the experiment should mimic the given world in all of its features.[8] If not, a Brunswickian view would caution against making any valid inferences.

Richard Thaler developed the importance of context further in his book *Misbehaving*.[9] He argued that human decision making is driven by a host of what he called SIFs (supposedly irrelevant factors). A SIF is a factor that should not matter according to a rational model of decision making. These factors could include physical elements of the context: the shape and size of the room, whether it was indoors or outdoors, how the furniture was arranged, the temperature, timing (weekday versus weekend, morning versus afternoon, season of the year), social surroundings (whether there were others physically present in the environment, whether those others were members of an in-group or an out-group, how crowded the environment was), or the manner in which information was presented (via visual representation, text, or numbers, framed as a gain versus framed as a loss, the medium that was used to deliver the message). Yet, we know from decades of research that all of these factors matter![10]

Taken together, this suggests that every documented effect in the academic literature is conditioned on a very specific set of contextual factors. Unless the practitioner knows that their world mimics this set of contextual factors, they will likely never be able to reliably obtain the same effects. The fragility of these documented effects as a function of their context is a helpful reminder of why the approach used by our three protagonists is fraught with danger. We liken our protagonists' approach to a consumer shopping in an apparel store (the "nudge-store"). Just as a consumer would browse through racks to look for clothes, a practitioner looks through the literature of published findings or the "nudge-store" to identify an intervention that accomplishes what they are trying to accomplish. However, these "off-the-shelf" solutions (solutions simply borrowed from elsewhere that are not adapted for the situation at hand) aren't always a good fit, and if the intervention fails to achieve the desired outcome, we run the risk of the entire "nudge-store" being written off as a source for solutions.

A different approach to getting new apparel is to get a tailored, custom-fitted outfit (see Figure 3.1). This approach is more complex – it involves multiple visits to a tailor to select fabric, get measured, do a trial, and then collect the final outfit. It is also likely to be a longer and more expensive process. However, the end product fits better and works well. Hence, we always recommend a tailored

Figure 3.1. Off-the-shelf versus tailored approaches to intervention design

NUDGE STORE

TAILOR: MEASURE, TRY, MEASURE, ADAPT

approach to designing behavioral interventions. In organizations, the idea should be to start with the literature to identify candidates for interventions, but then go through a process of understanding contextual differences as well as the specific bottlenecks in the organizations' context, adapt the intervention, test it in the right context, and iterate as needed. This is slower, but the tailored approach is the key to success.

Tailored designing of interventions can be expensive, as it involves designing and running trials in multiple contexts. Nonetheless, practitioners can reduce the costs of each trial by careful choice of samples. Moreover, cost of failure in smaller trials is much lower than cost of failure in larger interventions rolled out without running any in-situ trials. Overall, the long-term benefits of custom-designed interventions are likely to surpass the initial cost of such tailored designing.

Another key consideration when using research is the fact that studies typically employ specific groups of individuals, which can be unintentional (due to convenience) or intentional (to achieve the strongest result). However, subpopulations within a larger population might behave differently or may operate in different contexts. This resulting heterogeneity could cause interventions to be effective for some but not others in the broader population. These two issues – context dependence and individual heterogeneity – are central to the challenges in translating and scaling the results of behavioral experiments and pilots.

We will illustrate these challenges by briefly describing three field studies which highlight the way in which these two issues – context dependence and heterogeneity within a population – could alter the results of well-meaning interventions. We will then use a published paper that highlights the role of information framing on the productivity of workers as a basis for discussing ways in which some of these translational and scaling challenges might arise. We will also argue that the best way of overcoming these challenges is to relentlessly test before translating and scaling, and in particular to focus on what we refer to as in-situ testing (testing in the context in which the intervention will be used). We will also call for researchers and report writers to be explicit about identifying elements of the context in which the original study was created so that a practitioner can make better judgments about the fit between the context of the original work and theirs.

CREDIT CARD REMINDERS IN SOUTH KOREA

Research shows that consumers tend to spend more when using a credit card than when paying with cash or check.[11] One reason for this "credit card premium" is that, when people use a credit card to make purchases, it weakens their memory of these expenditures. Therefore, one way to reduce spending related to credit card use is to provide people with reminders of how much they have already spent. This improves people's ability to mentally track their expenses and mitigates this increased spending.[12]

In 2010, the government in South Korea was concerned about consumers' mounting credit card debt. The government, being aware of previous research, mandated that credit card providers introduce a text-messaging service that would remind consumers about their recent transactions. The expectation was that introducing a credit card spending text alert would enable people to better control their spending and reduce their credit card balances. However, upon evaluating the intervention, the government found that the policy had the intended outcome for only about 12% of the population, the heavy spenders. For the remaining 88%, the policy actually resulted in an increase in spending.[13]

First, this backfiring effect may come from important contextual differences between the original experiments and the context in which it was used in South Korea. The manner in which the reminder was delivered in the studies, where it was available on the same screen as the spending decisions were made, differed from the scaled-up intervention, where it appeared on a mobile device. This created a degree of "digital dependency":[14] consumers believed that they could easily access their past spending if they needed to, thereby reducing the motivation to track it mentally. Second, this backfiring effect may come from important heterogeneity within the larger population. Clearly, this intervention was successful for heavy spenders, but not for those who spend less. The text alert may have warned those that spend quite a bit to slow down their spending, but at the same time it provided a license to spend for those that spend less.

By unwittingly applying previous research to this new context, the intervention did not have the desired effect. Further, given that heterogeneity within the larger population was not fully explored by prior research, the government of South Korea assumed that this intervention should work for everyone.

WHEN A POPULAR BEHAVIORAL INTERVENTION (SOMETIMES) BACKFIRED

Mexico is facing an elderly-poverty crisis.[15] Salaried employees in Mexico are required to make a 6.5% contribution to their pension, while projections show that they need to make an additional 5% voluntary contribution in order to retire comfortably. Unfortunately, the voluntary contribution rate in Mexico is abysmally low.

Prior research shows that simplifying communications and making them more engaging increases the likelihood that recipients will consume the information and act on it.[16] Working with the pension authority in Mexico, Shah and co-authors[17] redesigned the quarterly pension statement that every salaried employee in Mexico receives. Accordingly, the redesigned statement was significantly more engaging than the original and differed in two ways. First, it provided a simplified visual illustration showing that the current pension savings were inadequate for retirement. Second, it included one of several well-known behavioral interventions (gain versus loss framing, a wallet cut-out to increase implementation intentions, an appeal that made the family's welfare salient, and an intervention encouraging recipients to start saving after a particular temporal landmark) that had been shown to be successful elsewhere. In a large-scale field trial, the members of two pension funds were selected as participants. Results showed that the intervention was a success among individuals of one fund (it increased the contribution incidence, the contribution amounts, and the contribution frequency) but backfired in the other. Why did this happen?

Backfiring happened because of an important contextual factor within a specific design feature unique to the Mexican pension system. Mexicans need to first choose a pension fund and then make contribution decisions. Importantly, these funds differ in terms of their performance. In the quarterly pension statements, the performance of each fund is displayed in a tabular form. By making these statements more engaging, the researchers increased the attention that was being paid to the table. If the fund was high performing, then the engaging statement ended up improving voluntary contributions because it increased the motivation to save. If, on the other hand, the recipient had chosen a low-performing fund, then the improved engagement of the statement actually resulted in demotivation because it highlighted attention to the low performance of the fund. Similar to the previous example, seemingly innocuous contextual features where the intervention was used resulted in unintended consequences.

FAMILY APPEALS APPEAL ONLY TO FAMILIES

Again, in ongoing work with the pension authority in Mexico to improve savings, Shah and co-authors[18] compared three groups: a group where no interventions were employed, a group in which recipients received the redesigned statement described above, and a third group that received the redesigned statement in addition to a text message. It was believed that the third group would outperform the other two groups, as text reminders have been shown to successfully move people from intention into action.[19]

The overall results of the field trial were mixed. For the third group that received both the redesigned quarterly statement and text messages, only recipients that received a text message emphasizing their family's financial security increased contribution rates compared to the other groups. However, is it fair to say that this intervention was successful for the overall population? Might the effect differ depending on the relevance of family considerations? What about people that do not have families? Does age matter? These questions raised concerns for the researchers about how heterogeneous subpopulations within the broader population may or may not be receptive to the intervention. Using machine learning techniques,[20] the researchers were able to identify heterogeneous effects across the larger population. Their results showed that the family security text message increased contribution rates for people who were aged between 28 and 42. It did not have a significant effect for people above the age of 43, and it had a backfiring effect for people under the age of 27. For those between the ages of 28 and 42, the intervention was most successful, as this is the age that individuals begin to get married and have children.

By identifying that heterogeneity within the population may play a role, the research was able to provide actionable insights for the Mexican pension authority. Knowing exactly for whom the family security text message was most effective, the Mexican pension authority can now target the subsegments of the population properly and customize the content of the text messages to these different subsegments accordingly. Successful scaling, in this case, embraces heterogeneity by using a group of interventions, each targeted to segments where it might be most effective.

WATCHING OUT FOR CHALLENGES: AN ILLUSTRATION

We next illustrate how some of these scaling challenges, highlighted above, might play a role if an intervention from the academic literature were to be scaled up and applied in other organizations.

Hossain and List[21] used one of the most robust findings from behavioral science – the framing of monetary outcomes as gains or losses. Tversky and Kahneman[22] discovered that an individual's choice over the same outcomes changes as a function of the way in which the choices are framed. Applying these insights in a field setting, a high-tech manufacturing facility, the researchers altered the manner in which a productivity bonus was presented to workers. In particular, workers were randomly split into three groups: a group where a bonus was presented as a potential gain (they were promised the bonus if they met a quota), a group where the same bonus was presented as a potential loss (they were endowed with the bonus and would lose it if a quota was unmet), and a baseline group that received no intervention. This research found that both the gain and loss framing of incentives increased productivity compared to the baseline group where there were no incentives. Incentives clearly worked! However, framing the incentive as a potential loss had a small but significant increase in productivity over presenting the same bonus as a potential gain.

Even though loss framing only had a small increase in productivity compared to gain framing, it is quite important that this change in productivity happened in a real work setting. The fact that this effect was demonstrated in a real-world environment instead of a lab may lead us to conclude that this is a candidate for a scalable intervention. If this small gain in productivity can be scaled up to large populations of workers, it would indeed make a significant impact on welfare. However, the question remains: will scaling up this loss-framed incentive have the same effect or will there be a voltage drop? Is it possible that the intervention might even backfire?

First, we'll examine the contextual features of the study. In this study, each intervention was implemented for only about a month. While the impact was evident over the duration of the experiment, framing incentives as a loss might not be successful if this change were to be permanent or much longer in duration. For example, continuously framing an incentive as a loss might have negative emotional consequences on a workforce in the long run. The effectiveness of loss framing may also depend on the size of the economic incentives. In Hossain and List, the size of the bonus was above 20% of any of the workers' base salary. The treatment effect for smaller-sized incentives may be insignificant or opposite in direction.[23] Furthermore, as the impact of loss aversion on productivity depends on the interaction of the framing and the underlying incentive scheme, incentives have to be deployed along the dimension of productivity that the policymaker is interested in.[24] Hence, while scaling up, one needs to be careful in choosing the economic part of the intervention to ensure that it does not backfire.

Second, heterogeneity within the work force may also lead to unintended consequences if the loss-framing intervention is scaled up. It is noteworthy that Hossain and List did not find any significant framing effects for individual workers, but rather the effect of loss framing was only significant for work teams. This suggests that loss framing is more effective at increasing productivity among employees who work in teams, but it may not increase productivity, or worse, it could backfire, for those who work alone.

These potential issues do not suggest that this type of incentive scheme is not a candidate for a scaled-up intervention. Rather, they should highlight some of the potential considerations to take into account before scaling is done to ensure that the intervention is a good candidate for the context and the population that will be targeted by the intervention.

HOW CAN WE OVERCOME THE HETEROGENEITY IN POPULATION AND CONTEXT?

Thus far we have provided examples that illustrate when the two challenges – heterogeneity within a population and contextual differences between academic work and scaled-up interventions – can lead to unintended consequences. We have also demonstrated, using Hossain and List's research, the ways that academic work should be carefully interpreted and applied before being scaled up. We conclude by recommending that the best way to overcome these challenges is to test before scaling interventions, and in particular, we suggest in-situ testing. We also suggest that there is an onus on researchers and report writers to be explicit about the elements of the context (setting, details of the intervention, and the sample selected) in which the original study was created. That way practitioners can not only better ascertain the fit between the original context and their own but also get a better sense of the conditions that are required to achieve the large effects that academic papers report (see Chapter 2).

After carefully considering how the context and sample used to test an intervention may differ from other contexts, next is to test the intervention. In-situ testing here refers to testing an intervention in the context in which it will be employed. We strongly suggest that this be done to ensure that precious resources are not needlessly spent on scaled-up interventions that may not work or that may even backfire. While it will be disappointing if an intervention does not have the intended consequences during in-situ testing, it could be catastrophic if interventions are scaled up without any due diligence. Another source of a voltage drop, which we have not explicitly discussed, can be the fallacy of composition. An intervention that is very successful when introduced by one organization may not be as successful in inducing behavioral change when all organizations adopt it, making it rather commonplace. In-situ testing can also help by making the intervention more common and familiar to people.

Customized interventions will take time and many tweaks in order to get the best-fitting intervention for the given context. Testing may require multiple iterations, as it is not wise to change multiple components of an intervention at once. It will become difficult to identify what aspect of the adapted intervention may be leading to certain effects. Therefore, testing carefully, and ideally over multiple trials, is imperative.

However, we understand that in-situ testing is sometimes unrealistic for many reasons, be they finances, time, or human capital. Researchers should therefore also be held responsible for articulating all the dimensions of the context or features of the situation under which their documented effects hold. Preferably, researchers should test for the effect under different contexts and with different populations, as Shah and co-authors[25] did in their research. When testing under different contexts is not possible, researchers should be given the opportunity to speculate on when a scaled-up intervention would hold and when it would not. Finally, in-situ testing constraints on the part of the practitioner and researcher present an opportunity for partnerships to gain these necessary insights. The goal of both researchers and practitioners should be to create a mutually beneficial relationship to generate an understanding of when interventions are helpful and when they could be unintentionally hurtful. By detailing information in the original experiments and providing new testing contexts from practitioners, we can begin to overcome the challenges of scaling up well-meaning interventions.

NOTES

1 Thaler, R.H., & Benartzi, S. (2004). Save more tomorrow™: Using behavioral economics to increase employee saving. *Journal of Political Economy*, 112(S1), S164–S187. https://doi.org/10.1086/380085.

2 Johnson, E.J., & Goldstein, D.G. (2003). Do defaults save lives? *Science*, 302, 1338–9. https://doi.org/10.1126/science.1091721.

3 Ganzach, Y., & Karsahi, N. (1995). Message framing and buying behavior: A field experiment. *Journal of Business Research*, 32(1), 11–17. https://doi.org/10.1016/0148-2963(93)00038-3.

4 Kilbourne, A.M., Neumann, M.S., Pincus, H.A., Bauer, M.S., & Stall, R. (2007). Implementing evidence-based interventions in health care: Application of the replicating effective programs framework. *Implementation Science*, 2(1), 1–10. https://doi.org/10.1186/1748-5908-2-42; Al-Ubaydli, O., Lee, M.S., List, J.A., Mackevicius, C.L., & Suskind, D. (2021). How can experiments play a greater role in public policy? Twelve proposals from an economic model of scaling. *Behavioural Public Policy*, 5(1), 2–49. https://doi.org/10.1017/bpp.2020.17.

5 See also Yeung, C., & Tham, S. (2021). Behavioral science in policy and government: A roadmap. In *The Behaviorally Informed Organization* (pp. 272–90). University of Toronto Press.

6 Context dependence was first used by Tversky & Simonson (1993) to refer to precise effects of additional options on choice between two focal options, but is now used more broadly. See Tversky, A., & Simonson, I. (1993). Context-dependent

preferences. *Management Science, 39*(10), 1179–89. https://doi.org/10.1287/mnsc.39.10.1179.

7 James, W. (1890). The perception of reality. *Principles of Psychology, 2,* 283–324.

8 Brunswik, E. (1947). *Systematic and representative design of psychological experiments; with results in physical and social perception.* University of California Press.

9 Thaler, R.H., & Ganser, L.J. (2015). *Misbehaving: The making of behavioral economics.* W.W. Norton.

10 See Soman, D. (2015). *The last mile: Creating social and economic value from behavioral insights.* University of Toronto Press; Thaler & Ganser (2015); and Halpern, D. (2016). *Inside the nudge unit: How small changes can make a big difference.* Random House.

11 See Feinberg, R.A. (1986). Credit cards as spending facilitating stimuli: A conditioning interpretation. *Journal of Consumer Research, 13*(3), 348–56. https://doi.org/10.1086/209074; Prelec, D., & Simester, D. (2001). Always leave home without it: A further investigation of the credit-card effect on willingness to pay. *Marketing Letters, 12*(1), 5–12. https://doi.org/10.1023/A:1008196717017; and Soman, D. (2001). Effects of payment mechanism on spending behavior: The role of rehearsal and immediacy of payments. *Journal of Consumer Research, 27*(4), 460–74. https://doi.org/10.1086/319621.

12 Soman (2001).

13 Kim, J.K., Yoon, J.H., Choi, Y.H., & Soman, D. (2020). Do text reminders about credit card spending help reduce spending? A quasi-experimental evaluation. Working Paper.

14 Sparrow, B., Liu, J., & Wegner, D.M. (2011). Google effects on memory: Cognitive consequences of having information at our fingertips. *Science, 333*(6043), 776–8. https://doi.org/10.1126/science.1207745.

15 Fertig, A., Fishbane, A., & Lefkowiz, J. (2018). Using behavioral science to increase retirement savings in Mexico: A look at what we have learned over three years. http://www.ideas42.org/wp-content/uploads/2018/11/I42-1046_MetLifeLatAm_paper_ENG_Final.pdf.

16 Bhargava, S., & Manoli, D. (2015). Psychological frictions and the incomplete take-up of social benefits: Evidence from an IRS field experiment. *American Economic Review, 105*(11), 3489–3529. https://doi.org/10.1257/aer.20121493.

17 Shah, A., Osborne, M., Lefkowitz, J., Fishbane, A., & Soman, D. (2020). The simplification paradox: When reducing cognitive complexity can impede retirement savings contributions. Working Paper.

18 Shah, A., Osborne, M., Lefkowitz, J., Fishbane, A., & Soman, D. (2019). Can making family salient increase financial savings? Quantifying heterogeneous treatment effects in retirement contributions using a field experiment in Mexico. Working Paper.

19 Karlan, D., McConnell, M., Mullainathan, S., & Zinman, J. (2016). Getting to the top of mind: How reminders increase saving. *Management Science, 62*(12), 3393–3411. https://doi.org/10.1287/mnsc.2015.2296.

20 Athey, S., & Imbens, G. (2016). Recursive partitioning for heterogeneous causal effects. *Proceedings of the National Academy of Sciences, 113*(27), 7353–60. https://doi.org/10.1073/pnas.1510489113.

21 Hossain, T., & List, J.A. (2012). The behavioralist visits the factory: Increasing productivity using simple framing manipulations. *Management Science, 58*(12), 2151–67. https://doi.org/10.1287/mnsc.1120.1544.

22 Tversky, A., & Kahneman, D. (1980). The framing of decisions and the rationality of choice. *Science, 211*, 453–8.
23 Hoffmann, C., & Thommes, K. (2020). Using loss aversion to incentivize energy efficiency in a principal-agent context – Evidence from a field experiment. *Economics Letters, 189*, 108984. https://doi.org/10.1016/j.econlet.2020.108984.
24 Hong, F., Hossain, T., & List, J.A. (2015). Framing manipulations in contests: A natural field experiment. *Journal of Economic Behavior & Organization, 118*, 372–82. https://doi.org/10.1016/j.jebo.2015.02.014.
25 Shah et al. (2019).

CHAPTER FOUR

The Last Yard Problem: Tailoring of Behavioral Interventions for Scale

Piyush Tantia, Saugato Datta, Alissa Fishbane, and Cassie Taylor

Behavioral science practitioners have successfully applied hundreds of behavioral interventions to solve various real-world problems. For example, ideas42 and other practitioners have helped people conserve energy and water, take up government benefits, show up to court,[1] and save more.[2] We now have the opportunity to scale these successful solutions to other institutions and geographies; however, doing so is harder than it seems.

Scaling may seem like a simple matter of disseminating and replicating interventions, but our experience at ideas42 has shown otherwise. To successfully scale, we find that interventions need "last yard" tailoring to work. Every detail of how the intervention is implemented matters. The fundamental behavioral insight, say peer comparison, may transfer as is, but how it is packaged and delivered often does not. Those delivery elements include things like the tone of an email, the timing and frequency of a text message, how frontline staff execute a new protocol, or even the graphics on a poster. Sometimes even the behavioral insight itself doesn't transfer to a seemingly similar context,[3] but in this chapter we will focus only on the first challenge of the "last yard," the tailored approach (see also Chapter 3) to design.

We have successfully scaled up interventions across different organizations and countries by paying close attention to all the delivery details. We find that those delivery details are themselves behavioral challenges to be solved, such as local differences in mental models. As such, every *scalable* intervention has many layers of behavioral solutions, and some of those layers need to be adapted to the local context when we take it to a different institution or geography. Below, we will illustrate this concept with two case studies and then draw generalizable lessons from them for practitioners aspiring to scale behavioral interventions.

CASE STUDY: FREE APPLICATION FOR FEDERAL STUDENT AID (FAFSA)

Affordability and financial access are some of the biggest barriers facing American students seeking to complete college degrees, and yet students leave more than $2.9 billion dollars in free federal grants on the table each year simply because they do not apply for them. In 2016, ideas42 found that just 18% of continuing students at Arizona State University (ASU) submitted their FAFSA before the priority deadline, which would ensure that they could receive the maximum financial aid package.[4] We developed a cost-effective and scalable solution to increase FAFSA submissions: a series of emails for the students and their parents incorporating a number of behavioral interventions. These emails broke the task down into small steps, helped create a sense of progress, prompted active choice, and more. Families receiving these emails were 3% more likely to submit the FAFSA, and 72% more likely to file by the priority deadline.[5]

Based on the success of this intervention at ASU, we sought to replicate it for students at the City University of New York (CUNY). Even though the design was simple, procedural, and designed to scale, we quickly learned that it needed to be modified in three key ways:

1. **Adapting to the audience.** At ASU, a four-year school with a traditional student body, a core component of the intervention's success was emailing not just students but also their parents. But at CUNY, students tend to be older, commonly with children of their own, and are often the first in their families

to attend college. Emailing these students' parents about the FAFSA deadline would not have been effective or appropriate in this new context.

2. **Tone.** The original emails were written in a friendly, casual tone that ASU students found to be approachable and unintimidating. However, CUNY students – who see college as providing a service more than an experience – felt that this informal tone was unprofessional and untrustworthy.

3. **Contexts may vary even across different parts of the same organization.** Even within the CUNY system, where we were working through the central office in an attempt to efficiently scale the intervention across all campuses, we learned that the messages and their delivery still needed to be tailored to each campus's individual needs and priorities.

We identified these necessary changes early on through in-situ user testing and conversations with CUNY students and staff. We also tested the impact of the redesigned intervention and then continuously refined it, ultimately adding an SMS component. Of course, this labor-intensive approach on its own has clear limitations for widespread scale. We are now exploring how to provide schools with not only the intervention design but also scaffolded adaptation guidance for them to make the necessary modifications without expert assistance. This guidance seeks to walk schools through the changes we know they'll need to make, but also to help them ask the right questions and adapt the design in ways that only they, as the local experts, can uncover.

CASE STUDY: CASH TRANSFERS

Much of our work with large-scale government cash transfer programs in sub-Saharan Africa has focused on providing program beneficiaries with decision-making aids and prompts that encourage them to see saving as "normal," identify their financial goals, make concrete plans to achieve them, and then follow through on these plans. As such, most intervention packages we've designed have had some common elements, including posters depicting peers' saving behavior, goal-setting activities, planning tools to help people allocate their funds between short-term consumption and savings or investments, and "savings pouches" to help them follow through on these plans.

Even in Tanzania and Kenya – two neighboring countries in East Africa with many social and cultural similarities – user testing uncovered a variety of ways in which these conceptually similar intervention components had to be tailored in terms of content, delivery, and even imagery. Careful in-situ user testing is therefore critical to ensure that images, content, and other details are context-appropriate, not unintentionally misleading or exclusionary, and have the best possible chance of achieving their desired impact.

1. **The same principle or design concept needed to be operationalized in different ways depending on the context.** In both Tanzania and Kenya, beneficiaries were provided with a "savings pouch" that provided a physical way to segregate funds by use. In Tanzania, where the transfer was given as cash, this pouch had two compartments: one for savings, and one for consumption funds. However, in Kenya, where the transfer was given electronically, it was no longer critical to have beneficiaries "separate" cash for savings from other expenses whenever they withdrew some transfer funds. As a result, the "savings pouch" had only one compartment.
2. **The same kind of activity might have to be delivered quite differently in different settings.** For example, the self-affirmation activity was originally delivered as an interactive activity whereby beneficiaries identified something they did very well, shared with a group of other beneficiaries, and publicly acknowledged each other's strengths. In Kenya, we observed that beneficiaries were not comfortable with doing this type of activity publicly. We adapted the intervention into one of self-reflection assisted by posters with aspirational stories of people relatable to cash transfer beneficiaries. These protagonists described strengths that helped them achieve their goals.

3. **Social and cultural differences led to different designs for the same "intervention."** Kenya and Tanzania proved to have sufficiently different social norms for financial behavior by gender. In Tanzania, a single gender-neutral version of the pouch with an image of a representative family was adequate. In Kenya, because of the association in people's minds between men and financial activities, we needed to design "male" and "female" variants. Had we not user-tested carefully, we might have wound up with a less effective design in Kenya, with the doubly worse outcome of unintentionally excluding women.

4. **Aligning images with people's identities is critical.** It is important to ensure that the way people are depicted in intervention materials makes it easy and intuitive for them to "see themselves" in these materials. In both Kenya and Tanzania, posters depicting savings behavior had to be carefully designed to ensure that this was the case. For instance, the program in Kenya targeted a variety of groups, including the disabled, orphans, older people, etc., and therefore posters needed to specifically depict these different groups to ensure that people did not dismiss the messages on the posters as "not for them." We had encountered a particularly telling example of the need for this kind of adaptation in an even earlier iteration of the savings poster intervention in Madagascar, where beneficiaries who participated in user testing pointed out that the images of beneficiaries were hard for them to identify with because they looked wealthier than actual program beneficiaries. On further probing, they explained that the people on the poster had teeth that were "too regular" – leading our team to adapt the posters to depict people with more "irregular," that is, "realistic," teeth.

5. **Program materials have to be tailored to the specificities of each context in order to avoid confusing (and potentially counterproductive) interpretations.** While we had plan-making activities for beneficiaries in both countries, the modalities of saving were different in each country, necessitating adaptation. In Tanzania, the program encourages the creation of savings groups – although people of course still saved at home. As a result, we noticed during user testing that when asked to make

savings plans, participants were confused about whether the savings had to be through the savings groups (which had pre-set savings amounts and frequencies) or individually. The final design therefore depicted both individual savings boxes (which usually have one padlock) and group savings boxes (which usually have three padlocks, each kept by a different member for security) to communicate to beneficiaries that they could select whichever means they preferred to save by. We also provided options for saving frequencies that accommodated both savings systems. This adaptation was not necessary in Kenya.

Encouragingly, we found positive results from the package of behavioral interventions in both countries, with significant increases in desired financial behaviors – including the likelihood of having a saving goal, saving a portion of the transfer, and – in the case of Tanzania – even making productive investments a short period of time after the interventions were delivered. In Kenya, the government is moving rapidly towards operationalizing these interventions across many more counties and eventually the entire country. No doubt, further tailoring will be needed as these interventions are taken to parts of Kenya that are different from those where they were originally tested.

LESSONS FOR PRACTITIONERS

The first lesson is that we need to adapt behavioral interventions to the local context. To learn what those adaptations might be, we must do in-situ testing of prototype designs with users, and sometimes even run pilot experiments in the field. Quickly collecting some data in the field in these ways often reveals differences in social norms, mental models, preferences, etc. that are not obvious on the surface. The adaptations are most commonly in how a behavioral intervention is packaged and delivered rather than in the fundamental behavioral insight being used. For example, in the cash transfers case study above, we used goal setting, partitioning, and other behavioral concepts in both countries.

There is also a second, more nuanced, lesson from our experience with scaling. Designing a successful field experiment to answer a research question is different from designing an intervention for scale. Adaptation challenges are more likely to emerge in the second case. For a scientific experiment, researchers can get around delivery problems *temporarily* at a high cost. For example, if they are struggling to get attention from enough subjects for an intervention, they can increase the sample size or pay people to take up their design. They can use very high touch delivery by research assistants to ensure that the intervention is delivered with high fidelity. For example, had we used research assistants in Tanzania, they could have simply explained that beneficiaries could save via groups or individually. We would not have needed to adapt the intervention materials. To design an intervention for impact at scale, we must solve these "secondary" behavioral problems at a low cost, and in such a way that implementers don't need any support from researchers to run the intervention at scale in the field. We must design not only the "core" behavioral intervention but also all the delivery details. That can add several layers of behavioral design in that some of the delivery challenges themselves benefit from behavioral interventions.

In designing the "last yard" of delivery, we see several behavioral barriers emerge, but four are very common. We would encourage practitioners wanting to implement behavioral solutions to **keep an eye out for these pesky problems** as they are adapting solutions for scale, but also as they're designing a behavioral intervention in the first place:

1. **Limited attention** is very common in any intervention where recipients must actively consume information, or some product or service. While it is outside the scope of this chapter to describe the typical challenges and solutions comprehensively, some solutions to try would be to change when or how often communications are delivered or ideally to deliver the intervention at moments when recipients are more likely to be paying attention and able to act. For example, ideas42 successfully implemented a peer benchmarking intervention for water

conservation in Costa Rica where the prompt was a sticker on the water bill, when the customers were already thinking about water consumption, rather than a separate communication.[6] Continual refinement helps to find the ideal frequency to intervene as well as the content of interventions. For example, our friends at EveryDay Labs increase school attendance by sending behaviorally informed letters to parents of frequently absent students. Originally, they sent four letters a year with a small number of variations in messaging.[7] Based on results from dozens of randomized controlled trials, they now deliver up to seven letters annually per family and more than 10,000 message variations,[8] and report double the impact of what they were doing originally.

2. **The behavioral intervention relies on customer-facing staff to do something differently.** For example, health care providers must present treatment options in a different way, bank staff must prompt clients to use a new savings product, or administrators need to collect new information. In these settings, we must design different behavioral interventions just to solve any barriers those staff members might face in changing their own behavior. For example, we worked with a large hospital to facilitate adoption of new medical protocols for the treatment of opioid use disorder among emergency room patients. Here, we inserted salient prompts in the electronic health record system, gave health providers "badge-backers" that created a visible norm of treatment as well as an easy access to treatment protocols, and sent monthly feedback emails. All of these treatments significantly increased adoption of the new protocol.[9]

3. **The behavioral intervention proves too long, complex, or unengaging for recipients.** In one example, we adapted a behavioral intervention teaching micro-entrepreneurs simple rules of thumb for financial management from an in-person training[10] to a more scalable approach of brief voice messages delivered weekly. In the initial pilot, the research assistants recorded the messages themselves, and we found that the recipients were hanging up before listening to the entire message. We then hired voice actors and scripted a more

engaging, conversational message, which boosted listening rates significantly.[11]

4. Where we are scaling an intervention across multiple locations like branches, schools, and government jurisdictions, we often encounter **limited attention among the administrators** at those sites. We may ship behaviorally designed posters that never get put up, or new medications that are never given out. In her previous role running Deworm the World, Alissa found that team members needed to be present in each country to work closely with administrators, whose attention was spread across many priorities, to help move along implementation at each level of government, from the ministry to the school.

CONCLUSIONS

A behavioral insight is just that – it is no more than the seed of a solution. We must carefully build the behavioral insight into a scalable behavioral intervention based on a thorough understanding of the context, and ample in-situ user testing. Then, we must tailor the last yard design elements to each new context where we scale. There are two important implications of recognizing this nuance about scaling:

1. Just as we cannot simply take and apply "off-the-shelf" solutions from the "nudge store" and hope to be successful, practitioners cannot simply "plug-and-play" intervention designs that worked elsewhere.
2. Practitioners must ideally learn enough behavioral design to be able to adapt interventions themselves, or they will need outside help.

We believe that the best long-term solution is to build capacity among practitioners for adapting behavioral interventions (or, for that matter, any innovations). That strategy may seem slow in the near term but will allow for much faster scaling of many more solutions in the long run. We already offer some training programs and have also partnered with universities in the Global South to offer practitioner training. Over time, we hope to see a growth in executive education programs that teach this skill set as well as university courses that are part of degree programs. The ideal programs will be experiential and allow practitioners to develop innovative adaptation skills while remaining in their jobs to implement them.

NOTES

1 Fishbane, A., Ouss, A., & Shah, A.K. (2020). Behavioral nudges reduce failure to appear for court. *Science, 370*(6517).

2 For more details and examples of applied behavioral interventions across a wide range of social issues, see ideas42.org; bhub.org; www.bi.team; Benartzi, S., Beshears, J., Milkman, K.L., Sunstein, C.R., Thaler, R.H., Shankar, M., ... & Galing, S. (2017). Should governments invest more in nudging? *Psychological Science, 28*(8), 1041–55; and DellaVigna, S., & Linos, E. (2020). *RCTs to scale: Comprehensive evidence from two nudge units.* Working Paper, UC Berkeley.

3 See Bronchetti, E.T., Dee, T.S., Hufman, D.B., & Magenheim, E. (2013). When a nudge isn't enough: Defaults and saving among low-income tax filers. *National Tax Journal, 66*(3), 609–34; and Beshears, J., Choi, J.J., Laibson, D., Madrian, B.C., & Milkman, K.L. (2015). The effect of providing peer information on retirement savings decisions. *Journal of Finance, 70*(3), 1161–1201.

4 ideas42. (2016). Nudging for success: Using behavioral science to improve the postsecondary student journey. https://www.ideas42.org/wp-content/uploads/2016/09/Nudging-For-Success-FINAL.pdf.

5 Ibid.

6 Miranda, J.J., Datta, S., & Zoratto, L. (2020). Saving water with a nudge (or two): Evidence from Costa Rica on the effectiveness and limits of low-cost behavioral interventions on water use. *World Bank Economic Review, 34*(2), 444–63.

7 Rogers, T., & Feller, A. (2018) Reducing student absences at scale by targeting parents' misbeliefs. *Nature Human Behavior, 2*(5), 335–42.

8 A Researcher's Take on Reducing Chronic Absenteeism, Future Ed Interview with Todd Rogers. (2019, December 16). *FutureEd*. Retrieved March 23, 2021, from https://www.future-ed.org/a-researchers-take-on-reducing-chronic-absenteeism/.

9 Martin, A., Baugh, J., Chavez, T., Leifer, J., Kao, L., Dutta, S., White, B., Hayes, B., Williamson, D., & Raja, A. (2020). Clinician experience of nudges to increase ED OUD treatment. *American Journal of Emergency Medicine, 38*(10), 2241–2.

10 Drexler, A., Fischer, G., & Schoar, A. (2014). Keeping it simple: Financial literacy and rules of thumb. *American Economic Journal: Applied Economics, 6*(2), 1–31.

11 See project page for more details: http://www.ideas42.org/blog/project/financial-management-training-mobile-phones/.

CHAPTER FIVE

The Limited Importance of External Validity in Experimental Economics

Colin F. Camerer

External validity refers to how valid the results are of an empirical inference from one setting to other settings "in the wild." The term was coined by Campbell and Stanley in their monumental book on experimental design.[1] Stanley had in mind educational research as a model "use case." In that case, external validity refers to how likely laboratory results testing, for example, the effectiveness of a new teaching method would actually work in schools. Similarly, Chapter 2 in this book examines the external validity of academic experiments by comparing their effectiveness to those of government experiments at scale.

As a running example I will use, from my own work, experimental tests of alternative theories to Nash equilibrium in games, and in particular "cognitive hierarchy (CH)" theories (a very close kin to level-k modelling).[2] In CH there is assumed to be a hierarchy of degrees of strategic thinking. Level 0 is a non-strategic level that chooses more salient strategies, or randomizes equally if no strategies are salient.[3] Those at level k>1 believe others will choose as if they are at levels 0 to k-1.

I will make the provocative case that in basic science, external validity is a concept of limited usefulness. It is not an unimportant property, but it is not worth spending much time debating. This is true for several reasons:

- External validity is not a single-dimensional quality. Internal validity is much easier – there is a checklist of mistakes that can be made in executing a treatment and control which undermine the quality of the inferences drawn. Every experimenter learns the checklist. The *generalizable scope* of an experimental result is a set of predictions about where an experimental result is most likely to explain behavior well or poorly. The scope is like a heatmap showing high and low generalizability scores on a historical timeline crossed with a globe of the world times a set of group portraits of people.
- External validity is not just a desirable property of lab experiments; it should also be used to judge *any* empirical result or *any* theory. In economics, in my long experience, external validity is used to critique lab experiments far more aggressively than it is used to critique empirics or theory.[4]
- External validity is essentially impossible to judge from features of an experiment itself. The claim that an experimental result is externally valid is a *prediction* about the range of different environments (time, place, population of people, etc.) in which a result will hold. If an experimenter predicts external validity, and a critic is doubtful, there is no way to figure out who is right.

I argued above that external validity is a concept of limited usefulness *in basic science*. In applied or policy science, it is entirely the opposite: We are almost always deeply interested in exactly where an experimental, empirical, or theoretical result is likely to hold or not. In this case it is certainly important to build up a map of the scope of generalizability.

Suppose a regulatory agency is interested in using CH game theory to figure out how gullible consumers are likely to be in falling for scams, and what to do about it. To help the regulators we could conduct an experiment which contains many lifelike features of scams, recruit the population the regulator wants to protect, and use the CH theory to make predictions from previous experiments (and new intuition) about what will happen. The theory should offer some guidance on what changes ("treatments" in experimental terminology, "policy changes" in regulator terminology) would protect consumers to achieve the regulator's objective.[5]

In an example like this, it *is* a key part of the experimenter's job to predict the likely scope of generalizability.

Now let's go back to our discussion of basic science generalizability. When the provocative essay "What Do Laboratory Experiments Measuring Social Preferences Reveal about the Real World?"[6] came out in economics, I asked a lot of Caltech science colleagues about how external validity concerns are discussed in their fields. Most of them were perplexed; a few smiled or laughed.

In the most mature and successful sciences, such as biology and chemistry, there is no central concept like external validity that is used to criticize a particular experimental finding. Instead, the sciences develop an understanding, from theory and examples, of how broadly results will generalize.

A good workhorse example is what are called "animal models" to study behaviors that are hoped to generalize to humans. For example, a colleague studies sleep in zebrafish larvae, which are transparent. You can see right inside them and take pictures of what's going on. The presumption of this animal model is that zebrafish sleep processes are informative, to some extent, compared to mammalian and human sleep ("evolutionarily conserved").

Another example is using non-human animal models, such as rodents, to develop drug treatments. Lots of nicotine research, for example, uses rodents, because enough has been established about common biological effects of nicotine on rodents and humans to make "external [cross-species] validity" plausible. But in fact, many promising therapeutics which work in animals *do not* work for humans. Not much time is spent debating the validity of the rodent-to-human generalization because it is not worth debating until you get to where you are actually designing human experiments. *Then*, the debate is crucial.

Now we have the "basic science" versus "policy" distinction firmly in mind.[7] The next question is far and away the most important question about generalizability: Who bears the burden of proof for predicting or establishing generalizability?

In law and economics there is a principle that liability should be placed on the "least cost avoider." On a ski slope the uphill skier is liable if they crash into a downhill skier, because it is generally easier for the uphill skier to see the accident conditions taking place (the downhill skier would have to look over their shoulder).

We can similarly ask whether an experimenter, a critic, referees (including an editor), or other people or systems should bear the burden of proof. Let's use the example of me submitting a study on cognitive hierarchy experiments with Caltech students to an economics journal.

I will generally claim that the cognitive hierarchy theory is generalizable because it can explain a lot of naturally occurring strategic behavior *better than competing equilibrium theories*. Note that this is a mild comparative claim, not a precise estimate. I would moderate that claim by noting that Caltech students are highly non-random because they are outstanding in science and general intelligence (they are also in a narrow age range, etc.). Therefore, it is likely that they think more strategically than people in other domains (e.g., people haggling at a flea market). Because there is a parameter τ which indexes the average depth of strategic thinking (higher is more depth), I would predict that in other populations τ would be smaller than in the submitted paper. If during the editorial process it becomes useful to replicate the experiment with a more random sample of people, that can – these days – often be done rather easily. (Pre-Amazon's Mechanical Turk, i.e. MTurk, crowdsourcing platform and internet, it was not at all easy.)

The problem with putting the burden on either the experimenter or the referees is a combination of knowledge and incentives. The experimenter will likely have stronger intuitions but also an incentive to overclaim generalizability. In some cases, referees may have better intuitions or knowledge, but one of the professional obligations in reviewing is to describe that knowledge (e.g., other published papers the author didn't know about) to close the gap. The practical problem now in economics is that competition for publication in the so-called "Top Five" general economics journals is gladiatorial, because of 5% acceptance rates which creep lower every year. So, it is conceivable – I think it's quite common – that referees raise vague concerns about external validity just as a pretext to reject a paper. And that concern is not one that is easily addressed.

A recent paper[8] claims that "while empirical economics has made important strides over the past half century, there is a recent attack that threatens the foundations of the empirical approach in economics: external validity" (abstract) and suggests a checklist of information that authors should include in their papers.[9] One of these items requires authors to describe "naturalness." That is defined as:

> Naturalness of the choice task, setting, and timeframe should be discussed. Does treatment reflect natural variability in choice task, setting, and timeframe as the target setting? Are subjects [participants] placed on an artificial margin[10] when making the choice or in the timeframe of choice? Generally, is the nature of the choice and outcome architecture exchangeable between research and target settings (similar norms, stakes, and effort/outcome ratios as well as familiarity of choice, individual versus group decision, etc.)?[11]

Notice that this definition refers to a "target setting." As discussed in other chapters in Part One of this book, that *should* be required for policy-oriented experiments (such as randomized control trials, i.e., RCTs, much as in medicine), but for basic science *there is no specific target setting*. My hypothetical cognitive hierarchy experiment, for example, is just providing information about general accuracy of different theories using the extraordinary control of the laboratory (and extraordinary ability to replicate, which is almost unheard of in field experiments).

Among experienced experimental economists, the default setting of where the burden of proof about generalizability should rest is with theory. In experimental economics our starting-point belief is that a theory should apply everywhere (Smith called this "parallelism")[12] ... *unless the theory itself specifies where it does and does not apply*. My opinion is that a large burden should be on the creator of a theory to lay out, in the presentation of the theory, the range of settings where it is likely to apply. The theory creator should have strong intuitions about what phenomena in the world the theory is meant to describe – what is it a theory *of*? Specifying those should be required in the editorial process.

SOME SPECIAL FEATURES OF THE EXTERNAL VALIDITY DEBATE IN EXPERIMENTAL ECONOMICS

I've been doing economics experiments since 1980. From then to now, there has been a never-ending reflexive criticism, from non-experimenters, about external validity.[13] The criticism is quietest and most constructive in seminar questions, and most ignorant and snarky when behind the veil of referee anonymity.

Two specific criticisms are heard again and again. One is whether we can generalize from typical convenience samples (e.g., college students). The second is whether behavior would change if the financial stakes were higher for the participants. The latter question is asked regularly both by the smartest first-year college frosh and by Nobel laureates.

Robustness to participants pool and motivation are perfectly legitimate questions that deserve an answer. What's annoying is that both concerns have been addressed by lots of empirical work, early and often.[14] It is also important because "concerns about external validity" are often used to reject papers from competitive economics journals. And this tendency seems to be at an all-time high.

Why are these criticisms so often aimed (by economists who have never done experiments) at laboratory experiments in economics? And why do these zombie criticisms seem to live forever?

There are two reasons, in my opinion: First, as a profession, economists are generally immersed in a culture of skepticism. Skepticism is often combined with various degrees of proud imperialism.[15] The result is a lot of variability in what experimental findings are judged to be likely to generalize – e.g., from students to investors, or from low to high stakes. Most experiments are too harshly criticized, but some results are also too readily accepted.

Second, there is no economics PhD program that I know of in which *all* PhD students are required to have substantial (e.g., multiple-week) training in experimental methods. Even at Caltech, in which more than half the social science faculty do experimental work, there was no *required* experimental training until 2019. It is a little different in modern times because econometrics students, and students in many applied fields, learn a lot about causal inference, which usually includes some discussion about RCTs and experimental control.

The result is that most economics PhDs are not knowledgeable about basic laboratory experimental methods. And even if they know a bit about methods, very few are educated in the long, impressive history of experimental economics. If they had taken even a single 10-week course they would *all* know how experimental economists have managed and addressed concerns about participant populations and stakes. Instead, hardly *any* of them know.

Two other aspects of external validity in experimental economics are important: classroom demonstrations; and design.

Classroom demonstrations. In the same PhD programs in which students are not required to learn about laboratory experimental methods, some of the faculty use experimental demonstrations in teaching, typically in an introductory "principles" course. This is an odd mismatch, when you think about it: It indicates that for a teacher, experimental data are a useful guide to explaining how textbook principles describe how the world actually works. At the same time, new economics PhD students don't need to be educated on how to produce new experimental data to describe how the world actually works.

Design. One way in which experiments are used is to "testbed" the design of new economic systems. The pioneer of this approach is my Caltech colleague Charlie Plott. His inspirations are wind tunnels and tow tanks. When engineers design an airplane wing, to explore its aerodynamic properties – even when theory is available – they build a prototype and put it in a wind tunnel. The wind tunnel simulates lots of different conditions an airplane might encounter. If the wing performs badly, then the theory underlying it did not produce a good design. Similarly, in designing boats and waterborne vehicles, prototypes are created and towed or motorized in a large pool (the tow tank). The tank is built so it can create changes in waves, temperature, etc. If boat designs sink, then the theory underlying them did not produce a good design.

Many successfully designed economic systems have come from laboratory economics experiments, which range from highly abstract to more lifelike testbeds. If these experiments were not "externally valid," designs based on their results would not work. (As economists say, they would "fail the market test.")

The most famous example is the design of government auctions of scarce bandwidth. In 1993 economists at the Federal Communications Commission (FCC) in the US suggested auctioning off scarce spectrum bandwidth to cell phone providers. This raises money, avoids wasteful lobbying and – in theory – gets the spectrum into the hands of the providers who can benefit consumers most, and hence profit, by bidding the highest.

The challenge was actually designing an auction which would bring out the best and highest bids. The FCC hired several experimental economists, including Plott, to testbed actual designs which were concocted by lots of clever auction theorists.[16] The auction designs that resulted worked rather well, and got better and better over time as more countries conducted auctions.[17]

The second example is prediction markets (PMs). In a PM people can buy and sell artificial securities which pay money after an event has been determined to have occurred or not. A common example, beginning in the 1980s, was bets on political events. For example, as of this writing Alexandria Ocasio-Cortez (AOC) is trading as if there is a 17% probability she will file to run for president before 2023 on the PredictIt platform.

The genesis of modern prediction markets was a highly abstract stream of experimental economics, about whether multiple sources of information held by asset traders would be aggregated into the price, as if the traders honestly shared information among themselves. Plott and Sunder was the breakthrough paper.[18] Bob Forsythe and Forrest Nelson, who were teaching at Caltech, took this basic idea from that breakthrough paper to Iowa in 1981. In 1988 they created real-money PMs for political experiments.[19]

The insights from Plott and Sunder's early experiments laid the groundwork for PMs which are now flourishing forty years later, predicting a wide range of events accurately.[20] Were those experiments "externally valid"? It seems like an odd question to even ask. And you know the answer.

NOTES

1 Campbell, D.T., & Stanley, J.C. (1963). *Experimental and quasi-experimental designs for research*. Rand McNally & Company.
2 See Camerer, C.F., Ho, T., & Chong, J.-K. (2004). A cognitive hierarchy model of games. *Quarterly Journal of Economics, 119*(3), 861–98; and Crawford, V.P., Costa-Gomes, M.A., & Iriberri, N. (2013). Structural models of nonequilibrium strategic thinking: Theory, evidence, and applications. *Journal of Economic Literature, 51*(1), 5–62. https://doi:10.1257/jel.51.1.5.
3 Obviously, completing the model as defined this way requires a plug-in theory of what is salient. Li and Camerer (2019) describe one approach where games are visualized; see Li, X., & Camerer, C.F. Predictable effects of bottom-up visual salience in experimental decisions and games (December 10, 2020). Available at SSRN: https://ssrn.com/abstract=3308886 or http://dx.doi.org/10.2139/ssrn.3308886. Leyton-Brown and Wright (2014) present a computer science approach in which level 0's use some ensemble of strategies with different properties (e.g., maximin, or strategies with equal payoffs to players), which is then estimated from behavior; see Wright, J.R., & Leyton-Brown, K. (2014), Level-0 meta-models for predicting human behavior in games. *Proceedings of the Fifteenth ACM Conference on Economics and Computation.* https://doi:10.1145/2600057.2602907.
4 See the implicit debate between Levitt and List (2007) and Camerer (2015) at Levitt, S.D., & List, J.A. (2007). What do laboratory experiments measuring social preferences reveal about the real world? *Journal of Economic Perspectives, 21*, 153–74. https://doi: 10.1257/jep.21.2.153; and Camerer, C.F. (2015). The promise and success of lab-field generalizability in experimental economics: A critical reply to Levitt and List. In G.R. Fréchette & A. Schotter (Eds.), *Handbook of experimental economic methodology* (pp. 249–95). Oxford University Press.
5 See Wang, Spezio, et al. (2010) for a lab example loosely modelled on "upselling" in Wang, J.T., Spezio, M., & Camerer, C.F. (2010). Pinocchio's pupil: Using eyetracking and pupil dilation to understand truth telling and deception in sender-receiver games. *American Economic Review, 100* (3), 984–1007. https://doi:10.1257/aer.100.3.984; and Brown, Camerer, et al.'s (2012) field study on consumer naïveté based on quality disclosure in Brown, A.L., Camerer, C.F., & Lovallo, D. (2012). To review or not to review? Limited strategic thinking at the movie box office. *American Economic Journal: Microeconomics, 4*(2), 1–26. https://doi: 10.1257/mic.4.2.1.
6 Levitt & List (2007).
7 List (2020) makes a similar distinction between Wave 1 and Wave 3 studies. See List, J.A. (2020). Non est disputandum de generalizability? A glimpse into the external validity trial. National Bureau of Economic Research. Working Paper Series, No. 27535. http://www.nber.org/papers/w27535.pdf.
8 Ibid.
9 See ibid., abstract, p. 2. The four items in the transparency checklist include Selection (how participants were selected and their representativeness of the target group), Attrition (how many participants drop out), Naturalness, and Scaling (what is non-negotiable while scaling).

10 Being "placed on an artificial margin" is an insider economist phrase that functions like a secret club member handshake. A "margin" is a change in a decision variable. In labor, whether or not to work is called the "extensive margin" and how much you work (if you choose to work at all) is the "intensive margin." An artificial margin is a made-up term, which means a decision about whether or how much that you would not make in everyday life.

11 List (2020), p. 42.

12 Smith, V.L. (1976). Experimental economics: Induced value theory. *American Economic Review, 66*(2), 274–9. http://www.jstor.org/stable/1817233.

13 To be sure, I am told by others that generalizability is a common criticism of findings in economic history and also in development economics. For example, is the result of an RCT that had an interesting effect in, say, Mexico or Laos likely to generalize to other countries? As noted, this is an important concern if the point of the experiments is to guide policy in a specific time and place.

14 On incentives, see Camerer, C.F., & Hogarth, R.M. (1999). The effects of financial incentives in experiments: A review and capital-labor-production framework. *Journal of Risk and Uncertainty, 19*, 7–42. https://doi.org/10.1023/A:1007850605129; and Enke, B., Gneezy, U., Hall, B., Martin, D., Nelidov, V., Offerman, T., & van de Ven, J. (2020). Cognitive biases: Mistakes or missing stakes? CESifo Working Paper No. 8168. SSRN: https://ssrn.com/abstract=3564873. And on subject pools, see Fréchette, G.R. (2015). Laboratory experiments: Professionals versus students. In *Handbook of experimental economic methodology*, Oxford University Press, pp. 360–90; Fréchette, G.R. (2016), Experimental economics across subject populations. In *The handbook of experimental economics* (vol. 2, pp. 435–80). Princeton University Press; Cason, T., & Wu, S. (2019). Subject pools and deception in agricultural and resource economics experiments. *Environmental and Resource Economics, 73*(3), 743–58. https://doi.org/10.1007/s10640-018-0289-x; and Snowberg, E., & Leeat, Y. (2021), Testing the waters: Behavior across participant pools. *American Economic Review, 111*(2), 687–719. https://doi: 10.1257/aer.20181065.

15 Lazear, E.P. (1999). Economic imperialism. *Quarterly Journal of Economics, 115*(1), 99–146. https://doi.org/10.1162/003355300554683.

16 See, for example, Bykowsky, M.M., Cull, R.J., & Ledyard, J.O. (2000), Mutually destructive bidding: The FCC auction design problem. *Journal of Regulatory Economics, 17*, 205–28. https://doi.org/10.1023/A:1008122015102; and Plott, C.R., Lee, H., & Maron, T. (2014). The continuous combinatorial auction architecture, *American Economic Review, 104*(5), 452–6. https://doi:10.1257/aer.104.5.452.

17 See, for example, Kwerel, E.R., & Rosston, G.L. (2000). An insiders' view of FCC spectrum auctions. *Journal of Regulatory Economics, 17*, 253–89. https://doi .org/10.1023/A:1008126116011; and Milgrom, P. (2004), *Putting auction theory to work*. Cambridge University Press.

18 Plott, C., and Sunder, S. (1982). Efficiency of experimental security markets with insider information: An application of rational-expectations models. *Journal of Political Economy, 90*(4), 663–98. https://dx.doi.org/10.1086/261084.

19 Berg, J., Forsythe, R., & Rietz, T. (1997). What makes markets predict well? Evidence from the Iowa electronic markets. In W. Albers, W. Güth, P. Hammerstein, B. Moldovanu, & E. van Damme (Eds.), *Understanding Strategic Interaction*. Springer, Berlin, Heidelberg. https://doi.org/10.1007/978-3-642-60495-9_34.

20 Pro tip: If you enjoy the suspense at awards shows like the Oscars or "American Idol," do not look at PMs before watching; almost all the winners are accurately predicted by the markets.

PART TWO

Some Popular Behavioral Interventions

Why Many Behavioral Interventions Have Unpredictable Effects in the Wild: The Conflicting Consequences Problem

Indranil Goswami and Oleg Urminsky

Changing the behavior of a well-functioning car is straightforward. Pressing the gas pedal has one simple effect, accelerating the car, while pressing the brake has the opposite effect, decelerating the car. Changing the behavior of the driver is a different matter. Pushing a behavioral "pedal" to induce safer driving won't necessarily have a single predictable effect. Drivers wearing a seat belt are more likely to survive a crash. So, it might seem straightforward that mandating seat belt usage should simply save lives. However, mandating seat belt usage can have the additional effect of more careless driving, partially offsetting the beneficial effects.[1]

More recently, similar concerns have resulted in much debate about attempts to mitigate the COVID pandemic by encouraging face-mask wearing.[2] Concerns that requiring people to wear masks might make them less careful about following social distancing norms or might increase face touching played a role in the initial guidance against mask wearing in the United States.[3] In this case, the concern was overblown, as mask wearing is effective[4] and does not seem to reduce social distancing.[5] However, multiple studies on "risk compensation" across various domains[6] find a wide range of results, illustrating the difficulty of knowing the effect of a particular intervention in advance.

We provide a framework for understanding why promising behavioral interventions can have inconsistent and unpredictable outcomes. We describe how the net effect of a single intervention often results from a balance between multiple potentially conflicting psychological consequences of the intervention. The framework can help practitioners make sense of the differences they observe in the results of nudges across field implementations, as well as to be better calibrated regarding the uncertainty inherent in behavior change tactics. We argue that behavioral interventions validated in one setting can seldom be taken "off the shelf" (see Chapter 1) and successfully applied to a different context, and we encourage practitioners to use in-context field experiments to determine how the various consequences of a behavioral intervention net out in their given situation.

THE PROBLEM OF MULTIPLE CONFLICTING CONSEQUENCES

As popularized in the idea of "nudges," behavioral interventions may seem simple, as if intervening on people's decision process would shift their decisions in one particular direction. However, that seeming simplicity may be deceptive. Consider the example of descriptive social norms – a widely used nudge based on the idea that people are motivated to match their peers' desirable behaviors. Accordingly, people who are doing less of a desirable behavior can be influenced to do more by showing them information about their peers' behavior. Interventions using such social norms have been shown to be effective in the areas of tax compliance,[7] recycling,[8] energy conservation,[9] water conservation,[10] and other prosocial behaviors. However, in practice, such interventions are not equally effective across implementations. Identifying the forces at work in such interventions can help us understand why and how the effectiveness of descriptive norm interventions varies across contexts and populations.

For example, Opower leverages the principle of descriptive social norms by providing consumers with information about how their energy consumption compares with that of their neighbors to motivate the conservation of electricity.[11] According to the theory underlying the descriptive norm intervention, presenting norm information (e.g., the average amount of electricity used) emphasizes that many people conserve and use a modest amount of electricity, motivating consumers to begin or continue to engage in the same desired behavior. However, the information can also lead to or strengthen a belief that some people do not engage in the behavior (i.e., that some fail to conserve electricity), which can reduce the motivation to engage in the behavior, giving people the "license" to likewise fail to conserve.[12]

Whether the intervention is effective overall then depends on the relative strength of these conflicting consequences. If a person reading the information focuses more on the other people who do engage in the desired behavior and is primarily motivated to join them, then the intervention will increase the behavior (e.g., energy conservation) for that person. If, on the other hand, the person reading the information also focuses on those other people who do not engage in the behavior and is equally demotivated by these people, the two consequences may cancel, resulting in no observed effect of the intervention for that person. In fact, for a person who primarily focuses on those who don't engage in the behavior and is demotivated (or licensed) by this information, the intervention could even backfire, reducing the person's energy conservation. After all, few people want to be the sucker who is engaging in costly prosocial behavior that seems pointless because others take the easy way out and avoid doing their part.

DIFFERENT CONSEQUENCES AMONG DIFFERENT PEOPLE AND IN DIFFERENT CONTEXTS

On its own, the problem of multiple consequences does not have to be a major impediment to reliably applying behavioral science. To know whether an intervention with multiple conflicting consequences will be successful overall, we simply need to know whether the positive effects are larger than the negative ones. If a rigorous experiment finds positive effects of the intervention (e.g., providing electricity usage norms reduces usage), then we can conclude that, on average, the positive effects (motivation to conserve from knowing that many others do so) outweigh the negative effects (demotivation from knowing that some others don't). In fact, such an experiment could even help us quantify the relative impact of the two factors.

However, deciding to implement an intervention based on the results of a study in another setting requires assuming that the relative impact of the multiple consequences is stable over populations and contexts. This strong assumption is typically not true. Indeed, several examples in this book in domains ranging from savings behavior (Chapter 1), credit card debt (Chapter 3), pension contributions (Chapter 3), energy savings (Chapter 1), and welfare programs (Chapter 4) highlight the perils of assuming the stability of settings in translating knowledge.

As illustrated in Figure 6.1, in one application where the positive effect of consequence A outweighs the negative effect of B, a net effect results, while no net effect is observed in another application where the two consequences are equal and cancel each other. Research on psychological factors that influence preferences and choices typically identifies a wide variety of moderators – factors that make a particular psychological process more or less likely to occur and make the process stronger or weaker when it does occur. As a result, the mix of consequences of the same intervention often varies across contexts.

A recent empirical investigation found that Opower's norm-based nudges to promote energy conservation yielded differing net results across implementations. In particular, the intervention yielded significantly higher energy savings in their first 10 sites than in their next 101 replications.[13] In general, the available information about the effectiveness of interventions may not be representative. Organizations developing a new program might target the initial tests for the most promising locations. Organizations with a more successful ongoing program might be more willing to do a program evaluation field experiment, while those who think evaluations could undermine their credibility would be less willing.[14] Successful

Figure 6.1. The conflicting consequences problem

The same intervention could yield different results in different applications based on the relative strengths of consequences A and B on the desired behavior.

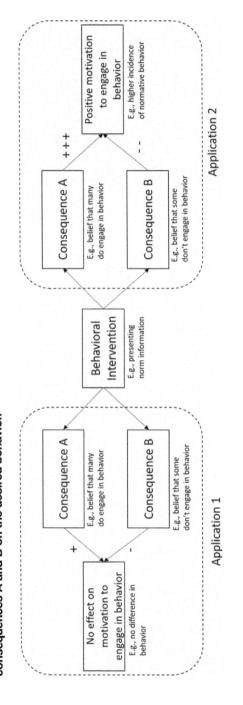

interventions are also more "newsworthy" and may be more likely to be publicized.[15]

To understand how the effects of descriptive norms may differ, we can identify some likely factors that contribute to differences in the relative strength of the multiple consequences of this intervention across people and contexts. Before the intervention, some people used less energy than others. Those who used less energy might have assumed that others were like them, carefully conserving energy. As a result, these conservationists might then be surprised to learn that the average person uses far more energy than they had thought, leading them to focus on those not conserving and to feel demotivated. Among those using more energy, on the other hand, the relative strength of the motivating and demotivating effects is likely to depend on pre-existing attitudes. For those non-conservers who endorse the goal and don't feel threatened by the implicit rebuke the information provides, the motivating effects are likely to dominate, as intended. However, those who do not endorse the goal or who are defensive about their non-normative behavior may avoid the intervention, reducing its efficacy.[16] Even more problematically, they may feel more licensed not to engage in the behavior themselves when they know that there are others who do not engage in the behavior.[17] Consistent with this possibility, descriptive norms are more effective at reducing electricity consumption among liberals than conservatives.[18]

In theory, if an intervention only has a single simple effect, decisions about using it are simpler, even when the magnitude of the effect varies by context. As long as the cost of the intervention is low, implementation can be justified by the potential benefit if successful and the minimal risk otherwise (because nothing will change if it is unsuccessful). However, this justification no longer holds when the intervention has multiple *conflicting* (i.e., both positive and negative) consequences that vary in relative strength. In such situations, the risk is that the negative consequences could dominate in a particular implementation, resulting in a negative net effect.

Our general framework applies to any situation in which a successful intervention from one study is used in a different setting, as illustrated using three case studies.

CASE 1: USING TEMPORARY INCENTIVES TO MOTIVATE USEFUL BEHAVIOR

Material incentives (including financial rewards, such as salaries) are perhaps the most basic way to motivate behavior because of the simple fact that people will do more of an activity that is more rewarding. However, a highly influential literature has raised concerns about a conflicting consequence when using temporary incentives to motivate useful behavior (e.g., going to the gym, eating healthy, giving nutritional supplements to children in developing countries). Researchers in psychology, based on lab experiments, have argued that although such incentives boost compensated behavior, they also undermine people's own intrinsic motivation to do useful or enjoyable activities without compensation.[19] As a result, practitioners have been warned[20] that once rewards are taken away, people's long-term engagement and performance might be lower than if incentives had not been used. This view has been quite influential, limiting the use of temporary incentives as a tool to motivate behavior, particularly in the context of education.

However, our framework recognizes that a *potential* conflicting effect of reducing intrinsic motivation is not a sufficient reason to abandon the use of temporary incentives. Instead, the question is how the potential motivating and demotivating consequences of temporary incentives balance out to produce the net effect of the intervention on the specific outcome of interest in a given context. In fact, field experiments that measured the effects of temporary incentives on people's behavior days, weeks, or months after the incentive ended reported no such detrimental net effects, contrary to the immediate negative effects found in lab experiments.[21] For example, temporary cash awards for students raising their first-year GPA had either no effect or a positive effect on GPA the subsequent year.[22]

Our research confirms that temporary incentives have two separate conflicting effects on post-incentive motivation and engagement.[23] However, the potential adverse effects are not due to a long-term loss of intrinsic motivation. Instead, decision makers are motivated to take a "break" after exerting additional effort to earn the reward. When a moderately rewarding temporary incentive is provided, we find a momentary break from task engagement when the reward ends, but the net effect differs over a longer time horizon, as people quickly return to their baseline activity level. A sufficiently rewarding incentive can increase liking of the task because of positive reinforcement from the rewards. Indeed, when the temporary incentive is more generous, we observe less of a momentary decrease in engagement immediately after the incentive ends, and people's engagement can increase to above their pre-reward levels over time. As a result, the net effect will systematically depend on both the magnitude of the reward and the time-frame of the outcome (e.g., immediately after the incentive ends versus longer-term).

Identifying the actual conflicting consequences allowed us to reconcile past research and better predict the effects of temporary incentives. We applied this approach in a café field study where we used a discount to incentivize lunchtime customers to buy soup. As predicted, soup sales dropped significantly on the first day after the discount ended (without advance notice) but then increased back to the pre-incentive sales level over the next few days.[24]

CASE 2: CAN DEFAULTS INCREASE CHARITABLE CONTRIBUTIONS?

Cass Sunstein, the co-author of the book *Nudge*, has stated that if there were an Olympic medal for the most effective tool in behavioral economics, the clear winner would be decision defaults,[25] a view supported by a review comparing behavioral interventions.[26] Defaults define one option as the action to take unless the person selects a different course of action. In some settings (e.g., organ donation,[27] saving for retirement,[28] etc.), a major reason why defaults are effective is that many people don't make a decision and instead let the default occur.

However, defaults can affect outcomes even when people actively make decisions and a default course of behavior cannot be imposed, such as in fundraising appeals. For example, people might treat the default as an implicit recommendation or norm, or they might be averse to change and prefer the status quo.[29] Most philanthropic organizations solicit donations online or via mail, where it is trivial to implement a non-binding default or "suggested amount." Our review of fundraising practices of top charities found that less than half used a pre-selected default contribution in their menu of amount options. Of those who had a default-ask, the vast majority used the lowest or second-lowest menu amount as the default donation option. We conducted a series of studies to test the net effect on the funds raised of defaulting potential donors to a particular donation amount.

Prior experimental research on suggested donation amounts had revealed a confusing set of seemingly contradictory results, with suggested amounts sometimes resulting in more donations, sometimes in less, and sometimes making no difference. Our investigation revealed that the effect of default nudges on the funds raised by a charitable solicitation could not be understood as a single effect, or even a single effect that varies in strength.[30] Instead, in a series of lab and online studies, we found that two separate conflicting consequences consistently operated in tandem, systematically varying with the defaulted donation amount, such that their joint effect determines whether implementing a particular default "suggested donation" raises more funds than the baseline of no default.

First, defaults suggest to the donor an amount to give. So, the straightforward (and typically intended) effect of defaulting or suggesting an amount is that people give that amount or a similar amount. Thus, among those who donate, setting a higher default would be expected to yield larger donations, on average, and we find that it usually does. In fact, this consequence results in a risk that setting too low a default – asking donors for less than they would otherwise be willing to give – could reduce donations. Donors asked to donate $10, for example, may think to themselves, "I was willing to give $50, but since you say that all you need is $10, it's a win-win: I get to feel good about helping, for less!" If this were the only effect of defaults, the prescription would be clear: set a high donation amount as the default.

However, we find that there is also a second effect of suggested amounts, conflicting with the first: suggesting a donation amount impacts whether or not people donate at all. Even when people can donate any amount they choose, suggesting a large amount typically reduces donations, and suggesting a small amount increases donations, relative to the baseline. It's as if potential donors would rather not participate than give a "wrong" amount. Donors reassured by the suggestion of a small donation are more likely to open their wallets, while those asked for a large donation move on instead of giving the small amount they would have otherwise been willing to donate.

As a result, the net effect of setting a particular donation amount as the default is not obvious. Asking for a smaller amount than the typical donation will encourage people to donate, but they may give less than they would have given without a default. In contrast, asking for an above-average amount may result in fewer people participating but giving more. Given that the net funds raised are the product of participation and average donation amount, how the joint effect of these two consequences balances out will determine whether a particular suggested amount results in more funds, less funds, or the same amount as without the suggested amount. A re-analysis found that the seemingly contradictory results of past studies were largely explained as the net of these two conflicting consequences varying by the suggested amount.

Furthermore, the relative sensitivity of participation rates and averaged donation amounts to the default intervention may differ across people and donation contexts, resulting in even greater uncertainty about the net effect of an intervention in a given context. In particular, among prior donors who give regularly, participation may be less sensitive, and donation amount may be relatively more sensitive to the default, while the reverse may be the case among donors who often fail to give.

Results of two separate field experiments conducted with the University of Chicago Booth School of Business annual fundraising campaign validated these insights and demonstrated the usefulness of the framework. In the first experiment, conducted at the end of the annual campaign, we varied the presence and amount of a "suggested" donation level in solicitations sent to prior donors who had not yet given in response to three mailers sent earlier that academic year. Among these unlikely donors, setting the lowest amount as the default raised more funds than the no-default appeal, while the higher default amounts were not effective. The low default did result in lower donation amounts among those who gave, but this was more than compensated for by a 128% increase in the (low) rate of giving.

In a follow-up study, we conducted the same experiment at the start of a new annual campaign in solicitations sent to all past donors, including the donors who give regularly that had been excluded in the first study.[31] The low default, which had been the best performer in the prior campaign, instead did the worst, reducing funds raised compared to the no-default baseline. This outcome was the result of the net effect from a different balance between the two conflicting outcomes: the low default substantially reduced the donation amounts among those who gave but had only a small positive effect on the (already much higher) participation rate in this population.

The experiment targeting frequent donors found a net effect of the low-amount default that was the *opposite* of the effect in the study targeting infrequent donors. While these findings can provide guidelines for thinking about how suggested amounts might be beneficial or harmful for a charity to use, a particular organization cannot readily know how a particular suggested amount would affect the funds raised. Even when we believe that we understand the underlying process, the variability of the relative impact of conflicting consequences leaves us uncertain and unable to predict the net effect of a specific default intervention when targeting a particular pool of donors for a given charity.

CASE 3: THE FAILURE OF A PROMISING MATCHING MECHANISM IN FUNDRAISING

It may turn out that the conflicting consequences problem is occurring in practice, even when conflicting consequences were not identified in advance, and the proposed intervention may have seemed as if it would have straightforward positive effects. Research that we have conducted regarding matching solicitations in charitable fundraising (e.g., every dollar donated is matched by an extra dollar from a benefactor) provides a demonstration of this principle.[32]

Matching appeals have been described as a staple of fundraising and are routinely used.[33] Theoretical models of altruism identify two benefits to the donor: the charity having more funds to do its work (regardless of the source) and the "warm glow" that the donor gets from being personally responsible for giving.[34] In this model, matching appeals motivate donors by enabling them to direct more funds to the charity than just the donation they personally give, increasing the impact of the person's donation on the funds available to the charity, and thereby motivating them to give more.[35] Based on this theoretical framework, we developed a novel approach to making matches more effective: reframing the match as the benefactor helping the donor give more (i.e., as opposed to the benefactor making their own separate matching donation). The idea behind this "giving credit" match framing is to increase the "warm glow" the donor feels from giving, in addition to increasing the objective benefit to the charity. Consequently, the new framing would be predicted by theoretical models to increase donations from the match. A sample of fundraising experts whom we surveyed overwhelmingly predicted that the "giving credit" framing would be effective, and most believed it would be more effective than the standard match framing.

However, despite its basis in academic theory and the favorable intuitions of fundraising experts, our novel "giving credit" framing was a failure when tested in practice in two fundraising campaigns for a Chicago arts non-profit targeting prior donors. The participation rate among potential donors who received the "giving credit" version of the matching appeal was almost half of the participation rate using the standard matching description and, as a result, the campaign raised significantly less funds.

Why did this promising, vetted intervention fail? While our field experiments did not collect the data needed to conclusively identify the underlying cause, it seems clear that the "giving credit" framing had a conflicting negative consequence on donors' motivations that far outweighed the intended positive effect of giving the donors a reason to feel "warm glow" from the benefactor's match.

Table 6.1. Summary of the cases discussed in this chapter

	Consequence A	Consequence B
Case 1: Using temporary incentives to motivate useful behavior	Longer-run return to baseline after "break" is over. Positive spillover from reinforcement, habit formation also possible.	Short-run decrease in engagement after incentives end because the option of a "break" is salient and easy to justify.
Case 2: Using defaults to increase charitable contributions	Lower defaults motivate participation as donors earn "warm glow" from the act of giving.	Lower default amount licenses people to donate a smaller amount.
Case 3: "Giving credit" match framing intended to improve fundraising outcomes	Increase in "warm glow" from donors' match.	Unidentified: could be confusion, perceived manipulativeness, or a reduction in accountability.

It is possible that the "giving credit" framing seemed weird or manipulative to the prospective donors. Alternatively, encouraging the potential donor to see the benefactor's funds as their own donation may have had the reverse effect, reducing perceived personal accountability for one's own donation because of the suggested "comingling" of funds. In any case, a promising intervention failed in practice, at least in the setting in which it was tested, because the intervention that was assumed to have a single positive motivational impact instead involved multiple conflicting potential consequences, resulting in a net effect mispredicted by us as well as by fundraising experts.

The "giving credit" framing might not be harmful or could even be successful in a different fundraising context. To know if that is the case, we would need first to identify all the conflicting consequences of framing matching appeals that way and then develop a means to predict how the relative impact of the conflicting consequences varies across implementation contexts. In the absence of this complete understanding of the intervention, a policymaker simply cannot generalize from observing either success or failure in another context to determine whether an intervention with potentially conflicting consequences would be beneficial, inconsequential, or harmful in their own context.

Table 6.2. Decision aid to identify potential conflicting consequences: Ask yourself the following five questions to start

	Factors suggesting multiple consequences
Question 1	Do people differ in relevant experience (e.g., high versus low engagement, prior experience, or expertise)?
Question 2	Do people differ in relevant values or attitudes (e.g., identifying with a pro-environment agenda or not)?
Question 3	Can short-term and long-term effects differ (e.g., due to forgetting, fatigue, habit formation, or satiation over time)?
Question 4	Does the targeted behavior involve multiple distinct decisions (e.g., whether to give and how much to donate)?
Question 5	Do the intervention cues have multiple plausible interpretations (e.g., as information or allocation of responsibility or an attempt to manipulate)?

THE PATH FORWARD

The problem of conflicting consequences prescribes a different approach to using behavioral insights in practice from what is often the case. Experimental evidence that an intervention has beneficial effects in another context, whether from academic research or observed in practice, validates the intervention as a *hypothesis to be tested* in the intended context, not as a policy to be adopted. Absent a complete understanding of how the potential conflicting consequences net out in a given context, which we typically do not have, we cannot predict the consequences of implementing even seemingly "proven" interventions. For academics, this suggests a need to go beyond "proof of concept" research and develop detailed and robust models of the most promising interventions.

For practitioners, even the most promising new behavioral intervention should be subjected to substantial field testing in one's own context, across the factors varying in that context, before changing to a new policy. The common reluctance many organizations have to test initiatives experimentally with appropriate controls and the preference instead to simply set policy and act can have serious hidden costs when interventions have conflicting consequences, perpetuating costly mistakes and impeding context-specific informed decision making.

NOTES

1 See Peltzman, S. (1975). The effects of automobile safety regulation. *Journal of Political Economy, 83*(4), 677–725. https://doi.org/10.1086/260352; and Cohen, A., & Einav, L. (2003). The effects of mandatory seat belt laws on driving behavior and traffic fatalities. *Review of Economics and Statistics, 85*(4), 828–43. https://doi .org/10.1162/003465303772815754.

2 Randall, I. (n.d.). *Wearing face masks makes people more careless and less likely to follow social distancing guidelines.* Daily Mail Online. Retrieved March 15, 2021, from https://www.dailymail.co.uk/sciencetech/article-8659487/Wearing-face-masks -makes-people-careless-likely-follow-social-distancing-guidelines.html.

3 Fact check: Outdated video of Fauci saying "there's no reason to be walking around with a mask." (n.d.). Reuters. Retrieved March 15, 2021, from https://www.reuters .com/article/uk-factcheck-fauci-outdated-video-masks/fact-checkoutdated -video-of-fauci-saying-theres-no-reason-to-be-walking-around-with-a-mask -idUSKBN26T2TR.

4 Mitze, T., Kosfeld, R., Rode, J., & Wälde, K. (2020). Face masks considerably reduce COVID-19 cases in Germany. *Proceedings of the National Academy of Sciences, 117*(51), 32293–301. https://doi.org/10.1073/pnas.2015954117.

5 Seres, G., Balleyer, A.H., Cerutti, N., Friedrichsen, J., & Süer, M. (2020). *Face mask use and physical distancing before and after mandatory masking: Evidence from public waiting lines* (SSRN Scholarly Paper ID 3641367). Social Science Research Network. https:// doi.org/10.2139/ssrn.3641367.

6 See Mantzari, E., Rubin, G.J., & Marteau, T.M. (2020). Is risk compensation threatening public health in the COVID-19 pandemic? *BMJ, 370*, m2913. https:// doi.org/10.1136/bmj.m2913; and Esmaeilikia, M., Radun, I., Grzebieta, R., & Olivier, J. (2019). Bicycle helmets and risky behaviour: A systematic review. *Transportation Research Part F: Traffic Psychology and Behaviour, 60*, 299–310. https://doi:10.1016/j .trf.2018.10.026.

7 Thaler, R.H. (2012). Watching behavior before writing the rules. *New York Times, 7.*

8 Cialdini, R.B. (2003). Crafting normative messages to protect the environment. *Current Directions in Psychological Science, 12*(4), 105–9. https://doi.org/10.1111 /1467-8721.01242.

9 Allcott, H. (2011). Social norms and energy conservation. *Journal of Public Economics, 95*(9), 1082–95. https://doi.org/10.1016/j.jpubeco.2011.03.003.

10 Ferraro, P.J., & Price, M.K. (2013). Using nonpecuniary strategies to influence behavior: Evidence from a large-scale field experiment. *Review of Economics and Statistics, 95*(1), 64–73. https://doi.org/10.1162/REST_a_00344.

11 Rahim, S. (2010, June 21). Finding the "weapons" of persuasion to save energy. *New York Times.* https://archive.nytimes.com/www.nytimes.com/cwire/2010 /06/21/21climatewire-finding-the-weapons-of-persuasion-to-save-ene-8137 .html?pagewanted=1.

12 See Ozaki, T., & Nakayachi, K. (2020). When descriptive norms backfire: Attitudes induce undesirable consequences during disaster preparation. *Analyses of Social Issues and Public Policy, 20*(1), 90–117. https://doi.org/10.1111/asap.12195; Miller, D.T., & Prentice, D.A. (2016). Changing norms to change behavior. *Annual Review of Psychology, 67*(1), 339–61. https://doi.org/10.1146/annurev-psych-010814-015013; and Mollen, S., Rimal, R.N., Ruiter, R.A.C., & Kok, G. (2013). Healthy and unhealthy social norms and food selection. Findings from a field-experiment. *Appetite, 65*, 83–9. https://doi.org/10.1016/j.appet.2013.01.020.

13 Allcott, H. (2015). Site selection bias in program evaluation. *Quarterly Journal of Economics, 130*(3), 1117–65. https://doi.org/10.1093/qje/qjv015.

14 Pritchett, L. (2002). It pays to be ignorant: A simple political economy of rigorous program evaluation. *Journal of Policy Reform, 5*(4), 251–69. https://doi.org/10.1080/1384128032000096832.

15 Hummel, D., & Maedche, A. (2019). How effective is nudging? A quantitative review on the effect sizes and limits of empirical nudging studies. *Journal of Behavioral and Experimental Economics, 80*, 47–58. https://doi.org/10.1016/j.socec.2019.03.005.

16 Allcott, H., & Kessler, J.B. (2019). The welfare effects of nudges: A case study of energy use social comparisons. *American Economic Journal: Applied Economics, 11*(1), 236–76. https://doi.org/10.1257/app.20170328.

17 Ozaki & Nakayachi (2020).

18 Costa, D.L., & Kahn, M.E. (2013). Energy conservation "nudges" and environmentalist ideology: Evidence from a randomized residential electricity field experiment. *Journal of the European Economic Association, 11*(3), 680–702. https://doi.org/10.1111/jeea.12011.

19 Deci, E.L., Koestner, R., & Ryan, R.M. (1999). A meta-analytic review of experiments examining the effects of extrinsic rewards on intrinsic motivation. *Psychological Bulletin, 125*(6), 627–68. https://doi.org/10.1037/0033-2909.125.6.627.

20 See Pink, D.H. (2011). *Drive: The surprising truth about what motivates us.* Penguin; and Kohn, A. (1999). *Punished by rewards: The trouble with gold stars, incentive plans, A's, praise, and other bribes.* Houghton Mifflin Harcourt.

21 Goswami, I., & Urminsky, O. (2017). The dynamic effect of incentives on postreward task engagement. *Journal of Experimental Psychology: General, 146*(1), 1–19. https://doi.org/10.1037/xge0000206.

22 Angrist, J., Lang, D., & Oreopoulos, P. (2009). Incentives and services for college achievement: Evidence from a randomized trial. *American Economic Journal: Applied Economics, 1*(1), 136–63. https://doi.org/10.1257/app.1.1.136.

23 Goswami & Urminsky (2017).

24 Urminsky, O., & Goswami, I. (2016). One Size Does Not Fit All: Importance of Donor Type on setting Default Amounts for Charitable Donations. University of Chicago. Working Paper.

25 Sunstein, C.R. (2017, December 28). Don't underrate the power of the default option. *Bloomberg.Com.* https://www.bloomberg.com/opinion/articles/2017-12-28/don-t-underrate-the-power-of-the-default-option.

26 Hummel & Maedche (2019).

27 Johnson, E.J., & Goldstein, D. (2003). Do defaults save lives? *Science, 302*(5649), 1338–9. https://doi.org/10.1126/science.1091721.

28 Beshears, J., Choi, J.J., Laibson, D., & Madrian, B.C. (2009). The importance of default options for retirement saving outcomes: Evidence from the United States. In *Social security policy in a changing environment* (pp. 167–95). University of Chicago Press.

29 Defaults are not the same by default. (2019, April 16). *Behavioral Scientist.* https://behavioralscientist.org/defaults-are-not-the-same-by-default/.

30 Goswami, I., & Urminsky, O. (2016). When should the ask be a nudge? The effect of default amounts on charitable donations. *Journal of Marketing Research, 53*(5), 829–46. https://doi.org/10.1509/jmr.15.0001.

31 Urminsky & Goswami (2016).

32 Goswami, I., & Urminsky, O. (2020). No substitute for the real thing: The importance of in-context field experiments in fundraising. *Marketing Science, 39*(6), 1052–70. https://doi.org/10.1287/mksc.2020.1252.

33 Leonhardt, D. (2008, March 9). What makes people give. *New York Times*.

34 Andreoni, J. (1990). Impure altruism and donations to public goods: A theory of warm-glow giving. *Economic Journal, 100*(401), 464–77. https://doi.org/10.2307/2234133.

35 Karlan, D., & List, J.A. (2007). Does price matter in charitable giving? Evidence from a large-scale natural field experiment. *American Economic Review, 97*(5), 1774–93. https://doi.org/10.1257/aer.97.5.1774.

CHAPTER SEVEN

Norm Nudging: How to Measure What We Want to Implement

Cristina Bicchieri

In recent years, nudging has emerged as one of the most salient intervention techniques in behavioral science. The advantage of nudges over other forms of interventions is that they redirect behavior by reframing the choice architecture, without forbidding any option or significantly changing economic incentives.[1] They are low-cost interventions, but can be very effective. Work on nudging has focused on individual behavior change, for example by trying to induce individuals to save more in their pension plans,[2] apply for student financial aid,[3] adhere to diet or medication plans, and even become organ donors.[4] Some nudges may simply aim to induce behavior that benefits only the individual who performs it. Others may try to bring about behaviors that are socially beneficial. In this case, nudges employ social comparison, by informing people about what others do and/or approve or disapprove of in order to induce a change in behavior. The messages can be purely descriptive, telling individuals what others do or do not do; or they can be normative (injunctive), either by directly prescribing or proscribing a specific target behavior, or by informing about others' approval or disapproval of the target behavior. In some cases, descriptive and normative messages are combined. The expression "norm nudging" that we refer to when using social comparisons indicates that nudging's aim may be to focus individuals on an existing norm, in order to improve compliance (in the case of a positive norm) or abandon it (in the case of a negative norm). It may also aim to create a new norm, by convincing people that a majority already perform a target action, work towards a target goal, or approve of the behavior we want to implement.

These norm-nudging techniques were first introduced by Cialdini and colleagues, who experimented with sending descriptive or injunctive messages to curb littering in a variety of contexts.[5] More recent examples include alerting taxpayers that the majority of taxpayers pay on time,[6] comparing electricity consumption to that of neighbors,[7] or telling hotel guests that most other guests reuse unwashed towels.[8] Some of these interventions were at least temporarily successful: for example, comparing electricity consumption to that of neighbors effectively reduced consumption, and telling hotel guests that most other guests reuse unwashed towels led overall to more guests reusing their towels. Failures, however, are also common: a well-known example in one study realized that comparing average electricity consumption among neighbors led to no overall change, since below-average consumers were induced to use more electricity.[9] A more worrisome consideration is that even successful interventions may not be sustainable. A majority of studies found the effects of descriptive messages to be very short-lived, and a few found a diminishing effect even in a longer time window.[10] For example, Fielding and colleagues found that though there is a decreasing trend of daily water use per person in intervention groups that use descriptive messages, the household water use returned to pre-intervention levels 12 months after the intervention.[11] Another issue is the generalizability of the results. As Chapter 3 emphasized, context matters, and should be taken into account. For example, when the US intervention to induce hotel guests' reuse of towels was replicated in Europe, one study found that it actually backfired.[12] With the great influence context can have, it becomes very challenging to interpret the implications of an intervention's effect for other settings.

All the above difficulties are not uncommon in a new area of research, where we proceed by trial and error and refine our tools as we go along. What is more problematic is that the "norm-nudging" approach is still a black box one. There is an input (the norm message), and an output (behavior), but no model of what goes on in between. Since results are mixed, it is important to focus on what may be going on "inside the box," to understand why some messages fail and others succeed. This understanding is particularly important to help design successful interventions, especially when target behaviors create negative externalities for entire communities or groups, as in sanitation (open defecation, hand washing, vaccinating), child nutrition (refusing to give colostrum to newborns), or women's welfare (child marriage, FGC).

To work, norm nudging requires correctly identifying the mechanisms through which different types of information affect behavior, and understanding individuals' motivations to engage in specific behaviors. For example, do people litter out of convenience or just because they observe others litter? People may have different motivations, but a social norm approach presupposes that – with respect to a specific target behavior – most choices are conditional on social expectations.[13] That is, the expectations we hold about other people's behaviors and/or beliefs induce us to act in ways we may not consider without such expectations. The implicit assumption of norm nudging is thus that people will be responsive to social information because their behavior is influenced by the social expectations that the messages induce.[14] We may therefore describe a norm nudge as *a nudge whose mechanism of action relies on eliciting social expectations with the intent of inducing desirable behavior, under the assumption that individual preferences for performing the target behavior are conditional on social expectations.*

In order to successfully apply norm nudging, a first step then consists in deciding if the target behaviors are socially independent or interdependent. In other words, is behavior motivated by social expectations, or rather independent of them? Independent behaviors are simply behaviors that are not conditional on social expectations. Using umbrellas when it rains (a collective custom) or refusing to harm an innocent person (a moral injunction) are examples of independent behaviors: in both cases, we may expect these behaviors to be common, or approved of, but these expectations do not influence our choices. We are just moved by considerations of what we need or what is right, respectively. The fact that many people have the

Figure 7.1. Four types of behavior

	Independent Behavior (Unconditional Preferences)	Interdependent Behavior (Conditional Preferences)
Descriptive	*Custom* You **prefer** to do X because **you believe X meets your needs.** Your choice does <u>not</u> depend on others doing X or thinking that you should do X.	*Descriptive Norm* You prefer to do X because **you expect others to do X.** Your choice depends on your **empirical expectations** of others' behavior.
Injunctive	*Moral Rule* You **prefer** to do X because **you believe X is the right thing to do.** Your choice does <u>not</u> depend on others doing X or thinking that you should do X.	*Social Norm* You **prefer** to do X because **you expect others to do X <u>and</u> you believe that others think that you should do X.** Your choice depends on both empirical <u>and</u> normative expectations.

Source: C. Bicchieri, *Lectures at the Penn-UNICEF Summer Program on Advances in Social Norms and Social Change*, July 2012.

same needs and the same means to satisfy them, or share the same moral concerns, does not make these behaviors interdependent.

Fashions and fads, etiquette, conventions, and fairness rules are all examples of interdependence. In some cases, like fashion, what matters is just what others do. In a convention like coordinating on traffic signals, what matters are mutual expectations (what others do and expect us to do), whereas in other cases, such as fairness rules, what matters to our choice is both what others do and what they approve of. In Figure 7.1, I separate behaviors that are independent (left) from those that are interdependent (right). This distinction is important for interventions, as it draws on the presence or absence of conditional preferences, which are the causal link between expectations and behavior.

There is another, coarser definition that is commonly used, and it is represented by what lies above and below the horizontal dividing line. This is the distinction usually made by social psychologists between what they call descriptive and injunctive norms.[15] Descriptive simply refers to what is commonly done, whereas injunctive refers to what is commonly approved of. A custom like using umbrellas and a descriptive norm like traffic rules are grouped together as "descriptive norms," while a shared moral rule and a social norm proper are grouped under the heading "injunctive norms."

I adopt a finer distinction, and say that a behavioral rule satisfies the properties of a descriptive norm only if the individual prefers to follow the rule on the condition that they believe that sufficiently many others in their reference network also follow it (empirical expectation). A custom, on the contrary, is a pattern of behavior such that individuals prefer to conform to it because it meets their needs. The difference here is the presence or absence of conditional preferences. Similar considerations apply to the distinction between moral rules and social norms.

If we were to only measure expectations, the coarser description might seem adequate. Customs and descriptive norms just tell us what is commonly done, and empirical expectations are usually present in both. Both moral and social norms have an injunctive component, and people would normally have expectations of what others approve of. Yet the existence of conditional preferences is what makes the difference, as they tell us whether these expectations have causal relevance. This information is crucial for interventions, as conditionality implies that *changing expectations will change behavior*. This is precisely what norm nudging aims to do.

Highlighting just the injunctive component may have a further, significant drawback: not only does it blur the difference between the moral and the social, but it also downplays the reason why social norms proper need the presence of *both* empirical and normative expectations. Social norms usually emerge when there is tension between selfish and other-regarding goals, and the combination of the expectation that most people behave prosocially with the expectation that they disapprove of anti-social behavior and may punish it is necessary to induce compliance. Whereas it is in our interest to follow a descriptive norm (because it pays to imitate, coordinate with others, etc.), compliance with a social norm may be costly from the point of view of material self-interest. A distinguishing feature of behaviors that are regulated by social norms is that the motivation to undertake such behaviors is *conditional* on a person's belief about what is commonly done *and* what is commonly approved of within that person's reference network.[16] The

Figure 7.2. Diagnostic process to identify type of behavior and nudge

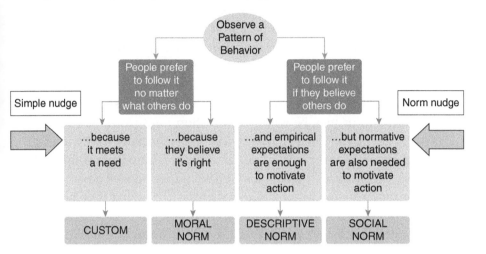

psychological foundation of such conditionality lies in the notion that humans naturally strive to obtain approval and avoid disapproval from others.[17] This combination of normative and empirical may be the reason why a message about water consumption in California that paired an injunctive message with information about the water consumption of one's neighbors reduced consumption more effectively than other descriptive or normative messages alone.[18]

Figure 7.2 presents a simple diagram that summarizes the diagnostic (and measurement) pattern we have to follow to decide the nature of the collective behavior we try to understand and possibly change. Independent behaviors can be nudged by reminding individuals of moral principles or values we know they hold, or by providing better means to satisfy a need they have. Norm nudging instead relies on interdependent behaviors, and on messages that elicit social expectations that have a causal influence on behavior.

WHICH NORM? DESCRIPTIVE VERSUS SOCIAL NORMS

Having said that what we care about are interdependent behaviors, let us summarize what a norm is or is not. A norm is a special type of behavioral rule that prescribes or proscribes a certain behavior to a specific group of people in a specific class of situations. We say that the rule satisfies the properties of a *social norm* if the individual prefers to follow the rule on the condition that (a) they believe that sufficiently many others in their reference network also follow it (empirical expectation) and (b) they believe that sufficiently many others in their reference network believe that one should follow the rule and/or may be willing to sanction transgressions (normative expectation).[19] Finally, we say that a social norm exists within a group of people if the rule is known to apply within that group, and people's normative expectations (i.e., what they believe others view as appropriate) and empirical expectations (i.e., what they believe others actually do) are *mutually consistent* (i.e., they all point to the same behavioral rule). A *descriptive norm* instead lacks condition (b), the normative condition.

An important point to be made is that our definition of a social norm allows us to separate the notion that a norm exists and the notion that it is followed (compliance), whereas this separation is impossible with a descriptive norm. The existence of a social norm depends on the mutual consistency of individuals' normative and empirical expectations. Since preference to comply with the norm is *conditional* on such expectations, a norm may exist without being followed at a particular time[20] because expectations may change or weaken. If transgressions become common, or are no longer disapproved of, the norm will weaken and eventually disappear. For instance, consider two communities that hold similar normative expectations about the appropriateness of recycling: in both cases, individuals believe that recycling is appropriate, i.e., a recycling norm exists. In one community, this general social approval for recycling is accompanied by evidence that recycling is frequent; empirical and normative expectations are both strong and aligned. In the other community, however, the approval of recycling is accompanied by widespread evidence that recycling is becoming uncommon. Empirical expectations of compliance are significantly weakened and observations are now incongruent with normative expectations, likely weakening them. If individuals in the latter community observe a sufficient number of transgressions, they may stop recycling, too, since their compliance is conditional upon what others actually do, not just what others say they *should* do. As a consequence, compliance (i.e., norm following) may become much lower in the latter community, even if all members previously held similar beliefs about what is socially appropriate. If recycling were just a descriptive norm, it would exist only when a sufficiently high number of community members are observed to recycle. Recycling would stop once numbers dwindle. The empirical expectations are the drivers of behavior, and once expectations change, behavior may suddenly disappear.

It is important to realize that social expectations are not generic, but refer instead to a particular reference network, people whose behavior and beliefs matter to the actor. Reference networks may vary from situation to situation. They may include people with whom individuals have daily interactions, as well as people who are distantly or indirectly related. Social network analysis is an important complement to the study of norms, as it characterizes the web of social relations around the individuals whose behavior we want to study. All the measures of social expectations we draw refer to a specific network, and norm nudging may succeed or fail if the message we send does not refer to the appropriate network. A successful example is an intervention by Hallsworth and colleagues to reduce antibiotic prescriptions among general practitioners (GPs) in the UK.[21] Overprescribing GPs were informed that they prescribed more than 80% of the GPs *in their area*, and this information significantly reduced antibiotic prescriptions. The important point here is that being compared to other GPs in the same area prevented self-serving interpretations: for example, one may think that those GPs who prescribe fewer antibiotics come from areas where there are fewer infectious diseases, smog, etc., thus justifying staying with one's choice. An example of how a wrong choice of reference network may backfire is the work done in various sub-Saharan African countries to improve newborn nutrition.[22] In almost all cases, the decision maker is the mother-in-law, and not realizing this fact has led to ineffective information campaigns that concentrated on young mothers. Closer to us, initial public messages about COVID-19 stressed that older people and people with serious preexisting conditions were most at risk. Younger people could not identify with that population, and were therefore less likely to adopt protective measures.

As we shall discuss later on, a key advantage of defining norms in terms of preferences and beliefs is that we can independently measure and quantify these primitive constructs (and hence norms) using the methodology of experimental economics. Belief-elicitation protocols[23] can be used to measure whether individuals hold sufficiently high and consistent empirical or normative expectations, and hence can be used to determine whether a majority believes that a norm applies to a given situation.

These considerations are relevant for norm-nudging interventions. Not only may we need to know if interdependencies exist, and of which type, but we may also consider if and how we can create them. It is important to understand what motivates a specific interdependent behavior, since different types of norm interventions will be in order. If only empirical expectations drive the target behavior, for instance paying taxes on time, it might be sufficient to design an intervention focused on a descriptive norm stating how many people pay their taxes on time. The behavior we broadcast may be common, and in this case it would be effective just to make the numbers public. If not, we should be able to create new expectations, and the method will differ. If instead the injunctive aspect is very important, for instance inducing people to refrain from bribing public officers, it might be necessary to broadcast a normative message. Here we would have to be careful about the type of normative message we relay. Do we aim to focus individuals on the right action? Or do we want to let them know what relevant others approve or disapprove of? Furthermore, we should be aware of the social inferences that individuals draw from empirical or normative information, and how the valence of the behavior (positive or negative) influences the inferences we draw.[24]

Finally, a rigorous causal analysis is needed to understand what kind of social norm interventions trigger appropriate changes in behavior.[25] The diagnostic schema I have proposed should help, but we need to rely on accurate measures, and to measurement we now turn.

MEASURING BEHAVIOR

Observing behavior, assessing practices, and identifying behavioral patterns is a useful starting point, but it is difficult if not impossible to infer that a social norm exists (or has been successfully created) from observation alone. An independent elicitation of social expectations should always accompany observation of target behaviors. As I mentioned at the outset, a norm is characterized by social expectations and conditional preferences. The presence of social expectations is not sufficient to conclude there is a social norm. These expectations must also motivate their holders to follow the norm. Measuring expectations is thus the first step. The next step is to measure the conditionality of preferences. Identifying reference networks is also crucial, as expectations are always specific to particular networks.

Empirical Expectations

To measure beliefs about behavior, we first need to measure the behavior of interest to assess how common or frequent it is. Sometimes this is a simple task. For instance, we can gauge how many households in a specific community have toilets, or how many people bring their own bags in a supermarket. We use monitors, as in the case of toilet use and maintenance,[26] but when direct observation is not possible, either we use proxies or the respondents may be directly asked if and how often they engage in the target behavior. For example, Fehr and Leibrandt measured the size of the holes in shrimping traps under the assumption that some shrimpers use larger holes to allow smaller shrimp to escape and reproduce.[27] Hole size was a proxy for cooperation among fishermen facing a common pool resource problem. Direct reporting of behavior is often subject to a social desirability bias. This happens, for example, when trying to determine the prevalence of domestic violence, sexual behaviors, or even recycling, when recycling is highly praised by the community. Here respondents tend to answer in ways that are considered appropriate from a moral, legal, or social standpoint, rather than expressing their true beliefs.

We may incentivize accuracy with spot checks, or by simply trying to hide the true response from the investigator. For example, responders anonymously write their answers on a piece of paper that they deposit in a box, and all information that identifies the responder is removed. Alternatively, one may use computerized measurement methods that provide respondents with relative anonymity and privacy.[28] One may also use questions that take away the social stigma from whatever behavior we are asking about; for example, we may say "In this neighborhood, some people recycle and some people do not. How often do you recycle?"[29] Another promising method is the randomized response technique.[30] Suppose we want to know the prevalence of recycling. Participants secretly toss a coin. If the coin toss comes up as tails, they must respond that yes, they recycle, and are instructed to tell the truth if it comes up heads. Since anonymity is guaranteed, it is assumed that those who get heads will tell the truth. And half of the population will say "yes," regardless of whether they recycle. Whatever the proportion of those who say "no," the true number is double that amount, since in a large sample, the two halves are approximately the same. This method makes the response completely private and enables the researcher to estimate the actual prevalence of the target behavior.

Once we have measured the prevalence of a behavior, we can measure empirical expectations, or what individuals believe about the collective behavior. A measure of empirical expectations tells if responders perceive the behaviors of interest as common, normal, and generally performed within their network. In this way, we gather information about the central tendency and dispersion of a collective behavior. A measure of empirical expectations should match the question that has been employed to measure the prevalence of a behavior. If not, then the two sets of measurements may measure two different behaviors. For example, imagine if a respondent's behavior is assessed by asking whether they have "ever recycled," and empirical expectations are measured by asking if members of their reference network "do frequently recycle." In this case, the empirical expectation question is too different from the behavioral measurement to check whether people's empirical expectations are accurate.[31] Another important consideration when measuring empirical expectations is how to frame the prevalence of a behavior. When we ask the "how many" question, we may use proportions, frequencies, or simple majority/minority and even most/few assessments. In a well-educated population, a numeric proportion or percentage estimate may be the most precise measurement. In our research on toilet use in India, with a population of largely uneducated responders, we found that the phrasing, "out of ten people, how many ..." was the easiest and most clearly understood way to assess prevalence.[32]

Knowing the prevalence of a behavior, we may test the accuracy of respondents' empirical expectations. We do not care if these prevalence perceptions are wrong. What we care about is that individuals focus and try to be sincere about what they believe others do. Accuracy here means expressing their true beliefs, not holding true beliefs. People may have confused ideas about others' behavior, or they may be susceptible to a social desirability bias. One might argue that people will be more ready to reveal what *others* are doing even if it is not socially desirable. Yet they may still be reluctant to admit that their community is doing something undesirable in the surveyors' eyes, especially when the community is small and close knit. Even if anonymity is provided, individuals may feel compelled to respond in ways that cast their community in a positive light. When accurate responses hold the promise of rewards, respondents are usually motivated to try harder to make accurate guesses.[33] For example, experiments on public goods games have shown that elicited expectations about other parties' contributions are more accurate when the elicitation is incentivized.[34] In the wild, in order to motivate responders to give an accurate response, we incentivize accuracy with rewards for "correct" estimates of the prevalence of behavior. For example, in a survey in Pakistan, respondents who accurately guessed the prevalence of open defecation were provided with 50 rupees via a popular cell phone payment system.[35]

A false consensus bias[36] is another reason why the perceived prevalence of a behavior may be inaccurate. In a recent study, it was found that individuals who practice open defecation overestimate its prevalence, whereas toilet users underestimate it.[37] In this case, the inaccurate perception may be relatively stable, and interventions should aim to reveal the true proportions of individuals who engage in a specific behavior. However, we should keep in mind that people tend to reject information inconsistent with their beliefs[38] and, even worse, will mistrust the messenger who offers information that is in conflict with what they already believe.[39] This may be a reason why some norm-nudging interventions backfire.

Personal Normative Beliefs

Assessing personal normative beliefs, or one's beliefs about whether one *should* engage in a behavior, allows one to determine the degree to which a behavior is endorsed. Before reviewing how a personal normative belief may be measured, it is first important to discuss the forms a personal normative belief takes and how it may differ from an attitude. An attitude[40] is more of an amorphous evaluative disposition towards a target (such as "liking ice cream" or thinking "one should not cheat"), and it includes personal normative beliefs as a subset.[41] Personal normative beliefs may give rise to evaluative feelings, but they should not be confused with them. When it comes to diagnosing collective behaviors, whether or not one "likes" a behavior is less important than whether one thinks people should engage in it.

We are specifically interested in *non-prudential* normative beliefs. For example, a prudential belief may state that people should not smoke because smoking causes cancer. A non-prudential one may state that we should not smoke because smoking pollutes the air of people who breathe the smoke. If we ask if one believes that people in the neighborhood should recycle, we should accompany a positive answer with a question asking for a reason why. Prudential normative beliefs refer to the (negative or positive) effects that an action has on the individual/s performing it, whereas non-prudential normative beliefs refer to the consequences that performing an action has on others. The positive or negative judgment in the latter case has to do with an evaluation of the external effects of the behavior in question. As we shall see, normative expectations, our second-order beliefs about the personal beliefs of others, only refer to non-prudential beliefs, to others' judgments of right or wrong, since only these judgments have the power to motivate us to conform to broadly approved behaviors.

We cannot incentivize truthful answers, as there is no way to directly monitor people's normative beliefs, and how one feels about a socially relevant behavior may be a sensitive topic. In this case, again, we can apply the same anonymizing techniques we used for assessing behavior and moderate possible demand effects. When asking about a respondent's personal rating of behaviors as appropriate/inappropriate, right or wrong, the precise language we use is even more important than it is when assessing a respondent's behavior. Most questions can be asked in a variety of ways. For example, we may ask the respondents: "Do you believe that people should ... because it is the right thing to do?" and "Do you think it is wrong not to do ...?" or "Do you approve of ...?" By taking the average response across a variety of questions, we reduce noise from both the question asked and participant response, increasing reliability. In order to get more detailed data, one can use a Likert scale rather than a simple Yes/No. This allows us to see more nuanced heterogeneity in the data.

Asking direct questions is not the only methodology available. There are other indirect measures that have been developed to reduce social desirability bias. One example is the implicit association test (IAT), which was recently used to assess the personal normative beliefs of women about female genital cutting.[42] The IAT was developed to measure implicit associations related to gender, race, or sexual orientation,[43] and it was deemed to be a better predictor of behavior than a self-report method. This test asks participants to pair two concepts (e.g., black and good, or white and good), and measures reaction times. The main idea is that when the implicit concept associations are strong (e.g., white is good), the response will be fast. Yet this test has engendered some controversy in the scientific literature.[44] For example, the racial bias studies have a test-retest reliability score of only 0.44, while the IAT overall is just around 0.5. Another major concern with the test has been its validity, as results from the test cannot accurately predict behaviors in real life. One reason may be that the test only assesses familiarity,[45] or just cultural knowledge irrespective of personal endorsement of that knowledge.[46]

Be that as it may, personal normative beliefs are important to measure because they form the basis for one's normative expectations (second-order beliefs about relevant others' personal normative beliefs). Very often, individuals' predictions about others' personal normative beliefs are accurate. However, normative expectations may also be false, as in the case of pluralistic ignorance,[47] where objective and perceived consensus on specific behaviors do not coincide. Such divergence is common in communities in which transparent communication is not possible or advisable. This is an important consideration when designing interventions, since if pluralistic ignorance is present, it may be effective to make public the extent of real support for the behavior we may want to change or implement.[48]

Normative Expectations

Many of the considerations that apply to the measurement of empirical expectations also apply to the measurement of normative expectations.[49] One must still be careful in framing the perceived prevalence of certain beliefs, and one may similarly want to motivate accuracy through incentivization. Additionally, a normative expectations measurement should mirror personal normative belief questions in the same way an empirical expectations measurement should mirror behavior measurements. For example, suppose we asked people about their personal normative beliefs about child marriage with the following question: "Some girls get married before they are 18 years old. Is this good?" and then ask the following ill-matched normative expectation question: "Do you think people in your community believe that it is a father's duty to marry off daughters as soon as possible?" Because this question does not match the personal-normative-belief question, it becomes impossible to evaluate the accuracy of the normative expectations.

There are a few aspects of normative expectations that make their measurement distinctive. Namely, sanctions stand in close relationship with normative expectations. In order to obtain a better understanding of normative expectations and their potential motivational weight, both should be measured. In fact, measuring beliefs about sanctions is often a proxy for measuring normative expectations, for sanctions often result from violations of these expectations. A social norm is present when people collectively engage in a behavior on the condition that they hold certain empirical and normative expectations. However, the probability that their behavior is conditional on holding certain normative expectations is likely strengthened by the combined expectations of negative sanctions should the rule of behavior be violated. In other words, the expectation of sanctions provides normative expectations with greater motivational weight and has important diagnostic value. Negative sanctions may come in a variety of forms and severity, from gossip to honor killing. Sanctions can be directly measured, and their intensity is a good proxy for a norm's strength and importance. More severe negative sanctions usually signal that the violated norm is central and well entrenched in the community.

Once we have successfully measured both personal normative beliefs and normative expectations, we should test for the existence of pluralistic ignorance. If personal normative beliefs and normative expectations align, then individuals' expectations are accurate: the target behavior is effectively endorsed by the majority of the population of interest. However, if the two diverge (and individuals' behavior is conditional on holding certain normative expectations), then pluralistic ignorance is present. In such a scenario, people follow a rule of behavior that they largely think one should not engage in because they wrongly think that relevant others endorse it. In this case, to change behavior we may just update respondents' normative expectations, as is often done with anti-binge-drinking campaigns.[50]

Norm-nudging interventions have often used normative messages. The effectiveness of such messages is unclear. First and foremost, we should differentiate between a normative message that tells what is the right thing to do and one that tells what *others* think is the right thing to do. In the first case, one might be reminded that, for example, littering is a bad choice, and in this case, even if faced with a littered environment, one may focus on the positive action.[51] In water conservation and electricity usage interventions, adding a small happy or unhappy face (or drop) was effective when accompanied by empirical information about what neighbors consumed.[52] What about adding information about what *others* approve or disapprove of? In this case, we aim to create normative expectations. If the normative message is in line with the empirical one, we may expect them to reinforce each other.[53] What if they are incongruent? This may happen frequently, as people often receive conflicting information. Corruption campaigns often mention how frequent corrupt behavior is, while at the same time revealing that large parts of the population condemn corruption.[54] More recently, the information we received about COVID-19-related behavior was often laced with comments about people not wearing masks, assembling in public places, and not keeping the recommended distance, but at the same time we were told that the majority of people approved of the public health measures. In an experimental setup, Erte Xiao and I have tested precisely the effects of incongruent information when the normative message (what others approve of) and the empirical one (what others do) go in opposite directions.[55] The result is sobering, as negative empirical information can win out over positive normative information.

One reason for this effect is that mentioning that many people engage in socially harmful behavior can normalize it. Studies show that commonness of behavior (empirical) can imply approval (normative).[56] That is, if behavior that is common is also perceived as normal, one would infer that people also consider it acceptable. Conversely, one may suppose that what people consider acceptable must also be common behavior. Information conveying what others do or what others approve of may seem prima facie to induce symmetrical inferences. This assumption is mistaken. Recent experimental data show that the social inferences we draw from empirical versus normative information are asymmetrical.[57] For example, we examined how giving participants different types of information (empirical or normative) about others' behavior or normative beliefs and then asking them to infer others' corresponding beliefs (or behavior) led to asymmetric inferences. If we tell participants that the majority of players in a game did not lie for their own benefit, they infer that the majority disapprove of lying. However, participants who were told that the majority disapprove of lying only infer that less than half of them did not lie for their own benefit. The approval rate of a behavior is not an indicator of its prevalence, whereas the prevalence of a behavior is often a good indicator of its endorsement. When the behavior is positive, individuals would follow a "common is acceptable" heuristic when making inferences.[58] Conversely, providing information about positive normative attitudes may not obtain the desired effect, as individuals are well aware that there is a difference between words and deeds, and tend to discount "cheap talk."

In a recent experiment we looked more carefully at norm inferences from positive *and* negative empirical or normative messages across a number of behavioral domains.[59] We found a double asymmetry in norm inferences: empirical information about positive behaviors leads to a parallel normative inference (i.e., most do the right thing implies most approve of it), while normative information about negative behaviors leads to a parallel empirical inference (i.e., most approve of the wrong behavior implies most do it). This evidence supports the mental association of "common" with "acceptable" found in several studies.[60] When the behavior is negative, the relative strength of the association between common and acceptable is reversed, and individuals infer others' undesirable behavior to a greater prevalence from their normative attitudes. Our finding about the asymmetric inferences from messages that target empirical or normative expectations suggests that the direction and relative strength of this association could be modulated by the valence of the behavior (positive/negative). Norm-nudging interventions should carefully consider these asymmetries. If norm inferences vary by the type of social expectation being elicited, information about positive behavior should produce a better effect than information about positive attitudes. When the behavior is negative, informing about the behavior is always counterproductive, but it may be less damaging than information about its endorsement.

Conditionality

As I mentioned at the outset, norm nudging only works when behaviors are interdependent. That is, the choice to engage in the target behavior depends upon holding certain social expectations. Conditionality of preferences is thus the critical component in assessing interdependence. With regard to any collective behavior, we may hold empirical and/or normative expectations, but that does not mean that we engage in the behavior *because* we hold those expectations. For example, surveys can tell us if normative expectations exist and are mutually consistent, but they may not be sufficient if the goal is to measure causal efficacy. Individuals who hold mutually consistent normative expectations may just share a moral rule, as many religious groups do. The fact that it is a shared rule does not imply that one would stop following it if others' behavior were to change. To assess the presence of a social norm, we still need to measure whether behavior *depends* on these expectations.

Unfortunately, assessing conditionality is one of the most difficult steps in the diagnostic process. To test whether behavior is conditional on social expectations, one must effectively *vary* those expectations. If relevant expectations change, does behavior follow? These variations are needed, since causal relations involve counterfactual dependence. In simple words, we say that event A causes event B if they both occurred, but if A had not occurred (and B had no other sufficient cause), B would not have occurred either. Imagine that A are the social expectations that we have measured and B is the behavior, which we have also measured. How do we know that social expectations have causal influence on the behavior we observe? Behavioral experiments allow us to answer that question, in that we can present participants with information aimed at inducing or changing empirical and/or normative expectations and check if behavior changes in predictable ways. In the wild, we need to use other tools, substituting the direct manipulation of expectations with hypothetical questions and scenarios.

At first glance, it may seem that asking direct hypotheticals about the respondent may allow one to test whether behavior is conditional on expectations. For example, one might ask: "What would you do if your community no longer engaged in recycling? What if they disapproved of recycling?" However, there are several drawbacks to asking people to imagine counterfactual situations. Think of asking a father living in a community that practices child marriage what he would do *if* he were to realize that most people in his reference network have decided to abandon child marriage or have become strongly opposed to the practice. A likely answer from the father would be that this is not and probably will never be occurring, as he *knows* what people in his network do and believe. Hypothetical questions are difficult, as they require the capability to answer "what if" questions and imagine scenarios that may seem prima facie impossible. Contrary-to-fact hypotheticals, for example, require the ability to assume as true a claim that conflicts with what is accepted as true, and the lack of such ability may lead individuals to deny that the suggested scenario is possible.[61] It may be easier to answer hypothetical questions about fantasy characters than questions about actual family and friends. This is what vignettes accomplish.

Multiple versions of vignettes could be used to assess causality in much the same way as multiple conditions in an experiment.[62] A vignette tells a short story about fictitious characters in scenarios similar to those known to the respondents.[63] Asking respondents about these stories can effectively elicit beliefs and expectations: they are particularly useful when the questions being asked are socially sensitive and subject to social desirability biases.[64] These hypothetical scenarios provide an unthreatening and impersonal avenue for exploring respondents' attitudes or beliefs about a sensitive topic. Note that in the vignettes, we would be manipulating the social expectations of the protagonist of the story, and not those of the respondent. However, most individuals are subject to what is known as a "false consensus effect" in that, when not aware of person-specific information, they infer that a decision maker would behave as they themselves would when in that particular situation.[65] When respondents think about what the fictitious character would do, they imagine what they themselves would do if they were in the same position. Thus, vignettes indirectly teach us something about how the respondent would react. By manipulating the fictitious character's social expectations, it is as if we were manipulating the respondent's social expectations. In this sense, vignettes are quasi-experiments.

In a typical vignette, a respondent would be presented with one of four randomly selected versions of a short story describing a person deciding whether to conform to a behavioral rule. Each potential version of the story would have variable levels of empirical expectations (high or low) and normative expectations (high or low).[66] The fictitious character is described as moving from a location similar to the respondent's to a new location because it provides a reasonable circumstance for new social expectations to be introduced. The respondent is asked to predict what the fictional character will do. If, when presented with any of the four versions of the vignette, respondents provide the same behavioral response, then behavior is likely not conditional on social expectations, and is possibly a custom or even a moral/religious rule. However, if respondents give a different behavioral prediction when provided with a situation in which the fictitious character holds empirical *and* normative expectations that are different from the respondent's (versus the same as the respondent's), then the behavior is likely a social norm. If the respondent is willing to give a different prediction when only empirical expectations are varied (regardless of whether normative expectations change), then the behavior is more likely to be a descriptive norm.[67]

One final method of inferring conditionality, which has some strengths and drawbacks, is the use of multiple regression models. That is, we may combine the analysis of vignettes with regressing the respondents' behavior on their own social expectations. When there is sufficient variation in behavioral data, normative expectations, and empirical expectations, one would expect fluctuations in behavior across individuals to be predicted by variabilities in social expectations only if the rule of behavior is a norm. Similar to vignettes, if behavioral data is predicted solely by empirical expectations in a regression model, then one may assume the behavior is a descriptive norm. If the behavior is predicted by both empirical and normative expectations, the behavior may be a social norm. These inferences assume that one adequately controls for factors that may affect behavior but do not influence conditionality, such as personal normative beliefs and community-specific fixed effects.

The main concern with inferring causality from regression analyses of macro data is that one is only provided with correlational data. It could very well be the case that there is reverse causation, where people's behavior is driving their own empirical and normative expectations. These limitations can be addressed by combining regression analyses with vignettes in which we can exogenously vary the target's social expectations and check for conditionality.[68] If the results of both methods are positive and converge, we would feel reasonably confident in concluding that a norm exists.

CONCLUSION

Norm nudging – and social norm interventions in general – should be grounded in an understanding of causation and on preliminary measures of beliefs and social expectations. With the rise of norm nudging as a strategy for influencing behavioral change, as well as the potential consequences of misapplied or context-specific norm nudges, it is crucial that practitioners and researchers develop a clear understanding of the various beliefs and expectations surrounding the desired behavior they hope to change, as well as the causal interaction between these beliefs and expectations on the one hand and the behavior in question on the other. Norm nudges are a great, low-cost method for behavioral scientists to implement that hold the promise of changing behavior in a prosocial way, but fundamental understandings of how causality, context, and conditionality regarding reference networks influence the resulting behavior are crucial to the effectiveness/success of norm nudging.

NOTES

1 Thaler, R.H., & Sunstein, C.R. (2008). *Nudge: Improving decisions about health, wealth, and happiness.* Yale University Press.
2 Madrian, B., & Shea, D. (2001). The power of suggestion: Inertia in 401(k) participation and savings behavior. *Quarterly Journal of Economics, 116*(4), 1149–87.
3 Bettinger, E.P., Long, B., Oreopoulos, P., & Sanbonmatsu, L. (2012). The role of application assistance and information in college decisions: Results from the H&R Block Fafsa experiment. *Quarterly Journal of Economics, 127*(3), 1205–42.

4 For a more thorough review, see Benartzi, S., Beshears, J., Milkman, K., Sunstein, C., Thaler, R., Shankar, M., Tucker-Ray, W., Congdon, W., & Galing, S. (2017). Should governments invest more in nudging? *Psychological Science, 28*(8), 1041–55.

5 Cialdini, R.B., Reno, R.R., & Kallgren, C.A. (1990). A focus theory of normative conduct: Recycling the concept of norms to reduce littering in public places. *Journal of Personality and Social Psychology, 58*(6), 1015–26.

6 Hallsworth, M., List, J.A., Metcalfe, R.D., & Vlaev, I. (2017). The behavioralist as tax collector: Using natural field experiments to enhance tax compliance. *Journal of Public Economics, 148,* 14–31.

7 Allcott, H. (2011). Social norms and energy conservation. *Journal of Public Economics, 95*(9–10), 1082–95.

8 Goldstein, N.J., Cialdini, R.B., & Griskevicius, V. (2008). A room with a viewpoint: Using social norms to motivate environmental conservation in hotels. *Journal of Consumer Research, 35*(3), 472–82.

9 Schultz, P.W., Nolan, J.M., Cialdini, R.B., Goldstein, N.J., & Griskevicius, V. (2007). The constructive, destructive, and reconstructive power of social norms. *Psychological Science, 18*(5), 429–34.

10 Bird, K.A., Castleman, B.L., Denning, J.T., Goodman, J., Lamberton, C., & Rosinger, K.O. (2021). Nudging at scale: Experimental evidence from FAFSA completion campaigns. *Journal of Economic Behavior & Organization, 183,* 105–28.

11 Fielding, K.S., Spinks, A., Russell, S., McCrea, R., Stewart, R., & Gardner, J. (2013). An experimental test of voluntary strategies to promote urban water demand management. *Journal of Environmental Management, 114,* 343–51.

12 Reese, G., Loew, K., & Steffgen, G. (2014). A towel less: Social norms enhance pro-environmental behaviors in hotels. *Journal of Social Psychology, 154*(2), 97–100.

13 See, for example, Bicchieri, C. (2006). *The grammar of society: The nature and dynamics of social norms.* Cambridge University Press; and Bicchieri, C. (2016). *Norms in the wild: How to diagnose, measure and change social norms.* Oxford University Press.

14 Bicchieri, C., & Dimant, E. (2019). Nudging with care: The risks and benefits of social information. *Public Choice.* https://doi.org/10.1007/s11127-019-00684-6.

15 Cialdini, R.B., Reno, R.R., & Kallgren, C.A. (1990). A focus theory of normative conduct: Recycling the concept of norms to reduce littering in public places. *Journal of Personality and Social Psychology, 58*(6), 1015–26.

16 Bicchieri (2006).

17 See, for example, Sugden, R. (1998). Normative expectations: The simultaneous evolution of institutions and norms. In A. Ben-Ner & L. Putterman (Eds.), *Economics, values, and organization* (pp. 73–100). Cambridge University Press; Sugden, R. (2000). The motivating power of expectations. In J. Nida-Rümelin & W. Spohn (Eds.), *Rationality, rules, and structure.* Theory and Decision Library (Series A: Philosophy and Methodology of the Social Sciences), vol. 28. Springer; Brennan, G., & Pettit, P. (2004). *The economy of esteem.* Oxford University Press; Bicchieri (2006) and (2016).

18 Bhanot, S. (2018). Isolating the effect of injunctive norms on conservation behavior: New evidence from a field experiment in California. *Organizational Behavior and Human Decisions Processes, 163*(1), 30–42. https://doi.org/10.1016/j.obhdp.2018.11.002.

19 Bicchieri (2006).

20 Ibid.

21 Hallsworth, M., Chadborn, T., Sallis, A., Sanders, M., Berry, D., Greaves, F., Clements, L., & Davies, S.C. (2016). Provision of social norm feedback to high prescribers of antibiotics in general practice: A pragmatic national randomised controlled trial. *Lancet, 387*(10029), 1743–52.

22 Kakute, P.N., Ngum, J., Mitchell, P., Kroll, K.A., Forgwei, G.W., Ngwang, L.K., & Meyer, D.J. (2005). Cultural barriers to exclusive breastfeeding by mothers in a rural area of Cameroon, Africa. *Journal of Midwifery & Women's Health, 50*(4), 324–8.
23 See, for example, social expectations as proposed by Bicchieri, C., & Xiao, E. (2009). Do the right thing: But only if others do so. *Journal of Behavioral Decision Making, 22*(2), 191–208; Bicchieri, C., & Chavez, A. (2010). Behaving as expected: Public information and fairness norms. *Journal of Behavioral Decision Making, 23*(2), 161–78; and Krupka, E.L., & Weber, R.A. (2013). Identifying social norms using coordination games: Why does dictator game sharing vary? *Journal of the European Economic Association, 11*(3), 495–524.
24 Bicchieri, C., & Kuang, J. (2021). *Variability and patterns in the inferences from social norms messages.* Center for Social Norms and Behavioral Dynamics Discussion Paper.
25 See, for example, Bicchieri, C., & Ganegonda, D. (2016). Determinants of corruption: A socio-psychological analysis. In P. Nichols & D. Robertson (Eds.), *Thinking about bribery: Neuroscience, moral cognition and the psychology of bribery.* Cambridge University Press; and Yamin, P., Fei, M., Lahlou, S., & Levy, S. (2019). Using social norms to change behavior and increase sustainability in the real world: A systematic review of the literature. *Sustainability, 11*(20), 5847.
26 Bicchieri, C., Ashraf, S., Das, U., Kohler, H.P., Kuang, J., McNally, P., Shpenev, A., & Thulin, E. (2018, 2019). Social networks and norms: Sanitation in Bihar and Tamil Nadu, India. Gates Report, Center for Social Norms and Behavioral Dynamics, University of Pennsylvania.
27 Fehr, E., & Leibbrandt, A. (2011). A field study on cooperativeness and impatience in the Tragedy of the Commons. *Journal of Public Economics, 95*(9–10), 1144–55.
28 Chauchard, S. (2013). Using MP3 Players in surveys: The impact of a low-tech self-administration mode on reporting of sensitive attitudes. *Public Opinion Quarterly, 77*(S1), 220–31.
29 Bicchieri et al. (2018, 2019).
30 Greenberg, B., Abul-Ela, A., Simmons, W., & Horvitz, D. (1969). The unrelated question randomized response model: Theoretical framework. *Journal of the American Statistical Association, 64*(326), 520–39.
31 Although varying the language of behavioral measurements raises concerns, divergent estimates of behavior are considered useful. Assessing behavior using multiple methods allows for a possible convergence of measures (through "triangulation"; see Jick, T.D. (1979). Mixing qualitative and quantitative methods: Triangulation in action. *Administrative Science Quarterly, 24*(4), 602–11. https://doi .org/10.2307/2392366; Thurmond, V.A. (2001). The point of triangulation. *Journal of Nursing Scholarship, 33*, 253–8. https://doi.org/10.1111/j.1547-5069.2001.00253.x. If the measures converge, we may have more confidence that a behavior has been effectively assessed.
32 Bicchieri et al. (2018, 2019).
33 See, for example, Goetz, E.G., Tyler, T.R., & Cook, F.L. (1984). Promised incentives in media research: A look at data quality, sample representativeness, and response rate. *Journal of Marketing Research, 21*(2), 148–54; and Osband, K. (1989). Optimal forecasting incentives. *Journal of Political Economy, 97*(5), 1091–1112.
34 Gätcher, S., & Renner, E. (2010). The effects of (incentivized) belief elicitation in public goods experiments. *Experimental Economics, 13*(3), 364–77.
35 Haider, N., Bicchieri, C., Thulin, E., Marini, A., Gill, A., Usmani, A., Shahzad, F., Dastageer, G., Kamal, R., Badr-un-Nisa, Gillani, N., Jalal, S., Abbas, F., Khan, S., Khan, S., & Khanzada, N. (2016). Sector sustainability check: Rural open defecation

free (ODF) & rural (drinking) water supply schemes (RWSS) Punjab & Sindh Provinces. Penn Social Norms Group.

36 Ross, L., Greene, D., & House, P. (1977). The "false consensus effect": An egocentric bias in social perception and attribution processes. *Journal of Experimental Social Psychology, 13*(3), 279–301.

37 Kuang, J., Ashraf, S., Das, U., & Bicchieri, C. (2020). Awareness, risk perception, and stress during the COVID-19 pandemic in communities of Tamil Nadu, India. *International Journal of Environmental Research and Public Health, 17*(19), 7177.

38 See Bicchieri, C., & Mercier H. (2014). Norms and beliefs: How change occurs. *Iyyun: The Jerusalem Philosophical Quarterly, 63,* 60–82; and Frey, B.S., & Meier, S. (2004). Prosocial behavior in a natural setting. *Journal of Economic Behavior & Organization, 54*(1), 65–88.

39 Stibe, A., & Cugelman, B. (2016). Persuasive backfiring: When behavior change interventions trigger unintended negative outcomes. *Lecture Notes in Computer Science,* 65–77. https://dspace.mit.edu/handle/1721.1/108479.

40 Ajzen, I., & Fishbein, M. (1977). Attitude-behavior relations: A theoretical analysis and review of empirical research. *Psychological Bulletin, 84*(5), 888–918.

41 Bicchieri (2016).

42 Efferson, C., Vogt, S., Elhadi, A., Ahmed, H.E.F., & Fehr, E. (2015). Female genital cutting is not a social coordination norm. *Science, 359*(6255), 1446–7.

43 See, for example, Nosek, B.A. (2007). Implicit-explicit relations. *Current Directions in Psychological Science, 16*(2), 65–9; and Greenwald, A.G., McGhee, D.E., & Schwartz, J.L.K. (1998). Measuring individual differences in implicit cognition: The implicit association test. *Journal of Personality and Social Psychology, 74*(6), 1464–80.

44 See, for example, Azar, B. (2008). "IAT: Fad or fabulous?" *Monitor on Psychology, 39*(7), 44; and Blanton, H., & Jaccard, J. (2006). Arbitrary metrics in psychology. *American Psychologist, 61*(1), 27–41.

45 Ottaway, S.A., Hayden, D.C., & Oakes, M.A. (2001). Implicit attitudes and racism: Effects of word familiarity and frequency on the implicit association test. *Social Cognition, 19*(2), 97–144.

46 Arkes, H., & Tetlock, P. (2004). Attributions of implicit prejudice, or "Would Jesse Jackson 'Fail' the implicit association test?" *Psychological Inquiry, 15*(4), 257–78.

47 Prentice, D.A., & Miller, D.T. (1993). Pluralistic ignorance and alcohol use on campus: Some consequences of misperceiving the social norm. *Journal of Personality and Social Psychology, 64*(2), 243–56.

48 Berkowitz, A.D., & Perkins, H.W. (1987) Recent research on gender differences in collegiate alcohol use. *Journal of American College Health, 36*(2), 123–9.

49 See, for example, Bicchieri & Chavez (2010); and Krupka & Weber (2013).

50 See, for example, Schroeder, C.M., & Prentice, D.A. (1998). Exposing pluralistic ignorance to reduce alcohol use among college students. *Journal of Applied Social Psychology, 28*(23), 2150–80.

51 Cialdini, Reno, & Kallgren (1990).

52 See, for example, Schultz et al. (2007); and Bhanot (2018).

53 See, for example, Bicchieri & Xiao (2009); and Bicchieri, C., Fatas, E., Aldama, A., Casas, A., Deshpande, I., Lauro, M., Parilli, C., Spohn, M., Pereira, P., & Wen, R. (2021). In science we (should) trust: Expectations and compliance across nine countries during the COVID-19 pandemic. *Plos One,* under revision.

54 See, for example, Bicchieri, C. & Ganegonda, D. (2016) Determinants of corruption: A Socio-psychological analysis. In P. Nichols & D. Robertson (Eds.), *Thinking about Bribery: Neuroscience, Moral Cognition and the Psychology of Bribery.* Cambridge University Press; and Dimant, E., & Schulte, T. (2016). The nature of corruption: An interdisciplinary perspective. *German Law Journal, 17*(1), 53–72.

55 Bicchieri & Xiao (2009).
56 See, for example, Eriksson, K., Strimling, P., & Coultas, J. (2015). Bidirectional associations between descriptive and injunctive norms. *Organizational Behavior and Human Decision Processes, 127,* 59–69; Lindström, B., Jangard, S., Selbing, I., & Olsson, A. (2018). The role of a "common is moral" heuristic in the stability and change of moral norms. *Journal of Experimental Psychology. General, 147*(2), 228–42; and Bicchieri, C., Dimant, E., & Sonderegger, S. (2020). It's not a lie if you believe the norm does not apply: Conditional norm-following with strategic beliefs. CESifo Working Paper No. 8059. SSRN: https://ssrn.com/abstract=3529015.
57 Bicchieri, Dimant, & Sonderegger (2020).
58 Lindström et al. (2018).
59 Bicchieri & Kuang (2021).
60 Eriksson, Strimling, & Coultas (2015).
61 Luria, A.R. (1976). *Cognitive development: Its cultural and social foundations.* Harvard University Press.
62 Sorenson, S.B., & Taylor, C.A. (2005). Female aggression toward male intimate partners: An examination of social norms in a community-based sample. *Psychology of Women Quarterly, 29*(1), 78–96.
63 See, for example, Alexander, C.S., & Becker, H.J. (1978). The use of vignettes in survey research. *Public Opinion Quarterly, 42*(1), 93–104; and Finch, J. (1987). The vignette technique in survey research. *Sociology, 21*(1), 105–14.
64 Finch (1987).
65 See, for example, Mullen, B., Atkins, J.L., Champion, D.S., Edwards, C., Hardy, D., Story, J.E., & Vanderklok, M. (1985). The false consensus effect: A meta-analysis of 115 hypothesis tests. *Journal of Experimental Social Psychology, 21*(3), 262–83; and Ross, Greene, & House (1977).
66 Bicchieri, C., Lindemans, J.W., & Jiang, T. (2014). A structured approach to a diagnostic of collective practices. *Frontiers in Psychology, 5,* 1418.
67 Bicchieri et al. (2018, 2019).
68 Bicchieri et al. (2021).

CHAPTER EIGHT

The Fresh-Start Effect: Motivational Boosts beyond New Year's Resolutions

Jason Riis, Hengchen Dai, and Katherine L. Milkman

Over his 10 years building and molding Google's HR department (known in-house as People Operations), Lazlo Bock learned to pay attention to patterns. Google leans on innovation, and one innovative practice they're committed to is using behavioral science to understand how employees tick. When Bock left the company to start his own, he brought that mindset with him and soon noticed that his new company, Humu, was wasting a lot of money on training programs. Most of the time, employees weren't getting much out of the formal training they were offered at great expense. But there were three exceptions to this rule: new hires, people who were promoted to their first managerial role, and people who were just entering the C-suite.

What made those three groups of people particularly willing to pay attention to training and apply what they'd learned to their careers? They were motivated by what we call a fresh start.

The degree of change that is possible for most people to make to their lives, productivity, health, and happiness is really quite astounding. Within one year, most people have the capability to develop eating and exercise habits that can give them a noticeably more athletic appearance and significantly longer life expectancy. But during a typical year, most people's eating and exercise routines remain the same or get worse. Also within a year, with the unprecedented access to knowledge and technology available today, it's possible to master a new language, learn how to code, or put in enough effort at work to transform your career.

Yet, most of us don't accomplish these kinds of transformations. Behavioral science can help explain why. Most of our actions are habit- or impulse-driven, not directly goal-driven. We're present-focused, motivated more by our immediate temptations and distractions than by our goals.

And yet, there are some moments when we are a little more willing and able to rise to our goals. In those moments, we feel the need to step up, do better, and become our ideal self.

Sometimes, those moments involve new roles and the new responsibilities that come with them. The new responsibilities of parenthood or a career-defining promotion can make us step up. We know we must grow into these roles, and often we do. These are the moments Bock noticed in Humu's training programs. Life events – a new job or new responsibilities at work – motivated people to take opportunities for growth more seriously.

But these moments are relatively rare. More common are moments without a major new role or new set of responsibilities, but that may still feel special because they mark a new beginning on your calendar. Psychologists call these "temporal landmarks";[1] these are moments that stand out from the normal passage of time and create natural feelings of "before" and "after." In other words, these moments tend to partition the passage of time and elicit feelings of a fresh start.

In this chapter, we will explain how temporal landmarks motivate action, and how the power of a fresh start can be harnessed to encourage change in others.

TEMPORAL LANDMARKS CAN INCREASE GOAL PURSUIT

When we ask people to come up with an example of a temporal landmark, most name the same one: New Year's Day. Each year on January first, millions of people make resolutions to change something about their lives. It's without a doubt one of the most famous and powerful fresh-start moments in our culture. Many people initiate significant personal changes at New Year's (e.g., starting new careers, quitting smoking, and starting weight-loss programs). Gym sign ups and goal setting – as well as online searches for virtuous terms like "diet" – spike during this time.

But it's not just at New Year's when people are motivated to change by a fresh start. Such moments are more common than you may think. There are dozens of potentially transformative days each year. Research about the "mental accounting" of time shows that people think of time as having natural breaking points.[2] Instead of time existing as a continuum in our minds, the timelines in our heads break at certain turning points. New Year's Day is an obvious one, but our research has shown that there are other days on the calendar that also make people feel as if their previous mistakes are in the past and they can start again.

Our studies have shown that fresh starts arise not just at the New Year but also on birthdays, at the beginning of school semesters, on the first day of the month, and even on the first day of the week.[3] These are times when people are particularly motivated to take actions towards their goals because they feel as if they have a new beginning and a clean slate. We coined the term "the fresh-start effect" to describe this phenomenon.

In one set of studies we conducted, we looked at archived Google search data and found that searches for the term "diet" spiked not only at New Year's but also on Mondays, the first day of the month, and the first workday after a federal holiday (particularly after holidays that people rate as more like a fresh start).[4] We also looked at gym attendance. In a large dataset from a university gym, we saw a big spike in gym attendance after temporal landmarks. There wasn't a large New Year's spike because students weren't usually on campus until the semester started in mid- to late January. But there were increases in attendance at the beginning of the semester and at the start of the week or month, after school breaks, and after people's birthdays (with the notable exception of 21st birthdays, for reasons that are probably quite obvious).

Finally, we analyzed data from a goal-setting company called stickK (www.stickk.com). StickK sells people "goal contracts" as a way to motivate goal pursuit. For example, imagine that someone has a goal of saving $10,000, or perhaps of completing the first draft of a manuscript, by a certain date. To motivate themself, this person could sign up for a goal contract on stickK and make a commitment that, if they do not accomplish their goal by the deadline, they will owe a sum of money (say $1,000) to a friend or a charity or even an anti-charity (a nonprofit whose mission they dislike). The amount someone chooses to pre-commit can be anything (even $0), but the key idea is that the contract commits them to act or face a penalty.

We found evidence of the fresh-start effect in stickK data. People were more likely to create goal contracts at the beginning of the year, the beginning of the month, the beginning of the week, after national holidays that feel like a fresh start, and after their birthdays.

Subsequent research from other scholars has provided more evidence that the first day of the week and the first day of the month can have motivational pull. In one study, prospective dieters were more likely to start a new diet on the first day of the week and the first day of the month.[5] In another, whether a calendar showed Sunday or Monday as the first day of the week determined the day on which people felt more motivated to pursue a goal (whichever was labeled the start of the week was more motivating).[6]

There is power in knowing when people will feel more motivated to begin a challenge. Marketing, sales, corporate, or clinical programs could potentially all be built to leverage this natural fluctuation in motivation.

Many companies, organizations, and programs may already be harnessing the power of the New Year, with performance reviews, goal setting, sales, and promotions happening in January. But our research shows that there are many more potentially transformative days these groups may be missing. For example, in all the data we analyzed, we saw that Mondays are a powerful fresh start, and there are 52 Mondays each year. Imagine leveraging the power of even a few of those Mondays.

Given our research suggesting that fresh starts can motivate change, we were curious to explore how managers, marketers, salespeople, and others could take advantage of them. Our investigations found that messages matter.

MESSAGES MIGHT BOOST THE FRESH-START EXPERIENCE

In one experiment, we randomly assigned online survey respondents either to list a few reasons why New Year's felt ordinary to them (control condition) or to list a few reasons why New Year's felt meaningful to them (fresh-start condition).[7] We then gave them an opportunity to look through some websites that could help them achieve their personal goals. These included the previously mentioned goal commitment website (stickK.com), four popular goal-tracking websites, and a *New York Times* website featuring an article on how people can increase their chances of achieving their goals. All of the participants in our study were interested in pursuing a goal, but those in the fresh-start condition looked at three times as many goal-related websites and spent 46% more time reading our descriptions of those websites than those in the control condition.

Even though New Year's Day is already one of the most important fresh-start moments, it seems that reminding people that the New Year is a special time can make them feel more open to change.

We attempted to replicate a version of this effect in a large field experiment with the health insurer Humana.[8] Medication adherence is one of the leading problems in healthcare. A large percentage of people on medication don't take their prescriptions as often as they should, which leads to unnecessary hospitalizations, poor health, and even death. To help Humana address this problem, we mailed more than 13,000 customers reminders that they should be regularly taking their medication. Several thousand customers were randomly assigned to get reminders near New Year's, and half of those people got a fresh-start message suggesting that the new year was an opportunity to begin taking medications regularly. Unfortunately, medication adherence was no higher among people who got the reminder at New Year's than among those who got the reminder on a "random" day, and the additional fresh-start framing didn't help at all.

Null results like this are common in research. Things that might work in one setting don't always work in another. While we don't have the evidence to say what exactly went wrong, we have a number of ideas. Perhaps the mailed reminders did not attract as much attention as we had hoped. Or, perhaps medication adherence wasn't a strong enough goal to be triggered at temporal landmarks. Or, perhaps our mailing and messages, largely designed by researchers, not professional marketers, just were not compelling enough. Maybe momentum was lost because people didn't get the New Year's messages until the third week of January. Or maybe it didn't work because, unlike in our previous research, we did not encourage people to reflect on the new year as a special time and have them come to the realization that it was an opportunity for change. More research on this kind of messaging is needed.

MESSAGES MIGHT BOOST FRESH-START ANTICIPATION

Another approach to fresh-start messaging uses the fact that people seem to recognize the opportunity for change inherent in temporal landmarks. Messages that harness the anticipation of an upcoming temporal landmark to get people to opt into change programs that will begin on a fresh-start date can be valuable.

We first showed that people are willing to commit to changing their behavior on a future fresh-start date in two laboratory studies.[9] In the first study, we surveyed people who had expressed a prior interest in getting a "goal reminder" via email. All respondents were given a list of dates on which they could get the reminder, but we randomly assigned people to get lists that labeled March 20th either as "The Third Thursday of March" (ordinary condition) or as "The First Day of Spring" (fresh-start condition). When March 20 was labeled as a fresh-start date, more than three times as many people chose it as the date when they'd receive a reminder to start pursuing a personal goal.

Our second study had a similar design. This time we offered to send college students at the University of Pennsylvania (Penn) email reminders to pursue their goals over the summer. When May 14th (not otherwise a temporal landmark) was labeled as "The First

Day of Summer Break," people were more than three times as likely to choose it as the date for their reminder email than when it was labeled as "Penn's Administrative Day."

These results suggest that people find future temporal landmarks auspicious for kick-starting goal pursuit. More generally, making the landmark nature of an upcoming fresh-start date salient has an effect. This suggests that a practitioner need not wait for the New Year or a new month to harness the fresh-start effect. It can be harnessed in anticipation.

A version of this theory was supported by another field experiment conducted by two of us (Dai and Milkman) with other collaborators.[10] Several thousand university employees received letters inviting them to start contributing to a savings plan either now or at a future date. People saved 20–30% more money in the eight months following our mailings when they were invited to start saving after a fresh-start date (e.g., their next birthday, the start of spring) than when they were invited to start saving at the same time but with no explicit reference to a fresh-start date.

Generally, it's good to seek commitments from people "now," but in cases when "now" is not viable, or when an alternative must be given, or when "now" has been rejected, it appears that people may be more willing to commit to start "good behavior" on future dates that are framed as temporal landmarks.

TAKEAWAYS

Habits, routines, impulses, and a general tendency to focus more on getting through the present moment than on being successful in the future are among the many psychological forces that make it hard for people to achieve their goals.

The fresh-start effect characterizes one set of moments when people exhibit a natural uptick in motivation to pursue their goals.[11] Salespeople, marketers, managers, and caregivers can use this insight to help their audiences achieve more. And individuals can use it to achieve their own goals, too. Our prescriptive advice to practitioners is twofold. First, identify the most relevant fresh-start opportunities. Second, tinker with different ways to capitalize on the added motivation that these fresh starts bring.

1. Identify the Most Relevant Fresh-Start Opportunities

What goals does your audience have? Do they want to improve their health? Do they want to read more? Do they want to innovate more (but find it hard to start new things)? Whether your audience includes consumers, employees, a single patient, or a family member, if you feel that whatever you're offering is aligned with one of their goals, you may be able to use the fresh-start effect to nudge them towards it.

Humu, the company Laszlo Bock co-founded, works with organizations to nudge their employees towards greater job satisfaction and productivity, which (in theory) makes it easier for Humu's client companies to improve. Bock is well acquainted with our work and has told us that some of the nudges Humu delivers take advantage of the fresh-start effect. For example, Humu has sent out emails around the New Year encouraging people to reply with a goal or intention they want to act on in the coming months. Humu sent those replies back a few weeks later to either help employees track their progress or give them another boost of motivation to get started.

We know of one healthcare service provider that sees large sign-up spikes each New Year's. But the company didn't strategically use the full strength of the pattern until our work prompted them to look deeper. New Year's is undoubtedly one of the most important temporal landmarks associated with the fresh-start effect. Most businesses and employers should be able to find an opportunity here.

Practitioners can take advantage of industry or organizational restructuring to capitalize on the fresh-start effect. Whenever a client company reorganizes something about the way people work, Humu sends nudges prompting its client's employees to re-evaluate their habits and see if there are any improvements they want to make. This can also work on a more personal level. Say someone moves into a new office or shifts to a new desk – that might be an ideal time to suggest a change.

Birthdays are notable fresh-start opportunities, and we might expect decade birthdays to be even stronger than others. The problem with birthdays as fresh-start moments is that they're different for everyone, so they can be harder to leverage (though not impossible). Facebook, for example, started a "birthday fundraisers" program in 2017. Readers may have seen the prompts: Now, instead of just writing "Happy Birthday!" on a friend's Facebook wall, you can donate a few dollars to the cause of their choice. Several days before someone's birthday, Facebook sends a message saying "It's almost your birthday! Create a fundraiser to support a cause you care about." These messages wisely harness people's motivation to become kinder, more generous versions of themselves after a birthday, encouraging them to set up a fundraiser.

As more and more commerce takes place online, and people can shop anytime they're motivated, there is more opportunity to look for things like Monday Fresh-Start effects. Our research suggests that anyone hoping to spur change in others can *create* fresh-start moments if they frame a day as special in the right way. Most people may not otherwise take note of the first day of spring, but if your building posts signs saying that a building-wide recycling program will start on the first day of spring, you might pay closer attention.

2. Taking Advantage of Fresh Starts with Timing and Message Content

There are many ways to capitalize on temporal landmarks. Here are a few:

1. **Make it especially easy for people to sign up for new, smart defaults on fresh-start dates.** For example, a dieting program can make it easy for people to commit to future healthy eating with a program to "build a healthy cart" on Mondays. Similarly, a savings program can make it easy for people to commit to increased saving after an upcoming birthday.
2. **Pay attention to the timing of annual appointments.** Annual medical checkups are often scheduled around birthdays. This is good timing because, if the appointment happens very near

a birthday, the patient may be particularly receptive to health advice and even to committing to wellness programs. Relatedly, gyms are always ready for a New Year's blitz, but are health programs? With the rise of telemedicine, there may be novel wellness appointments that would be of particular interest to people at New Year's.

3. **Consider giving birthday gifts or recognition to boost motivation.** Birthday gifts are meant to celebrate and generally indulge the recipient. But there may be opportunities to give separate or additional gifts that take advantage of post-birthday motivation. Some companies and schools celebrate birthdays, some salespeople give clients birthday gifts. Gifts that line up with goal pursuit may be well received, especially in professional contexts, once the dust of the birthday celebration settles (e.g., books, subscriptions, workshop enrollment, art or other mementos that symbolize personal or professional ambition, etc.).

4. **Send check-in notes.** Salespeople, marketers, employers, clinicians, and teachers all have reasons to check in with their audiences through direct messages by email or over LinkedIn, Facebook, etc. Rather than sending a simple "Happy Birthday," "Happy New Year," or "Happy Monday" note, people can use temporal landmarks as opportunities to send goal-aligned messages. For example, you might write, "I saw your birthday pop up in my LinkedIn feed, and I thought of you when I saw this article on innovation – something we've talked about many times." That message can be personalized with a quote from the article if you have the time. A birthday wish that connects to a client's vision of their ideal entrepreneurial self may be well received.

5. **Ask for commitment on a future fresh-start date.** People recognize temporal landmarks as fresh-start opportunities. And, as the success of programs like Save More Tomorrow™ has shown,[12] people are willing to pre-commit to start good deeds in the future. Knowing these two facts, salespeople and other motivators might seek to take answers of "not now" as an opportunity to set up action on a fresh-start moment in the future. Rather than saying, "Okay, I'll reach out again in a few months,"

try saying something like "Okay, I'll try you again on Monday, April 2, the first workday of the new quarter. And in the hope that you're seriously considering this offer, I'll send a few notes in the meantime that will make it easier for us to hit the ground running."

6. **Optimally timed training programs.** People may be most interested in signing up for training programs at fresh-start moments. If you're planning a new training, think carefully about timing.

7. **Do you want to rock the boat?** In some situations, managers may not want to encourage or highlight fresh starts. For employees with recent strong performance, the introduction of a fresh start may hamper their motivation by reducing their confidence in achieving similarly strong records in a new time period.[13] And anticipation of a fresh start may harm employees' continued goal motivation by tempting them to wait to work towards their goals after an upcoming fresh start.[14]

Before we close, we would like to re-emphasize the point that others in this book have repeatedly made. Given that the success of an intervention seeking to capitalize on the fresh-start effect depends on the context, the recipient, and the implementation details, what has worked elsewhere might not have as strong an effect in a different setting. Therefore, we join the chorus of voices that recommends testing and iterating before an intervention is launched.

The fresh-start effect is not a silver bullet solution to all behavioral challenges. In the grand scheme of things, people often don't change their behavior either because it's complicated to do so or because they are simply not motivated. While many "nudge-like" interventions focus on the first of these obstacles to change, the fresh-start effect capitalizes on systematic temporal fluctuations in goal motivation. It's important to strike when the proverbial iron is hot. With a little tinkering and experimentation, fresh starts can be turned into an effective lever to propel positive change.

NOTES

1 Shum, M.S. (1998). The role of temporal landmarks in autobiographical memory processes. *Psychological Bulletin, 124*(3), 423–42. https://doi.org/10.1037/0033-2909.124.3.423.

2 Soman, D., & Ahn, H.-K. (2011). Mental accounting and individual welfare. In K. Gideon (Ed.), *Perspectives on framing* (pp. 65–92). Psychology Press.

3 Dai, H., Milkman, K.L., & Riis, J. (2014). The fresh start effect: Temporal landmarks motivate aspirational behavior. *Management Science, 60*(10), 2563–82. https://doi.org/10.1287/mnsc.2014.1901.

4 Ibid.

5 Hennecke, M., & Benjamin, C. (2017). Next week, next month, next year: How perceived temporal boundaries affect initiation expectations. *Social Psychological and Personality Science, 8*(8), 918–26. https://doi.org/10.1177/1948550617691099.

6 Davydenko, M., & Peetz, J. (2019). Does it matter if a week starts on Monday or Sunday? How calendar format can boost goal motivation. *Journal of Experimental Social Psychology, 82*, 231–7. https://doi.org/10.1016/j.jesp.2019.02.005.

7 Dai, H., Milkman, K.L., & Riis, J. (2015). Put your imperfections behind you: Temporal landmarks spur goal initiation when they signal new beginnings. *Psychological Science, 26*(12), 1927–36. https://doi.org/10.1177/0956797615605818.

8 Dai, H., Mao, D., Riis, J., Volpp, K., Relish, M.J., Lawnicki, V.F., & Milkman, K.L. (2017). Effectiveness of medication adherence reminders tied to "fresh start" dates: A randomized clinical trial. *JAMA Cardiology, 2*, 453–5. https://doi.org/10.1001/jamacardio.2016.5794.

9 Dai, Milkman, & Riis (2015).

10 Beshears, J., Dai, H., Milkman, K.L., & Benartzi, S. (2021). Using fresh starts to nudge increased retirement savings. Working Paper.

11 Dai, H., & Li, C. (2019). How experiencing and anticipating temporal landmarks influence motivation. *Current Opinion in Psychology, 26*, 44–8. https://doi.org/10.1016/j.copsyc.2018.04.012.

12 Thaler, R., & Benartzi, S. (2004). Save More Tomorrow™: Using behavioral economics to increase employee saving. *Journal of Political Economy, 112*(S1), S164–S187. https://doi.org/10.1086/380085.

13 Dai, H. (2018). A double-edged sword: How resetting performance metrics affects motivation and future performance. *Organizational Behavior and Human Decision Processes, 148*, 12–29. https://doi.org/10.1016/j.obhdp.2018.06.002.

14 Koo, M., Dai, H., Mai, K.M., & Song, C.E. (2020). Anticipated temporal landmarks undermine motivation for continued goal pursuit. *Organizational Behavior and Human Decision Processes, 161*, 142–57. https://doi.org/10.1016/j.obhdp.2020.06.002.

CHAPTER NINE

Reminders: Their Value and Hidden Costs

Christina Gravert

In a world where everyone wants our attention, reminders and notifications are omnipresent. Is there anyone who can live without their Google or Outlook calendar? And who doesn't receive hundreds of emails every day? App stores are bursting with clever reminders and to-do list features that help us micromanage our life and remind us to do trivial things like drink water or major things like submit our taxes on time. And let us not forget that companies like Google and Facebook make billions with their ability to capture our attention and affect our behavior.

It is evident that reminders work. They steer our attention towards a particular decision, and in many cases, they can be a powerful tool for motivation and behavior change. A reliable reminder can give us peace of mind and reduce our cognitive load. However, reminders also have a dark side – they distract us and turn our time into "time confetti" by pulling our attention away from what we are currently focusing on. They also have the potential to make us feel bad about the tasks we have not completed. Since reminders are here to stay, we need to understand how to design them better so we can increase their positive impact on behavior change and limit their negative effects.

I will draw on my research on reminders as well as the many great experiments done by colleagues. I will first give insights into why reminders work to change behavior. I will then discuss whether pure reminders can be improved upon with framing or other types of "nudges." I will briefly discuss the difference between physical and digital reminders. Next, I will discuss the optimal timing of reminders and what happens when they are used repeatedly. That leads me to the challenge of annoyance costs that reminders create, and I present evidence on how reminders can backfire. Lastly, I summarize what we have learned about designing reminders so far and what we need to investigate further.

WHY DO REMINDERS WORK?

Reminders change behavior in two steps. First, a reminder briefly shifts our attention towards a particular goal by making that goal more salient. Second, if the receiver's transaction costs of carrying out the action compared to the perceived benefit of the action are low enough, the receiver will carry out the behavior. This simple process was among others modeled by researchers who considered responses to donation requests: (1) A donation request reaches the receiver and (2) if the timing is convenient and the receiver feels generous, they make a donation and receives positive utility from their donation.[1] Transaction costs depend on whether the receiver is physically and/or cognitively able to carry out the task at the point in time when they are made attentive to it (i.e., they are not sitting in their car when they get a reminder to send a document to a colleague). The perceived benefit depends on the intrinsic or extrinsic motivation of doing the action (i.e., some desire to exercise or the fear of getting audited when not paying one's taxes).

More sophisticated reminder models take into consideration that the receivers are not just reacting to an external reminder but are also (more or less) aware of their inattention.[2] These models are usually from the perspective of the receiver of a reminder at a point in time before they receive the reminder. In one of my studies, the decision maker needs to trade off the benefit from reducing the risk of forgetting something that they wanted or have to do with the cost of being distracted or annoyed and the potential feeling of guilt for not acting on a reminder.[3] In another, we model the different channels through which reminders affect attention.[4] Our model considers three mechanisms: a pure attention shift, a shift in beliefs about the benefits of the behavior, and a shift in psychological utility from being reminded.

The first mechanism is straightforward and is inherent to any kind of reminder. Reminders focus the attention towards a behavior the receiver had at least some intention of carrying out but that, for some reason, was not at the top of mind. Whether the behavior that the reminders targets is "top of mind" depends partly on the importance of the behavior to the receiver (picking up their kids at school versus congratulating an acquaintance on their birthday) and partly on the overall cognitive load of the individual (a stressful day at work versus a Sunday afternoon).[5]

The two additional mechanisms don't have to be present with every reminder, but can have an influence on how reminders affect behavior. First, reminders might affect beliefs about how important or socially desirable an action is. This can be conveyed either through information or nudges, such as social proof, added to the reminder message, or by sending a reminder repeatedly and conveying urgency. Second, reminders could create psychological costs such as guilt for having forgotten and thus not having carried out a behavior or for not living up to a social norm or one's own self-image. This mechanism is most likely present in reminders about habits such as saving or going to the gym that the decision maker might have procrastinated on. It is less relevant for a reminder for a one-time action that is coming up, such as an Outlook notification five minutes prior to a meeting or a Facebook birthday reminder on the day.

FRAMING OF REMINDERS

Whether it is increasing savings,[6] meeting loan payments,[7] donating to charity,[8] going to the gym,[9] or adhering to medical treatment,[10] reminders have been proven to work in changing behavior in all types of contexts. Indeed, the fact that reminders will work is often a given, and hence the focus of much of our research efforts has been on the secondary question of how the effectiveness of a reminder can be increased by the way it is written. Karlan and colleagues sent reminders to bank customers in Peru, Bolivia, and the Philippines who had recently opened a commitment savings account to remind them to save.[11] They show that reminders helped increase savings. When the reminders mentioned the saving goal or the financial incentive to save, compliance increased. Framing the reminder in a positive versus a negative way had no differential effect on savings. Altmann and Traxler tested reminders to make a dental appointment. Within a month of receiving a reminder, the fraction of patients who make a check-up appointment at the dentist more than doubled.[12] The gain/loss framing of the reminders ("Go now and keep your smile" versus "Go now to not lose your smile") had no effect.[13] Likewise, we sent reminders to citizens in southern Sweden who had previously received an offer for a free two-week bus ticket. Twenty per cent of the receivers responded to the reminder, but the addition of a positively or negatively framed social norm ("72% of your neighbors travel by public transport" versus "Only 28% do not travel by public transport") had no additional effect compared to the reminder.[14]

If you are reading this book, then you have probably heard of the experiment by the Behavioural Insights Team in the UK, who sent reminders to taxpayers letting them know that "9 out of 10 people in their town/region/the UK have paid their taxes on time while they have not." The closer the reference group was, the higher their response rate. The popularity and simple design of this reminder type led to dozens of replications worldwide. A recent meta-study of 45 such tax reminder experiments[15] finds that overall, non-deterrence messages such as norms (as in the original study) or moral appeals have no significant additional effect compared to a basic reminder. Deterrence messages, such as reminders mentioning the penalty for not paying on time, on the other hand, did have a small but significant positive effect on compliance on top of the basic reminder. It would be wrong to conclude from these results that social proof doesn't work. However, it does highlight the fact that – like many of our popular interventions – social proof is susceptible to context, and that practitioners should pre-test to see whether social norms are relevant in a given context (see also Chapter 7). Even in classic social psychology studies, such as Robert Cialdini's famous study on social norms and towel reuse, the biggest effect comes from the reminder itself to reuse the towels.[16] In that context, though, the social norm, telling hotel guests that most guests reuse their towels, significantly increased the reminder effect.

But what about additional information meant to encourage a behavior, such as health tips or feedback? In one study, my collaborators and I investigate the effect of reminders on medication adherence of pregnant women in South Africa and whether exposure to reminders affects their demand for additional reminders to take their medicines.[17] We find that pure reminders ("Remember to take your medication") increase self-reported medication adherence. Exposure to these pure reminders increases the willingness to pay for more reminders. However, adding health information to the reminders had a negative effect on adherence and demand for reminders for our sample compared to the pure reminders. Others found a similar result in a field experiment in Brazil.[18] The parents of schoolchildren received either messages conveying information about their children's school absence (information) or messages that only highlighted the importance of attending school (salience). They find that most of the behavior change is driven by salience, not by a change in beliefs based on the information. A mega experiment on reminders to get a flu vaccine showed that the differences in message content on effectiveness were negligible compared to the pure effect of the reminder.[19] For policymaking, it is good news that the information effect in both studies is negative compared to the pure reminders. Pure reminders – for example, "Remember to take your pills"[20] – are not only effective but also more cost-effective, as their messages are easier to develop.

In sum, while additional information might have a significant positive effect on top of the reminder, the additional effort involved in finding the perfect social norm or information framing might not be worth the small and unreliable additional effects.

PHYSICAL REMINDERS VERSUS WRITTEN REMINDERS

The largest share of the academic literature evaluates digital (or letter-based) reminders versus physical reminders such as stickers or signs. Any sign that does not convey new information but helps to remind people about things that they should know, such as "Don't climb on the luggage carousel" or "No shouting in the hallways," can be considered as a reminder, and our world is full of them. For example, during the COVID-19 pandemic, reminders about hand washing, mask wearing, and social distancing were omnipresent. There are few studies systematically evaluating these kinds of reminders. Mostly, this is due to the inconvenience of randomization and data collection in the field. It is easier to register whether someone paid their taxes after receiving a letter with treatment "A" than it is to measure whether people are standing far enough apart in a supermarket queue.

A notable exception is a field experiment on hotel food waste at a breakfast buffet.[21] Putting up a reminder sign reduced food waste by 20.5% compared to the control groups (the same effect size as using smaller plate sizes). As with any type of reminder, a physical reminder needs to be closely connected to the place and point of time of an action. In the buffet case, the reminder was displayed next to the plates – the perfect time to say, "Take only what you can eat" and "You can go twice." However, physical reminders can also backfire when they bring to mind an action that was previously not even considered as a possibility. This is exemplified by a study in which signs in the Petrified Forest National Park in the US said, "Many past visitors have removed the petrified wood from the park, changing the state of the Petrified Forest." Theft of petrified wood *increased* compared to a more neutrally phrased sign.[22] These results highlight the problem of setting up a reminder for a behavior that otherwise might not even have crossed most people's minds. While it is challenging to execute, more research is needed to develop a better understanding of how physical reminders can best affect behavior.

TIMING AND FREQUENCY OF REMINDERS

How many reminders are needed to cause a behavior change and when should they be delivered? In an ideal world, one reminder at the right time when the receiver is willing and able to act on the reminder should do! Unfortunately, reminders are often sent when the transaction costs of acting are too high. For example, receiving a donation request reminder when you are in the middle of a meeting will not have an effect because you cannot act on it at that moment. Donation reminders sent via email either led to immediate donations (if timely) or no donations at all (if not), regardless of the length of the deadline.[23]

A one-size-fits-all claim about the timing of reminders is impossible to make. A reminder for medication adherence needs to come at a different time from a reminder to fill out tax returns or a reminder to not stand too close to the track on a platform. Digital apps provide plenty of opportunities to test and send perfectly timed reminders. Duolingo, a language learning app, does this by tracking the time a user practiced the day before and then sending a reminder at the same time the next day, assuming that if that time was convenient one day it might be convenient the next. If you haven't practiced for a week, it "gives up" on sending you daily reminders. A recent study shows the causal effect of sending a push notification on the probability of interacting with a commercial workplace well-being intervention app over the next 24 hours.[24] Relative to a control (no reminder) condition, users were 3.9% more likely to engage with the app when a tailored reminder was sent. This effect was slightly higher on weekends than on weekdays. A second study with the same app tested whether push notifications that gave information versus those that suggested an action led to more engagement.[25] Push notifications that suggest an action led to more engagement with the app. However, both studies show that prompts are not very effective in re-engaging individuals who have not interacted much with the app in the past days. Based on this evidence, the Duolingo approach in which reminders become more frequent for engaged users and become infrequent for less engaged users seems to be a good design.

REPEATED REMINDERS

The effect of repeated reminders has been further studied in several domains. One study testing the effects of repeated text message reminders on repaying microloans finds that reminders increase the probability of paying by 9%.[26] The reminders work particularly well for younger customers of the microloans. The text messages had approximately the same economic effect on late payments as a 25% reduction in the interest rate. The study finds no negative effects of repeated reminders.

A field experiment used simple weekly reminders to induce users of a gym to substantially increase their gym attendance.[27] Users' response to reminders is immediate, and each additional reminder triggers additional behavior for any subsequent reminder. Reminders raise the probability of attendance during the 24 hours following receipt of the email by 5.7% (when considering their entire sample) or 7.8% (when restricting the sample to low users). In another experiment with gym-goers,[28] weekly reminders sent to half of the sample increased total gym attendance by 13%. In both studies, participants with low attendance show greater behavior change, which is not surprising given that those who already train frequently have less scope to increase their training.

In partnership with the Smithsonian Institution in the US, we tried to understand the effect of repeated reminders on membership renewals and additional gifts.[29] The Smithsonian sends up to eight rounds of reminders to their members to get them to renew their yearly membership. We found that the first reminder was quite effective and led to a 23.2% response rate. However, we also found that subsequent reminders were much less effective. The fact that members are busy at different points in time and forget to renew their membership cannot explain the decline in the response rate. Instead, we show that the most generous and motivated donors are the ones who respond first, while the more marginal donors respond later, if at all.

Given the success of repeated reminders and the low costs of sending them via email, should we send repeated reminders, even if, as in the case of the Smithsonian, they become increasingly less effective? The answer is no, because there are hidden costs.

HIDDEN COSTS OF REMINDERS

While reminders are effective at generating behavior change, they can also impose moral costs if they draw attention to a decision that the decision maker would rather avoid or cannot act on.[30] If we see the reminder but do not have a chance to act on it at that point in time or deliberately choose not to act on it, then all we get are the distraction and the annoyance costs that come with the reminder. Well-meaning reminders from my gym telling me that they miss me during a stressful period at work make me feel bad about myself without getting me to act. The effect of the reminder on gym attendance is around 10%[31] – so what about all those who receive a reminder but do not change behavior? Is their decision utility affected by the reminder?

In a project with a Danish charity,[32] we found that reminder emails increase donations. However, we also found that the more emails the charity sent, the more people who had previously donated unsubscribed from the mailing list. While, for some people, the reminder came at a good time and helped them remember to donate to a charity they had previously supported, others felt annoyed and maybe even guilty for not giving. For the charity, this dual mechanism meant that they were losing valuable donors who might have donated at another point in time.

In a second experiment, the PS of the solicitation email announced for one group that they would receive only one reminder email in the next three months instead of the usual three. If receivers did not care for the charity anymore, then the change in frequency should not affect their decision to unsubscribe. We had another treatment in which we promised a special donation opportunity in the next newsletter. Both treatments reduced the unsubscribe rate compared to the baseline email while not affecting the rate of donations. This result can be seen as evidence for the trade-off between dealing with the annoyance costs of the reminder and the benefit of not missing out on an opportunity.

Researchers on another project asked whether customers would like to receive home energy reports reminding them to save energy and informing them how their energy consumption compared to their neighbors'.[33] A significant minority of customers were willing to pay not to receive any reminders. Both studies show that for at least some of the receivers, the reminders create a negative utility, and they would rather avoid them.

DESIGNING BEHAVIORALLY INFORMED REMINDERS

What is the optimal design of reminders? Overall, we can say that reminders work to change behavior. Compared to other types of nudges, reminders produce consistent significant effects. In some domains, such as charitable giving[34] or saving,[35] there is usually no action without a reminder. Behaviors in other domains, such as going to the gym or taking medication, can be influenced by reminders but are often already at high levels for the individuals who respond to the reminders. Nevertheless, in these cases, the reminders might help individuals overcome the cognitive costs of remembering for themselves and thus be warranted.

While some studies find that goal framing has a significant effect,[36] others[37] find no effects of framing of reminders. Yet others[38] even find that adding additional information to the reminder can lead to a worse outcome than a pure reminder. Adding social norms, framing, information, moral pressure, etc., does not produce consistent effects and has been shown to backfire. Given that the costs for detailed reminders are usually higher than for generic reminders, a generic reminder is a more cost-effective alternative. A clear outcome from all of my research and most of the other experiments is that basic demographics such as gender, age, income level, education level, and the like are not correlated with the effect of reminders. There is no use in segmenting reminders based on these observable characteristics. Segmentation should only happen based on behaviors or beliefs.

One of the big questions the literature still needs to answer is how reminders interact with each other and what the risks of crowding out attention are. From the perspective of a private company, the question should be easy to answer: Maximize the attention on the product. However, for policymakers, the question is much harder.

At any given moment, should citizens focus on avoiding food waste, saving energy, taking their medication, paying their taxes, saving for retirement, exercising, or donating to charity? Every reminder for one cause distracts from something else. Reminders should therefore be simple, and be used wisely.

NOTES

1 Huck, S., & Rasul, I. (2010). Transactions costs in charitable giving: Evidence from two field experiments. *BE Journal of Economic Analysis & Policy*, *10*(1).
2 Karlan, D., McConnell, M., Mullainathan, S., & Zinman, J. (2016). Getting to the top of mind: How reminders increase saving. *Management Science*, *62*(12), 3393–3411; Ericson, K.M. (2017). On the interaction of memory and procrastination: Implications for reminders, deadlines, and empirical estimation. *Journal of the European Economic Association*, *15*(3), 692–719; Damgaard, M.T., & Gravert, C. (2018). The hidden costs of nudging: Experimental evidence from reminders in fundraising. *Journal of Public Economics*, *157*, 15–26.
3 Damgaard & Gravert (2018).
4 Barron, K., Damgaard, M.T., & Gravert, C. (2021) Nudge me! The response to and demand for healthy habit reminders. CEBI Working Paper.
5 Mullainathan, S., & Shafir, E. (2013). *Scarcity: Why having too little means so much.* Macmillan.
6 Karlan et al. (2016).
7 Cadena, X., & Schoar, A. (2011). *Remembering to pay? Reminders vs. financial incentives for loan payments* (No. w17020). National Bureau of Economic Research.
8 Huck & Rasul (2010); Damgaard & Gravert (2018).
9 Calzolari, G., & Nardotto, M. (2017). Effective reminders. *Management Science*, *63*(9), 2915–32.
10 Vervloet, M., Linn, A.J., van Weert, J.C., De Bakker, D.H., Bouvy, M.L., & Van Dijk, L. (2012). The effectiveness of interventions using electronic reminders to improve adherence to chronic medication: A systematic review of the literature. *Journal of the American Medical Informatics Association*, *19*(5), 696–704; Altmann, S., & Traxler, C. (2014). Nudges at the dentist. *European Economic Review*, *72*, 19–38.
11 Karlan et al. (2016).
12 Altmann & Traxler (2014).
13 Karlan et al. (2016).
14 Gravert, C.A., and Olsson Collentine, L. (2021). When nudges aren't enough: Norms, incentives and habit formation in public transport usage. *Journal of Economic Behavior & Organization*, *190*, 1–14.
15 Antinyan, A., & Asatryan, Z. (2020). Nudging for tax compliance: A meta-analysis. Working Paper.
16 Goldstein, N.J., Cialdini, R.B., & Griskevicius, V. (2008). A room with a viewpoint: Using social norms to motivate environmental conservation in hotels. *Journal of Consumer Research*, *35*(3), 472–82.
17 Barron, Damgaard, & Gravert (2021).
18 Bettinger, E., Cunha, N., Lichand, G., & Madeira, R. (2020). Are the effects of informational interventions driven by salience? University of Zurich, Department of Economics, Working Paper 350. See https://www.econ.uzh.ch/static/wp/econwp350.pdf.

19 Milkman, K.L., Patel, M.S., Gandhi, L., Graci, H., Gromet, D., Ho, Q.D., ...
    Duckworth, A. (2021). A mega-study of text-message nudges encouraging patients
    to get vaccinated at their pharmacy. *SSRN Electronic Journal.* https://doi:10.2139
    /ssrn.3780356.
20 Barron, Damgaard, & Gravert (2021).
21 Kallbekken, S., & Sælen, H. (2013). "Nudging" hotel guests to reduce food waste as
    a win-win environmental measure. *Economics Letters, 119*(3), 325–7.
22 Cialdini, R.B., Demaine, L.J., Sagarin, B.J., Barrett, D.W., Rhoads, K., & Winter, P.L.
    (2006). Managing social norms for persuasive impact. *Social Influence, 1*(1), 3–15.
23 Damgaard, M.T., & Gravert, C. (2017). Now or never! The effect of deadlines on
    charitable giving: Evidence from two natural field experiments. *Journal of Behavioral
    and Experimental Economics, 66*, 78–87.
24 Bidargaddi, N., Pituch, T., Maaieh, H., Short, C., & Strecher, V. (2018). Predicting
    which type of push notification content motivates users to engage in a self-
    monitoring app. *Preventive Medicine Reports, 11*, 267–73.
25 Ibid.
26 Cadena & Schoar (2011).
27 Calzolari & Nardotto (2017).
28 Muller, P., & Habla, W. (2018). Experimental and non-experimental evidence on
    limited attention and present bias at the gym. *ZEW Discussion Papers, 18.*
29 Damgaard & Gravert (2018).
30 Ibid.
31 Calzolari & Nardotto (2017); Muller & Habla (2018).
32 Damgaard & Gravert (2018).
33 Allcott, H., & Kessler, J.B. (2019). The welfare effects of nudges: A case study of
    energy use social comparisons. *American Economic Journal: Applied Economics, 11*(1),
    236–76.
34 Damgaard & Gravert (2017).
35 Karlan et al. (2016).
36 Ibid.
37 Gravert & Olsson Collentine (2021); Altmann & Traxler (2014).
38 Barron, Damgaard, & Gravert (2021); Bettinger, Cunha, Lichand, & Madeira (2020).

PART THREE

Domain-Specific Behavior Change Challenges

Applying Behavioral Insights to Cultivate Diversity and Inclusion

Joyce C. He, Grusha Agarwal, and Sonia K. Kang

Leslie was recently hired as a chief diversity officer. They've tried the usual approach with diversity training and hiring targets, but they don't have the data to assess whether it was effective. Even without the data, it's clear that change in representation has been slow. The company is pushing them to move the needle and they need a solution fast.

Many managers are facing the same problem as Leslie: feeling an increased need and pressure from corporate for diversity and inclusion (D&I), but hitting a wall in terms of actual change. Diversity refers to numerical representation – in a nutshell, it's about having good representation across a number of different identities. We focus on gender and race in this chapter, but companies also need to think about diversity based on other identities like age, social class, sexual orientation, and all of their combinations. Inclusion, on the other hand, is about whether employees feel that they belong, that their voices are heard and valued, and that they have power.

Attention and calls for action on D&I are reaching new heights: for instance, nearly half of S&P 500 companies have a chief diversity officer, two-thirds of whom were appointed to that role in only the last three years.[1] Unfortunately, both research and practice suggest that these increased efforts have not been associated with actual improvement[2] and that progress has stagnated.[3] In this chapter, we'll break down *why* traditional initiatives fail, and provide concrete solutions based on behavioral science that have the potential for real change and have been shown to bring it about.

Part of the problem is the traditional focus on changing "individuals." By this, we mean trying to change behavior by changing how people think they should act, or controlling what is going on inside their heads. The "Lean In" approach[4] is one example of "fixing" the people who are being oppressed, specifically by advising women to take a more proactive role in advancing their own careers. While this aims to empower, we also know that women are seen as "too aggressive" when they advocate for themselves, while the same behavior among men is seen as perfectly acceptable and even applauded.[5]

Diversity training is a popular (and lucrative) example of trying to control biases inside people's heads – it's a multi-billion-dollar industry focused on educating people about their unconscious biases, in the hope that this will translate to behavioral change. Despite the billions of dollars and countless hours invested, rigorous research shows that these programs can *backfire* because they induce perceptions of unfairness.[6] For example, *mandatory* diversity training, as adopted in most organizations today, not only disrupts participants' sense of autonomy and self-determination but is also met with resistance and even hostility towards minority groups.[7] More surprisingly, diversity trainings can actually *reinforce* bias by making stereotypes and status hierarchies more salient in people's minds and, in some cases, leave them with new stereotypes that they may not have previously known or endorsed.[8] Worse yet, diversity-oriented initiatives can *legitimize and normalize* bias by giving a false reassurance that individuals and organizations partaking in such initiatives will come away "cured" of bias and/or that individuals cannot do anything to overcome bias because it is ingrained in human nature. As a result, people have reduced concerns about discrimination and, in turn, are more likely to engage in biased behavior and show skepticism when they hear about discrimination within the company.[9] At best, diversity training changes attitudes and intentions to be more inclusive but doesn't translate to actual behavioral change, and, at worst, it can have unintended negative consequences for minority group members.[10]

What, then, *actually* works? We argue that rather than trying to change people's minds or convincing them to act differently, we should redesign their *systems and environments*, so that biases have no place to hide. This approach – "behavioral approaches to diversity," or "structural interventions," or "equality by design"[11] – focuses on redesigning organizational policies, procedures, and norms to change behavior in line with D&I goals.

This approach uniquely harnesses insights from Nobel Prize–winning research in behavioral science[12] to the problem of bias and inequality. The main idea is that small changes may have big results – organizations can use easy-to-implement and economical interventions to change behaviors by structuring choices.

This chapter documents the exciting new world of research on behavioral approaches to diversity and inclusion to provide a list of concrete solutions that you can try out in your own organization. We explore each stage of the employee pipeline: from attraction and recruitment, to screening and selection, to promotion, advancement, and retention, and finally to organizational culture. For each of these stages, we provide a brief summary of research and the practical solution that it suggests. Finally, we provide specific takeaways in Table 10.1 at the end of this chapter.

ATTRACTION AND RECRUITMENT

Recruitment is one of the most essential stages of the pipeline, as it is the first time applicants come in contact with and learn about a company. Below, we describe some empirically derived tools that are designed to maximize inclusion and minimize bias when attracting minority candidates.

Reducing gendered language in job advertisements. A popular narrative is the "pipeline problem": that women (and minorities) simply choose not to apply.[13] This is more likely a system problem; advertisements for male-typed jobs use more masculine language (e.g., competitive, dominant, leader) than feminine language (e.g., sympathetic, caring, warm).[14] This makes women feel that they don't belong and that employers might not see them as "fitting" the job.

In response, women engage in impression-management strategies like using less feminine language to describe themselves.[15] Despite their best efforts to minimize backlash, these strategies work against them – making them less attractive to recruiters who are used to women fitting a stereotypical mold.

Companies can avoid this lose-lose situation for women and themselves by moving away from gendered wording towards more *neutral* wording. For example, we recently worked with an organization to replace masculine language in their job advertisements (i.e., words like "entrepreneurial," "strong") with neutral synonyms (i.e., "creative," "dedicated"), and found the "de-biased" job posting attracted more women, but also more people in general – in particular, men who were more weakly identified with their gender.[16] De-biasing job postings resulted in a 4% increase in the proportion of women in the applicant pool. While not a huge effect on its own, this type of intervention could be an important piece in a larger set of inclusive strategies. More research is needed to fully understand the scope and constraints of this strategy, but the evidence so far suggests that it is a relatively effortless way to be more inclusive in recruitment.

Key takeaway: *replace gendered language in job descriptions with neutral language.*

Making use of visual representation. One of the most important things that applicants (especially minority applicants) look for when applying for jobs is depictions of demographic diversity.[17] Companies can showcase their diversity through *visual* cues in recruitment materials. For example, pictures of diverse groups of employees in job advertisements attract more diverse candidates to apply without affecting the number of white applicants.[18]

But, what if your company doesn't have enough diversity for you to advertise? Don't fake it. Minority applicants negatively evaluate companies that engage in "counterfeit" diversity[19] for the sake of attracting them.[20] Thus, honesty is the best solution. Be honest about your employee demographic – even if diversity is low – but share aspirations and concrete plans for increasing diversity in the future.

Key takeaway: *incorporate visual cues for diversity that are authentic and honest, and outline aspirations and plans for improvement in the future.*

Tailoring job descriptions to be more specific and *show* **diversity.** The key to writing job descriptions that attract diverse applicant pools is *specificity* in qualifications and diversity statements. Compared to subjectively worded qualifications, concrete and objective qualifications (e.g., showing exact cut-offs) can increase application rates for women.[21]

Diversity statements – written statements that communicate an organization's commitment to diversity – are often included in job descriptions and can attract minorities by making them feel more valued.[22] With these statements, specificity again is key – specific, numeric diversity goals as opposed to vaguely worded statements, are more effective at increasing diversity in the application pool without deterring majority group members.[23]

Further, companies should "show" the diversity climate – such as employees' demographics and D&I policies – instead of just "telling" applicants about it.[24] Zurich, a UK-based firm, increased recruitment of women by switching their default for *all* job advertisements to have the terms "part-time," "job-share," or "flexible working," thereby signaling a culture that recognizes the challenge of work-family balance.[25] One caveat: employees must actually be able to exercise their flexible work options, and doing so shouldn't be at the discretion of managers.[26]

As tempting as it is to quickly implement these strategies, companies must practice caution. For example, statements emphasizing cultural diversity that attract minority men and white women might discourage minority women from applying.[27] Therefore, companies need to experiment: collect data, evaluate results, and assess the impact of diversity statements before rolling them out.

Key takeaway: *be specific and showcase inclusive climate in diversity statements, but do some testing first.*

SCREENING AND SELECTION

Attraction and recruitment efforts can go to waste if companies fail to engage in fair selection practices. So, once minority applicants have signaled their interest, how do we ensure that selection processes not only minimize bias but also foster inclusion?

Anonymizing selection. One of the most famous examples of de-biasing screening procedures is that of blind auditions in orchestras. Simply adding a screen to hide musicians' identities from the judges during auditions leads to more women being selected.[28] Of course, if you are actively targeting specific underrepresented groups for hiring, removing cues for the identities you are selecting for would make your efforts impossible.[29] Companies should therefore engage in anonymized selection procedures as long as the blind nature of the screening does not interfere with the actual hiring goal.

Key takeaway: *incorporate anonymization in your selection process to hide any demographic identities that you are not specifically looking to increase.*

Using structured selection and screening procedures. One of the best ways to reduce bias in interviews is to structure them by using the same questions in the same order for all applicants. Structured interviews not only reduce bias but are also better predictors of job performance.[30]

Companies can boost the effectiveness of structured interviews by developing scoring systems and detailed hiring criteria in advance.[31]

Key takeaway: *make the process structured and consistent; decide on scoring systems and evaluation criteria in advance.*

Evaluating sets of applications together, rather than individually. When you think of reviewing résumés or conducting an interview for a job, chances are that you imagine a series of individual evaluations. While this is usually the default, joint evaluations – comparing applicants side by side – help evaluators make more objective, performance-based, and less biased evaluations.[32] And even within these joint evaluations, companies benefit from comparing individual responses "horizontally." This means looking at one question or criterion for all applicants and then moving on to the next question or criterion,[33] rather than the traditional "vertical assessment" (i.e., looking at an applicant's entire application package and then moving to the next applicant). This horizontal versus vertical comparison prevents spillover and halo effects.

The promise of joint evaluations doesn't end there: when companies hire and select candidates in groups (or sets) instead of individually, they end up with a more gender-diverse group.[34] People notice diversity more when they're recruiting in groups or sets than when they're looking to select a single candidate.

Key takeaway: *wherever possible, hire in groups, not individually, and conduct joint evaluations horizontally.*

PROMOTION, ADVANCEMENT, AND RETENTION

The next crucial stages are promotion, advancement, and retention. While many organizations focus on increasing diversity at earlier stages, they sometimes neglect to nurture and grow D&I among their existing employees. Below, we suggest a few nudges for performance reviews, promotions, and negotiation.

Rethinking performance rating scales that are out of 10 or 100. Typically, performance ratings use scales out of 10 or 100. This might seem trivial, but these numbers are imbued with cultural associations of "brilliance" and "perfection,"[35] which is problematic because we tend to associate white men, and not people of other genders or racial groups, with brilliance.[36] Evaluators are actually less likely to give 10/10 – an indicator of perfection and brilliant performance – to high-performing women.[37]

A quick fix to this problem is to change the rating scale to a number that has less cultural baggage. For example, changing the top of a rating scale from 10 to 6 closed the gender gap on perfect scores – women were *just as likely* as men to receive a 6/6.[38] This could feed into downstream benefits, like more women being recommended for advancement opportunities.

Key takeaway: *swap out evaluation scales that are out of 10 or 100 for another number.*

Finding alternatives to self-evaluation, like behavior-based 360 review. Managerial evaluations are commonly coupled with employees' self-evaluation during performance reviews. Unfortunately, women self-promote less than men, even if they are objectively as competent.[39] For example, when asked to self-evaluate, women rated their performance lower than men, *even when they performed equally and were informed of their objectively high performance.*[40]

This research also shows that it's incredibly difficult to turn *off* this effect by redesigning self-evaluations.[41]

Organizations should ask themselves: Do self-evaluations contribute something unique that we can't get in any other way? Most of the time the answer is "no," which means they can be scrapped. If the answer is "yes" or "maybe," consider peer evaluations instead. For instance, systems like the 360-performance review system can be incredibly useful and effective.[42] A best practice is to couple these peer-review systems with behaviorally anchored scales;[43] rather than peers rating general attributes, peers should rate specific behaviors. Again, make sure the scale is not out of 10!

Key takeaway: *replace self-evaluation in performance reviews with behaviorally anchored peer reviews.*

Making use of "opt-out" promotions. Many promotions and other competitions in organizations require people to actively "apply" and self-nominate, with women being less likely than men to put themselves forward.[44] Rather than having "opt-in promotions" where one must self-nominate to be considered, why not use "opt-out" promotions where everyone is automatically considered unless they opt out? This way, the default is inclusion. The effectiveness of opt-out framing has already been demonstrated in domains like retirement savings plans,[45] and preliminary results show promise for effectiveness in this domain as well: while opt-in schemes give rise to the usual gender gap in competition, women are *just as likely* as men to compete in the opt-out scheme (where everyone is automatically competing unless they opt out).[46] Opt-out framing *eliminated* the gender gap![47]

In practice, "opt-out promotions" may come with an added burden on managers to select from a larger applicant pool. This could be mitigated by combining opt-out promotions with a qualification threshold, such that everyone who passes a predetermined, behaviorally anchored qualification threshold is automatically considered. This way, you can filter out those at the bottom and reduce the burden on your HR managers, while simultaneously capturing more of the top talent pool.

Key takeaway: *make use of promotions where everyone past a predetermined qualification threshold is automatically considered unless they opt out.*

Communicating norms to apply. In 2010, Google noticed that women software engineers were not getting promoted, so a senior leader sent out emails about promotion opportunities to eligible women, encouraging them to apply.[48] As a result, applications from women increased, as did women's overall promotion rates.[49]

Increasing the number of women and minorities in the applicant pool might be as easy as reminding them of the opportunity and the process and encouraging them to apply.[50] However, there is also some evidence that "encouragement" doesn't always work. For instance, researchers found that a "vote of confidence" from a sponsor (i.e., being tapped on the shoulder) increased *men's* likelihood to apply, but it didn't change women's likelihood, thereby maintaining the gender gap.[51]

These conflicting findings suggest that there is still work to be done to understand exactly how information and encouragement can be used to close the gender gap.

Key takeaway: *experiment with explicitly encouraging employees of different identities to apply for opportunities.*

Making norms around negotiation clear. Rules around negotiations are relatively ambiguous. Employers rarely tell employees that they can negotiate, so whether or not one *should* negotiate is up in the air. Researchers found that women were less likely than men to negotiate when there was no explicit statement about negotiations; however, women were just as likely, if not more likely, than men to negotiate when the job description explicitly stated that the salary was negotiable.[52] Other research has similarly found that the gender gap in negotiation is widest when there is ambiguity about appropriateness or the economic terms. Reducing ambiguity (e.g., by having clear and specific information about what would be a good final agreement) reduced the gender gap in negotiation.[53] This leads to a feasible, concrete change that companies can make to their job postings to lessen the gender salary gap: when negotiation is possible, state this explicitly.

Research also suggests that employers and companies should frame negotiations as "asking" rather than "negotiating." Whereas women are less likely than men to negotiate a higher salary when they are cued to "negotiate," they are just as likely to ask for a higher salary when they are cued to "ask" for one.[54]

Key takeaway: *make the option to negotiate explicit and couple it with a reframe from "negotiating" to "asking."*

ORGANIZATIONAL CULTURE

Everything that happens within an organization is a function of organizational culture and mindset – the whole is greater than the sum of its parts. In this section, we put forth a few concrete strategies to embed D&I within organizational culture.

Communicating a growth mindset. Many of us have come across psychologist Carol Dweck's work on fixed versus growth mindsets – for example, some believe that you are "born" with your intelligence (fixed mindset), whereas others believe that, with effort, you can "improve" your intelligence (growth mindset).[55]

Growth mindsets may also be a powerful tool for instilling inclusion. The kind of talent mindset that organizations espouse in their mission statements can directly influence culture – companies who endorse a more fixed mindset had cultures with less collaboration, innovation, and trust.[56] Worse, fixed mindsets can strengthen negative racial and gender stereotypes about ability and make overcoming them futile. Growth mindsets, on the other hand, can create more inclusive cultures. For example, while STEM faculty who believe that ability is fixed have a larger racial achievement gap in their classes, this gap *shrinks by nearly half* in the classrooms of faculty who believe that ability is malleable.[57]

Growth mindsets can be expressed via policies, norms, and leadership messages, but also in everyday actions; for example, in managerial feedback to individuals and teams.[58]

Key takeaway: *communicate and practice a growth mindset at the organizational level and in everyday actions.*

Practicing inclusive leadership. Leaders are key influencers of social norms and culture; their buy-in on D&I goals is incredibly important. People look to leaders to understand what "valued" or "acceptable" behavior is,[59] so leaders who openly champion D&I

issues are more likely to get buy-in from everyone and inspire action on these initiatives.[60]

Leaders of an organization not only enhance and promote diversity initiatives but are also *crucial* for instilling inclusion. Even when diversity initiatives and policies are in place, those policies don't benefit racial minorities unless there is inclusive leadership.[61] In addition, we've all heard about the benefits of diverse teams, but greater team diversity doesn't automatically yield creativity. Leaders are necessary to create and support an inclusive climate in which different team members are valued for what they bring to the team, and only with inclusive leadership do we reap the benefits of diversity, with a win-win for all.[62]

To practice inclusive leadership, make sure that everyone has a chance to speak at the table and that all voices are heard and valued. This creates a sense of psychological safety,[63] where everyone's opinions are respected, and where it is safe to share perspectives and make mistakes.[64] Inclusivity is not just about having everyone's voice at the table, but also valuing and respecting those voices.

Key takeaway: *make sure leaders actively endorse D&I and embody those values by creating safe spaces for voices that aren't normally heard.*

Instilling a culture of accountability and transparency. We can't stress enough the importance of accountability and transparency. Companies need to treat D&I as any other organizational initiative, with milestones, progress checks, and metrics. An important part of this is accountability and transparency. Accountability ensures that people make better and more careful decisions because they are required to justify them. It also comes hand in hand with transparency, which is being open and allowing access to information about how decisions are made. When firms use accountability and transparency in their pay decisions and performance-reward systems, they are able to close the pay gap internally for women, racial minorities, and immigrant workers.[65]

On a societal level, we see transparency laws being put forward that obligate organizations to disclose pay information.[66] Organizations can adopt similar rules and cultures around transparency and accountability.[67] These cultures will help close gender and racial gaps, but also are likely to benefit everyone in the organization.

Key takeaway: *incorporate accountability and transparency checks into key decisions like hiring and advancement.*

CONCLUSION

Researchers and practitioners alike are facing pressure to move the needle on D&I. Whereas previous efforts have focused on how to change "individuals" – whether it be by "fixing the sexists and racists" or by "fixing the women and minorities" – we highlight here the promise of behavioral insights that help "fix the system." We have provided a series of concrete, evidence-based solutions that organizations can implement and experiment with in their unique settings. This list is comprehensive but by no means exhaustive, and new insights and ideas will continue to emerge as research proliferates.

While the insights explored here are exciting and promising, we underscore the importance of testing them in-situ "in the wild" to understand their scope and boundary conditions. Many interventions that have worked in one context (or in a lab experiment setting) may not have the same effects in other settings, as outlined in Part One of this book. So, there is still much to be done to understand how these interventions work in practice.

For practitioners, we hope that you're inspired with some ideas to bring to your own organizations. These solutions are some potential tools for your toolkit, but they will need experimentation, measurement, and refinement to see if they work for you. Testing them out will require you to collect data, set milestones, hold people accountable, be willing to experiment, anticipate failing, and be ready to refine or pivot as necessary. While this process can happen internally, it is often helpful to partner with expert D&I researchers who can help you to rigorously design, test, and evaluate interventions.

Researchers also need to take stock of what works by venturing out into the wild. Research is informed not just by theory but also by phenomenon, and observing what happens in the field and partnering with practitioners will inform new and even more promising research ideas.

Table 10.1. Takeaways: Practical solutions for each stage of the employee pipeline

Stage of employee pipeline	Practical solution
Attraction and recruitment	Use gender-neutral language in job advertisements. Incorporate visual cues to diversity in job advertisements. Specificity is key in job descriptions; show rather than tell about your inclusive climate.
Screening and selection	Anonymize applicants in your selection process when appropriate. Practice structure and consistency; use predetermined selection criteria. Hire in groups, not individually; evaluate candidates "horizontally" rather than vertically.
Promotion, advancement, and retention	Swap out scales that are out of 10 or 100 to different numbers. Get rid of (or replace) self-evaluations. Automatically consider everyone past a predetermined qualification threshold for promotion unless they opt out. Explicitly encourage employees to apply for promotions. Make the option to negotiate explicit.
Organizational culture	Communicate and signal a growth mindset about performance. Leaders should actively endorse D&I and embody those values by creating safe spaces for voices that aren't normally heard. Incorporate accountability and transparency checks into key decisions.

While the allure of the "nudge" approach to D&I is its promise of small changes and big effects, it's unlikely that we can just nudge our way to equality. Nudges are but one tool among many, and inequality is a complex problem with many levers and knobs to work on. Other tools and approaches will be necessary, including larger policy changes and rehauling of systems; for example, tying executive pay to diversity goals.[68] However, nudges are a start for companies to take an active role in rectifying inequality, and to get creative about structural changes. Our goal is to start small but think big. We urge companies to look at their own seemingly neutral and meritocratic practices to see how bias might be hidden, and see how they can leverage our key takeaways to reduce bias. Although the strategies we've put forth so far are small concrete changes that can affect real behaviors, labeling them "best practices" – ones that yield positive results across the board – would be a myth. Eradicating bias and creating lasting D&I requires commitment, experimentation, and, most importantly, finding the right combination of tools that will create lasting change in your organization.

NOTES

1 Paikeday, T.S, Sachar, H., & Stuart, A. (2019, March 1). *A leader's guide: Finding and keeping your next chief diversity officer.* Russell Reynolds Associates. https://www .russellreynolds.com/insights/thought-leadership/a-leaders-guide-finding-and -keeping-your-next-chief-diversity-officer.
2 Newkirk, P. (2019). *Diversity, Inc.: The failed promise of a billion-dollar business.* PublicAffairs.
3 England, P., Levine, A., & Mishel, E. (2020). Progress toward gender equality in the United States has slowed or stalled. *Proceedings of the National Academy of Sciences, 117*(13), 6990–7. https://doi.org/10.1073/pnas.1918891117.
4 Sandberg, S. (2013). *Lean in: Women, work, and the will to lead.* Knopf Doubleday Publishing Group.
5 Rudman, L.A., & Phelan, J.E. (2008). Backlash effects for disconfirming gender stereotypes in organizations. *Research in Organizational Behavior, 28,* 61–79. https:// doi.org/10.1016/j.riob.2008.04.003.
6 Dobbin, F., & Kalev, A. (2016, July). Why diversity programs fail. *Harvard Business Review.* https://hbr.org/2016/07/why-diversity-programs-fail.
7 Ibid.
8 Amoroso, L.M., Loyd, D.L., & Hoobler, J.M. (2010). The diversity education dilemma: Exposing status hierarchies without reinforcing them. *Journal of Management Education, 34*(6), 795–822. https://doi.org/10.1177/1052562909348209; Kulik, C.T., Perry, E.L., and Bourhis, A.C. (2000). Ironic evaluation processes: Effects of thought suppression on evaluations of older job applicants. *Journal of Organizational Behavior, 21,* 689–711. https://doi.org/10.1002/1099 -1379(200009)21:6 < 689::AID-JOB52 > 3.0.CO;2-W; Duguid, M.M., & Thomas-Hunt, M.C. (2015). Condoning stereotyping? How awareness of stereotyping prevalence impacts expression of stereotypes. *Journal of Applied Psychology, 100*(2), 343–59. https://doi.org/10.1037/a0037908.
9 Brady, L.M., Kaiser, C.R., Major, B., & Kirby, T.A. (2015). It's fair for us: Diversity structures cause women to legitimize discrimination. *Journal of Experimental Social Psychology, 57,* 100–10. https://doi.org/10.1016/j.jesp.2014.11.010; Kirby, T.A., Kaiser, C.R. & Major, B. (2015). Insidious procedures: Diversity awards legitimize unfair organizational practices. *Social Justice Research, 28,* 169–86. https://doi .org/10.1007/s11211-015-0240-z.
10 Chang, E.H., Milkman, K.L., Gromet, D.M., Rebele, R.W., Massey, C., Duckworth, A.L., & Grant, A.M. (2019). The mixed effects of online diversity training. *Proceedings of the National Academy of Sciences, 116*(16), 7778–83. https://doi.org/10.1073 /pnas.1816076116; Kalinoski, Z.T., Steele-Johnson, D., Peyton, E.J., Leas, K.A., Steinke, J., & Bowling, N.A. (2013). A meta-analytic evaluation of diversity training outcomes. *Journal of Organizational Behavior, 34*(8), 1076–1104. https:// doi.org/10.1002/job.1839.
11 Bohnet, I. (2016). *What works.* Harvard University Press.

12 Thaler, R.H., & Sunstein, C.R. (2009). *Nudge: Improving decisions about health, wealth, and happiness*. Penguin.
13 Kang, S.K., & Kaplan, S. (2019). Working toward gender diversity and inclusion in medicine: Myths and solutions. *Lancet, 393*(10171), 579–86. https://doi.org/10.1016/S0140-6736(18)33138-6.
14 Gaucher, D., Friesen, J., & Kay, A.C. (2011). Evidence that gendered wording in job advertisements exists and sustains gender inequality. *Journal of Personality and Social Psychology, 101*(1), 109–28. https://doi.org/10.1037/a0022530.
15 He, J., & Kang, S. (2019). Covering in cover letters: Gender and self-presentation in job applications. *Academy of Management Proceedings, 2019*(1), 15481. https://doi.org/10.5465/AMBPP.2019.275.
16 Engendering Success in STEM (ESS). (2020). *De-biasing Job Advertisements*. Engendering Success in STEM (ESS). https://successinstem.ca/wp-content/uploads/2020/10/De-Biasing-Job-Advertisements.pdf.
17 Thomas, K.M., & Wise, P.G. (1999). Organizational attractiveness and individual differences: Are diverse applicants attracted by different factors? *Journal of Business and Psychology, 13*(3), 375–90. https://doi.org/10.1023/A:1022978400698.
18 Avery, D.R., & McKay, P.F. (2006). Target practice: An organizational impression management approach to attracting minority and female job applicants. *Personnel Psychology, 59*(1), 157–87. https://doi.org/10.1111/j.1744-6570.2006.00807.x; Avery, D.R. (2003). Reactions to diversity in recruitment advertising – Are differences black and white? *Journal of Applied Psychology, 88*(4), 672–9. https://doi.org/10.1037/0021-9010.88.4.672; Perkins, L.A., Thomas, K.M., & Taylor, G.A. (2000). Advertising and recruitment: Marketing to minorities. *Psychology & Marketing, 17*(3), 235–55. https://doi.org/10.1002/(SICI)1520-6793(200003)17:3<235::AID-MAR3>3.0.CO;2-#.
19 Kroeper, K.M., Williams, H.E., & Murphy, M.C. (2020). Counterfeit diversity: How strategically misrepresenting gender diversity dampens organizations' perceived sincerity and elevates women's identity threat concerns. *Journal of Personality and Social Psychology*. https://doi.org/10.1037/pspi0000348.
20 Wilton, L.S., Bell, A.N., Vahradyan, M., & Kaiser, C.R. (2020). Show don't tell: Diversity dishonesty harms racial/ethnic minorities at work. *Personality and Social Psychology Bulletin, 46*(8), 1171–85. https://doi.org/10.1177/0146167219897149.
21 Coffman, K.B., Collis, M., and Kulkarni, L. When to apply? Harvard Business School Working Paper, No. 20–062, November 2019. (Revised January 2021.)
22 Highhouse, S., Stierwalt, S.L., Bachiochi, P., Elder, A.E., & Fisher, G. (1999). Effects of advertised human resource management practices on attraction of African American applicants. *Personnel Psychology, 52*(2), 425–42. https://doi.org/10.1111/j.1744-6570.1999.tb00167.x; Williams, M.L., & Bauer, T.N. (1994). The effect of a managing diversity policy on organizational attractiveness. *Group & Organization Management, 19*(3), 295–308. https://doi.org/10.1177/1059601194193005; Kim, S.S., & Gelfand, M.J. (2003). The influence of ethnic identity on perceptions of organizational recruitment. *Journal of Vocational Behavior, 63*(3), 396–416. https://doi.org/10.1016/S0001-8791(02)00043-X.
23 Kirgios, E.L., Silver, I.M., Chang, E.H. Do concrete diversity goals attract or repel job applicants? Evidence from the field. Working Paper.
24 Wilton, Bell, Vahradyan, & Kaiser (2020); Casper, W.J., Wayne, J.H., & Manegold, J.G. (2013). Who will we recruit? Targeting deep- and surface-level diversity with human resource policy advertising. *Human Resource Management, 52*(3), 311–32. https://doi.org/10.1002/hrm.21530.
25 Burd, H., Davidson, S., & Hacohen, R. (2020, November 17). Switching the default to advertise part-time working boosts applications from women by 16%. Retrieved

from https://www.bi.team/blogs/switching-the-default-to-advertise-part-time-working-boosts-applications-from-women-by-16/.

26 Kelly, E.L., & Kalev, A. (2006). Managing flexible work arrangements in US organizations: Formalized discretion or "a right to ask." *Socio-Economic Review*, *4*(3), 379–416. https://doi.org/10.1093/ser/mwl001.

27 Rau, B.L., & Hyland, M.M. (2003). Corporate teamwork and diversity statements in college recruitment brochures: Effects on attraction. *Journal of Applied Social Psychology*, *33*(12), 2465–92. https://doi.org/10.1111/j.1559-1816.2003.tb02776.x.

28 Goldin, C., & Rouse, C. (2000). Orchestrating impartiality: The impact of "blind" auditions on female musicians. *American Economic Review*, *90*(4), 715–41. https://doi.org/10.1257/aer.90.4.715.

29 Behaghel, L., Crépon, B., & Le Barbanchon, T. (2015). Unintended effects of anonymous résumés. *American Economic Journal: Applied Economics*, *7*(3), 1–27. https://doi.org/10.1257/app.20140185.

30 Kutcher, E.J., & Bragger, J.D. (2004). Selection interviews of overweight job applicants: Can structure reduce the bias? *Journal of Applied Social Psychology*, *34*(10), 1993–2022. https://doi.org/10.1111/j.1559-1816.2004.tb02688.x; Bragger, J.D., Kutcher, E., Morgan, J., & Firth, P. (2002). The effects of the structured interview on reducing biases against pregnant job applicants. *Sex Roles*, *46*(7), 215–26. https://doi.org/10.1023/A:1019967231059.

31 Uhlmann, E.L., & Cohen, G.L. (2005). Constructed criteria: Redefining merit to justify discrimination. *Psychological Science*, *16*(6), 474–80. https://doi.org/10.1111/j.0956-7976.2005.01559.x.

32 Bohnet, I., Van Geen, A., & Bazerman, M. (2016). When performance trumps gender bias: Joint vs. separate evaluation. *Management Science*, *62*(5), 1225–34. https://doi.org/10.1287/mnsc.2015.2186.

33 Bohnet, I. (2016, April 18). How to take the bias out of interviews. Retrieved from https://hbr.org/2016/04/how-to-take-the-bias-out-of-interviews.

34 Chang, E.H., Kirgios, E.L., Rai, A., & Milkman, K.L. (2020). The isolated choice effect and its implications for gender diversity in organizations. *Management Science*, *66*(6), 2752–61. https://doi.org/10.1287/mnsc.2019.3533.

35 Rivera, L.A., & Tilcsik, A. (2019). Scaling down inequality: Rating scales, gender bias, and the architecture of evaluation. *American Sociological Review*, *84*(2), 248–74. https://doi.org/10.1177/0003122419833601.

36 Bian, L., Leslie, S.-J., Murphy, M.C., & Cimpian, A. (2018). Messages about brilliance undermine women's interest in educational and professional opportunities. *Journal of Experimental Social Psychology*, *76*, 404–20. https://doi.org/10.1016/j.jesp.2017.11.006; Leslie, S.J., Cimpian, A., Meyer, M., & Freeland, E. (2015). Expectations of brilliance underlie gender distributions across academic disciplines. *Science*, *347*(6219), 262–5. https://doi.org/10.1126/science.1261375.

37 Rivera & Tilcsik (2019).

38 Ibid.

39 Moss-Racusin, C.A., & Rudman, L.A. (2010). Disruptions in women's self-promotion: The backlash avoidance model. *Psychology of Women Quarterly*, *34*(2), 186–202. https://doi.org/10.1111/j.1471-6402.2010.01561.x.

40 Exley, C.L., & Kessler, J.B. (2019). The gender gap in self-promotion (No. w26345). National Bureau of Economic Research. https://doi.org/10.3386/w26345.

41 Ibid.

42 Antonioni, D. (1996). Designing an effective 360-degree appraisal feedback process. *Organizational Dynamics*, *25*(2), 24–38. https://doi.org/10.1016/S0090-2616(96)90023-6; Atkins, P.W.B., & Wood, R.E. (2002). Self- versus others'

ratings as predictors of assessment center ratings: Validation evidence for 360-degree feedback programs. *Personnel Psychology, 55*(4), 871–904. https://doi .org/10.1111/j.1744-6570.2002.tb00133.x.

43 Hom, P.W., DeNisi, A.S., Kinicki, A.J., & Bannister, B.D. (1982). Effectiveness of performance feedback from behaviorally anchored rating scales. *Journal of Applied Psychology, 67*(5), 568–76. https://doi.org/10.1037/0021-9010.67.5.568.

44 Bosquet, C., Combes, P.P., & García-Peñalosa, C. (2019). Gender and promotions: Evidence from academic economists in France. *Scandinavian Journal of Economics, 121*(3), 1020–53. https://doi.org/10.1111/sjoe.12300.

45 Thaler, R.H., & Benartzi, S. (2004). Save More Tomorrow™: Using behavioral economics to increase employee saving. *Journal of Political Economy, 112*(S1), S164–S187. https://doi.org/10.1086/380085.

46 See He, J., Kang, S., & Lacetera, N. (2019). *Leaning in or not leaning out? Opt-out choice framing attenuates gender differences in the decision to compete* (Working Paper 26484). National Bureau of Economic Research; and Bock, L. (2015). *Work rules! Insights from inside google that will transform how you live and lead.* John Murray Press.

47 He, Kang, & Lacetera (2019).

48 Bock (2015).

49 Kang, C. (2014). Google data-mines its approach to promoting women. *Washington Post.* https://www.washingtonpost.com/news/the-switch/wp/2014/04/02 /google-data-mines-its-women-problem/.

50 Li, H. (2018). Do mentoring, information, and nudge reduce the gender gap in economics majors? *Economics of Education Review, 64*, 165–83. https://doi.org /10.1016/j.econedurev.2018.04.004.

51 Baldiga, N.R., & Coffman, K.B. (2018). Laboratory evidence on the effects of sponsorship on the competitive preferences of men and women. *Management Science, 64*(2), 888–901. https://doi.org/10.1287/mnsc.2016.2606.

52 Leibbrandt, A., & List, J.A. (2015). Do women avoid salary negotiations? Evidence from a large-scale natural field experiment. *Management Science, 61*(9), 2016–24. https://doi.org/10.1287/mnsc.2014.1994.

53 Bowles, H.R., Babcock, L., & McGinn, K.L. (2005). Constraints and triggers: Situational mechanics of gender in negotiation. *Journal of Personality and Social Psychology, 89*(6), 951. https://doi.org/10.1037/0022-3514.89.6.951.

54 Small, D.A., Gelfand, M., Babcock, L., & Gettman, H. (2007). Who goes to the bargaining table? The influence of gender and framing on the initiation of negotiation. *Journal of Personality and Social Psychology, 93*(4), 600. https://doi.org /10.1037/0022-3514.93.4.600.

55 Murphy, M.C., & Reeves, S.L. (2019). Personal and organizational mindsets at work. *Research in Organizational Behavior, 39*, 100121. https://doi.org/10.1016/j .riob.2020.100121.

56 Canning, E.A., Murphy, M.C., Emerson, K.T., Chatman, J.A., Dweck, C.S., & Kray, L.J. (2020). Cultures of genius at work: Organizational mindsets predict cultural norms, trust, and commitment. *Personality and Social Psychology Bulletin, 46*(4), 626–42. https://doi.org/10.1177/0146167219872473.

57 Canning, E.A., Muenks, K., Green, D.J., & Murphy, M.C. (2019). STEM faculty who believe ability is fixed have larger racial achievement gaps and inspire less student motivation in their classes. *Science Advances, 5*(2). https://doi.org/10.1126/sciadv.aau4734.

58 Murphy & Reeves (2019).

59 Cialdini, R.B., & Goldstein, N.J. (2004). Social influence: Compliance and conformity. *Annual Review of Psychology, 55*, 591–621. https://doi.org/10.1146/annurev.psych .55.090902.142015.

60 Subašić, E., Hardacre, S., Elton, B., Branscombe, N.R., Ryan, M.K., & Reynolds, K.J. (2018). "We for she": Mobilising men and women to act in solidarity for gender equality. *Group Processes & Intergroup Relations, 21*(5), 707–24. https://doi.org /10.1177/1368430218763272.
61 Jin, M., Lee, J., & Lee, M. (2017). Does leadership matter in diversity management? Assessing the relative impact of diversity policy and inclusive leadership in the public sector. *Leadership & Organization Development Journal, 38*(2), 303–19. https:// doi.org/10.1108/LODJ-07-2015-0151.
62 Ashikali, T., Groeneveld, S., & Kuipers, B. (2020). The role of inclusive leadership in supporting an inclusive climate in diverse public sector teams. *Review of Public Personnel Administration,* 0734371X19899722. https://doi.org/10.1177 /0734371X19899722.
63 Carmeli, A., Reiter-Palmon, R., & Ziv, E. (2010). Inclusive leadership and employee involvement in creative tasks in the workplace: The mediating role of psychological safety. *Creativity Research Journal, 22*(3), 250–60. https://doi.org/10.1080/10400419. 2010.504654; Hirak, R., Peng, A.C., Carmeli, A., & Schaubroeck, J.M. (2012). Linking leader inclusiveness to work unit performance: The importance of psychological safety and learning from failures. *Leadership Quarterly, 23*(1), 107–17. https://doi .org/10.1016/j.leaqua.2011.11.009.
64 Edmondson, A. (1999). Psychological safety and learning behavior in work teams. *Administrative Science Quarterly, 44*(2), 350–83. https://doi.org/10.2307/2666999.
65 Castilla, E.J. (2015). Accounting for the gap: A firm study manipulating organizational accountability and transparency in pay decisions. *Organization Science, 26*(2), 311–33. https://doi.org/10.1287/orsc.2014.0950.
66 Bennedsen, M., Simintzi, E., Tsoutsoura, M., & Wolfenzon, D. (2019). *Do firms respond to gender pay gap transparency?* (No. w25435). National Bureau of Economic Research. https://doi.org/10.3386/w25435; Gamage, D.K., Kavetsos, G., Mallick, S., and Sevilla, A. (2020). Pay transparency initiative and gender pay gap: Evidence from research-intensive universities in the UK. IZA Working Paper 13635. https:// papers.ssrn.com/abstract=3682949; Baker, M., Halberstam, Y., Kroft, K., Mas, A., and Messacar, D. (2019). Pay transparency and the gender gap. NBER Working Paper 25834. https://doi.org/10.3386/w25834.
67 BEworks. (n.d.). *BEworks choice architecture report 2021.* Retrieved April 15, 2021, from https://go.beworks.com/car2021.
68 McDonald's ties executive pay to diversity, releases data. (2021, February 18). *Bloomberg.Com.* https://www.bloomberg.com/news/articles/2021-02-18 /mcdonald-s-ties-executive-pay-to-diversity-goals-releases-data; Microsoft to tie executive bonuses to company diversity goals. (2016, November 17). *Bloomberg.Com.* https://www.bloomberg.com/news/articles/2016-11-17 /microsoft-to-tie-executive-bonuses-to-company-diversity-goals.

CHAPTER ELEVEN

Sustainable Nudges for the Wild: Recommendations from SHIFT

*David J. Hardisty, Katherine White, Rishad Habib,
and Jiaying Zhao*

INTRODUCTION

This chapter of *Behavioral Science in the Wild* looks at behavioral insights *for* the wild. Our well-being and our economy depend on our most precious asset: nature. Yet, our exploitation of nature is endangering both current and future generations of human beings and other life on this planet that we share.[1] Extinction rates, for example, are 100 to 1,000 times higher than the replacement rate, and are increasing.[2] Just as human decisions have caused the environmental crisis, so too must sustainable human choices be part of the solution. Thus, we need *sustainable nudges*, that both (1) shift people to make more sustainable choices, and (2) maintain those improvements for the long term. Easier said than done! Fortunately, the science of behavioral insights has diagnosed the key challenges and identified promising solutions.

CHALLENGES

When applying academic behavioral insights research to sustainable behavior change in the wild, there are two key challenges: *social desirability bias* and the *intention-action gap*. The social desirability bias is the idea that people often say what "sounds good" (or is socially valued) more than what they truly believe.[3] For example, someone may *say* that they care about nature conservation "very much" in a survey, but in reality perhaps they only care "somewhat." This bias means that we should be skeptical of studies that rely solely on self-report measures of environmental behavior, as these reports may not be honest. A second, more insidious challenge is the intention-action gap,[4] in which people fully intend to make sustainable choices and report that they will do so, and yet the promised action never materializes. For example, a consumer might intend to buy more plant-based meat, but yet still choose animal-based meat when they are in the grocery store. This happens because environmental benefits are often distant and abstract, and struggle to compete with immediate concerns such as price, convenience, flavor, and ingrained habits.[5]

GUIDELINES

In light of these challenges, behavioral insights practitioners should follow these guidelines for selecting, interpreting, and applying academic research on sustainable behavior change:

1. **Look for field studies measuring real sustainability behavior.** Ideally such studies should use randomized controlled trials (RCTs), which allow comparisons between an experimental and a control group – these are the gold standard for what will work in the wild. (This is always a good guideline in behavioral insights practice more broadly, and it is especially true for sustainable nudges.) For example, one famous study provided homeowners with information about how their energy usage compared to that of their neighbors, plus positive feedback (smiley faces) for conserving more than the average, and measured actual energy usage.[6] They found that households change their energy conservation to match or exceed that of their neighbors, a result that has subsequently been replicated over 200 times in other field studies across 27 US states.[7]

2. If field studies measuring natural behavior are not available, **lab experiments (where participants sign up to participate in a study) using objective "behavioral measures" are the next best thing.** These "behavioral measures" could take the form of a skills test (e.g., proper waste disposal), measures of actual consumption (e.g., how much does someone take), real donations to an environmental charity, or other objectively measured behaviors. For example, a recent lab-based study tested a digital sorting game that provides immediate feedback on recycling and composting decisions.[8] Student participants learned to be more accurate in the game, and this translated into actual increased composting rates and reduced contamination in student residences. Thus, this was an initial lab study with a behavioral measure and was later validated in the field. Another study tested the Phylo game in the lab to promote biodiversity conservation behaviors and found that the game increased real donations to prevent negative environmental events (e.g., wildfires, oil spills) compared to a passive slideshow.[9]

3. **Interpret self-report studies with caution.** They can still be useful to identify promising interventions, but self-reports of environmental behavior are likely to be exaggerated (often unintentionally; the "intention-action gap" at work!). For example, we ran a pair of studies examining the efficacy of "10-year cost" labels to nudge consumers to choose more energy-efficient, but more expensive, lightbulbs. In a self-report study with hypothetical scenarios, 56% of people in the control condition and 84% of people in the "10-year cost" condition said they would choose the efficient lightbulb. In a field study of actual consumer purchases in drugstores, using exactly the same lightbulbs and labels, the actual rates of environmental choices were much lower: only 12% of people in the control condition chose the efficient bulb, and 48% of people in the "10-year cost" condition chose the efficient bulb.[10]

In some cases, behavioral evidence is impossible to obtain, and in these cases self-report evidence is better than no evidence at all. For example, in political elections and referendums, it is extremely difficult to conduct an RCT with objective behavioral measures. One of the critical policy issues of our time is the need to establish appropriate carbon pricing, which requires the support of the citizenry. How should we craft and frame carbon pricing? Our research suggests that "carbon tax" framing (versus other frames such as a mandatory "carbon offset") is less likely to receive support among US citizens, especially among self-identified Republicans.[11] While overall support for carbon pricing is likely lower than indicated by these self-report results, it is also likely that the policy frames that are more popular among voters in these studies would also perform better when voters consider real policy proposals. In this case, the toxicity of the "tax" frame in US politics perhaps explains the relative popularity of "cap and trade" or "green new deal" subsidy proposals over the carbon tax policies that are recommended by economists.

THE SHIFT FRAMEWORK FOR SUSTAINABLE BEHAVIOR CHANGE

With these challenges and guidelines in mind, we recently reviewed 320 academic articles on sustainable consumer behavior change.[12] We identified five factors that lead to successful behavior change: Social influence, Habit formation, Individual self, Feelings and cognition, and Tangibility. This forms the handy acronym SHIFT. In the following paragraphs, we explain each SHIFT factor, and give an example of a study employing that factor and measuring its impact on real behavior.

Social Influence

As detailed in Chapter 7 on norm nudging, humans are social animals, and respond strongly to what others are doing ("descriptive" social norms) and what others approve or disapprove of ("injunctive" social norms). Communicating what *relevant* others are doing or what they think should be done can influence sustainable behaviors, especially when the collective self is activated or when language mentions "we," "our," or "the community."[13] These social norms act not only on individuals but also at the level of groups: competition with outgroups is a powerful motivator to change behavior.[14] More broadly, consumers try to make a positive impression on others, and therefore the social desirability of sustainable behaviors is a critical factor. All of these norms can be harnessed by making sustainable behavior more public and observable where possible.

But what do we do when a sustainable behavior is not yet the norm? Just as a high norm can motivate behavior, so too can a low norm backfire. One solution here is to communicate *dynamic* norms. People will be inclined to join a rising trend, even if it isn't (yet) in the majority. In one study, researchers were seeking to increase the selection of meatless options by customers at a restaurant.[15] One group of customers read a message with a *static norm* that "30% of Americans make an effort to limit their meat consumption"; a second group read a *dynamic norm* message that "30% of Americans have started to make an effort to limit their meat consumption"; and a third group read a control message without any norm information. The researchers measured participants' actual lunch orders and calculated the percentage of meat versus meatless entrees ordered. The results showed that participants in the dynamic-norm condition chose the meatless lunch 34% of the time, significantly more than participants in the static-norm condition (17%) or the control condition (21%). Thus, while a low norm (30% of Americans limit meat) can discourage behavior change, a low norm that is dynamic (30% of Americans have started to limit meat) can encourage behavior change.

Tools for social influence:

- Use descriptive social norms (e.g., "Most of your neighbors are recycling; join in and recycle too").
- Use injunctive social norms (e.g., "Your community wants to recycle; recycling is something you should do for your community").
- Communicate using collective pronouns (e.g., "We can make a difference").
- Promote healthy competition between groups (e.g., "Computer science/Business students are recycling the most").

- Communicate dynamic norms (e.g., "30% of Americans have started to make an effort to limit their meat consumption").

Habit Formation

Although some sustainable behaviors (such as choosing to buy an electric car over a gas-powered car) only require a one-time action, many other sustainable behaviors (such as driving less and taking public transit more) must be repeated over time and so require new habit formation.

Changing habits requires breaking old unsustainable habits, which can be done most easily when people are experiencing a big life change. For example, when moving to a new location, entering a new relationship, or breaking up from a relationship, people are more likely to alter their environmental behaviors.[16] Another tip for breaking bad habits is that penalties generally have more impact than rewards.[17] For example, a five-cent plastic bag tax is likely to be more effective than a five-cent reward for bringing reusable bags.

To establish new habits, implementation intentions and plans are a good first step,[18] but should be supported by making the environmental behavior as easy as possible,[19] and providing timely prompts,[20] incentives,[21] and feedback[22] (for details see Chapters 8 and 9).

One of the most powerful behavioral insights tools is quite simply to "make it easy" and encourage the formation of a sustainable habit by changing the default, so that the environmental behavior is the pre-set behavior, and it takes additional effort to switch to the non-environmental behavior (for details see Chapter 6). For example, in one field study, changing the default energy source from "grey" energy to "green" energy increased customer green energy choices from approximately 1% before the default change to 99% after the default change.[23]

Tools for habits:

- Harness moments of change when people are most receptive to change (e.g., share local transit maps with people moving to a new city).

- Use penalties to discourage repeated unsustainable behaviors (e.g., a five-cent charge for plastic bags).
- Provide timely prompts (e.g., a prompt before people leave the house to remind them to bring a reusable bag).
- Provide real-time feedback (e.g., a meter for water usage while in the shower).
- Make sustainable behavior easy by making it the default (e.g., change the default energy source to green energy).

Individual Self

Most people pay special attention to themselves and the impacts and consequences that affect themselves, and sustainable decision making is no exception. Therefore, interventions that appeal to the self will often be more effective. This can be accomplished in several different ways, such as targeting people's self-concept,[24] self-consistency,[25] self-interest,[26] or self-efficacy.[27] People respond more to actions that make them feel positive about themselves, and are less likely to engage in actions that make them feel bad about themselves, such as throwing products linked to their identity in the trash.[28] They also try to act in a consistent way, leading to positive spillover effects, and are most responsive when they feel they can make a difference.[29]

Of course, some people have stronger environmental values, and appeals to those individuals will be more successful.[30] Furthermore, priming or reminding people of their own self-standards can increase sustainable behaviors.[31] Conversely, a mismatch between identity and the environmental message can produce backfire effects. For example, threats to Republican self-identity can lead to backfire effects such that Republicans decrease support for climate change mitigation policies in response to climate change communications[32] and are less likely to choose an eco-friendly option.[33] However, matching environmental messaging with identity can increase sustainable behavior. For instance, Republicans donated more to the Environmental Defense Fund when they saw messages reflecting patriotism and love for their country and less when they saw messages emphasizing harm, fairness, and justice.[34]

On the positive side, targeting individuals with stronger environmental values or a more communal orientation can bring increased effectiveness. In a field study, researchers aimed to influence climate action by including communally oriented members through conscious group formation. Indeed, collective village groups in Indonesia, Peru, and Tanzania conserved about 51% more trees by ensuring that half of the group members were women.[35]

Tools for individual self:

- Tailor messages to appeal to different identities (e.g., Republicans responded well to a message saying, "Show your love to your country by joining the fight to protect the purity of America's natural environment").
- Do not threaten an important identity (e.g., highlighting environmental values can threaten a Republican identity and reduce support for climate action).
- Target those with strong environmental and communal values (e.g., creating groups including women led to more trees being conserved).
- Link products with a desired identity (e.g., cups with the American flag printed on them were more likely to be recycled by those who strongly identified with being American).

Feelings and Cognition

We group feelings and cognition together because they represent the two general routes to communicating about sustainable behavior change: one that is more linked to emotions and one that is more driven by thinking.[36] Behavioral insights practitioners need to be sure to consider both modes of decision making, and interventions that target one or the other, depending on the context. Negative emotions such as guilt, fear, and sadness can be powerful when used in small amounts,[37] but can also backfire when they are too intense or overbearing.[38] Thus, the effect of negative emotions on behavior change is described by an "inverted-U" shape, where extremely low or extremely high levels of negative emotion are ineffective, and modest use of negative emotions is most effective. Conversely, positive emotions such as hope, "warm glow," and "affinity towards nature" have been found to motivate behavior change and can be used more liberally.[39]

Turning to cognitions, some amount of basic information communication, education, and knowledge improvement may be useful for behavior change.[40] However, research also reveals that interventions providing information and education only (see Chapter 17 for the financial domain) are often not enough to spur long-term sustainable changes.[41] Because of this, combining information with other tactics can be more effective.[42] When doing so, it is critical to frame information in a compelling way. For example, communicating energy costs is generally more effective in encouraging conservation than communicating energy savings, even though the underlying information is the same.[43] Once the proper framing has been determined, eco-labeling is a useful way to reach consumers with the right information, at the right time, in a trusted format.[44] Eco-labels are seen as more transparent and unbiased if they are certified by a third party that validates the sustainability claims.[45]

A recent study examined the effectiveness of carbon labeling for food. The results showed that consumers generally underestimated the greenhouse gas (GHG) emissions associated with their food choices (especially meat), and that labels communicating the GHG of each menu option (in a familiar reference unit: light-bulb minutes) led to fewer beef purchases.[46]

Tools for feelings and cognition:

- Use negative emotions like guilt, fear, and sadness in moderation (e.g., "Our fair trade teas allow us to ensure fair wages for tea producers in developing nations").
- Avoid explicit guilt messages (e.g., "How can you enjoy a cup of tea knowing that the people who produce it are not being treated fairly?").
- Frame information to highlight costs (e.g., communicate energy costs rather than savings).
- Use eco-labels that people trust (e.g., include third-party verifications on labels).

- Communicate information clearly (e.g., show the total greenhouse gas emissions from different foods in an easy-to-understand unit or format, such as "light-bulb minutes").

Tangibility

Many environmental outcomes can seem vague, abstract, and distant, yet consumers are more motivated by tangible, concrete, and immediate consequences. Therefore, practitioners should consider using tangibility techniques to nudge consumers to care more about the environment and take action.

One solution to the intangibility problem is to communicate the local and immediate environmental impacts associated with a behavior. For example, communications that relate the more immediate consequences of pro-environmental behaviors for a given city, region, or neighborhood can make environmental actions and outcomes seem more tangible and relevant.[47] Another solution to the intangibility problem is simply to make sustainability more tangible, such as through vivid imagery, analogies, and narratives;[48] a photograph of glacier retreat will generally have more impact than a graph communicating glacier retreat statistics.

A novel solution to the intangibility problem is to move the consciousness of the consumer into the future. For example, asking someone to consider their legacy ("How will you be remembered?") mentally moves their ego into the future, and has a greater impact than merely asking them to consider future generations.[49]

Lastly, an important challenge for sustainable behavior change is to shift consumers from the desire for material goods to the pursuit of experiences. This process has been called "dematerialization,"[50] and can include consumption of experiences,[51] digital products,[52] or services,[53] provided those options are sustainable.

A recent study examined the effect of tangible representations on recycling rates at outdoor events and residences. While participants in the control condition were informed about which plastics were recyclable, those in the experimental conditions also learned what products the recycled materials could become, after the recycling process. For example, they might see that a bottle could be recycled into another bottle, or that a bottle could be recycled into a jacket. In either case, these tangible representations of recycling improved recycling rates from 51% in the control condition to 80% in the tangible representation conditions.[54]

Tools for tangibility:

- Communicate local and immediate impacts (e.g., rising sea levels can harm island residents).
- Make sustainability more tangible and concrete (e.g., clearly show new products made from recycled products).
- Encourage people to think about their own importance in the future (e.g., consider how you will be remembered).
- Encourage people to focus on non-material options (e.g., experiences, digital products and services).

CONCLUDING THOUGHTS AND ADVICE FOR BEHAVIORAL INSIGHTS PRACTITIONERS

One question that we often get asked by practitioners is which factor or tool works the "best" in encouraging sustainable behavior change. The answer depends on the context, the target audience, and the characteristics of the behavior itself; and the tools chosen need to be tailored accordingly. Based on the behavior the practitioner wants to influence, the barriers and benefits associated with the behavior, and the target audience, it might become clear that a certain factor in the SHIFT framework should be considered. For example, if your preliminary research tells you that a key barrier to doing the focal action is that it is unfamiliar and the perception is that nobody else is doing it, then communicating social norms might be an impactful strategy. If the existing behavior is very habitual, automatic, and difficult to change, using habit-formation techniques may be most efficacious. If the desired action is seen by the target market as time-consuming, unpleasant, or costly to the self, devising ways to appeal to the individual self might be most important.

As described above, the SHIFT framework provides five distinct pathways to nudge consumers towards more sustainable choices. Yet, when crafting an intervention, there is no need to limit yourself to only one factor; many of the best behavioral insights interventions combine several principles.[55] Indeed, a review of energy conservation interventions by power companies found that each intervention combined at least two (and often more) behavioral insights tools.[56] For example, the Cape Light Compact used a web interface to change energy behavior by combining seven techniques: the availability heuristic, competition, feedback, gamification, goal setting, fairness, and modelling. The result? Customers' energy savings ranged from 7.8% to 8.8% on average. Thus, while academic papers generally seek to isolate a single, "clean" intervention and psychological process, practitioners may consider combining multiple factors that apply to their context together in a "kitchen sink" approach. That being said, there is a caveat here – sometimes combining factors can "crowd" one another out. For example, while intrinsic appeals that appeal to environmental values to act sustainably can work well in isolation, combing these with extrinsic appeals to look good to others or save money may reduce effectiveness.[57] Thus, once you have narrowed down your perfect behavioral insights intervention, we suggest conducting a small in-situ pilot test to determine efficacy before you take it to full scale.

Moreover, just as practitioners should consider using multiple tools to craft an effective intervention, they might also consider measuring multiple behaviors (when possible) to assess the efficacy of the intervention. In some cases, there may be unanticipated "positive spillover," wherein one good environmental deed may establish a "foot in the door" in the mind of the consumer, and lead to further pro-environmental behaviors in the future.[58] Conversely, in other cases, one pro-environmental behavior can lead to "negative spillover" and "license" the consumer to slack off environmentally on another behavior.[59] When do you get one or the other? Our research suggests that small, "token" public actions such as a social media post supporting environmentalism can lead to negative spillover, while larger, effortful actions and/or private actions such as a home energy audit can lead to positive spillover.[60]

Finally, keep in mind that nudges are but one tool in the larger behavior change system.[61] We are big believers in behavioral insights, but there is a risk that people may see them as the only sustainability solution and neglect other economic and policy tools.[62] Therefore, behavioral insights should be used as a complement and support to regulatory and economic interventions such as tracking and disclosure requirements, taxes, subsidies, and outright prohibition.

Happy nudging!

NOTES

1 Dasgupta, P. (2021). *The economics of biodiversity: The Dasgupta Review. Headline messages.* HM Treasury. https://assets.publishing.service.gov.uk/government/uploads/system/uploads/attachment_data/file/957629/Dasgupta_Review_-_Headline_Messages.pdf.

2 Ibid.

3 Vesely, S., & Klöckner, C.A. (2020). Social desirability in environmental psychology research: Three meta-analyses. *Frontiers in Psychology, 11,* 1395. https://doi.org/10.3389/fpsyg.2020.01395.

4 See Carrington, M.J., Neville, B.A., & Whitwell, G.J. (2014). Lost in translation: Exploring the ethical consumer intention–behavior gap. *Journal of Business Research, 67*(1), 2759–67; and White, K., Habib, R., & Hardisty, D.J. (2019). How to SHIFT consumer behaviors to be more sustainable: A literature review and guiding framework. *Journal of Marketing, 83*(3), 22–49. https://doi.org/10.1177/0022242919825649.

5 Barr, N., Thomson, D.R., Peters, K., and Mazar, N. (forthcoming). Improving the effectiveness of time-of-use pricing on sustainable electricity consumption with behavioral science. *Behavioral Science and Policy, 2021.*

6 Schultz, P.W., Nolan, J.M., Cialdini, R.B., Goldstein, N.J., & Griskevicius, V. (2007). The constructive, destructive, and reconstructive power of social norms. *Psychological Science, 18*(5), 429–34. https://doi.org/10.1111/j.1467-9280.2007.01917.x.

7 Jachimowicz, J.M., Hauser, O.P., O'Brien, J.D., Sherman, E., & Galinsky, A.D. (2018). The critical role of second-order normative beliefs in predicting energy conservation. *Nature Human Behaviour, 2*(10), 757–64. https://doi.org/10.1038/s41562-018-0434-0.

8 Luo, Y., Zelenika, I., & Zhao, J. (2019). Providing immediate feedback improves recycling and composting accuracy. *Journal of Environmental Management, 232,* 445–54. https://doi.org/10.1016/j.jenvman.2018.11.061.

9 Callahan, M.M., Echeverri, A., Ng, D., Zhao, J., & Satterfield, T. (2019). Using the Phylo card game to advance biodiversity conservation in an era of Pokémon. *Palgrave Communications, 5*(1) https://doi.org/10.1057/s41599-019-0287-9.

10 Hardisty, D.J., Shim, Y., Sun, D., & Griffin, D.W. (2020). Encouraging energy efficiency: Product labels activate temporal tradeoffs. Available at SSRN 3576266. https://dx.doi.org/10.2139/ssrn.3576266.

11 Hardisty, D.J., Johnson, E.J., & Weber, E.U. (2010). A dirty word or a dirty world? Attribute framing, political affiliation, and query theory. *Psychological Science, 21*(1), 86–92. https://doi.org/10.1177/0956797609355572.

12 White, Habib, & Hardisty (2019).

13 White, K., & Simpson, B. (2013). When do (and don't) normative appeals influence sustainable consumer behaviors? *Journal of Marketing, 77*(2), 78–95. https://doi.org/10.1509/jm.11.0278.

14 White, K., Simpson, B., & Argo, J.J. (2014). The motivating role of dissociative outgroups in encouraging positive consumer behaviors. *Journal of Marketing Research, 51*(4), 433–47. https://doi.org/10.1509/jmr.12.0335.

15 Sparkman, G., & Walton, G.M. (2017). Dynamic norms promote sustainable behavior, even if it is counternormative. *Psychological Science, 28*(11), 1663–74. https://doi.org/10.1177/0956797617719950.

16 See, for example, Bamberg, S. (2006). Is a residential relocation a good opportunity to change people's travel behavior? Results from a theory-driven intervention study. *Environment and Behavior, 38*(6), 820–40. https://doi.org/10.1177/0013916505285091; Verplanken, B., Walker, I., Davis, A., & Jurasek, M. (2008). Context change and travel mode choice: Combining the habit discontinuity and self-activation hypotheses. *Journal of Environmental Psychology, 28*(2), 121–7. https://doi.org/10.1016/j.jenvp.2007.10.005; and Walker, I., Thomas, G.O., & Verplanken, B. (2015). Old habits die hard: Travel habit formation and decay during and after relocation. *Environment and Behavior, 47*(10), 1089–1106. https://doi.org/10.1177/0013916514549619.

17 See, for example, Fullerton, D., & Kinnaman, T.C. (1995). Garbage, recycling, and illicit burning or dumping. *Journal of Environmental Economics and Management, 29*(1), 78–91. https://doi.org/10.1006/jeem.1995.1032; and Krause, R.M. (2009). Developing conditions for environmentally sustainable consumption: Drawing insight from anti-smoking policy. *International Journal of Consumer Studies, 33*(3), 285–92. https://doi.org/10.1111/j.1470-6431.2009.00769.x.

18 Kurz, T., Gardner, B., Verplanken, B., & Abraham, C. (2015). Habitual behaviors or patterns of practice? Explaining and changing repetitive climate-relevant actions. *Wiley Interdisciplinary Reviews. Climate Change, 6*(1), 113–28. https://doi.org/10.1002/wcc.327.

19 See, for example, Brothers, K.J., Krantz, P.J., & McClannahan, L.E. (1994). Office paper recycling: A function of container proximity. *Journal of Applied Behavior Analysis, 27*(1), 153–60. https://doi.org/10.1901/jaba.1994.27-153; and Gamba, R.J., & Oskamp, S. (1994). Factors influencing community residents' participation in commingled curbside recycling programs. *Environment and Behavior, 26*(5), 587–612. https://doi.org/10.1177/0013916594265001.

20 Lehman, P.K., & Geller, E.S. (2004). Behavior analysis and environmental protection: Accomplishments and potential for more. *Behavior and Social Issues, 13*(1), 13–33. https://doi.org/10.5210/bsi.v13i1.33.

21 Wilhite, H., & Ling, R. (1995). Measured energy savings from a more informative energy bill. *Energy and Buildings, 22*(2), 145–55. https://doi.org/10.1016/0378-7788(94)00912-4.

22 See, for example, Chiang, T., Mevlevioglu, G., Natarajan, S., Padget, J., & Walker, I. (2014). Inducing [sub]conscious energy behaviour through visually displayed energy information: A case study in university accommodation. *Energy and Buildings, 70*, 507–15. https://doi.org/10.1016/j.enbuild.2013.10.035; Fischer, C. (2008). Feedback on household electricity consumption: A tool for saving energy? *Energy Efficiency, 1*(1), 79–104; and Karjalainen, S. (2011). Consumer preferences for feedback on household electricity consumption. *Energy and Buildings, 43*(2), 458–67.

23 Pichert, D., & Katsikopoulos, K.V. (2008). Green defaults: Information presentation and pro-environmental behaviour. *Journal of Environmental Psychology, 28*(1), 63–73. https://doi.org/10.1016/j.jenvp.2007.09.004.

24 Trudel, R., Argo, J.J., & Meng, M.D. (2016). The recycled self: Consumers' disposal decisions of identity-linked products. *Journal of Consumer Research*, 43(2), 246–64. https://doi.org/10.1093/jcr/ucw014.
25 Van der Werff, E., Steg, L., & Keizer, K. (2014). I am what I am, by looking past the present: The influence of biospheric values and past behavior on environmental self-identity. *Environment and Behavior*, 46(5), 626–57. https://doi.org/10.1177/0013916512475209.
26 Green, T., & Peloza, J. (2014). Finding the right shade of green: The effect of advertising appeal type on environmentally friendly consumption. *Journal of Advertising*, 43(2), 128–41. https://doi.org/10.1080/00913367.2013.834805.
27 White, K., MacDonnell, R., & Dahl, D.W. (2011). It's the mind-set that matters: The role of construal level and message framing in influencing consumer efficacy and conservation behaviors. *Journal of Marketing Research*, 48(3), 472–85. https://doi.org/10.1509/jmkr.48.3.472.
28 Trudel, Argo, & Meng (2016).
29 Spielmann, N. (2020). Green is the new white: How virtue motivates green product purchase. *Journal of Business Ethics*. https://doi.org/10.1007/s10551-020-04493-6.
30 Verplanken, B., & Holland, R.W. (2002). Motivated decision making: Effects of activation and self-centrality of values on choices and behavior. *Journal of Personality and Social Psychology*, 82(3), 434–47. https://doi.org/10.1037/0022-3514.82.3.434.
31 Peloza, J., White, K., & Shang, J. (2013). Good and guilt-free: The role of self-accountability in influencing preferences for products with ethical attributes. *Journal of Marketing*, 77(1), 104–19. https://doi.org/10.1509/jm.11.0454.
32 Hart, P.S., and Erik, C.N. (2012). Boomerang effects in science communication: How motivated reasoning and identity cues amplify opinion polarization about climate mitigation policies. *Communication Research*, 39(6), 701–23. https://doi.org/10.1177/0093650211416646.
33 Gromet, D.M., Kunreuther, H., and Larrick, R.P. (2013). Political ideology affects energy-efficiency attitudes and choices. *Proceedings of the National Academy of Sciences*, 110(23), 9314–19. https://doi.org/10.1073/pnas.1218453110.
34 Wolsko, C., Ariceaga, H., & Seiden, J. (2016). Red, white, and blue enough to be green: Effects of moral framing on climate change attitudes and conservation behaviors. *Journal of Experimental Social Psychology*, 65, 7–19. https://doi.org/10.1016/j.jesp.2016.02.005.
35 Cook, N.J., Grillos, T., & Andersson, K.P. (2019). Gender quotas increase the equality and effectiveness of climate policy interventions. *Nature Climate Change*, 9, 330–4. https://doi.org/10.1038/s41558-019-0438-4.
36 Shiv, B., and Fedorikhin, A. (1999). Heart and mind in conflict: The interplay of affect and cognition in consumer decision making. *Journal of Consumer Research*, 26(3), 278–92. https://doi.org/10.1086/209563.
37 Peloza, White, and Shang (2013).
38 Kollmuss, A., and Agyeman, J. (2002). Mind the gap: Why do people act environmentally and what are the barriers to pro-environmental behavior? *Environmental Education Research*, 8(3), 239–60. https://doi.org/10.1080/13504620220145401.
39 See, for example, Giebelhausen, M., Chun, H.H., Cronin Jr, J.J., and Hult, G.T.M. (2016). Adjusting the warm-glow thermostat: How incentivizing participation in voluntary green programs moderates their impact on service satisfaction. *Journal of Marketing*, 80(4), 56–71. https://doi.org/10.1509/jm.14.0497; Peter, P.C. and Honea, H. (2012). Targeting social messages with emotions of change: The call for optimism. *Journal of Public Policy & Marketing*, 31(2), 269–83. https://doi.org/10.1509/jppm.11.098; and

Kals, E., Schumacher, D. and Montada, L. (1999). Emotional affinity toward nature as a motivational basis to protect nature. *Environment and Behavior*, *31*(2), 178–202. https://doi.org/10.1177/00139169921972056.

40 McKenzie-Mohr, D. (2000). New ways to promote proenvironmental behavior: Promoting sustainable behavior: An introduction to community-based social marketing. *Journal of Social Issues*, *56*(3), 543–54. https://doi.org/10.1111/0022-4537.00183.

41 See, for example, Abrahamse, W., Steg, L., Vlek, C., and Rothengatter, T. (2005). A review of intervention studies aimed at household energy conservation. *Journal of Environmental Psychology*, *25*(3), 273–91. https://doi.org/10.1016/j.jenvp.2005.08.002; and Osbaldiston, R., and Schott, J.P. (2012). Environmental sustainability and behavioral science: Meta-analysis of proenvironmental behavior experiments. *Environment and Behavior*, *44*(2), 257–99. https://doi.org/10.1177%2F0013916511402673.

42 See, for example, Kahan, D.M., Peters, E., Wittlin, M., Slovic, P., Ouellette, L.L., Braman, D., & Mandel, G. (2012). The polarizing impact of science literacy and numeracy on perceived climate change risks. *Nature Climate Change*, *2*(10), 732–5. https://doi.org/10.1038/nclimate1547; McKenzie-Mohr, D. (2011). Fostering sustainable behavior: An introduction to community-based social marketing. *New Society Publishers*; Peattie, K., and Peattie, S. (2009). Social marketing: A pathway to consumption reduction? *Journal of Business Research*, *62*(2), 260–8. https://doi.org/10.1016/j.jbusres.2008.01.033; and Stern, P.C. (1999). Information, incentives, and proenvironmental consumer behavior. *Journal of Consumer Policy*, *22*(4), 461–78. https://doi.org/10.1023/A:1006211709570.

43 See, for example, Bull, J. (2012). Loads of green washing – can behavioural economics increase willingness-to-pay for efficient washing machines in the UK? *Energy Policy*, *50*, 242–52. https://doi.org/10.1016/j.enpol.2012.07.001; and Min, J., Azevedo, I.L., Michalek, J., & de Bruin, W.B. (2014). Labeling energy cost on light bulbs lowers implicit discount rates. *Ecological Economics*, *97*, 42–50. https://doi.org/10.1016/j.ecolecon.2013.10.015.

44 Parguel, B., Benoît-Moreau, F., & Larceneux, F. (2011). How sustainability ratings might deter "greenwashing": A closer look at ethical corporate communication. *Journal of Business Ethics*, *102*(1), 15. https://doi.org/10.1007/s10551-011-0901-2.

45 Manget, J., Roche, C., & Münnich, F. (2009). Capturing the green advantage for consumer companies. *The Boston Consulting Group*, 13. https://bcg.com/publications/capturing-the-green-advantage.

46 Camilleri, A.R., Larrick, R.P., Hossain, S., & Patino-Echeverri, D. (2019). Consumers underestimate the emissions associated with food but are aided by labels. *Nature Climate Change*, *9*, 53–8. https://doi.org/10.1038/s41558-018-0354-z.

47 See, for example, Leiserowitz, A. (2006). Climate change risk perception and policy preferences: The role of affect, imagery, and values. *Climatic Change*, *77*(1), 45–72. https://doi.org/10.1007/s10584-006-9059-9; and Scannell, L., & Gifford, R. (2013). Personally relevant climate change: The role of place attachment and local versus global message framing in engagement. *Environment and Behavior*, *45*(1), 60–85. https://doi.org/10.1177%2F0013916511421196.

48 Marx, S.M., Weber, E.U., Orlove, B.S., Leiserowitz, A., Krantz, D.H., Roncoli, C., & Phillips, J. (2007). Communication and mental processes: Experiential and analytic processing of uncertain climate information. *Global Environmental Change*, *17*(1), 47–58. https://doi.org/10.1016/j.gloenvcha.2006.10.004.

49 Zaval, L., Markowitz, E.M., & Weber, E.U. (2015). How will i be remembered? Conserving the environment for the sake of one's legacy. *Psychological Science*, *26*(2), 231–6. https://doi.org/10.1177%2F0956797614561266.

50 Csikszentmihalyi, M. (2000). The costs and benefits of consuming. *Journal of Consumer Research, 27*(2), 267–72. https://doi.org/10.1086/314324.
51 Van Boven, L. (2005). Experientialism, materialism, and the pursuit of happiness. *Review of General Psychology, 9*(2), 132. https://doi.org/10.1037%2F1089-2680.9.2.132.
52 See, for example, Atasoy, O., & Morewedge, C.K. (2018). Digital goods are valued less than physical goods. *Journal of Consumer Research*, in press, https://doi.org/10.1093/jcr/ucx102; and Belk, R.W. (2013). Extended self in a digital world. *Journal of Consumer Research, 40*(3), 477–500. https://doi.org/10.1086/671052.
53 Lovelock, C.H. (1983). Classifying services to gain strategic marketing insights. *Journal of Marketing, 47*(3), 9–20. https://doi.org/10.1177%2F002224298304700303.
54 Winterich, K.P., Nenkov, G.Y., & Gonzales, G.E. (2019). Knowing what it makes: How product transformation salience increases recycling. *Journal of Marketing, 83*, 21–37. https://doi.org/10.1177%2F0022242919842167.
55 Thaler, R.H., & Benartzi, S. (2004). Save More Tomorrow™: Using behavioral economics to increase employee saving. *Journal of Political Economy, 112*(S1), S164–S187. https://doi.org/10.1086/380085.
56 Consortium for Energy Efficiency, Inc. (2017). Behavior insights and tools: How social science has been – and could be – applied to connected programs. https://library.cee1.org/system/files/library/13330/2017_CEE_Connected_Behavior _Insights__Tools_-_public.pdf.
57 Edinger-Schons, L.M., Sipilä, J., Sen, S., Mende, G., & Wieseke, J. (2018). Are two reasons better than one? The role of appeal type in consumer responses to sustainable products. *Journal of Consumer Psychology, 28*(4), 644–64. https://doi.org/10.1002/jcpy.1032.
58 Spielmann (2020).
59 Noblet, C.L., & McCoy, S.K. (2018). Does one good turn deserve another? Evidence of domain-specific licensing in energy behavior. *Environment and Behavior, 50*(8), 839–63. https://doi.org/10.1177/0013916517718022.
60 Kristofferson, K., White, K., & Peloza, J. (2014). The nature of slacktivism: How the social observability of an initial act of token support affects subsequent prosocial action. *Journal of Consumer Research, 40*(6), 1149–66. https://doi.org/10.1086/674137.
61 Naito, R., Zhao, J., & Chan, K.M.A. (2021, February 16). An integrative framework for transformative social change: A case in global wildlife trade. https://doi.org/10.31235/osf.io/5zmxd.
62 Hagmann, D., Ho, E.H., & Loewenstein, G. (2019). Nudging out support for a carbon tax. *Nature Climate Change, 9*(6), 484–9. https://doi.org/10.1038/s41558 -019-0474-0.

START Communicating Effectively: Best Practices for Educational Communications

Jessica Lasky-Fink and Carly D. Robinson

Imagine for a moment that you are a parent or guardian[1] of two school-age children. Each child's school sends you report cards or progress reports four times per year; monthly, or even weekly, notices regarding upcoming field trips, activities, and school events; and requests for parent-teacher conferences a few times per year. Not to mention the emails, text messages, or robocalls you receive whenever your child is absent. And these are just the standard school communications. You receive dozens of other communications from their teachers, the school district, and the extracurricular activities they are involved in.

Each individual communication may convey important information to help you better support your children and their education. But how do you pay attention to, keep track of, and act upon so much information?

Behavioral scientists recognize this dilemma and, over the past decade, have tested many different approaches for improving school-to-family communications. Effective and efficient communications are crucial for supporting family engagement and student success at all levels. This chapter highlights five key evidence-based principles for improving school-to-family communications. While we focus specifically on school-to-family communications, these principles can also help guide school leaders and educators in improving communications more broadly.

Most educators would agree that parental support and engagement are critical for children's academic success. And all parents want their children to succeed. But, like all of us, parents are human – they are busy, and they do not always have time, energy, knowledge, information, or resources to support their children's education in the way they or educators want.

School-to-family communications are one of the main methods through which educators and districts attempt to engage families to support students' success. In fact, policies increasingly require schools and teachers to communicate regularly with parents and to provide information that allows parents to make well-informed choices about their children's education. The challenge is that a lot of these communications – just like many non-educational communications – seem to be designed without the recipients' day-to-day realities in mind.

First, parents have limited time and attention to devote to processing and acting upon the information they receive.[2] Thinking back to the example we started this chapter with: Even if each piece of information parents receive about their children is important and useful, it is simply impossible to pay close attention to everything, let alone remember it all – especially amidst work, family, and other life responsibilities.

Second, over 40% of US adults also have limited literacy, which means they read at an eighth-grade reading level, or below.[3] This can make it even more difficult and time consuming to understand complex communications.[4] Additionally, many parents, especially in urban districts, may be non-native English speakers, which also can affect their ability to process lengthy or complex written communications.

Third, while all parents want their children to succeed academically, they often don't know how.[5] Schools have the ability, via their communications, to influence parents' sense of efficacy, and to guide parents towards actions that will help their children succeed.[6]

Finally, parents tend to hold upwardly biased beliefs about their children's performance.[7] Everyone thinks their child is above average. Nearly 90% of parents believe that their child's achievement is at or above grade level, despite data showing that only one-third of children actually perform at that level.[8] Overconfidence in their children's achievement may drive lower parental engagement and involvement, especially in the absence of communications that aim to correct these misbeliefs.

Research suggests that making communications Simple, easy to Take up, Actionable, Reliable, and Timely can help parents overcome these barriers, and increase the likelihood that they pay attention to, understand, and act upon the critical information they receive. By applying the START principles, school leaders can increase family engagement and improve a range of student outcomes through more effective communications.

SIMPLE

Think about the last letter or email you received. How much time did you spend reading it?

If you're like most of us, the answer is probably less than about ten seconds. When people are busy, they do not have the time to thoroughly read and keep track of every individual letter, email, and text message, especially when these messages are overly long or complex. This is especially problematic for communications that are requesting – either explicitly or implicitly – that the reader take an action. If a reader cannot understand the purpose of a communication in the limited time they allot to reading it, they are, of course, less likely to take the requested action.

Take, for instance, truancy notifications. All 50 states require that students attend school.[9] When students miss too many days of school without a verified or valid excuse, a so-called "unexcused absence," states deem them "truant." Most states require that schools notify parents when their children accrue too many absences and hit this threshold. In some states, this requirement takes the form of a written, mailed letter.

In a 2015 study, researchers worked with a large urban public school district in a state that requires written notification to parents when their child becomes truant.[10] As shown in Figure 12.1, the standard truancy notification was over 350 words long, written at a

Figure 12.1. Standard and simplified state-mandated truancy notifications

(a) Standard truancy notice; and (b) improved notice, which was modified and simplified using behavioral insights. The improved notice reduced student absences compared to the standard notice by 0.07 days in the one month following each truancy notice mailing.

Source: Lasky-Fink, Robinson, Chang, & Rogers (2021).

a

Condition A (Control)
Standard Notice

School Name
Address
City, State Zip

Date

Parent Name
Parent Address
RE: Student Name
City, State Zip

Student ID#: XXXXX

Dear Parent/Guardian:

Good attendance is required for academic excellence. [STATE] Education Code determines what types of absences are excused or unexcused. When a child is absent from school and/or tardy in excess of 30 minutes on three (3) occasions in one school year without a valid excuse, the law considers that child to be truant. The law and district policy requires all schools to notify parents when this occurs. The [DISTRICT] central office automatically sends these letters based on school records so that parents are aware of absences and can address these concerns.

School records indicate that your child was absent from school without a valid excuse on occasions, beginning with the following dates:

Thursday, September 12, 2015
Thursday, September 19, 2015
Thursday, September 27, 2015

Figure 12.1. (Continued)

Our goal is to partner with families to ensure that students are attending school every day. Although the following consequences may appear harsh we are mandated by Education Code Article 48260.5 to inform you of the following:

- That the parent or guardian is obligated to compel the attendance of the pupil at school.
- That parents or guardians who fail to meet these obligation may be guilty of an infraction and subject to prosecution pursuant to Article 6 (commencing with Section 48290) of Chapter 2 or Part 27.
- That alternative education programs are available in the district.
- That the parent or guardian has the right to meet with appropriate school personnel to discuss solutions to the pupil's truancy.
- That the pupil may be subject to prosecution under Education Code Section 48264.
- That the pupil may be subject to suspension, restriction, or delay of the pupil's driving privilege pursuant to Section 13202.7 of the Vehicle Code.
- That it is recommended that the parent or guardian accompany the pupil to school and attend classes with the pupil for one day.

Please recognize that we are required to monitor attendance and notify parents of potential problems with student attendance. If you have concerns about your child's attendance, or if you believe there is an error in this notice, contact the school at [PHONE NUMBER]. The designated attendance personnel will work with you to resolve this issue. We look forward to assisting you.

Sincerely,
Principal Signature
Principal Name

Figure 12.1. (Continued)

b   **Condition D**
                             Add-up Notice

We need your help. [STUDENT NAME]'s absences from school are concerning, and your partnership is critical. Students who miss just one or two days of school each month can fall seriously behind.

[STUDENT NAME] is now "truant" because [SHE/HE] missed school (or was more than 30 minutes late) without a valid excuse on:

Thursday, September 12, 2015
Thursday, September 19, 2015
Thursday, September 27, 2015

Being absent can lead to doing poorly in school. Students who miss many days of school are more likely to:
- Fail their classes
- Drop out from high school
- Have poor relationships with parents and teachers

We are required by [STATE] law to send you this letter and to warn you of the consequences of additional unexcused absences (see sidebar).

Please remember that every absence matters and just a couple days each month adds up. **You are key** to improving [STUDENT NAME]'s attendance.

Sincerely,
Principal X

Truancy- [STATE] Education Code School administrators determine what types of absences are excused or unexcused based on state law and on the facts of the pupil's circumstances. When a child is absent from school and/or tardy in excess of 30 minutes on three (3) occasions in one school year without a valid excuse, the law considers that child to be truant.
Education Code Section 48260.5 requires us to inform you of the following:

Figure 12.1. (Continued)

- *That the parent or guardian is obligated to compel the attendance of the pupil at school.*
- *That parents or guardians who fail to meet these obligations may be guilty of an infraction and subject to prosecution pursuant to Article 6 (commencing with Section 48290) of Chapter 2 or Part 27.*
- *That alternative education programs are available in the district.*
- *That the parent or guardian has the right to meet with appropriate school personnel to discuss solutions to the pupil's truancy.*
- *That the pupil may be subject to prosecution under Education Code Section 48264.*
- *That the pupil may be subject to suspension, restriction, or delay of the pupil's driving privilege pursuant to Section 13202.7 of the Vehicle Code.*
- *That it is recommended that the parent or guardian accompany the pupil to school and attend classes with the pupil for one day.*

If you have concerns about your child's attendance or if you believe our records are inaccurate contact the school at [PHONE NUMBER].

10th-grade reading level, and full of legal language that highlighted the potential consequences of missing additional school, including possible prosecution for parents and suspension for students. Understandably, parents reported finding the language threatening.[11]

Working with the school district and the state Attorney General's office, the researchers created a simplified version of the truancy notification. The simplified version was less than 150 words, was written at a fifth-grade reading level, emphasized parental efficacy, and highlighted the potential consequences of missing just a few days of school each month. In the month following receiving a truancy notification, this simplified version was 40% more effective at reducing student absenteeism than the standard notice. The communication still included all the required legal information, but in fine print at the bottom of the letter. This design allowed parents – even those who merely skimmed the letter – to quickly and easily understand the message's purpose.

Simplifying educational communications can increase the likelihood that busy parents, as well as those with low literacy, are able to quickly and easily understand the message in order to decide if and how to take action.

EASY TO TAKE UP

Simplifying educational communications helps increase the likelihood that parents read and understand them – but only if they receive them in the first place. Parents face many competing demands on their time and resources, and a communication program that involves a lengthy or complex enrollment process almost guarantees that families will not receive the messages. The process of receiving communications must be made as easy as possible in order for them to be effective.

Seemingly small barriers, or "frictions," can prevent people from adopting useful and beneficial programs.[12] Over the past decade, schools around the country have started using learning platform technologies. These platforms have online portals through which parents can track their student's progress. Many can also send automated email or text message alerts to parents updating them on their children's academic performance.

When implementing these technologies, most school districts ask parents to actively sign up to receive text or email alerts.[13] This approach seems reasonable: Surely, parents should be able to decide whether they receive weekly messages from the school or not. However, this seemingly small friction – the act of signing up for text or email updates – presents an obstacle for many parents who might otherwise benefit from, and elect to receive, such communications. Conversely, simplifying the enrollment process can be a powerful way to increase adoption.[14]

A study run in 12 middle and high schools in Washington, DC, randomized the method by which parents were asked to enroll in a text message alert program that would send weekly updates about their children's progress.[15] As is often standard practice, one group of parents were told that they could log into the district's online parent portal and enroll in the weekly text message alert program. Fewer than 1% of these parents ultimately enrolled in the program.

Other parents were sent a text message and told they could enroll by simply replying "START." Eleven per cent of these parents enrolled in the program. Reducing the barriers to enrollment by allowing parents to sign up via a single text message, as opposed to having to log into the portal, increased enrollment tenfold.

Finally, the last group of parents were sent a text message and told that they had automatically enrolled in the program, but could opt out of this default at any point by responding to the text message with "STOP." In this group, 95% of parents remained enrolled.

Not only did simplifying the enrollment process increase take-up of the communication program, it also increased average achievement among children whose parents were automatically enrolled. The average grade point average (GPA) of children whose parents were automatically enrolled in the text message program increased by 0.06 points, and one in four students did not fail a class they otherwise would have failed.

The point here is not that the communication program was more effective for these students; the program was similarly effective for children whose parents enrolled by any method. Rather, when take-up of beneficial programs is low, the programs fail to reach enough students to yield improvements in average student achievement. As a result, when frictions prevent parents from adopting a communication program, it may seem as if the communication itself is ineffective when, in reality, it is the enrollment process that is ineffective.

Making a communication easy to understand and easy to receive is a necessary, but insufficient, first step towards improving its efficacy. In order for a communication to affect parent behavior – and thus, children's success – it is equally important that the message is actionable and easy to follow through on.

ACTIONABLE

Parents are critical partners in ensuring student success.[16] But parents looking for advice on how to support their children's education often receive vague communications like "Get involved with the school" or "Help with your child's homework." These types of messages are, at best, well-meaning, but nebulous and hard to quantify. At worst, they can feel overwhelming to parents – particularly those who do not have the resources or skills to act upon them – and actually become demotivating. So how can schools mobilize and support parents to act?

To make communications actionable, parents (1) need to know precisely what they are being asked to do; (2) need to believe they can do it, and that their efforts will have a positive impact; and (3) then must both decide to and be able to take action.

First, communications must be explicit about what parents are being asked to do. In one study run during a summer school program, some parents were randomly assigned to receive weekly one-sentence text messages from their children's teacher.[17] Half of these parents received messages that communicated positive feedback, while the other half received messages that highlighted an area where their children needed improvement. The needs-improvement messaging provided parents with more specific and actionable information than the positive feedback, and increased the percentage of students who earned course credit in the summer school program by nine points.

The more specific and discrete the guidance for parents, the better, especially when parents may not feel confident in their ability to help their children academically. For instance, parents can play a large role in improving young children's literacy.[18] But helping someone learn to read is not necessarily an intuitive task, and many parents do not know where to start. A text-message-based intervention aimed to break down the complex task of teaching children to read into discrete and manageable steps. The intervention then offered parents strategies for enacting each incremental step.[19] For eight months, parents received three texts per week that (1) highlighted the importance of a particular literacy skill, (2) offered directions on specific educational activities, and (3) provided positive encouragement. Parents who received these text messages, which provided specific and discrete strategies for helping their children learn to read, became more involved in supporting their children's reading acquisition, and, in turn, their children scored higher on literacy assessment scores at the end of the year. In particular, the intervention increased children's abilities to recognize letters and sounds, and these gains were largest for those who started off the year with the lowest literacy skills.

Second, when schools clearly communicate how they want parents to be involved in their children's education, it demonstrates that they are inviting parents to be partners in promoting student success.[20] Parents tend to be motivated to engage when they feel invited by the school to do so.[21] For instance, inviting parents to set their own goals – as opposed to imposing goals upon them – may increase the likelihood that they follow through on specific education-promoting behaviors. One study found that asking parents to set weekly goals for reading with their children using an electronic tablet, and subsequently sending automated reminders about these goals, doubled the amount of time parents spent reading with their children. Notably, these parents continued reading more to their children three months after they stopped receiving communications.[22]

Finally, the easier it is for a parent to take a requested action, the higher the likelihood they'll both decide to and be able to act. In one of the best-known examples of this, researchers tested the impact of helping college-bound adults and parents of college-bound children fill out the Free Application for Federal Student Aid (FAFSA) form. The FAFSA form includes over 100 questions that students (and their parents, for young adults) must answer in order to be eligible for need-based financial aid programs. The complexity of the process is often cited as a deterrent that prevents many low-income individuals from accessing higher education.[23] In a randomized experiment, low-income adults receiving help preparing their annual taxes were offered concurrent assistance to complete the FAFSA for themselves or their children.[24] Much of the information required for the FAFSA is also required for tax forms, which helped streamline the process for applicants. Assisting applicants with preparation and submission of their FAFSA forms increased both the percentage of people who applied for financial aid and the number who attended college and received aid.

Successful educational communications clearly highlight what parents can *do* (e.g., sound out that word, make sure your child does not miss more school than they have to), and, in doing so, increase parents' sense of efficacy for helping their children and the likelihood that they take action. Making this action easy to follow through on further increases the likelihood that parents will act.

RELIABLE

So far, we have made the case that parents are busy and often do not know how to support their children academically or believe that doing so will have an impact. As a result, educational communications should be simple and clear about what parents are being asked to do, and should reinforce parents' important role in their children's education. However, educational communications also need to be reliable – particularly if they are to rise above the tidal wave of emails, texts, calls, tweets, direct messages, and the many other communications parents receive on a near-constant basis.

Reliable communications are accurate and from a trusted source. In the context of school-to-family communications, this means that the information being shared is consistently up to date, relevant, and purposeful. If parents receive inaccurate, irrelevant, or unnecessary communications from their children's school, they may stop viewing the school as a reliable messenger of important information and, ultimately, begin to ignore school communications entirely.

Two large-scale randomized experiments found that sending parents mailers containing personalized and up-to-date information on their children's attendance reduced chronic absenteeism by 10–15%.[25] These mailings were sent an average of five times per year on behalf of the school – a trusted messenger – and conveyed accurate and personalized information that many parents did not otherwise have access to. A similar intervention that used text messages to provide preschool parents with objective feedback on their children's attendance decreased chronic absenteeism over an 18-week period.[26]

In all three of these examples, the reliability of these messages is particularly important, given that most parents tend to believe their children are above average. For instance, 80% of parents of students with below average attendance believe their children's attendance is average or above average.[27] Similarly, parents of students with high rates of absences underestimate the number of school days their children have missed by almost double. Thus, to successfully recalibrate parents' beliefs and motivate them to take action, parents must perceive both the sender and the information provided as reliable and credible.

TIMELY

Reliable communications can only encourage parental action if they are received at a point when parents can still intervene. Report cards, for instance, are reliable but are often received at the end of a semester – at which point, there is nothing parents can do to help their children increase their final semester grades. On the other hand, the three studies described above that sent parents consistent and regular messages about their children's absenteeism delivered these communications at critical junctures throughout the school year. When parents received these communications, they still had time to act to ensure that their children attended school as much as possible for the remainder of the school year.

Recent research shows that technology that automatically sends routine text message alerts to parents with timely and reliable information about their children's academic progress can meaningfully increase student success.[28] Specifically, sending weekly alerts informing parents about their children's recent missing assignments, low average course grades, and recent class absences decreased course failures, increased GPAs, and reduced absenteeism. One can imagine that if the same information were delivered only at the end of the semester, like report cards, it would have little to no impact, since parents would be unable to take any action at that point to help their children correct course.

Notably, the timing of messages must also be responsive to parents' realities.[29] If the goal of a message is for parents to encourage their children to complete a missing homework assignment, sending a text message about it during the workday may backfire, since it is likely that parents will forget about it by the time they see their children that night. Conversely, a text around dinner time may not be effective for parents who work the night shift. One study found it was more effective to text families of low-performing students (who may face more challenges) on the weekends, whereas texting families of high-performing students is more effective on weekdays.[30]

While it is obviously impossible to tailor the timing of communications to an individual parent's lifestyle, the key to sending timely educational communications is to consider (a) the timeline in which parents must act to be effective, and (b) the time at which a majority of parents will actually be able to take the requested or necessary action.

PUTTING THE START PRINCIPLES INTO PRACTICE

For school leaders and educators looking to put the START principles into practice, we offer specific and actionable advice for implementing each principle in Table 12.1. By considering the goal of each communication they send, schools can design the communication accordingly and maximize the likelihood that they achieve their desired purpose.

We understand that sometimes schools want to share more information than might be possible in the "short and sweet" messages we are proposing. In those cases, we recommend first taking inventory of the information: Which pieces of information are the most important for parents to know? Which pieces of information are nice to know, but not critical for what the communication is asking parents to do? So as not to overwhelm parents with a wall-of-text message, the most important pieces of information should be clearly and concisely outlined in the main body of the message – using the START principles. The nitty-gritty, "nice to know" details can then be included as an extra page or "more information" section for those who are interested and have the time to read on.

Taking a step back, schools should take stock of the entirety of their communication program, from district communications to teacher communications to automated parent portal messages. In particular, they should consider the parent experience. As communicators, we often write as if our message is the only one our readers have to contend with. It is easy to forget that parents actually receive a full program of communication from their children's school district. In

Table 12.1. A guide for using the START principles

Principle	Objective	Strategies for implementation
Simple	The purpose of the message is clear and easy to quickly understand, even for skimmers or readers with low literacy.	• Use www.readable.com to check for language complexity and reading level. • Aim for a fifth-grade reading level (or lower) whenever possible. • Cut unnecessary words. • Clearly state and draw attention to the purpose of the communication by placing it at the top of the message and/or using formatting to highlight it.
Easy to Take up	The communication is easy to receive, and the requested action is easy to follow through on.	• When possible, automatically (i.e., by default) enroll parents in communication programs and give them the chance to opt out if they wish. • When automatic enrollment is not desirable or possible, minimize the number of steps parents have to take in order to enroll in a communication program. • Minimize the number of steps parents have to take in order to follow through on a requested action. • Make foreign-language translations easily accessible for non-English speakers.
Actionable	Invite parents to act, set clear expectations, and reinforce efficacy to help them feel capable of taking the requested action.	• Be explicit about the action being requested. • Make guidance specific and discrete. • Break down tasks into simple, easy-to-achieve steps.
Reliable	Information is accurate and from a trusted and credible source.	• Share accurate and relevant information. • Make communications purposeful. • Send communications only to those for whom they are relevant. • Highlight the sender to establish trust.
Timely	Deliver communications at times when action is both feasible and beneficial.	• Identify critical times for parents to take a necessary or requested action, and deliver communications before these times. • Account for parents' busy lives, and deliver communications at times when parents will be most able to act. • Ask parents when they want to receive communications.

reexamining their program of communication from the perspective of a parent, schools might realize that some communications are duplicative or unnecessary, or that the timing should be adjusted so that communications are received in a logical order.

Although it may not always be obvious, there is a cost associated with each communication. Because parents have limited time and attention, shifting their focus to reading or acting upon a particular message means that effort is necessarily taken away from some other behavior. In one study, encouraging parents to talk with their children specifically about science did increase conversations about science – but it also decreased other parent-child interactions, including conversations about other school-related topics.[31] Strategically planning the timing and content for a full program of communication can help school leaders ensure that parents receive the most critical information at the most opportune times.

A final note: While improving the efficacy of school-to-family communications can have a real and meaningful impact on parental engagement and student success, it is also important to have realistic expectations about the size of the effect, as outlined in Chapter 2 of this book. Many of the most powerful educational interventions have relatively small average effects. Yet, small average effects accrue to have significant impact when interventions are implemented at scale for thousands (or hundreds of thousands) of students and parents. Improving school-to-family communications is certainly not a "silver bullet" solution for equalizing and accelerating educational outcomes, but it is a relatively low-cost and easy-to-implement strategy for affecting small change.

Behavioral insights will never be sufficient to overcome structural barriers in education, but as a tailored approach they are a powerful tool for helping overcome the common cognitive barriers that parents face in supporting their children's education. If combined with iterative, in-situ testing, using the START principles to improve the effectiveness of educational communications at scale can meaningfully mobilize lasting family engagement and, in turn, increase the likelihood that students succeed.

NOTES

1 Henceforth referred to as "parents," although we acknowledge the wide variety of caregivers in children's lives.
2 DellaVigna, S. (2009). Psychology and economics: Evidence from the field. *Journal of Economic Literature, 47*(2), 315–72.
3 National Center for Education Statistics (NCES). (2003). *National assessment of adult literacy (NAAL).* Retrieved from https://nces.ed.gov/naal/kf_demographics.asp.
4 Bohler, S.K., Eichenlaub, K.L., Litteken, S.D., & Wallis, D.A. (1996). Identifying and supporting low-literate parents. *Reading Teacher, 50*(1), 77–9.
5 Hoover-Dempsey, K.V., Bassler, O.C., & Brissie, J.S. (1992). Explorations in parent-school relations. *Journal of Educational Research, 85*(5), 287–94.
6 Hoover-Dempsey, K.V., Walker, J.M., Sandler, H.M., Whetsel, D., Green, C.L., Wilkins, A.S., & Closson, K. (2005). Why do parents become involved? Research findings and implications. *Elementary School Journal, 106*(2), 105–30.
7 Bergman, P., & Chan, E.W. (2021). Leveraging parents through low-cost technology: The impact of high-frequency information on student achievement. *Journal of Human Resources, 56*(1), 125–58; Bergman, P. (2021). Parent-child information frictions and human capital investment: Evidence from a field experiment. *Journal of Political Economy, 129*(1), 286–322.
8 Learning Heroes. (2018). Parents 2018: Going beyond good grades. Retrieved from https://bealearninghero.org/research/.
9 National Center for Education Statistics (NCES). (2017). State education reforms (SER). Retrieved from https://nces.ed.gov/programs/statereform/tab5_1.asp.
10 Lasky-Fink, J., Robinson, C.D., Chang, H., & Rogers, T. (2021). Using behavioral insights to improve school administrative communications: The case of truancy notifications. *Educational Researcher.* https://doi:10.3102/0013189X211000749.
11 Lambert, D. (2017, October 29). Should parents be able to take their kids out of school without getting a truancy letter? *Sacramento Bee.* Retrieved from https://www.sacbee.com/news/local/education/article181277431.html.
12 Sunstein, C. (2013). Impersonal default rules vs. active choices vs. personalized default rules: A triptych. Unpublished manuscript. https://dash.harvard.edu/handle/1/9876090.
13 Bergman, P., Lasky-Fink, J., & Rogers, T. (2020). Simplification and defaults affect adoption and impact of technology, but decision makers do not realize it. *Organizational Behavior and Human Decision Processes, 158,* 66–79.
14 Madrian, B.C., & Shea, D.F. (2001). The power of suggestion: Inertia in 401 (k) participation and savings behavior. *Quarterly Journal of Economics, 116*(4), 1149–87; Johnson, E.J., & Goldstein, D. (2003). Do defaults save lives? *Science, 302*(5649), 1338–9.
15 Bergman, Lasky-Fink, & Rogers (2020).
16 Mapp, K.L., Johnson, V.R., & Davies, D. (2007). *Beyond the bake sale: The essential guide to family-school partnerships.* New Press.
17 Kraft, M., & Rogers, T. (2015). The underutilized potential of teacher-to-parent communication: Evidence from a field experiment. *Economics of Education Review, 47,* 49–63.
18 Hart, B., & Risley, T.R. (1995). *Meaningful differences in the everyday experience of young American children.* Paul H Brookes Publishing.
19 York, B.N., Loeb, S., & Doss, C. (2019). One step at a time: The effects of an early literacy text-messaging program for parents of preschoolers. *Journal of Human Resources, 54*(3), 537–66.

20 Montemayor, A. (2019). Family engagement for school reform. IDRA EAC-South. https://www.idraeacsouth.org/wp-content/uploads/2019/08/Lit-Review-Family -Engagem ent-for-School-Reform-IDRA.pdf.
21 Hoover-Dempsey, Bassler, & Brissie (1992).
22 Mayer, S.E., Kalil, A., Oreopoulos, P., & Gallegos, S. (2018). Using behavioral insights to increase parental engagement: The parents and children together intervention. *Journal of Human Resources*, 0617–8835R.
23 Dynarski, S., & Scott-Clayton, J. (2006). The cost of complexity in federal student aid: Lessons form optimal tax theory and behavioral economics. *National Tax Journal, 59,* 319–56.
24 Bettinger, E.P., Long, B.T., Oreopoulos, P., & Sanbonmatsu, L. (2012). The role of application assistance and information in college decisions: Results from the H&R Block FAFSA experiment. *Quarterly Journal of Economics, 127*(3), 1205–42.
25 Rogers, T., & Feller, A. (2018). Reducing student absences at scale by targeting parents' misbeliefs. *Nature Human Behaviour, 2,* 335–432; Robinson, C., Lee, M., Dearing, E., & Rogers, T. (2018). Reducing student absenteeism in the early grades by targeting parental beliefs. *American Educational Research Journal, 26*(3), 353–83.
26 Kalil, A., Mayer, S.E., & Gallegos, S. (2019). Using behavioral insights to increase attendance at subsidized preschool programs: The show up to grow up intervention. *Organizational Behavior and Human Decision Processes.* In press.
27 See Rogers & Feller (2018); and Robinson et al. (2018).
28 See, for example, Bergman & Chan (2019); and Bergman (2021).
29 Austin, J., Sigurdsson, S.O., & Rubin, Y.S. (2006). An examination of the effects of delayed versus immediate prompts on safety belt use. *Environment and Behavior, 38*(1).
30 Cortes, K.E., Fricke, H., Loeb, S., Song, D.S., & York, B. (2019). When behavioral barriers are too high or low – How timing matters for parenting interventions. NBER Working Paper No. w25964. https://papers.ssrn.com/sol3/papers .cfm?abstract_id=3405151
31 Robinson, C.D., Chande, R., Burgess, S., & Rogers, T. (2020). Parent engagement interventions are not costless: Opportunity cost and crowd out of parental investment. (EdWorkingPaper 20–282). Retrieved from Annenberg Institute at Brown University.

CHAPTER THIRTEEN

A Psychological "Vaccine" against Fake News: From the Lab to Worldwide Implementation

Sander van der Linden and Jon Roozenbeek

The spread of false or misleading information – variously described as "fake news" – poses a significant threat to the well-being of individuals, democracies, and societies around the world.[1] We will use the term "misinformation" throughout this chapter to refer to any kind of (deliberately) false or misleading information circulating online. Nonetheless, the fact that scholars, practitioners, and journalists can barely agree on a conceptual taxonomy of fake news highlights the complexity of the problem.[2] Of course, it's not difficult to think of examples of unambiguously false information having adverse consequences, for instance when people set fire to mobile phone masts based on a mistaken belief that 5G radiation exacerbates the symptoms of COVID-19.[3] Yet, in many cases, the distinction between true and false (or harmful and not harmful) isn't always clear, and any effort to curb the spread of misinformation through algorithms, legislation, or censorship comes with backfire potential[4] and inevitably evokes difficult discussions about freedom of speech.[5] Accordingly, much enthusiasm has been expressed for the role of the behavioral sciences in reducing the spread of misinformation by empowering people to better discern fact from fiction.

In this chapter, we explain how behavioral science has been leveraged to tackle the issue of misinformation in recent years, with a particular focus on developing a psychological "vaccine" against misinformation. We will walk the reader through how our own program of research grew from a theoretical idea into a large multinational collaboration with social media companies, governments, and international organizations to evaluate its efficacy at-scale "in the wild."

THE MISINFORMATION PROBLEM

Belief in misinformation is widespread. Estimates vary, but anywhere between 22% and 85% of people profess belief in at least one conspiracy theory about COVID-19.[6] Importantly, belief in such misinformation is associated with key behavioral outcomes such as lower self-reported willingness to get vaccinated, potentially compromising future herd immunity.[7] More generally, a majority of Americans and Europeans feel that fake news is a threat to democracy and causes confusion over basic facts.[8] The harmful consequences of misinformation can be seen in the proliferation of anti-vax groups on Facebook,[9] misinformation about climate change,[10] acts of vandalism committed based on false conspiracy theories about COVID-19,[11] and the way in which misinformation can exacerbate ethnic tensions and incite offline violence.[12] Accordingly, research in the behavioral sciences has increasingly focused on ways to try to counter misinformation.

LESSONS FROM BEHAVIORAL SCIENCE: COUNTERING MISINFORMATION

Perhaps the most obvious way to try to combat misinformation is through the use of fact checking and debunking; that is, attempting to correct misinformation after the fact. Unfortunately, doing so comes with several well-known problems. First, meta-analyses have shown that fact checking is not always effective,[13] particularly because correcting misinformation doesn't completely undo the damage:[14] people continue to rely on false information even after a correction has been provided, a phenomenon known as the "continued influence effect."[15] Second, the spread of false information can outpace credible information on social media, making it difficult for fact checks to reach the same number of people as the original misinformation.[16] Third, the so-called "illusory truth effect" shows that repeated exposure to misinformation can increase people's belief in it, possibly rendering fact checks less effective if people are exposed to the same (mis)information repeatedly from multiple sources.[17] In other words, while fact checking is a worthwhile endeavor, it is insufficient as a solution to eradicate the problem of online misinformation.

This raises an obvious question: if correcting misinformation after the fact is less than ideal, maybe scientists can leverage behavioral insights to prevent people from falling for it in the first place? When it comes to reducing susceptibility to misinformation, scientists have branched out into three main directions: providing people with short reminders (sometimes called "nudges" or "primes") to subtly induce them to share less misinformation;[18] providing media literacy training;[19] and pre-emptively debunking (or *prebunking*) misinformation by means of psychological "vaccines." Our program of research has focused predominantly on the last branch, so we will review its background briefly below.

INOCULATION THEORY

The idea of developing a psychological "vaccine" is based on a framework from the 1960s called inoculation theory.[20] At the time, the US government became fascinated with the question of how soldiers might be brainwashed when captured by enemy troops, and social psychologist William McGuire started to wonder how resistance to propaganda and persuasion might come about. In search of a "vaccine for brainwash," McGuire posited that pre-emptive exposure to a weakened dose of a persuasive argument could confer psychological resistance against future exposure to persuasive attacks, as a medical vaccine confers physiological resistance against infection.[21] Such a psychological inoculation generally consists of two components: (1) a forewarning of an impending attack on one's beliefs, and (2) a pre-emptive refutation (or "prebunk") of the persuasive argument.[22]

What's interesting about McGuire's inoculation theory is that, although the original paradigm has proved highly replicable,[23] it was never actually tested in the context that inspired its conception: propaganda. Moreover, rather than losing its relevance over the years, with the viral spread of misinformation amidst a worldwide "infodemic,"[24] the psychological vaccination analogy seems more apt today than ever before. Crucially, however, many interesting questions about inoculation theory have remained unanswered.[25] We have sought to address these open questions in our research program in several progressive stages, which we will describe below with the assistance of a framework we developed for practitioners and policymakers interested in applying behavioral insights.

Specifically, in collaboration with NASA scientists, we have called for scholars to evaluate the "readiness" of their research findings for "launch" into the wild. Yet, as opposed to NASA's readiness levels (which are uniquely suited to rocket science), we have translated these levels into the five phases of the "THEARI" quality of evidence rating system.[26] The system starts with a Theoretical idea and then gradually moves to Empirical testing in the field (including preliminary evidence, i.e., pilots), to generating Applicable insights (pre-registered randomized trials) and Replication (successful replications across different contexts) to the final stage of Impact (application at scale through real-world testing).

The interventions and insights we developed over the years have impacted millions of people, have won several awards, are part of education programs the world over, are promoted by global organizations such as the World Health Organization (WHO) and the United Nations (UN) as well as various governments, and have been used by social media companies such as Google and WhatsApp as part of their anti-misinformation efforts. This process of transforming a basic idea into a series of practical interventions took years to complete. We hope that describing this process (including the challenges we faced) is of help to practitioners seeking guidance on how to translate and scale research ideas to a practical context. To do so, we will walk the reader through the five THEARI phases of our research program: Theory and the lab, the pilots (and the "do no harm" principle of Empirical testing), randomized controlled testing to produce Applicable insights, cross-cultural validation through Replication across contexts, and finally the implementation of our findings "in the wild" to create Impact.

PHASE 1: TESTING INOCULATION THEORY IN THE LABORATORY

For his initial "proof-of-concept" experiments, McGuire believed that inoculation theory was most suitable for so-called "germ-free beliefs" or "cultural truisms" such as the idea that brushing your teeth is beneficial.[27] This reasoning was based on the observation that the inoculation treatments needed to be purely prophylactic (pre-emptive), in the sense that people had no prior exposure to the persuasive argument that they would be inoculated against. In other words, most people have never faced persuasive counterarguments to the idea that brushing your teeth is beneficial (a truly pre-emptive test case). A crucial challenge with this assumption is that you can only test it under highly stylized laboratory conditions by pre-screening people into the experiment based on their prior attitudes towards an issue. The "no prior exposure" clause is also an unrealistic assumption in the context of real-world misinformation, as people commonly have prior beliefs (e.g., about politics) that misinformation taps into, and there's often no way of knowing if and how often people have already been exposed to a myth.[28] Researchers therefore began to explore the feasibility of *therapeutic* inoculations, or the idea that inoculation could be effective even for the "already afflicted," consistent with the medical use of therapeutic vaccines.[29]

Our first step was therefore to establish whether inoculation theory could be applied in the context of influential misinformation where people clearly have differing prior attitudes. We considered climate change to be a useful test case because of how polarizing the topic is, especially in the United States.[30] To make sure that the inoculation treatment had ecological validity, we first conducted a national poll to identify what misinformation about climate change people found persuasive. What surfaced was a false petition claiming that thousands of scientists had declared global warming a hoax. Incidentally, this petition also formed the basis of an actual viral misinformation campaign on Facebook in 2016.[31] We then screened over 2,000 Americans according to their prior attitudes towards climate change. These participants were subsequently randomized into one of six conditions: a baseline control condition containing no information, a misinformation condition (a screenshot of the bogus petition), a facts condition emphasizing the scientific consensus on climate change, a false-balance condition (containing both the facts and the misinformation side by side), and two inoculation conditions (a forewarning-only inoculation condition, where participants were forewarned that politically motivated actors seek to mislead people on climate change, and a full inoculation condition, where the forewarning was accompanied by an additional preemptive refutation). This preemptive refutation mentioned that participants may see a petition casting doubt on climate change but that they should know that the signatories are bogus and include people like the Spice Girls and Charles Darwin. Afterwards, all groups were exposed to the full dose of misinformation: the petition website.

What we found was alarming: misinformation had a significant negative impact on public opinion, and in the false-balance condition, exposure to misinformation completely neutralized the influence of facts. Importantly, however, the inoculation conditions proved effective and significantly immunized people against the misinformation *regardless* of their prior attitudes.[32] The treatment effect was impressive by common standards,[33] but it is important to note that such large effects are obtained under controlled laboratory conditions and, as such, may not generalize to the real world. Nonetheless, the randomized trial provided evidence that inoculation (a) can be applied in the context of influential misinformation and (b) may still work irrespective of people's prior attitudes. Subsequent

pre-registered direct and conceptual replications have largely validated these initial findings.[34]

PHASE 2: PRELIMINARY EMPIRICAL TESTING (FROM LAB TO THE FIELD)

Following these promising results, practitioners reached out to us,
wondering how to implement and scale this intervention. Until this
point, inoculation research had often been exclusively issue-based,
in the sense that study participants were inoculated against specific
unwanted persuasive arguments[35] or a set of related arguments.[36]
However, following conversations with practitioners, it dawned
on us that such an issue-based approach isn't very scalable, as it's
impossible to inoculate people against every individual piece of
misinformation circulating online.[37] Together with our colleagues,
we hypothesized that we might be able to inoculate people against
the *techniques* that underpin the production of misinformation more
generally, as this would, in theory, cultivate resistance across a wide
range of issues.[38] For example, if you're aware that people sometimes quote fake experts to lend credibility to a particular argument,
you're less likely to be duped by Dr. Hyde T. Paine's recommendation to eat pickled onions to help prevent COVID-19 infection.

We also started to explore how we might move the intervention
"out of the lab." Interestingly, McGuire himself hypothesized early
on that so-called "active" inoculation, where people generate their
own defenses against persuasive attacks, might engender greater
resistance than "passive" treatments[39] in which the preemptive refutation is already provided (as in our climate experiment). Around
the same time that we began to explore what an active inoculation
intervention might look like, some acquaintances of ours received
seed funding from a Dutch public journalism fund to set up DROG, a
creative anti-misinformation platform. DROG's idea was to develop
a card game in which players roleplay as a type of fake news pro-
ducer (such as a conspiracy theorist or a clickbait monger) and put
together a news article about a contentious topic in line with their
character's goals and motivations.

This gave us an idea: maybe games are a suitable avenue for active, technique-based inoculation. The fake news card game we designed prompted players – in weakened form – to think about *how* a conspiracy theorist, say, might go about manipulating their audience. Moreover, games are more interactive and cognitively demanding than a reading exercise, and so could serve as the "active" component of the inoculation treatment. In collaboration with the Dutch media literacy foundation Stichting Mediawijsheid Scholen (bonus points for pronouncing that correctly), DROG wanted to run a workshop with the fake news card game in a high school in the Netherlands. This school visit provided us with a great opportunity to pilot-test the idea of using active inoculation as a way to improve people's ability to spot misinformation in a relatively controlled but more realistic "field" setting. We designed a short test in which students aged 16 to 19 were asked to rate the reliability of a (fictitious) news article about immigration that made use of various misinformation techniques. We hypothesized that game players would find this article significantly less reliable than non-players. Our collaborators agreed to split the students into two groups: a treatment group and a control group that watched an unrelated video. The results of this first pilot were encouraging: not only did we find support for our hypothesis (students who played the game found the misinformation article significantly less reliable), but participants also indicated that they found the game entertaining, particularly the part where they took on the perspective of fake news creators.[40] Although this was promising, several issues also became evident. While our school contact, Dr. Wim Hilberdink, was knowledgeable about experimental design, not all of the students showed up to the workshop, so we ended up with 95 students (with 57 assigned to the treatment and 38 to the control group). Moreover, the study took a long time to plan and organize. Going into one school at a time proved to be a painstaking research exercise. We therefore decided to take our efforts online, because it would greatly enhance our ability to scale the intervention. In collaboration with DROG, we developed an online version of the card game, which became known as *Bad News* (www.getbadnews.com; Figure 13.1).

Figure 13.1. *Bad News* landing page (*left*) and gameplay

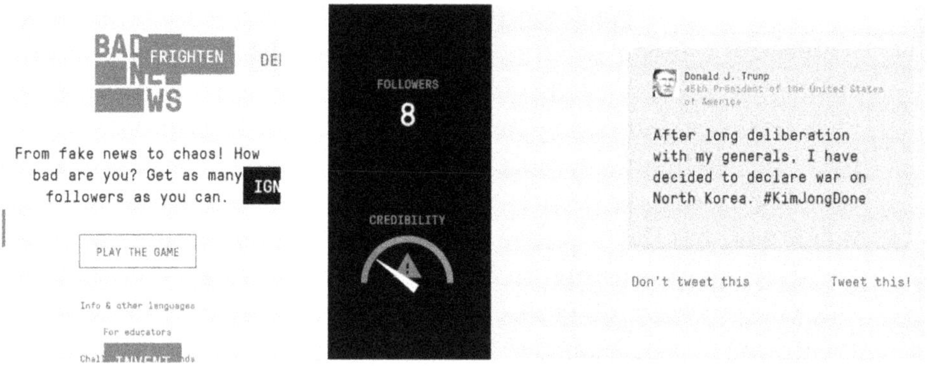

Source: www.getbadnews.com

Although we retained the basic idea of letting players take on the role of fake news creators, we shifted our focus towards several common misinformation techniques ("the six degrees of manipulation"), such as impersonating people online (e.g., experts), using excessively emotional language (e.g., fearmongering), floating conspiracy theories, discrediting people (e.g., ad hominem attacks), fueling polarization, and trolling people.[41] Prior research had shown that making people aware of their own vulnerability and unveiling the manipulative intentions of others is a powerful way to help people resist persuasion.[42] In keeping with the original inoculation analogy, over the course of six levels, *Bad News* players are forewarned of the dangers of misinformation and exposed to weakened doses of each of these techniques in a simulated social media environment. Throughout the 15 or so minutes of gameplay, players learn how these techniques work by gradually going from being an anonymous social media user to running their own fake news empire. The goal of the game is to build a follower base whilst maintaining your credibility. We wanted the game to be as entertaining as possible, so we included plenty of jokes and cultural references, to make sure that people were exposed to sufficiently weakened doses of misinformation: strong enough to trigger resistance but not so convincing as to actually dupe them. We also wanted people to actually enjoy the game rather than see it as only an educational exercise.

Because we only had our pilot results to go on, launching the browser game as a free intervention was a bit of a gamble: what if *Bad News* inspired the formation of a roving gang of fake news producers? From research, we know that people tend to spread misinformation mainly for political or monetary reasons.[43] So after careful deliberation, we made sure to keep the game as politically neutral as possible and we refrained from illustrating how to make money by spreading fake news. We decided that the potential harm of the *Bad News* game was therefore minimal. We also relied on research into the link between video games and behavior, which generally shows that playing video games causes little (if any) harm.[44] The ethics committee agreed: the benefits of gathering data about how to help people spot fake news outweighed potential harms. The key element in all of this, however, was our second pilot experiment: we implemented a pre-post survey within the *Bad News* game environment to measure people's ability to spot misinformation before and after gameplay. What we did not anticipate was the response that *Bad News* evoked: two days after launch in early 2018, the press release went viral and more than 80,000 people had played it. Thanks to the in-game survey, we were able to collect a dataset of about 15,000 individuals and found that the game significantly reduced perceived reliability of misinformation after gameplay, but that there was no meaningful effect for "real news," or social media content that doesn't contain any manipulation techniques. In other words, playing the game improved people's ability to spot misinformation, but it did not affect how people viewed news from credible sources.[45]

PHASE 3: APPLICABLE INSIGHTS THROUGH RANDOMIZED AND PRE-REGISTERED TESTING

Although our two pilot studies showed that our "broad-spectrum" inoculation interventions caused no discernible harm and were even potentially beneficial, we had not yet tested them in a randomized controlled setting. Doing so was key to establishing how *Bad News* performed against a control intervention (in our case *Tetris*), and also allowed us to answer other important questions about the game's efficacy. Our first randomized controlled study further confirmed our pilot results using a much larger battery of test items, showing that *Bad News* players found misinformation in social media content significantly less reliable than the control group post-gameplay. We also found that players became significantly more confident in their own ability to spot misinformation.[46] In a second (pre-registered) study, we examined the longevity of the inoculation effect conferred by the game, and found that players remained significantly better than a control group at detecting misinformation for up to three months if given regular reminders (or "booster shots").[47] The in-game data collection system also proved extremely useful. The *Bad News* player base remained stable for a long period of time, and the survey kept collecting data, allowing us to answer several other rather technical questions about item and testing effects.[48] The randomized testing phase thus strengthened our conviction that our initial intuition about the potential efficacy of active inoculation interventions was correct. We were onto something and now getting ready to talk to governments and social media companies.

PHASE 4: CROSS-CULTURAL REPLICATION

After the launch of *Bad News*, we were asked to collaborate with the Foreign, Commonwealth and Development Office of the United Kingdom on the translation of the game into a large variety of foreign languages. We also began a collaboration with Professor Thomas Nygren at the University of Uppsala to translate the game into Swedish. These collaborations allowed us to investigate whether the results we found for the English-language game would replicate in other linguistic and cultural settings. To do so, we implemented in-game surveys – similar to the English version – in all translations. Although not every version of the game was equally successful in terms of attracting players, after a few months we had enough data to assess the game's efficacy in four languages: Swedish, German, Greek, and Polish. Although there was some slight cultural variation, the results were robust and highly similar to the English version of the game.[49]

PHASE 5: WIDER IMPLEMENTATION AND IMPACT

Thus far, we had focused our efforts primarily on answering various open questions about active inoculation and resistance to misinformation, for which *Bad News* was an excellent vehicle. However, *Bad News* is limited to six misinformation techniques, and a 15-minute game couldn't feasibly inoculate people against all misinformation that exists in the world. Having established the empirical rigor of our gamified approach, we felt comfortable expanding into other issue domains where misinformation is a problem, always accompanied by further testing. First, we started working with WhatsApp to create an adapted version of *Bad News* about the types of misinformation used in direct messaging apps, which in the past has led to serious problems such as lynchings and even deaths.[50] Second, ahead of the 2020 US presidential elections, we worked with the Cybersecurity and Infrastructure Security Agency (CISA) at the Department of Homeland Security and the US Global Engagement Center (GEC) to create *Harmony Square* (www.harmonysquare. game), a game about political misinformation during elections. Our randomized controlled trial with this game replicated previous findings and showed that people who played *Harmony Square* were less willing to share misinformation with other people in their social network than a control group.[51] The game is currently being translated into Spanish, French, Dutch, and German. Third, to help combat the growing problem of misinformation about COVID-19, we, in collaboration with DROG and the UK Cabinet Office with support from the WHO and the UN, created *Go Viral!* (www.goviralgame.com), in which players learn how to resist COVID-related misinformation by slowly becoming the leader of a conspiratorial social media group. We ran a large experimental study with the game in English, French, and German, which showed highly robust inoculation effects.[52] Lastly, we realized that the same basic principles can be applied to other important issues, such as extremism.

Figure 13.2. *Harmony Square, Go Viral!,* and *Radicalise* landing pages

We worked with the Nudge Unit in Lebanon to create *Radicalise,* a game about the persuasion strategies used by extremists to recruit members into their organizations, which was effective in improving people's ability to spot these strategies and the characteristics that make individuals vulnerable to extremist recruitment.[53] We recently presented these results at the UN. Screenshots from the *Harmony Square, Go Viral!,* and *Radicalise* games are shown in Figure 13.2.

Although games are entertaining and can be scaled to millions of people, they are difficult to implement directly on social media platforms. After all, not everyone wants to interrupt scrolling through their feed to play a game. In collaboration with Google Jigsaw, we therefore developed a series of short animated inoculation videos that expose common misinformation techniques. Our study into the effectiveness of these videos found that they significantly improve people's ability to spot these techniques in social media content.[54]

Of course, our journey isn't over. Now that the interventions are being scaled across millions of people worldwide, we are going back to the lab to think about herd immunity. Ultimately, the main goal of the vaccination analogy is that if enough people are vaccinated in an online community, misinformation no longer has a chance to spread.[55] But our research has found that psychological inoculation is different from the process of biological inoculation: people never really receive full immunity, and the vaccine wears off over time without booster shots. In other words, we do not know how many people need to be vaccinated – and at what level – for

herd immunity to be realistic. We are currently building computa-
tional models to try to provide preliminary answers to these exciting questions. Other important questions also remain. For example,
participation in the games largely relies on voluntary self-selection.
Will those who need the "vaccine" the most volunteer to participate
in our interventions? And are the interventions effective amongst
those who are more susceptible to misinformation in the first place?
We have provided some preliminary answers to these questions.
For example, in our 2019 field pilot we found that those individuals
with the lowest pre-test performance on the misinformation items
actually improved the most post-gameplay.[56] To get around the self-
selection problem, which could lead to a voltage drop (see Chapter 3),
we are teaming up with social media companies and international
organizations. For example, the videos we have developed with
Google could be deployed as non-skippable YouTube ads to prebunk harmful content across the whole platform. Information volunteers from the United Nation's *Verified* team are able to identify
and distribute our *GoViral!* game to audiences who might particularly benefit from it. Individuals who spread misinformation can
also be targeted with ads on social media linking to the interventions. Future research should find ways to further evaluate the efficacy of inoculation interventions with audiences at risk of receiving
or spreading misinformation.

CONCLUSION

Our research program started out with an idea, and eventually grew
into a multinational collaborative effort to tackle misinformation in
several key issue domains. A few factors that we see as key elements
in the success of our approach are worth discussing here. First of all,
it is important to start out carefully, and establish that an intervention at the very least does no measurable harm, and preferably some
measurable good. To do so, we made sure to do rigorous empirical in-situ pilot testing and collect feedback from key stakeholders.
Second, we have always emphasized the entertainment value of our
games and other interventions. If people are interested in engaging

with an intervention by themselves because it's fun, the intervention is much more likely to be successful and adopted widely. There are numerous ways to achieve this goal; for us, using humor was one of them. Third, we have fostered strong collaborations with strategic partners, including design companies, governments, international organizations, and social media giants, whose creativity and flexibility we cannot emphasize enough as a key factor in the success of these interventions. Our final recommendation is that behavioral interventions, however effective, are only one tool in a larger toolbox. But a highly adaptable tool is likely to become a toolbox mainstay. One of the benefits of our approach is that our interventions are "living," so we can continuously adapt and tailor them with our partners to new challenges and contexts as they arise. In the words of the infamous Professor Severus Snape, "our defenses must be as flexible and inventive as the arts we seek to undo."

NOTES

1 Lewandowsky, S., Ecker, U.K.H., & Cook, J. (2017). Beyond misinformation: Understanding and coping with the "post-truth" era. *Journal of Applied Research in Memory and Cognition, 6*(4), 353–69. https://doi.org/10.1016/j.jarmac.2017.07.008; and Lewandowsky, S., & van der Linden, S. (2021). Countering misinformation and fake news through inoculation and prebunking. *European Review of Social Psychology, 32*(2), 348–84. https://doi.org/10.1080/10463283.2021.1876983.

2 See, for example, Molina, M.D., Sundar, S.S., Le, T., & Lee, D. (2021). "Fake news" is not simply false information: A concept explication and taxonomy of online content. *American Behavioral Scientist, 65*(2), 180–212. https://doi.org/10.1177/0002764219878224; Lazer, D.M.J. (2018, March 9). The science of fake news. *Science, 359*(6380). https://science.sciencemag.org/content/359/6380/1094; Vraga, E.K., & Bode, L. (2020). Defining misinformation and understanding its bounded nature: Using expertise and evidence for describing misinformation. *Political Communication, 37*(1), 136–44. https://doi.org/10.1080/10584609.2020.1716500; and van der Linden, S., & Roozenbeek, J. (2020). Psychological inoculation against fake news. In R. Greifeneder, M. Jaffe, E. Newman, & N. Schwarz (Eds.), *The psychology of fake news: Accepting, sharing, and correcting misinformation.* Routledge.

3 Jolley, D., & Paterson, J.L. (2020). Pylons ablaze: Examining the role of 5G COVID-19 conspiracy beliefs and support for violence. *British Journal of Social Psychology, 59*(3), 628–40. https://doi.org/10.1111/bjso.12394.

4 van der Linden & Roozenbeek (2020).

5 Rainie, L., & Anderson, J. (2017). *The future of free speech, trolls, anonymity, and fake news online*, 82. Pew Research Center. https://assets.pewresearch.org/wp-content/uploads/sites/14/2017/03/28162208/PI_2017.03.29_Social-Climate_FINAL.pdf.

6 See Roozenbeek, J., Schneider, C.R., Dryhurst, S., Kerr, J., Freeman, A.L.J., Recchia, G., van der Bles, A.M., & van der Linden, S. (2020). Susceptibility to misinformation about COVID-19 around the world. *Royal Society Open Science, 7*(10), 201199.

https://doi.org/10.1098/rsos.201199; Miller, J.M. (2020). Do COVID-19 conspiracy theory beliefs form a monological belief system? *Canadian Journal of Political Science*, 53(2), 319–26. https://doi.org/10.1017/s0008423920000517; and Enders, A.M., Uscinski, J.E., Klofstad, C., & Stoler, J. (2020). The different forms of COVID-19 misinformation and their consequences. *Harvard Kennedy School Misinformation Review.* https://doi.org/10.37016/mr-2020-48.

7 See Roozenbeek et al. (2020); and Loomba, S., de Figueiredo, A., Piatek, S.J., de Graaf, K., & Larson, H.J. (2021). Measuring the impact of COVID-19 vaccine misinformation on vaccination intent in the UK and USA. *Nature Human Behaviour*, 5(3), 337–48. https://doi.org/10.1038/s41562-021-01056-1.

8 Barthel, M., Mitchell, A., & Holcomb, J. (2016, December 15). Many Americans believe fake news is sowing confusion. *Pew Research Center's Journalism Project.* https://www.journalism.org/2016/12/15/many-americans-believe-fake-news-is -sowing-confusion/; and Eurobarometer. Final results of the Eurobarometer on fake news and online disinformation. *ec.europa.eu* (2018). Available at: https://ec.europa .eu/digital-single-market/en/news/final-results-eurobarometer-fake-news-and -online-disinformation (accessed February 26, 2021).

9 See Johnson, N.F., Velásquez, N., Restrepo, N.J., Leahy, R., Gabriel, N., El Oud, S., Zheng, M., Manrique, P., Wuchty, S., & Lupu, Y. (2020). The online competition between pro- and anti-vaccination views. *Nature*, 582(7811), 230–3. https://doi .org/10.1038/s41586-020-2281-1; and Hoffman, B.L., Felter, E.M., Chu, K.-H., Shensa, A., Hermann, C., Wolynn, T., Williams, D., & Primack, B.A. (2019). It's not all about autism: The emerging landscape of anti-vaccination sentiment on Facebook. *Vaccine*, 37(16), 2216–23. https://doi.org/10.1016/j.vaccine.2019.03.003.

10 van der Linden, S., Leiserowitz, A., Rosenthal, S., & Maibach, E. (2017). Inoculating the public against misinformation about climate change. *Global Challenges*, 1(2), 1600008. https://doi.org/10.1002/gch2.201600008.

11 Jolley & Paterson (2020); and BBC News (2020). Ofcom: Covid-19 5G theories are "most common" misinformation. www.bbc.co.uk.

12 See Vasudeva, F., & Barkdull, N. (2020). WhatsApp in India? A case study of social media related lynchings. *Social Identities*, 26(5), 574–89. https://doi.org/10.1080 /13504630.2020.1782730; and Warofka, A. (2018, November 6). An independent assessment of the human rights impact of Facebook in Myanmar. *About Facebook.* https://about.fb.com/news/2018/11/myanmar-hria/.

13 Walter, N., Cohen, J., Holbert, R.L., & Morag, Y. (2020). Fact-checking: A meta-analysis of what works and for whom. *Political Communication*, 37(3), 350–75. https://doi.org/10.1080/10584609.2019.1668894.

14 Chan, M.S., Jones, C.R., Hall Jamieson, K., & Albarracín, D. (2017). Debunking: A meta-analysis of the psychological efficacy of messages countering misinformation. *Psychological Science*, 28(11), 1531–46. https://doi.org/10.1177/0956797617714579.

15 Ecker, U.K.H., Lewandowsky, S., & Chadwick, M. (2020). Can corrections spread misinformation to new audiences? Testing for the elusive familiarity backfire effect. *Cognitive Research: Principles and Implications*, 5(1), 41. https://doi.org/10.1186 /s41235-020-00241-6; and Lewandowsky, S., Ecker, U.K.H., Seifert, C.M., Schwarz, N., & Cook, J. (2012). Misinformation and its correction: Continued influence and successful debiasing. *Psychological Science in the Public Interest*, 13(3), 106–31. https:// doi.org/10.1177/1529100612451018.

16 Vosoughi, S., Roy, D., & Aral, S. (2018). The spread of true and false news online. *Science*, 359(6380), 1146–51. https://doi.org/10.1126/science.aap9559.

17 See Fazio, L. (2020). Pausing to consider why a headline is true or false can help reduce the sharing of false news. *Harvard Kennedy School Misinformation Review.* https://doi

.org/10.37016/mr-2020-009; and Fazio, L.K., Brashier, N.M., Payne, B.K., & Marsh, E.J. (2015). Knowledge does not protect against illusory truth. *Journal of Experimental Psychology: General, 144*(5), 993–1002. https://doi.org/10.1037/xge0000098.

18 See Fazio (2020); and Pennycook, G., McPhetres, J., Zhang, Y., Lu, J.G., & Rand, D.G. (2020). Fighting COVID-19 misinformation on social media: Experimental evidence for a scalable accuracy-nudge intervention. *Psychological Science, 31*(7), 770–80. https://doi.org/10.1177/0956797620939054.

19 See Guess, A.M., Lerner, M., Lyons, B., Montgomery, J.M., Nyhan, B., Reifler, J., & Sircar, N. (2020). A digital media literacy intervention increases discernment between mainstream and false news in the United States and India. *Proceedings of the National Academy of Sciences, 117*(27), 15536–45. https://doi.org/10.1073/pnas.1920498117; and Carlsson, U. (Ed.). (2019). *Understanding Media and Information Literacy (MIL) in the digital age: A question of democracy.* UNESCO.

20 McGuire, W.J. (1961). Resistance to persuasion conferred by active and passive prior refutation of the same and alternative counterarguments. *Journal of Abnormal and Social Psychology, 63*(2), 326–32. https://doi.org/10.1037/h0048344; and McGuire, W.J. (1964). Inducing resistance to persuasion: Some contemporary approaches. In C.C. Haaland and W.O. Kaelber (Eds.), *Self and society. An anthology of readings* (pp. 192–230). Ginn Custom Publishing, 1981. https://opus4.kobv.de/opus4-Fromm/frontdoor/index/index/docId/16094.

21 See McGuire (1964); and Compton, J. (2013). Inoculation theory. In J.P. Dillard & L. Shen (Eds.), *The SAGE handbook of persuasion: Developments in theory and practice* (pp. 220–36). SAGE Publications. https://doi:10.4135/9781452218410.

22 See Compton (2013); and Compton, J., & Pfau, M. (2005). Inoculation theory of resistance to influence at maturity: Recent progress in theory development and application and suggestions for future research. *Annals of the International Communication Association, 29*(1), 97–146. https://doi.org/10.1080/23808985.2005.11679045

23 Banas, J.A., & Rains, S.A. (2010). A meta-analysis of research on inoculation theory. *Communication Monographs, 77*(3), 281–311. https://doi.org/10.1080/03637751003758193.

24 Zarocostas, J. (2020). How to fight an infodemic. *Lancet, 395*(10225), 676. https://doi.org/10.1016/S0140-6736(20)30461-X.

25 Eagly, A.H., & Chaiken, S. (1993). *The psychology of attitudes.* Harcourt Brace Jovanovich College Publishers.

26 Ruggeri, K., Linden, D.S., van der, Wang, C., Papa, F., Riesch, J., & Green, J. (2020). Standards for evidence in policy decision-making. *Nature Research Social and Behavioural Sciences, 399005.* go.nature.com/2zdTQIs.

27 McGuire (1964).

28 Lewandowsky & van der Linden (2021).

29 Compton, J. (2020). Prophylactic versus therapeutic inoculation treatments for resistance to influence. *Communication Theory, 30*(3), 330–43. https://doi.org/10.1093/ct/qtz004; and Wood, M.J., Douglas, K.M., & Sutton, R.M. (2012). Dead and alive: Beliefs in contradictory conspiracy theories. *Social Psychological and Personality Science, 3*(6), 767–73. https://doi.org/10.1177/1948550611434786.

30 van der Linden, S., Maibach, E., Cook, J., Leiserowitz, A., & Lewandowsky, S. (2017). Inoculating against misinformation. *Science, 358*(6367), 1141–2. https://doi.org/10.1126/science.aar4533.

31 Readfearn, G. (2016, November 29). *Revealed: Most popular climate story on social media told half a million people the science was a hoax.* DeSmog. https://www.desmogblog.com/2016/11/29/revealed-most-popular-climate-story-social-media-told-half-million-people-science-was-hoax.

32 van der Linden, Leiserowitz, et al. (2017).
33 Banas & Rains (2010).
34 Cook, J., Lewandowsky, S., & Ecker, U.K.H. (2017). Neutralizing misinformation through inoculation: Exposing misleading argumentation techniques reduces their influence. *PLOS ONE, 12*(5), e0175799. https://doi.org/10.1371/journal.pone.0175799; Maertens, R., Anseel, F., & van der Linden, S. (2020). Combatting climate change misinformation: Evidence for longevity of inoculation and consensus messaging effects. *Journal of Environmental Psychology, 70,* 101455. https://doi.org/10.1016/j.jenvp.2020.101455; and Williams, M.N., & Bond, C.M.C. (2020). A preregistered replication of "Inoculating the public against misinformation about climate change." *Journal of Environmental Psychology, 70,* 101456. https://doi.org/10.1016/j.jenvp.2020.101456.
35 Compton (2013).
36 Parker, K.A., Rains, S.A., & Ivanov, B. (2016). Examining the "blanket of protection" conferred by inoculation: The effects of inoculation messages on the cross-protection of related attitudes. *Communication Monographs, 83*(1), 49–68.
37 van der Linden & Roozenbeek (2020).
38 Cook, Lewandowsky, & Ecker (2017); and Roozenbeek, J., & van der Linden, S. (2019a). The fake news game: Actively inoculating against the risk of misinformation. *Journal of Risk Research, 22*(5), 570–80. https://doi.org/10.1080/13669877.2018.1443491.
39 McGuire (1961).
40 Roozenbeek & van der Linden (2019a).
41 Roozenbeek, J., & van der Linden, S. (2019b). Fake news game confers psychological resistance against online misinformation. *Palgrave Communications, 5*(1), 65. https://doi.org/10.1057/s41599-019-0279-9.
42 Sagarin, B.J., Cialdini, R.B., Rice, W.E., & Serna, S.B. (2002). Dispelling the illusion of invulnerability: The motivations and mechanisms of resistance to persuasion. *Journal of Personality and Social Psychology, 83*(3), 526–41. https://doi.org/10.1037/0022-3514.83.3.526.
43 Tandoc, E.C., Lim, Z.W., & Ling, R. (2018). Defining "fake news": A typology of scholarly definitions. *Digital Journalism, 6*(2), 137–53. https://doi.org/10.1080/21670811.2017.1360143.
44 See Lee, E.-J., Kim, H.S., & Choi, S. (2020). Violent video games and aggression: Stimulation or catharsis or both? *Cyberpsychology, Behavior, and Social Networking, 24*(1), 41–7. https://doi.org/10.1089/cyber.2020.0033; and Thompson, D., Baranowski, T., Buday, R., Baranowski, J., Thompson, V., Jago, R., & Griffith, M.J. (2010). Serious video games for health: How behavioral science guided the development of a serious video game. *Simulation & Gaming, 41*(4), 587–606. https://doi.org/10.1177/1046878108328087.
45 Roozenbeek & van der Linden (2019b).
46 Basol, M., Roozenbeek, J., & van der Linden, S. (2020). Good news about bad news: Gamified inoculation boosts confidence and cognitive immunity against fake news. *Journal of Cognition, 3*(1). https://doi.org/10.5334/joc.91.
47 Maertens, R., Roozenbeek, J., Basol, M., & van der Linden, S. (2021). Long-term effectiveness of inoculation against misinformation: Three longitudinal experiments. *Journal of Experimental Psychology: Applied, 27*(1), 1–16. https://doi.org/10.1037/xap0000315.
48 Roozenbeek, J., Maertens, R., McClanahan, W., & van der Linden, S. (2021). Disentangling item and testing effects in inoculation research on online misinformation: Solomon revisited. *Educational and Psychological Measurement, 81*(2), 340–62. https://doi.org/10.1177/0013164420940378.

49 Roozenbeek, J., van der Linden, S., & Nygren, T. (2020). Prebunking interventions based on "inoculation" theory can reduce susceptibility to misinformation across cultures. *Harvard Kennedy School Misinformation Review*, 1(2). https://doi.org/10.37016//mr-2020-008.

50 Vasudeva & Barkdull (2020); Phartiyal, S., Patnaik, S., & Ingram, D. When a text can trigger a lynching: WhatsApp struggles with incendiary messages in India. Reuters UK (2018); and Roozenbeek, J., Basol, M. & van der Linden, S. (2019). WhatsApp wants researchers to tackle its fake news problem – here's our idea. *The Conversation*.

51 Roozenbeek, J., & van der Linden, S. (2020). Breaking *Harmony Square*: A game that "inoculates" against political misinformation. *Harvard Kennedy School Misinformation Review*. https://doi.org/10.37016/mr-2020-47.

52 Basol, M., Roozenbeek, J., Berriche, M., Uenal, F., & van der Linden, S. (2021). Towards psychological herd immunity: Cross-cultural evidence for two prebunking interventions against COVID-19 misinformation. *Big Data and Society*. https://doi.org/10.5194/egusphere-egu21-12138.

53 Saleh, N., Roozenbeek, J., Makki, F., McClanahan, W., & van der Linden, S. (2021). Active inoculation boosts attitudinal resistance against extremist persuasion techniques – A novel approach towards the prevention of violent extremism. *Behavioural Public Policy*, 1–24. https://doi:10.1017/bpp.2020.60.

54 Roozenbeek, J., van der Linden, S., Goldberg, B., & Lewandowsky, S. (2021). Scaling psychological inoculation against misinformation techniques. *Science Advances*.

55 van der Linden, Maibach, et al. (2017).

56 Ibid.

CHAPTER FOURTEEN

Developing Effective Healthy Eating Nudges

Romain Cadario and Pierre Chandon

OK. You have heard the demand for change and want to help your customers eat better but without curtailing their freedom to indulge if they want to and without going out of business. What can you do? A large number of interventions have been suggested to promote healthy eating.[1] However, many of these various "nudges" have only been tested in laboratory or online studies, and, as we have heard in the first part of this book, there are several important reasons why they may not necessarily translate into successful behavioral change. It is also not easy to decipher the scientific literature.

This chapter, which is based on two of our recent articles, summarizes what we know about which healthy eating nudges are most effective at changing food choices in the field, in supermarkets or restaurants.[2] In addition, it examines another aspect of the debate: whether customers are likely to welcome these nudges.

THINKING, FEELING, DOING: THE TRILOGY OF NUDGES

Since Thaler won the Nobel prize in economics for his work on nudging, every marketing intervention has been rebranded as a nudge. However, a discount is not a nudge, and neither is traditional awareness or image-based advertising, for example. According to Thaler and Sunstein, a nudge can be defined as "any aspect of the choice architecture that alters people's behavior in a predictable way (a) without forbidding any options, or (b) significantly changing their economic incentives.[3] Putting fruit at eye level counts as a nudge; banning junk food does not."

Even this restricted definition of nudges encompasses a wide variety of interventions, including various labeling schemes, changes to the visibility of different foods, or reductions of plate and portion size. In this first section, we provide a framework to classify nudges. We draw on the classic tripartite classification of mental activities into cognition (thinking), affect (feeling), and behavior (doing). This so-called trilogy of mind has long been adopted in psychology and marketing to understand consumer behavior and predict the effectiveness of marketing actions.[4]

We distinguish between (a) cognitively oriented nudges that seek to influence what consumers think, (b) affectively oriented nudges that seek to influence how consumers feel without necessarily changing what they know, and (c) behaviorally oriented nudges that seek to influence what consumers do (i.e., their motor responses) without necessarily changing what they know or how they feel. Within each type, we further distinguish subtypes that share similar characteristics, ending with seven nudges overall (see Table 14.1).

Thinking: Informing the Brain about What Is Healthy with Cognitive Nudges

There are three types of cognitive nudges. The first type, "descriptive nutritional labeling," provides calorie counts or information about other nutrients, be it on menus or menu boards in restaurants, or on labels on the food packaging or near the foods in self-service cafeterias and grocery stores.

The second type, "evaluative nutritional labeling," typically (but not always) provides nutrition information but also helps consumers interpret it through color coding (e.g., red, yellow, green as nutritive value increases) or by adding special symbols or marks (e.g., heart-healthy logos or smileys on menus) or by simplifying schemes (e.g., Nutri-Score's A to E categories).

Although the third type, "visibility enhancement," does not directly provide health or nutrition information, it is a cognitively

Table 14.1. Overview of the three nudge types (cognitive, affective, behavioral) and their subtypes

Nudge type	Definition and example
	Cognitive nudges: Thinking
Descriptive nutritional labeling	Labels in supermarkets, cafeterias, and fast-food restaurants with calorie and nutrition facts. For example, the shelf label or the menu board provides information about calorie, fat, sugar, and salt content.
Evaluative nutritional labeling	Labels in supermarkets, cafeterias, and fast-food restaurants providing color-coded nutrition information that easily identifies healthier foods. For example, the shelf label or the menu board provides information about calorie and fat content and a green sticker if the food is healthy or a red sticker if the food is unhealthy.
Visibility enhancements	Supermarkets, cafeterias, and fast-food restaurants make healthy food more visible and unhealthy food less visible. For example, supermarkets place healthy food rather than unhealthy food near cash registers and cafeterias or restaurants make healthy food visible and easy to find on their menus and unhealthy food harder to find.
	Affective nudges: Feeling
Healthy eating calls	Staff in supermarkets, cafeterias, and fast-food restaurants prod consumers to eat more healthily. For example, supermarket or cafeteria cashiers or restaurant waiters ask customers if they would like to have fruits or vegetables.
Pleasure appeals	Supermarkets, cafeterias, and fast-food restaurants make healthy food more appealing and unhealthy food less appealing. For example, healthy foods are displayed more attractively in cafeteria counters or are described in a more appealing and appetizing way on menus.
	Behavioral nudges: Doing
Convenience enhancements	Cafeterias and fast-food restaurants include healthy food as a default in their menu, and supermarkets make unhealthy food physically harder to reach on the shelves. For example, vegetables are included by default in combo meals or in fixed menus in cafeterias and chain restaurants, but customers can ask for a replacement.
Size enhancements	Supermarkets, cafeterias, and fast-food restaurants reduce the size of the packages or portions of unhealthy food that they sell and increase those of the healthy foods. For example, cafeterias and restaurants serve smaller portions of fries and larger portions of vegetables, or supermarkets sell smaller candy bars and larger strawberry trays.

oriented intervention because it informs consumers of the availability of healthy options by increasing their visibility on grocery or cafeteria shelves (e.g., placing healthy options at eye level and unhealthy options on the bottom shelf) or on restaurant menus (e.g., placing healthy options on the first page and burying unhealthy ones in the middle).

Feeling: Seducing the Heart with Affective Nudges

The first type of affectively oriented interventions, which we call "healthy eating calls," directly encourages people to do better. This can be done by placing signs or stickers (e.g., "Make a fresh choice," or "Have a tossed salad for lunch!") or by asking food service staff to verbally encourage people to choose a healthy option (e.g., "Which vegetable would you like to have for lunch?") or to change their unhealthy choices (e.g., "Your meal doesn't look like a balanced meal" or "Would you like to take half a portion of your side dish?").

The second type, "pleasure appeals," seeks to increase the hedonic appeal of healthy options by using vivid hedonic descriptions (e.g., "twisted citrus-glazed carrots") or attractive displays, photos, or containers (e.g., "pyramids of fruits").

Doing: Manipulating the Hands with Behavioral Nudges

The third group consists of two types of interventions that aim to impact people's behaviors without necessarily influencing what they know or how they feel, often without people being aware of their existence. "Convenience enhancements" make it physically easier for people to select healthy options (e.g., by making them the default option or placing them in faster "grab & go" cafeteria lines) or to consume them (e.g., by pre-slicing fruits or pre-serving vegetables), or make it more cumbersome to select or consume unhealthy options (e.g., by placing them later in the cafeteria line when trays are already full or by providing less convenient serving utensils).

The second type, which we call "size enhancements," modifies the size of the plate, bowl, or glass, or the size of pre-plated portions, either increasing the amount of healthy food they contain or, most commonly, reducing the amount of unhealthy food.

HANDS ABOVE HEARTS ABOVE BRAINS: WHICH TYPE OF NUDGE WORKS BEST?

We tested this framework with a meta-analysis of published field experiments, which allows us to measure the average effectiveness of a given nudge type across many studies.[5] Our meta-analysis reviewed real-life experiments rather than lab- or online-based studies because, when it comes to food choices, there's an important intention-action gap between what people say they eat and what they actually eat when no one is watching. Overall, the meta-analysis covered 96 field experiments published in 90 academic articles.

We collated information about the experiments and measured the effectiveness of each type of nudge using the standardized mean difference (also known as Cohen's d), which allows us to pool the results across various units of measurements and foods. To get a more intuitive grasp of nudge effectiveness, we converted them into the daily energy equivalent, expressed in number of sugar cubes. For example, if a nudge can reduce consumption by 100 calories a day, it's the equivalent of 10 fewer sugar cubes.

Our key finding is that the effectiveness of nudges increases as they shift from cognition/thinking (d = 0.12, −64 kcal) to affect/feeling (d = 0.24, −129 kcal) to behavior/doing (d = 0.39, −209 kcal). In other words, the hand is stronger than the heart, which is stronger than the brain. Figure 14.1 summarizes the average effectiveness of our seven identified heathy eating nudges, measured in daily decrease in energy intake transformed into sugar cube equivalents.

The Disappointing Effects of Cognitive Nudges

Descriptive labeling. Information alone, that is, nutritional facts with no color-coding or symbols to help people interpret the numbers, does not move the dial very much in terms of making healthy choices. Expected calorie reduction = five sugar cubes.

Figure 14.1. Average nudge effectiveness from the meta-analysis

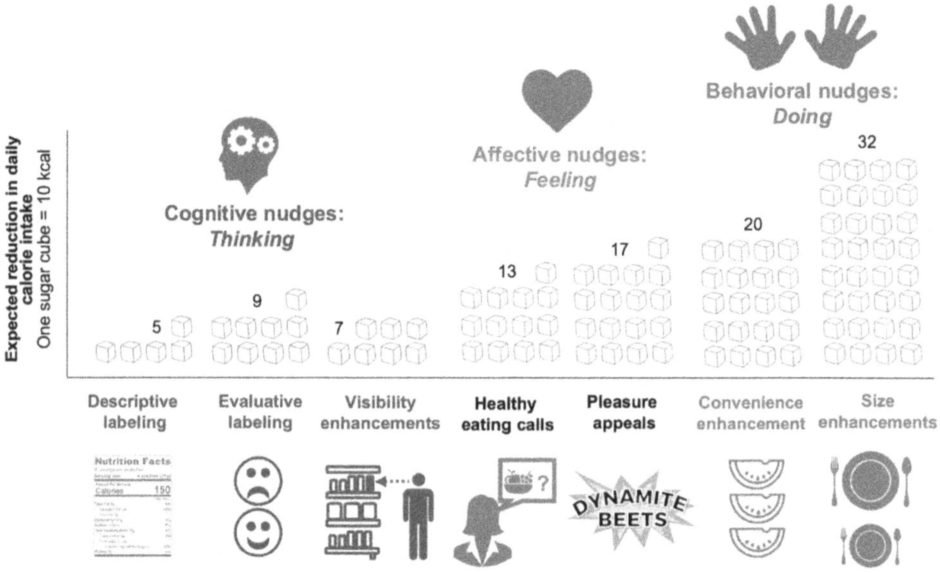

Source: Cadario & Chandon (2020)

Evaluative labeling. When we know how healthy something is in relation to something else, in the form of a summary score, a smiley face, or traffic-light food labeling, the information has some impact on our choices. We understand that a red light means "stop," even in the grocery store. In fact, a large randomized controlled trial in 60 supermarkets showed that simplified front-of-pack nutrition labels help sell good foods.[6] However, they did not reduce the sales of "bad" foods, and there was a significant "voltage-drop": their effects were 17 times lower overall than in comparable laboratory studies. Expected calorie reduction = nine sugar cubes.

Visibility enhancements. Another nudge that informs our brains is one that puts the healthiest product in the most visible place – at eye level on a shelf or on the best place in the middle of a menu. Still, it didn't have a significant impact on making better choices. Expected calorie reduction = seven sugar cubes.

In conclusion, targeting thinking is not enough! Cognitive nudges are trying to inform us about the healthiness of the food options, either by displaying nutrition information or traffic-light symbols or by placing the healthiest foods right where we will see them. Clearly, they are not ideal. Nudges that inform only have a small impact on our food decisions, reducing our intake by the equivalent of five to nine sugar cubes per day. This is not as surprising as it sounds, since people already know that they should replace calorie-dense snacks with fruits and vegetables or sodas with water. The difficulty is converting this knowledge into action, and that requires the motivation to act and aids that help to follow through on one's intentions. This is where affective and behavioral nudges can help.

Affective Nudges: Social Pressure and Pleasure as Allies of Healthy Eating

Healthy eating calls. This type of nudge can be implemented by asking the cashier to ask customers if they want a salad with their burger or by placing signs up encouraging people to "make a fresh choice." On average, these nudges can expect a daily calorie reduction of nearly 13 sugar cubes.

  Pleasure appeals. These nudges emphasize the taste or the sensory characteristics of the food. Instead of telling us that carrots are rich in antioxidants, the menu describes them as "twisted citrus-glazed carrots" to draw attention to how they might taste or feel. Expected calorie reduction = 17 sugar cubes.

  Instead of informing people about nutrition or the availability of healthier options, as cognitive/thinking nudges do, affective nudges try to motivate us to eat foods that we already know are better for us by playing up their delicious taste or texture or by leveraging social pressure. These tend to be effective, reducing our calorie intake by the equivalent of 13 to 17 sugar cubes.

Behavioral Nudges: When Doing Beats Seducing and Informing

Convenience enhancements. These nudges make selecting or consuming healthier foods the easy option. It can be done by placing indulgent foods at the end of the cafeteria line, when our tray is already full of healthier foods. Another convenience enhancement is to pre-cut and pre-plate fruit or vegetables. After all, it's much easier to eat peeled and chopped pineapple than a whole one. Expected calorie reduction = nearly 20 sugar cubes.

Size enhancements. The most effective nudges directly change how much food is put on plates or the size of the bottle. This is still technically a nudge as long as the unit price stays the same. Although there have been inconsistent results, simply reducing the size of the plate or glass may also help, if people use it as a cue to decide how much to serve themselves. Expected calorie reduction = 32 sugar cubes.

In conclusion, behavioral nudges try to influence what we do directly, without changing what we know or what we want. They are by far the most effective, as they can save us up to 32 sugar cubes' worth of calories. At least when it comes to eating, feelings beat thinking and doing beats feelings. If public policy and food businesses want to help consumers eat better, our findings suggest focusing on developing behavioral nudges.

MANIPULATIVE BUT EFFECTIVE: CONSUMER APPROVAL OF HEALTHY EATING NUDGES

If behavioral nudges are so much more effective than cognitive or even affective ones, why are most policy debates about how to best inform people, for example, with nutrition labels, rather than about how to shrink package size or downsize restaurant food portions? The answer is fear of consumer reactance. Developing effective healthy eating nudges should not be driven only by effectiveness considerations. We must take into account consumer approval. This is what we did in a second study, for which we recruited American participants to evaluate the seven healthy eating nudges presented in the previous section.[7]

Measuring Consumer Approval of Nudges

Each nudge was presented with a specific scenario, as shown in the table below. We first showed the nudge type, logo, and description of one the seven nudges, selected in random order. We then measured nudge approval using binary scales ("Do you approve or disapprove of the following policy?", Approve/disapprove) and perceived effectiveness ("Do you think that this policy will make people eat better?", Yes it will/No it will not). We obtained similar results when asking people to rate the nudge on a 13-point scale labeled from to A+ to F. Last, we asked people who would be the primary beneficiary of each nudge, from three options: (1) "Primarily consumer health (little or negative impact on business)," (2) "Primarily business (little or negative impact on health)," (3) "It will be a win-win (both health and business will benefit)."

Effective or Accepted: Tradeoffs in Selecting Nudges

Our results found only moderate acceptance of the seven healthy eating nudges. The average approval rate was 64% for women and 52% for men. To further examine the relationship between these scores and the actual effectiveness of the nudge, we plotted on the Y-axis of Figure 14.2 the percentage of respondents who approved the nudge. The X-axis shows the actual effect size of each nudge estimated in the meta-analysis presented in the previous section. The cognitive nudges are represented with circles, the affective nudges with triangles, and the behavioral nudges with squares.

Figure 14.2 shows that the actual effectiveness of these nudges was inversely related to their mean approval rating (r=−.57). Whereas 85% approved of descriptive labeling, the least effective nudge, only 43% approved portion size changes, the most effective one. In additional analyses, we examined the drivers of consumer approval, as function of actual nudge effectiveness and perceived nudge effectiveness, as well as perceived beneficiary of the nudge. We found that that approval was positively associated with the perceived effectiveness of the nudge. Importantly, we found that healthy eating nudges perceived as a "win-win" for business and health had higher approval than interventions perceived as benefiting either health or business, and that there were no differences in approval between each of these respectively. That is, the more people expected a nudge to be effective, and the more they perceived it

Figure 14.2. Nudge effectiveness is inversely related to consumer approval

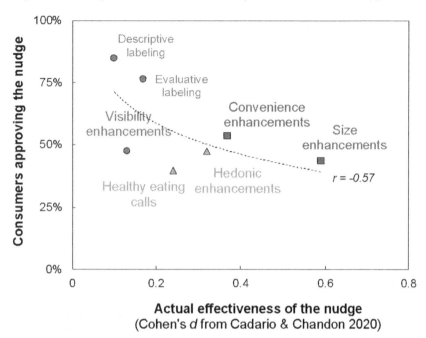

Source: Cadario & Chandon (2019)

to be a win-win for both business and health, the more likely they were to approve of the nudge.

KEY TAKEAWAYS AND IMPLICATIONS

In conclusion, we find clear evidence that not all nudges are created equal. This is true in terms of their effectiveness and their acceptance by citizens and consumers alike. In our view, it is time to move beyond discussing the value of nudging in general to consider both the expected effectiveness and the public acceptance of specific types of nudges.

At first glance, our results seem to lead to a conundrum. On the one hand, we find that the effectiveness of healthy eating interventions increases as their focus shifts from cognition to affect to behavior. On the other hand, we find that consumer approval of the nudges decreases with their effectiveness. Unless one is a benevolent dictator, a parent for example, this suggests that managers or public servants who are beholden to the support of their clients or citizens cannot simply go with "what works best." Simply being transparent about nudges can impair their implementation, as the majority of people are likely to disapprove of them.

Yet, our results also offer a solution. The crux of the problem is not that people dislike being nudged, or that they disapprove of nudges that help businesses, but that they are poor judges of which nudges are effective. So, the first conclusion is that we first need to listen to consumers to find out what they think of the nudges that we intend to implement. The second conclusion is that we must frame nudges appropriately, highlighting their effectiveness as well as highlighting that they can be a win-win for all.

Given this, priority should go to nudges that achieve multiple goals, such as "Epicurean nudges" focused on the pleasure (versus health benefits) of portion control, which deliver both business and health benefits because pleasure in food does not increase with quantity, but with quality and savoring.[8] Since people tend to approve of the nudges that they perceive to be effective, approval rates for powerful nudges like size and convenience enhancements can be improved if people learn that they are three times more effective than descriptive or prescriptive labeling.

Overall, healthy eating nudges are a valuable addition to the traditional public policy toolbox of tax incentives and regulations.[9] However, the controversy over the newsfeed experiments conducted at Facebook without explicit consent reminds us that we can no longer assume that people will accept being nudged as long as the objective of the nudge is commendable.[10] Rather than framing the debate as nudging versus traditional tools, specific nudges should be compared to specific tools on both their effects and their acceptance.

NOTES

1 Hollands, G.J., Shemilt, I., Marteau, T.M., Jebb, S.A., Lewis, H.B., Wei, Y., Higgins, J.P.T., & Ogilvie, D. (2015). Portion, package or tableware size for changing selection and consumption of food, alcohol and tobacco. *Cochrane Database of Systematic Reviews, 9.* https://doi.org/10.1002/14651858.CD011045.pub2.

2 See Cadario, R., & Chandon, P. (2020). Which healthy eating nudges work best? A meta-analysis of field experiments. *Marketing Science, 39*(3), 465–86. https://doi.org/10.1287/mksc.2018.1128; and Cadario, R., & Chandon, P. (2019). Effectiveness or consumer acceptance? Tradeoffs in selecting healthy eating nudges. *Food Policy, 85*, 1–6. https://doi.org/10.1016/j.foodpol.2019.04.002.

3 Thaler, R.H., & Sunstein, C.R. (2009). *Nudge: Improving decisions about health, wealth, and happiness.* Penguin.

4 See, for example, Hanssens, D.M., Pauwels, K.H., Srinivasan, S., Vanhuele, M., & Yildirim, G. (2014). Consumer attitude metrics for guiding marketing mix decisions. *Marketing Science, 33*(4), 534–50. https://doi.org/10.1287/mksc.2013.0841.

5 Cadario & Chandon (2020).

6 Dubois, P., Albuquerque, P., Allais, O., Bonnet, C., Bertail, P., Combris, P., Lahlou, S., Rigal, N., Ruffieux, B., & Chandon, P. (2021). Effects of front-of-pack labels on the nutritional quality of supermarket food purchases: Evidence from a large-scale randomized controlled trial. *Journal of the Academy of Marketing Science, 49*(1), 119–38. https://doi.org/10.1007/s11747-020-00723-5.

7 Cadario & Chandon (2019).

8 Cornil, Y., & Chandon, P. (2016). Pleasure as a substitute for size: How multisensory imagery can make people happier with smaller food portions. *Journal of Marketing Research, 53*(5), 847–64. https://doi.org/10.1509/jmr.14.0299.

9 Benartzi, S., Beshears, J., Milkman, K.L., Sunstein, C.R., Thaler, R.H., Shankar, M., Tucker-Ray, W., Congdon, W.J., & Galing, S. (2017). Should governments invest more in nudging? *Psychological Science, 28*(8), 1041–55. https://doi.org/10.1177/0956797617702501.

10 Verma, I.M. (2014). Editorial expression of concern: Experimental evidence of massive-scale emotional contagion through social networks. *Proceedings of the National Academy of Sciences, 111*(29), 10779. https://doi.org/10.1073/pnas.1412469111.

CHAPTER FIFTEEN

Wellness Rewarded: A "How To" on Designing Behavioral Science–Informed Financial Incentives to Improving Health (That Work)

Marc Mitchell and Renante Rondina

Carrot Rewards was a free-to-use commercial mobile health application (mHealth app) that was available in Canada from 2016 to 2019. Grounded in behavioral economics, it used financial incentives to reward its users for engaging in healthy behaviors (e.g., walking, smoking cessation, immunization). Regarding physical activity promotion, by far the app's most popular feature, it used the available technology in modern smartphones to measure its users' daily step count in real time and reward them immediately upon achieving realistic, individualized goals ($0.03 US per day, or about $8 US per year). By promising to improve population-level physical activity for just pennies a day, Carrot Rewards was able to secure funding from Canadian federal and provincial governments to pay for the incentives. However, due in part to its runaway success in the wild (e.g., 1.5+ million users and very high engagement rates) – the opposite of the voltage drop outlined in Chapter 3 *of this book – resulting in rising costs of total payouts, some government partners chose to discontinue funding. Unfortunately, and despite its great potential as a health behavior change tool, Carrot Rewards went out of business in 2019.*

WE AREN'T HEALTHY

In many ways, we have never been less healthy. Nearly 100 million adults in the United States are obese.[1] At any given time, almost 13 million adults in the United Kingdom show symptoms of anxiety or depression.[2] In Canada, just about half of adults have at least one of the 10 major chronic diseases (e.g., arthritis, diabetes).[3] Several modifiable behaviors, like unhealthy eating, smoking, and excessive drinking, predispose us to these debilitating chronic diseases.[4] By far, though, the most common one is physical inactivity, with a whopping 85% of adults not achieving the recommended 150 minutes of moderate-intensity activity per week (e.g., walking briskly).[5] Physical activity is simply not something most of us engage in on a regular basis. For good reason too – it's hard, our built environments discourage it (think cars, desks, etc.), and the health benefits are, for the most part, delayed. Sadly, these risk factors may be exacerbated in the COVID-19 pandemic, forcing many to stay and work from home, become more sedentary,[6] and increase their food and alcohol consumption in response to unprecedented stressors.[7] These may have knock-on effects on important health outcomes in the future (a pandemic shadow if you will). Luckily, recent advances in mobile technology and behavioral science have spurred new research in this area that may help more of us start *and stick with* healthier, more active lifestyles.

DIGITAL SOLUTIONS

This year, more than 2.5 billion people worldwide will own a smartphone.[8] The number of mobile health applications (mHealth apps) published in the major app stores continues to rise, with 325,000 published in 2017, up 34% from the previous year.[9] This increase in part reflects evolving smartphone capabilities (e.g., "built-in" motion sensors called accelerometers, GPS). Access to accelerometer data in particular has transformed physical activity promotion. For the first time ever, the majority of adults (approaching 90%) in the US and Canada, for example, carry a physical activity monitoring device most of the time.[10] This presents an unprecedented opportunity to deliver more precise health interventions and bridge well-worn physical activity divides (e.g., women walk less than men), using instantaneous physical activity data to set and adjust realistic goals, provide immediate feedback, link users with friends to support long-term change, and so on. Not surprisingly, physical activity apps make up the bulk of all mHealth apps (30%, or roughly 100,000 apps).[11] Unfortunately, low app engagement leading to small effects and little sustainability remain industry hallmarks. For example, 90% of people who download an mHealth app delete it within 30 days.[12] Similarly, while many large corporations offer their employees digital wellness platforms, most (i.e., 90–95%) do not engage meaningfully. In response, many large corporations have incorporated financial health incentives (e.g., paying people for health screenings, to quit smoking, etc.).[13] Accumulating evidence, though, suggests deficiencies in the way digital health programs are designed. Most notably, these behavior modification programs are almost never grounded in behavioral science. In other words, road maps exist and no one is using them!

BETTER FINANCIAL INCENTIVES WITH BEHAVIORAL SCIENCE

Wellness programs based on financial incentives continue to be popular with 56% of large US employers[14] (and at least 15% of European employers),[15] for instance, offering monetary rewards worth $946 US per year to employees for participating in healthy activities. An obvious concern is that financial health incentives are prohibitively costly with limited scalability potential. Stronger behavioral science application has the potential to reduce the cost of incentives and allow practitioners to operate realistically within finite corporate or government budgets, as illustrated in our recent meta-analysis in the *British Journal of Sports Medicine*.[16]

Knowing more about behavioral economics, the theoretical foundation for incentive interventions, is an important first step. Behavioral economics has shown that systematic errors in thinking, called "decision biases," can lead to poor health outcomes.[17] The "present bias" is the most relevant example when thinking about incentives.[18] Sometimes referred to as "temporal discounting," present bias describes how the value a person sets on a reward (e.g., better health) decreases the further away in time the reward is realized.[19] Put another way, people tend to respond more to the immediate costs and benefits of their actions than to those experienced in the future. In the case of physical activity, for example, the *cost* of the behavior (e.g., time out of a busy schedule, discomfort/sweatiness) is usually experienced in the present and thus overvalued, while the *benefits* (e.g., health, longevity) are often delayed and thus discounted, tipping daily decisional scales towards inactivity.

According to behavioral economics, *immediate* incentives may be useful in emphasizing a short-term physical activity benefit and motivate more people to choose to be active today. Maintaining fidelity to the "present bias" in designing incentive programs (i.e., not delaying incentives by months/weeks or even days/hours) may increase effectiveness. In fact, immediate incentives have been shown to drive the cost of physical activity rewards way, way down to pennies a day, or about $8 US a year! Applying a broader range of behavioral economics concepts in the design of incentive programs may further reduce costs while maintaining effects. According to our recent meta-analysis, the financial incentive size being tested in clinical trials has dropped from $10 US per day a few years ago to $1.50 US per day now, with some studies determining that financial rewards worth less than $0.10 US per day increase physical activity.[20] A dime a day may indeed keep the doctor away!

Which raises the question, *how have behavioral scientists and practitioners been able to save so much on the cost of health rewards while maintaining effects?*

This newfound efficiency is due in large part to recent technological advances that have made tracking and rewarding physical activity easier and more immediate, as well as a broader application of potent behavioral economics decision biases such as "loss aversion" and "commitment" (for an overview of common decision biases and potential interventions, see Table 15.1).

Table 15.1. Overview of common decision biases and potential interventions

Decision bias	Description	Intervention examples
Present bias	Preference for a payoff close to the present time rather than in the future	Monitoring behavior in real time and rewarding users immediately upon reaching a goal
Loss aversion	Preference for avoiding losing something over acquiring an equal gain	Endowing users with incentives at the beginning of a week and taking some of it back whenever they fail to reach a goal
Over-optimism	Over-estimating the probability of positive events	Rewarding users for reaching a goal with a chance to win a lottery-based prize
Salience	Information that stands out, is novel, or seems relevant is more likely to affect our actions	Personalized feedback is more salient than generic feedback
Herd behavior	Doing what others are doing instead of making independent decisions	Using leaderboards and collaborative goals to nudge behavior
Commitment	Preference for a consistent self-image, best achieved by making a commitment or pre-commitment	Promising a friend to reach a goal, or agreeing to consequences if failing to do so (e.g., making a bet)
Fresh start	Aspirational behavior around temporal landmarks (e.g., New Year's, birthdays)	Resetting the clock on reaching a goal every Monday
Gamification	The application of game-design elements and game principles in non-game contexts	Points, leaderboards, challenges or "quests," in-app currencies, badges, or trophies, etc.
Payment transparency	Forms of payment that are further removed from physical currency are less salient	Rewarding users with points that can be converted into cash or used to purchase virtual goods in an in-app store

The *Carrot Rewards* app (see vignette above) is a good example of a commercial attempt to provide behavioral economics-driven financial incentives on a population scale. Amongst other things, *Carrot Rewards* rewarded Canadians for walking a little bit more than normal.[21] *Carrot Rewards* exploited a number of predictable biases in human decision making. For example, the app offered immediate incentives ("present bias") in the form of loyalty points ("payment transparency") for personalized ("salience") and longer-term team-based ("fresh start" and "herd behavior") physical activity achievements and in doing so drove incentive costs down to pennies a day ($0.03 US per day, or $8 US per year). Unfortunately, with over one million registered users (two-thirds of whom used the app every single day!), these costs started to rack up and so were then deemed too high for a singular, publicly funded healthy living program, mainly because financial incentives were (incorrectly) designed to be offered indefinitely.[22] We urge you to please learn from our mistakes!

LEARN FROM OUR MISTAKES!

Despite its early success, the *Carrot Rewards* app is an important cautionary tale. The longer-term benefits of the *Carrot Rewards* initiative, such as healthcare system savings (a health economic impact study is underway and preliminary results are very promising), may have been superseded in a policy context by shorter-term priorities. *Carrot Rewards* worked because it leveraged behavioral economic principles. However, one of the reasons it was discontinued was because of its success. A more sustainable strategy might have been to evolve the app into a platform in which daily financial incentives would have been only a temporary feature. Despite the prevailing sentiment that incentives only work while in place,[23] our recent paradigm-shifting meta-analysis[24] suggests that moving from small, daily financial incentives to larger, less frequent ones, *and then none at all*, may be one way of driving sustained behavior change in a cost-conscious manner. While behavioral economics describes situations that might *stimulate* change, a look over at another theory of human motivation (called self-determination theory) provides practical suggestions for designing incentives for *lasting* change. In particular, self-determination theory suggests that extrinsic rewards (a) that are not overly large/controlling (imagine how much pressure a $1000 US reward might be to a lower-income mother of two!), (b) that are contingent on realistic goals ("Forget about 10,000 steps, just do 500 more *than you normally do*!"), and (c) that promote social interaction (team goals are great for that) may actually help develop the intrinsic motivations needed for long-term change.[25]

In other words, the latest evidence suggests that well-designed extrinsic rewards can lead to internalized motivation ("Hey, I actually really enjoy going for a walk!") and quality behavior change.

The *Carrot Rewards* app also included other behavioral science–informed elements that have been previously suggested to promote sustained change, such as passive tracking, biofeedback, adaptive goal setting, and gamification features (e.g., points, goals, challenges, collaborations, competitions). In the future, these elements, along with a short-term financial incentive "dose," should be considered by others looking to match *Carrot Rewards'* rare level of engagement without being hamstrung by a larger than necessary program/policy price tag. Insights from our health economic impact study may also help practitioners target interventions at population segments for maximum efficiency. For example, we determined that *Carrot Rewards* was most cost-effective for females, highly engaged users, and adults aged 35–64 years. For older adults (65+ years), the app actually saved the healthcare system money!

A HARD NUT TO CRACK

Changing health behaviors is definitely a hard nut to crack – but it can be cracked with a little behavioral science on your side. We have described how financial incentives can be optimized using behavioral economics, self-determination theory, and cost-effectiveness analyses, as well as our own experience developing a popular commercial mHealth app. We now boil it all down to five practical incentive design suggestions. Apply these to your practice and your chances of success will skyrocket.

1. **Do not delay rewards.** Leverage the latest in smartphone technology to reward your people immediately for engaging in a healthy behavior. Maintaining fidelity to the behavioral economics principle "present bias" with a simple push notification or alert each time a reward is earned will pay big dividends.
2. **Reward a personalized behavior.** Too often people bite off more than they can chew. Ask your people which modifiable health

behavior they want to improve (e.g., physical activity, smoking, etc.) and use the latest technology to help them set and strive for realistic goals. Realistic goals lead to mastery experiences, which increase confidence – a critical ingredient in all great behavior change recipes.

3. **Clear the sludge.** Behavior change programs nowadays need to be virtually seamless. Any preventable friction or "sludge" (e.g., unnecessarily onerous sign-up processes, extra steps to redeem rewards, manual health data entry, etc.) must be removed.

4. **Zero in on engagement.** Pay close attention to engagement at critical junctures: (a) uptake (e.g., percentage of eligible people signing up), (b) seven-day (e.g., percentage of people daily and weekly active users), and (c) 30-day (e.g., percentage of monthly active users). Programs that can "hook" people at these key timepoints are much more likely to drive sustained engagement and improve health.

5. **Reward prescriptions.** Financial health incentives are a lot like medicine. Decisions around type, dose, timing, etc. need to be made for maximal therapeutic effect. Use the checklist in Table 15.2 to make purposeful incentive design decisions.[26] Pay close attention to incentive feature 12, "Duration," and decide how long you want to reward healthy behavior. Six months is the theoretical threshold for behavior maintenance.[27] Slowly weaning people off rewards around the six-month mark is a nice rule of thumb.

CONCLUSION

This chapter represents the next step for financial health incentives. We have moved from answering the question "Do incentives work?" to "When do incentives work best?" Drawing on our research and experience with *Carrot Rewards*, we have shared evidence-based strategies to enhance the design of more effective and scalable financial health incentive programs. Specifically, we argue that reward sizes can be driven way down by using technology to monitor and reward users in real time and that the role of incentives should be minimized as time passes to maximize sustainability. Some of the

Table 15.2. Checklist for purposeful incentive design decisions

Incentive features	Possible incentive attributes
☐ 1. Form	(a) Cash ($10 cash, cheque)
	(b) Voucher (iTunes, grocery, transit, Amazon)
	(c) Specific good/service (gym shoes, dietician consultation)
	(d) Reimbursement (existing expense reimbursed, e.g., gym membership fee or health insurance premium)
	(e) Donation (value of incentive earned donated to charity of choice)
☐ 2. Magnitude	Continuous variable (often expressed as dollars (US) per week or month)
☐ 3. Target	(a) Self-regulatory behavior (self-monitoring, scheduling, seeking social support)
	(b) Behavior (exercise, medication adherence)
	(c) Outcome (BMI < 25 kg/m2, BP<140/90)
☐ 4. Timing of assessment	(a) Completion of incentive program (six months)
	(b) Set intervals (daily/weekly assessments)
	(c) Random intervals (10 assessments over six months)
	(d) Dependent intervals (varying intervals based on previous performance)
☐ 5. Type of assessment	(a) Self-report (exercise diary submission)
	(b) Objective, direct (face to face)
	(c) Objective, indirect (pedometer, photo of weight on scale)
☐ 6. Reward immediacy	Continuous variable (often expressed as days or weeks between assessment and reward)
☐ 7. Certainty	(a) Certain ($50 for meeting A1C target)
	(b) Certain chance (one in four chance of $25)
	(c) Uncertain chance (one in 100 chance of $500)
	(d) Mix ($50 and one in 100 chance of $500)
☐ 8. Schedule	(a) Uniform ($50 lump sum for meeting goal)
	(b) Indexed ($1 for each gym visit)
	(c) Escalating ($1 for first 10 gym visits, $2 for next 10, etc.)
	(d) Random ($1 to $50 for gym visit)
☐ 9. Dispensing type	(a) Resetting (discrete reward at time of each achievement)
	(b) Aggregative ("passbook saving" – information on running tally given)
	(c) Mix (accumulated incentives lost if discrete goal not met, "go back to zero if missed gym visit")
☐ 10. Participant investment	(a) Opportunity cost only (time)
	(b) Deposit contract (own money lost if fail to achieve goal)
	(c) Matching ("double or nothing") ($50 of own money lost if fail, $50 extra gained if successful)

(Continued)

Table 15.2. Continued

Incentive features	Possible incentive attributes
☐ **11. Information disclosure**	(a) Factual (information given about meeting or failing to meet goal) (b) Counterfactual (information given about reward lost by failing to meet goal, i.e., regret)
☐ **12. Duration**	Continuous variable (often expressed in weeks or months incentive available; maybe indefinitely)
☐ **13. Source**	(a) Self or significant others (spouse, friend) (b) Group members (incentive plan members) (c) Government (d) Employer (e) Insurance company (f) Other (non-insurance) companies
☐ **14. Recipient**	(a) Individual (cash for weight lost) (b) Group (reward for >50% group attendance) (c) Significant other(s) (spouse, parent) (d) Charitable organization

lessons learnt here (e.g., the immediacy of personalized feedback is key) may be applicable to the design of other incentive types too (e.g., social incentives like sharing progress on social media, or non-monetary incentives like virtual badges). Financial incentive–based wellness programs should aim to leverage wearable technologies and embrace behavioral insights for a healthier future.

NOTES

1 Adult Obesity Facts. Available at: https://www.cdc.gov/obesity/data/adult.html.
2 Fundamental facts about mental health 2016. https://www.mentalhealth.org.uk /publications/fundamental-facts-about-mental-health-2016.
3 PHAC. Prevalence of chronic diseases among canadian adults. https://www .canada.ca/en/public-health/services/chronic-diseases/prevalence-canadian -adults-infographic-2019.html.
4 PHAC. Chronic disease risk factors. https://www.canada.ca/en/public-health /services/chronic-diseases/chronic-disease-risk-factors.html.
5 Colley, R., Garriguet, D., Janssen, I., Craig, C.L., Clarke, J., & Tremblay, M.S. (2011). Physical activity of Canadian adults: Accelerometer results from the 2007 to 2009. Canadian Health Measures Survey, Health Reports/Statistics Canada, *Canadian Centre for Health Information/Cent. Can. Inf. sur la Santé, 22*, 7–14.
6 Tison, G.H., Avram, R., Kuhar, P., Abreau, S., Marcus, G.M., Pletcher, M.J., & Olgin, J.E. (2020). Worldwide effect of COVID-19 on physical activity: A descriptive study. *Annals of Internal Medicine, 173*(9), 767–70. https://doi.org/10.7326/M20-2665.
7 CAMH (2020, October 14). COVID-19 pandemic adversely affecting mental health of women and people with children. https://www.camh.ca/en/camh-news-and -stories/covid-19-pandemic-adversely-affecting-mental-health-of-women-and -people-with-children.

8 Silver, L. (2019, February 5). Smartphone ownership is growing rapidly around the world, but not always equally. *Pew Research Center's Global Attitudes Project.* https://www.pewresearch.org/global/2019/02/05/smartphone-ownership-is-growing-rapidly-around-the-world-but-not-always-equally/.

9 Grand View Research. (2019, June). mHealth apps market size, share & trends analysis report by type (fitness, lifestyle management, nutrition & diet, women's health, medication adherence, healthcare providers/payers), and segment forecasts, 2019–2026.

10 Silver (2019, February 5).

11 Research2Guidance. (2017). *mHealth economics 2017 report: Current status and future trends in mobile health.* Research2Guidance. https://research2guidance.com/product/mhealth-economics-2017-current-status-and-future-trends-in-mobile-health/.

12 Ibid.

13 Willis Towers Watson. (2018). *23rd Annual Best Practices in Health Care Employer Survey.* Willis Towers Watson. https://www.willistowerswatson.com/-/media/WTW/Insights/2018/10/wtw-23rd-annual-best-practices-in-health-care-employer-survey-executive-summary.pdf.

14 Ibid.

15 Mercer. (2019). *How benefits are shaping the future of work: 2019 Europe corporate wellness trends.*

16 Mitchell, M.S., Orstad, S.L., Biswas, A., Oh, P.I., Jay, M., Pakosh, M.T., & Faulkner, G. (2020). Financial incentives for physical activity in adults: Systematic review and meta-analysis. *British Journal of Sports Medicine, 54*(21), 1259–68. https://doi.org/10.1136/bjsports-2019-100633.

17 Camerer, C.F., & Loewenstein, G. (2003). Behavioral economics: Past, present, future. In *Advances in behavioral economics* (pp. 1–61). Princeton University Press. https://resolver.caltech.edu/CaltechAUTHORS:20110204-152338626.

18 Ibid.

19 Ibid.

20 Mitchell, Orstad, et al. (2020).

21 Mitchell, M., Lau, E., White, L., & Faulkner, G. (2020). Commercial app use linked with sustained physical activity in two Canadian provinces: A 12-month quasi-experimental study. *International Journal of Behavioral Nutrition and Physical Activity, 17*(1), 24. https://doi.org/10.1186/s12966-020-00926-7.

22 Rondina, R. II, Pearson, E.K., Prapavessis, H., White, L., Richard, S., & Mitchell, M.S. (2020). Bright spots, physical activity investments that (almost) worked: Carrot Rewards app, driving engagement with pennies a day. *British Journal of Sports Medicine, 54*(15), 927–9. https://doi.org/10.1136/bjsports-2019-100969.

23 Promberger, M., & Marteau, T.M. (2013). When do financial incentives reduce intrinsic motivation? Comparing behaviors studied in psychological and economic literatures. *Health Psychology, 32*(9), 950. https://doi.org/10.1037/a0032727.

24 Mitchell, Orstad, et al. (2020).

25 Deci, E.L., & Ryan, R.M. (2004). *Handbook of self-determination research.* University of Rochester Press.

26 Mitchell, M.S., Goodman, J.M., Alter, D.A., Oh, P.I., & Faulkner, G.E.J. (2015). Development of the Health Incentive Program Questionnaire (HIP-Q) in a cardiac rehabilitation population. *Translational Behavioral Medicine, 5*(4), 443–59. https://doi.org/10.1007/s13142-015-0330-3.

27 Prochaska, J.O., & Velicer, W.F. (1997). The transtheoretical model of health behavior change. *American Journal of Health Promotion, 12*(1), 38–48. https://doi.org/10.4278/0890-1171-12.1.38.

Increasing Blood and Plasma Donations: Behavioral and Ethical Scalability

Nicola Lacetera and Mario Macis

KEY IDEA

Blood banks around the world often struggle to collect sufficient quantities of blood, plasma, and other blood components to meet the needs of the large and growing number of patients who rely on transfusions and blood-derived therapies for their survival. Several blood collection organizations have explored the use of both behavioral nudges and economic incentives, with varying degrees of success. Economic incentives are often perceived as being in conflict with the core mission of blood banks, with donors' altruistic motivation, and, more generally, with moral values. Research, however, shows that properly designed economic incentives do boost donations. In some countries, moreover, paying donors is legal. In the United States, for example, plasma donors receive financial compensation, and the plasma industry is a thriving business that results in 70% of the world supply of plasma-derived therapies. In fact, millions of patients in countries that do not allow payment to plasma donors rely on imports of life-saving, plasma-derived medicinal products from the US. In this chapter, we begin by describing the unique features of the "market" for blood and blood components, emphasizing the mix of moral and material motivations that typically characterizes donors, and the mission-driven nature of blood-collecting organizations. Next, we report findings from empirical research that studied the impact of behavioral nudges and economic incentives provided to blood and plasma donors, with focus on the effects of these interventions on the quantity and quality of collections as well as on donor motivation. By comparing and contrasting donations of whole blood for transfusion (a largely altruistic system chronically affected by shortages) with donations of plasma for the production of medical therapies (a large-scale business that reliably supplies millions of patients around the world), we discuss the tradeoffs that societies face when deciding how to organize the procurement of blood and plasma. Similar to Chapter 14 on healthy eating nudges, we also discuss the importance of assessing the public's opinion as an input into the legislative and regulatory deliberations, particularly concerning the role of and limits to market-based incentives and mechanisms.

INTRODUCTION

The American Association of Blood Banks estimates that, annually, about seven million people donate whole blood in the United States, with about 13.6 million units of whole blood and red blood cells collected. Blood donors are generally unpaid, and giving blood is viewed as a virtuous, selfless act performed by generous individuals who want to save lives. Yet, despite the involvement of many individuals (donors, health workers) and organizations, it has proven difficult to guarantee that the availability of blood for transfusions satisfies the needs of patients. In particular, although the need for blood is roughly constant throughout the year, its availability is often seasonal, and the maximum storage for blood is only a few weeks. Temporary and longer-term shortages are often severe in middle- and low-income countries. Alongside this system of altruistic whole blood donations, a market for a blood component, plasma, exists in the United States. Plasma, the liquid part of blood that remains after removing red blood cells, white blood cells, platelets, and other cellular components, can be directly transfused as well as used for the production of therapies to treat patients with chronic diseases and disorders such as primary immunodeficiency, hemophilia, and genetic lung disease. The global need for plasma-derived therapies (PDTs) is large and growing. In the United States, plasma donors receive financial compensation – between $20 and $50 per donation. In 2019, five million donors made a total of 53.5 million donations of plasma in the US. This supply far exceeds domestic needs, and exports of PDTs account for 1.6% of total annual US exports.[1] Apart from a few exceptions, most countries run a constant deficit of plasma for therapeutic uses. In fact, many countries where plasma donors are not paid rely on PDTs produced with paid-for plasma from the US to meet the needs of their patients.

The objective of this chapter is threefold. First, we describe the different institutional arrangements and underlying behavioral considerations that characterize the systems of procurement and allocation of blood and plasma, including the implications for the supply and availability of these life-saving products. Second, we review the evidence on behaviorally informed policies and interventions to motivate the donation of blood and plasma with various incentives that lie between the sole reliance on altruism on the one hand and the use of monetary payments on the other. Third, we stress that, especially when it comes to transactions concerning the human body or its parts, the selection of the most effective institutional regime does not respond only to behavioral considerations about individual motivations. The legal status and regulation of these transactions depends also on the societal support for exchanges to occur through a market mechanism as opposed to other arrangements not based on prices. Concerns about individual exploitation, coercion, or unfairness, as well as about the violation of "sacred values" such as human dignity, characterize many transactions, but they are particularly salient if a transaction concerns the human body. The consideration of these ethical dimensions adds layers of complexity for public and organizational policies meant to encourage blood and plasma donations, and require the solution of additional tradeoffs in the decision process. We discuss these issues first with reference to blood and then with reference to plasma. Finally, we further elaborate on political and organizational challenges in balancing economic, behavioral, and ethical considerations in the institutional design of the procurement and allocation of blood and plasma.

BLOOD PROCUREMENT: GRATUITY, INCENTIVES, AND A LABORATORY OF BEHAVIORAL INTERVENTIONS

Blood transfusions allow medical providers to address emergencies such as massive blood loss due to trauma, blood replacement during surgeries, and the treatment of premature babies, as well as to treat certain types of cancer and blood-related diseases. Population ageing and the increase in surgical procedures such as organ transplants are further increasing the demand for blood.

Interventions targeting altruistic motives. According to the guidelines of the World Health Organization (WHO), the objective of national blood procurement and allocation systems is to "obtain all blood supplies from voluntary non-remunerated donors."[2] There are several ethical and behavioral foundations at the origin of this stance. The first and most important one is a strong reliance on the power of altruism as a motivator of blood donation. In fact, in this particular case, all the various ways in which scholars have defined and interpreted altruistic motivations may play an important role, compounding the positive effects. People might help others because of a genuine desire to increase their well-being, even at the expense of their own. In his 1759 book *The Theory of Moral Sentiments*, Adam Smith claims that this "virtue of beneficence" derives from a natural human "sympathy." Individuals may derive a benefit from the act *itself* of giving, rather than from (or in addition to) the increased welfare of the recipients; behavioral scientists call this tendency "warm glow" or "impure altruism." Another strong underlying source of altruistic behavior is the desire to signal to others (or to oneself) that one is a "good person," and to improve one's reputation or prestige in a community. Yet another source of altruism derives from reciprocal feelings, whereby a person behaves altruistically with the expectation that the recipient will reciprocate in the future should the need and opportunity arise.

Blood banks routinely leverage one or more of these sources of altruistic motivations, and a few studies have investigated their effectiveness. In Sweden, for example, in 2015 Stockholm's blood service began to send text messages to blood donors to inform them that a recent transfusion included the blood they had recently donated. The objective of this and similar campaigns is to lever-age on multiple altruistic drivers: the desire to help others, "warm glow," and boosting donors' self-esteem. Evidence from random-ized experiments shows some positive effects of these initiatives,[3] but also some backfiring,[4] because the message may actually "exhaust," for example, the need for self-esteem instead of stimu-lating more altruistic activities. The largest organ donor organiza-tion in Italy rewards donors who have reached certain donation milestones with pins and medals of symbolic value. In some cases, rewards are handed out in a public ceremony. Evidence from these programs shows a particularly strong reaction, in terms of donation frequency, to the provision of "public" symbolic rewards, indicating that social-image concerns are likely to be relevant in this context.[5] In a related context, i.e., promoting organ donation, organ procure-ment agencies have also leveraged people's sense of reciprocity. In Canada, for example, Trillium Gift of Life and Service Ontario have introduced new signup forms that promote reciprocal altruism with the question *"If you needed a transplant would you have one?"*[6]

Interventions applying economic incentives. The second key behavioral claim at the basis of the promotion of purely altruistic donations is that material rewards or compensation might actually have, in the case of altruistic activities in general and the donation of body parts and fluids in particular, perverse effects that do not correspond to the "rational agent" view according to which the higher the reward for an activity, the more an individual will make an effort in that task. In his 1970 book *The Gift Relationship*, Brit-ish scholar Richard Titmuss claimed that material rewards might change a donor's perception of the nature of their act from being altruistic to resembling a market exchange. This could reduce peo-ple's altruistic drive without a counterbalancing increase in material incentives (especially if the amount of the reward is small). Titmuss also argued that monetary incentives would attract donors with a higher risk of carrying infectious diseases; monetary rewards are appealing especially to low-income individuals who are, in turn, more likely to be affected by blood-transmissible diseases (e.g., because they engage in unhealthy lifestyles and risky behaviors). Moreover, he was concerned that compensation for an activity like blood donation would erode prevailing values in society, such as a "sense of community," and could therefore spread negative moral consequences on society overall. The World Health Organization's appeal to a fully unpaid blood procurement system also refers to the risk of erosion of overall moral values in society.[7]

The strong objections to providing any form of compensation to blood donors, therefore, derives from multiple considerations and concerns. At the same time, both in the Western world and even more so in low- and middle-income countries, guaranteeing the availability of blood for transfusions to satisfy immediate needs has proven difficult. The seasonality of the blood supply compared to the constant need, moreover, adds to the difficulty of keeping an adequate inventory level. Even in contexts where the organization of procurement and allocation is very advanced, therefore, relying on and eliciting altruism is often insufficient to cover the demand for blood.

This conundrum has stimulated legislative and organizational efforts to devise incentive programs that would minimize potential "crowding out" effects as well as address ethical concerns and gain social support. In Italy, for example, employees have the right to a paid day off work on the day they donate. We investigated the effectiveness of this policy, and found that those who benefit from it (employees as opposed to, for example, self-employed individuals or people out of the labor force) donate more frequently.[8] This implicit economic incentive, however, is expensive (we estimated that each additional unit of blood collected thanks to the day-off incentive would cost about 400 Euros) and may perhaps not be "scalable" to other contexts. In the United States, American Red Cross blood drives sometimes offer rewards such as t-shirts, lottery tickets, and gift cards to those who donate. In a retrospective study of about 14,000 in Ohio, and in a large randomized controlled trial with about 100,000 individuals again in collaboration with the ARC in Ohio, together with Bob Slonim we found that these rewards did increase show-ups and actual donations, with rewards of higher economic value resulting in more additional donations than rewards of smaller value. There was no impact on deferral rates (percentage of donors who turned out not eligible to donate), our measure of the "quality" of donors. We also found that part of the increase in donations at blood drives offering rewards came from a reduction in turnout at neighboring blood drives that were not offering any extra incentive to donate. Moreover, people modified the timing of their donations, switching them to coincide with periods when incentives were provided.[9] If, on the one hand, these additional findings highlight the importance of carefully distributing rewards across geographic areas in order to avoid competition among drives (which might result in cannibal-ization with small or no net increases in donations), on the other hand the temporal effects imply that the use of rewards in peri-ods with lower seasonal supply might help reduce the imbalances when this is a more pressing need. Our calculations indicated that small economic rewards increase donations in a cost-effective way. For example, the cost of one extra unit of whole blood collected using a $5 gift card as an incentive was $22.[10] In recent years, the American Red Cross has offered gift cards with a large array of use (e.g., Amazon.com cards) during periods of low supply, for exam-ple in the winter season. In an intervention that we conducted in collaboration with an Argentine blood bank, together with Victor Iyaja and Bob Slonim, we found again that gift cards motivated additional donations, whereas social-image stimuli, that is, t-shirts with designs that indicated that the owner was a blood donor, were not effective in this context.[11] Evidence from similar trials in Switzerland show that lottery tickets were an effective motivator for blood donors, whereas offering a free cholesterol test was not.[12] More recently, one study found positive and sizeable effects from offering free, comprehensive health check-ups to blood donors in Germany.[13]

There are a few common features in these different interventions and initiatives. First, the rewards are often offered one time only or in sporadic fashion. Second, the incentives, even when they have economic value, are typically in-kind, not direct cash. Third, donors usually qualify for the rewards by only presenting to a donation center, and not if they actually donate. Fourth, the framing of the rewards is typically that of a gift or a "thank you" rather than a pay-ment for a service rendered.[14]

Overall, the evidence that we discussed demonstrates that certain explicit incentives do not have negative consequences in terms of quantity and quality of collections. People respond in a rather standard way (e.g., higher-value rewards have bigger effects than lower-value rewards), even in the case of this archetypal altruistic activity. The fact that several organizations and jurisdictions allow and make broad use of (appropriately framed) economic reward incentive programs suggests that there are opportunities to leverage on other motives in addition to altruism, in a way that is socially and ethically acceptable.

THE MARKET FOR PLASMA

Plasma is the liquid part of blood that remains after removing red blood cells, white blood cells, platelets, and other cellular components.[15] There are some differences between plasma and whole blood in terms of how the donation occurs, and, especially, in how the two products are used. Whole blood is primarily used for transfusion, the donation takes between 10 and 20 minutes, and donors must wait at least 56 days between consecutive donations. Although plasma is also used for direct transfusion (e.g., in about 15% of Newborn Intensive Care Unit [NICU] patients to prevent bleeding),[16] most of the plasma collected goes into manufacturing plasma-derived therapies (PDTs). Millions of patients around the world rely on PDTs, and the global market for these therapies was estimated to be worth about $25.7 billion in 2018 and is projected to grow to $35.5 billion by 2023.[17] The treatment of some diseases requires a large number of plasma donations – for example, up to 900 per year for genetic emphysema, and up to 1,200 for hemophilia.

During a plasma donation, blood is drawn from one arm and channeled through a machine that filters the plasma and returns the remaining blood components to the donor. The procedure can take between one and three *hours* – so significantly longer than a blood donation. Because a donor receives back their red blood cells and platelets, they may donate plasma more frequently than whole blood – up to twice per week in the United States.

Paying plasma donors is illegal in most countries around the world. There are four countries that allow it: Austria, the Czech Republic, Germany, and the United States. These are also the only countries that are self-sufficient in their supply of many PDTs.[18]

In the United States, plasma donors receive between $20 and $50 per donation. The payment is often framed as a reward for the donor's time and effort.[19] Some plasma banks devise compensation schemes that reward regular, high-frequency donors, for example with bonuses for those who give twice per week. Some advertise that "donors can earn up to $700 a month" from giving plasma.[20] In the United States, more than 50 million plasma donations are made annually.[21] About 70% of the immunoglobulin used in Australia and Canada derives from paid plasma donors from the United States. Similarly, in Europe several countries rely on PDTs imported from Germany or the United States.[22]

Because of the rising demand for PDTs, many countries are searching for strategies to increase their supply of source plasma. In recent years, attempts to introduce paid plasma centers in Australia and Canada prompted heated public debates, and in some cases, legislative action by policymakers. Canada had no paid plasma centers until 2016. In 2012, a plasma company announced plans to open in Ontario, but two years later, the provincial government passed legislation prohibiting payments to plasma donors. Between 2016 and 2017, commercial plasma centers opened in the provinces of Manitoba, New Brunswick, and Saskatchewan.[23] Following this, several provinces introduced legislation to prohibit compensation for plasma donors, and recently there has been a debate about banning compensation for plasma donors at the federal level.[24] Opponents of paid plasma justify the ban on compensation by citing similar reasons to those discussed in the realm of whole blood donations above: safety concerns and ethical issues related to exploitation of the poor and vulnerable.

Yet, countries that prohibit payments are not self-sufficient and rely on imported PDTs from countries that do pay plasma donors. So, the ethical argument is not fully consistent. What is more, relying on imports is costly and increases the risk of facing shortages, for example in the case of international supply chain disruptions.[25]

In the face of such a dilemma, it is important to understand how the citizens of a country perceive the tradeoffs involved and how they reason about whether or not to allow donors to be paid. Evidence about the degree of social support (or disapproval) for morally controversial transactions is scant. In recent work, we studied the attitudes of a representative sample of Canadian citizens towards paying plasma donors.[26] We found that a large majority of respondents (70%) support paying plasma donors in Canada. The highest-rated motive for legalizing plasma-donor compensation was to guarantee a stronger domestic supply. The majority of respondents who were in favor of legalizing compensation believed that paying donors would not run against mainstream Canadian moral and societal values.[27]

CONCLUSION: IL FAUT CHOISIR – WE HAVE TO CHOOSE!

Table 16.1 summarizes the main findings of the field experiments referenced in our chapter. While the table gives an overview of what interventions have been tested and to what extent they have worked, it does not answer the question of whether societies should organize the procurement of blood and blood components as a purely altruistic system, or whether they should rely on prices and the market mechanism. The answer is not obvious; it varies across and within countries, it depends on a complex set of considerations, and it involves important tradeoffs. Also, hybrid systems that leverage the "good" of each approach while avoiding the "bad" might be achievable.

Despite the similarities of the collection processes and the underlying individual motivations to donate blood and plasma, the organization of the procurement and allocation of these two life-saving products has evolved in different directions. In the case of blood, most if not all national systems interpret and regulate the donation activity as voluntary and non-remunerated. In order to enhance donations and address shortages, various countries and organizations, often in collaboration with behavioral scientists, have introduced programs to emphasize certain motives or provide additional

Table 16.1. Overview of referenced field study findings

Study	Method and sample	Incentives/Nudges	Outcome variable(s)	Findings	
				Quantity	Safety
English and Jaworski (*Unpublished manuscript 2020*)	Observational data. City-level data on plasma and whole blood donations in selected cities in Canada and the United States,	Introduction of commercial (paid) plasma banks in three US and three Canadian cities.	Donations of plasma and whole blood.	Positive effect on plasma donation. No displacement effects on (unpaid) whole blood donation.	No effect of paid plasma on quality of plasma or whole blood collected.
Goette et al. (*Transfusion 2009*)	Field experiment. N=2,825 non-donors; N=8,269 Red Cross donors in Switzerland.	Cholesterol test.	Individual blood donations.	No effect.	N/A
Gemelli et al. (*Transfusion 2018*)	Field experiment. N=2605 whole blood donors in Australia.	Donors received a post-donation SMS informing them that their blood had been utilized.	Blood donation within 12 months since the intervention.	Positive effect of the SMS on returning to donate.	N/A
Goette and Tripodi (*JEBO 2020*)	Field experiment. N=8,591 blood donors in Italy.	Donors were provided feedback (by e-mail) on successful utilization of their blood donation.	Blood donation within 7 months since the intervention.	Negative effect on subsequent donations.	N/A

Study	Setting/Sample	Incentive	Outcome measure	Effect on donations	Effect on rejected/ineligible
Goette and Stutzer (*JEBO* 2020)	Natural field experiment. N=12,268 Red Cross blood donors in Switzerland	Lottery ticket (CHF5, US$4.30) cholesterol test.	Individual usable donations, rejected donations.	Positive effect of lottery tickets on usable donations. No effect of cholesterol test. No reduction in donations after the experiment.	No effect of lottery on rejected donations.
Iajya et al. (*Soc Sci and Med* 2013)	Field experiment. N=17,238 randomly selected subjects in Argentina.	AR$20/60/100 (US$5/15/25) supermarket vouchers, t-shirt, newspaper mention.	Individual blood donations, ineligible donors, rejected donations.	Positive effect of AR$60/100 vouchers. No effect of other incentives.	No effect of incentives on ineligible/ rejected.
Lacetera and Macis (*JEBO* 2010)	Observational data. N=2009 Italian blood donors observed in 2002-06.	Symbolic awards (medals) given to donors when they reach certain donation quotas. Some medals are awarded privately whereas other medals are given in a public ceremony.	Interval between consecutive individual blood donations.	Positive effect of publicly awarded medals (increased frequency of donation as the threshold for earning the medals approach).	N/A
Lacetera, Macis, Slonim (*AEJ* 2012)	Observational data. N=13,707 American Red Cross drives in N. Ohio.	Material gifts (T-shirts, coupons, mugs, sweaters, jackets, beach blankets, coolers, etc.).	Drive-level turnout, usable units, deferrals.	Positive effect on turnout and usable units, increasing in the value of the reward.	No effect of incentives on deferral rates.
Lacetera, Macis, Slonim (**Man Sci 2014**)	Field experiment. N=98,278 American Red Cross donors in N. Ohio.	$5/10/15 gift cards.	Individual usable blood donations.	Positive effect, increasing in the value of the reward.	N/A

(Continued)

Table 16.1. Continued

Study	Method and sample	Incentives/Nudges	Outcome variable(s)	Findings	
				Quantity	Safety
Lacetera and Macis (*JLEO 2013*)	Observational data. N=289 Italian blood donors observed in 1985-89 and 2002-06.	One-day paid leave of absence from work.	Individual blood donations.	Positive effect (donations increase from 2 per year to 3 per year).	N/A
Leipnitz et al. (*IJRM 2018*)	Field experiments. N = 53,257 and N = 31,522 German Red Cross blood donors.	Donors were offered a comprehensive blood health check.	Individual blood donations.	Positive effect. No evidence of "wear out" effects from multiple exposure to the incentive.	N/A
Robitaille et al. (*J Marketing 2021*)	Field experiment. N = 3,330 prospective organ donor registrants.	Four behavioral interventions: (1) information brochure, (2) reciprocal altruism persuasive message, (3) first-person emotional perspective-taking message, (4) third-person emotional perspective-taking message.	Decision to register as an organ donor.	Positive effect of information brochure and reciprocal altruism persuasive message.	N/A
English & Jaworski (2020)	Observational data. City-level data on plasma and whole blood donations in selected cities in Canada and the United States	Introduction of commercial (paid) plasma banks in three US and three Canadian cities	Donations of plasma and whole blood	Positive effect on plasma donation. No displacement effects on (unpaid) whole blood donation	No effect of paid plasma on quality of plasma or whole blood collected

Study	Sample/Design	Intervention	Outcome	Effect	
Goette et al. (2009)	Field experiment. N=2,825 non-donors; N=8,269 Red Cross donors in Switzerland	Cholesterol test	Individual blood donations	No effect	N/A
Gemelli et al. (2018)	Field experiment. N=2605 whole blood donors in Australia	Donors received a post-donation text message informing them that their blood had been utilized	Blood donation within 12 months since the intervention	Positive effect of the SMS on returning to donate	N/A
Goette & Tripodi (2020)	Field experiment. N=8,591 blood donors in Italy	Donors were provided feedback (by email) on successful utilization of their blood donation	Blood donation within seven months since the intervention	Negative effect on subsequent donations	N/A
Goette & Stutzer (2020)	Natural field experiment. N= 12,268 Red Cross blood donors in Switzerland	Lottery ticket (CHF5, US$4.30) cholesterol test	Individual usable donations, rejected donations	Positive effect of lottery tickets on usable donations. No effect of cholesterol test. No reduction in donations after the experiment	No effect of lottery on rejected donations
Iajya et al. (2013)	Field experiment. N=17,238 randomly selected subjects in Argentina.	AR$20/60/100 (US$5/15/25) supermarket vouchers, t-shirts, newspaper mentions	Individual blood donations, ineligible donors, rejected donations	Positive effect of AR$60/100 vouchers. No effect of other incentives	No effect of incentives on ineligible/ rejected

(Continued)

Table 16.1. Continued

Study	Method and sample	Incentives/Nudges	Outcome variable(s)	Findings	
				Quantity	Safety
Lacetera & Macis (2010)	Observational data. N=2009 Italian blood donors observed in 2002–6	Symbolic awards (medals) given to donors when they reach certain donation quotas. Some medals are awarded privately whereas other medals are given in a public ceremony.	Interval between consecutive individual blood donations	Positive effect of publicly awarded medals (increased frequency of donation as the threshold for earning the medals approaches)	N/A
Lacetera, Macis, & Slonim (2012)	Observational data. N=13,707 American Red Cross drives in N. Ohio	Material gifts (T-shirts, coupons, mugs, sweaters, jackets, beach blankets, coolers, etc.)	Drive-level turnout, usable units, deferrals	Positive effect on turnout and usable units, increasing in the value of the reward	No effect of incentives on deferral rates
Lacetera, Macis, & Slonim (2014)	Field experiment. N=98,278 American Red Cross donors in N. Ohio	$5/10/15 gift cards	Individual usable blood donations	Positive effect, increasing in the value of the reward	N/A

Lacetera & Macis (2013)	Observational data. N=289 Italian blood donors observed in 1985–9 and 2002–6	One-day paid leave of absence from work	Individual blood donations	Positive effect (donations increase from two per year to three per year)	N/A
Leipnitz et al. (2018)	Field experiments. N = 53,257 and N = 31,522 German Red Cross blood donors	Donors were offered a comprehensive blood health check.	Individual blood donations	Positive effect. No evidence of "wear out" effects from multiple exposure to the incentive	N/A
Robitaille et al. (2021)	Field experiment. N = 3,330 prospective organ donor registrants	Four behavioral interventions: (1) information brochure, (2) reciprocal altruism persuasive message, (3) first-person emotional perspective-taking message, (4) third-person emotional perspective-taking message	Decision to register as an organ donor	Positive effect of information brochure and reciprocal altruism persuasive message	N/A

economic rewards beyond the altruistic drive of donors. For plasma, in some countries (notably the United States), a large for-profit collection industry that relies on compensated donors coexists with a non-profit system of non-remunerated donations. Although plasma donor compensation and the operation of for-profit plasma collection entities is legal only in some jurisdictions, the plasma collected from compensated donors is exported to countries who do not allow it because the latter suffer systematic domestic supply shortages.

At a first look, there seem to be many contradictions both between and *within* the organization of the procurement and allocation of the two products. Why, for example, have most countries converged on a voluntary non-remunerated system for the donation of blood, but not for plasma? And why do countries that prohibit compensation for plasma donors allow the import of pharmaceuticals made out of plasma coming from paid donors?

In fact, these differences are not necessarily surprising, given the varieties of economic, behavioral, and ethical issues that surround these activities. Unlike whole blood, for example, plasma is used not only for direct transfusions but also as a key input in many therapeutic products. As such, the (for profit) pharmaceutical industry is an integral part in the supply chain and the whole organizational and institutional ecosystem. Moreover, the quantity of plasma needed for the production of these therapies is massive. The introduction of a set of actors with different legal statuses, objectives, and incentives, and the sheer size of the supply requirements, imply the consideration of a more complex set of behavioral issues, as well as the need to balance different moral principles that societies recognize as important in the way the human body and its parts are treated. We should expect, as a consequence, to observe different regulatory regimes coexisting and interacting with each other. Regarding whole-blood donation, the widespread reliance on a non-remunerated supply did not prevent several countries and organizations from experimenting with and successfully developing behaviorally informed interventions that would elicit motivations beyond altruism alone, while remaining within the WHO guidelines and being ethically viable and socially supported.

In 2018, Health Canada released the report "Immune Globulin Product Supply and Related Impacts" that an ad hoc expert panel elaborated on. The objective of this report was to assess Canada's immune globulin product supply, the effect of the expansion of plasma collection capabilities in the country, and practices in other countries. A key, overall conclusion of the report resonates with our own beliefs after years of research in this area: guaranteeing a steady supply of blood and plasma entails complex choices that need to balance health requirements with economic and moral viability and scalability. Interventions based on insights from behavioral sciences have proven to be fruitful ways to address these delicate balances and at scale in the wild. Properly designed surveys and experiments, in addition, allow for the assessing of public opinions about the moral and social acceptability of various initiatives and regulatory choices concerning the organization of the supply and allocation of blood and plasma. For example, in our study of Canadians' attitudes towards paying plasma donors, we found no evidence of widespread societal opposition, somewhat in contrast with the recent legislative bans on compensation in several provinces.[28] The ultimate choices, of course, reside with the legislative and regulatory authorities of a country; because of the complexities that we described, different regulatory frameworks between jurisdictions or even between products within the same jurisdiction have emerged. Behaviorally informed interventions and the ability to test the "pulse" of public opinion are essential ingredients for well-founded, informed deliberations.

NOTES

1 *Economist* (2018, May 12). America's booming blood-plasma industry.
2 See WHO (2009). Report on Global Consultation: 100% voluntary non-remunerated donation of blood and blood components, Melbourne, Australia, 9 to 11 June 2009 (Geneva); and WHO (2012). Expert consensus statement on achieving self-sufficiency in safe blood and blood products, based on voluntary non-remunerated blood donation (VNRBD), Geneva.
3 Gemelli, C.N., Carver, A., Garn, A., Wright, S.T., & Davison, T.E. (2018). Evaluation of the impact of a personalized post donation short messaging service on the retention of whole blood donors. *Transfusion, 58*(3), 701–9.

4 Goette, L., & Tripodi, E. (2020). Does positive feedback of social impact motivate prosocial behavior? A field experiment with blood donors. *Journal of Economic Behavior & Organization*, 175, 1–8.

5 Lacetera, N., & Macis, M. (2010). Social image concerns and prosocial behavior: Field evidence from a nonlinear incentive scheme. *Journal of Economic Behavior & Organization*, 76(2), 225–37.

6 Robitaille, N., Mazar, N., Tsai, C.I., Haviv, A., & Hardy, E. (2021). Increasing organ donor registrations with behavioral interventions: A field experiment. *Journal of Marketing*, 85(3), 168–83. https://doi.org/10.1177%2F0022242921990070.

7 See WHO (2009); and WHO (2012).

8 Lacetera, N., & Macis, M. (2013). Time for blood: The effect of paid leave legislation on altruistic behavior. *Journal of Law, Economics, & Organization*, 29(6), 1384–1420; Lacetera, N., Macis, M. and Slonim, R. (2012). "Will there be blood? Incentives and substitution effects in pro-social behavior." *American Economic Journal: Economic Policy*, 4(1), 186–223.

9 See Lacetera, Macis, & Slonim (2012); and Lacetera, N., Macis, M., and Slonim, R. (2014). Rewarding volunteers: A field experiment. *Management Science*, 60(5), 1107–29.

10 Lacetera, Macis, & Slonim (2014).

11 Iajya, V., Lacetera, N., Macis, M., and Slonim, R. (2013). The effects of information, social and financial incentives on voluntary undirected blood donations: Evidence from a field experiment in Argentina. *Social Science & Medicine*, 98, 214–23.

12 Goette, L., Stutzer, A., Yavuzcan, G., & Frey, B.M. (2009). Free cholesterol testing as a motivation device in blood donations: Evidence from field experiments. *Transfusion*, 49(3), 524–31; Goette, L., and Stutzer, A. (2020). Blood donations and incentives: Evidence from a field experiment. *Journal of Economic Behavior & Organization*, 170, 52–74.

13 Leipnitz, S., de Vries, M., Clement, M., & Mazar, N. (2018). Providing health checks as incentives to retain blood donors – Evidence from two field experiments. *International Journal of Research in Marketing*, 35(4), 628–40.

14 Lacetera, N., Macis, M., & Slonim, R. (2013). Economic rewards to motivate blood donations. *Science*, 340(6135), 927–8.

15 See https://www.redcrossblood.org/donate-blood/dlp/plasma-information.html (last accessed February 27, 2021).

16 Keir, A.K., & Stanworth, S.J. (2016). Neonatal plasma transfusion: an evidence-based review. *Transfusion Medicine Reviews*, 30(4), 174–82.

17 See https://www.grifolsplasma.com/en/about-plasma-donation/plasma-a-source-of-life (last accessed February 27, 2021).

18 English, W., & Jaworski, P.M. (2020). The introduction of paid plasma in Canada and the US has not decreased unpaid blood donations. Available at SSRN.

19 See, for example, https://plasma.prometic.com/why-donate-plasma/ (last accessed February 27, 2021).

20 See https://www.cslplasma.com/rewards-for-current-donors (last accessed February 27, 2021).

21 See https://www.statista.com/statistics/756229/number-of-annual-plasma-collections-in-the-us/ (last accessed February 27, 2021).

22 "To date, Italy cannot yet be defined as self-sufficient in terms of plasma collection. Italy today depends on foreign countries from which it imports plasma-derived medicines." https://fidas.it/tag/plasmaderivati/ (last accessed February 27, 2021).

23 English & Jaworski (2020).

24 See Canadian Press (2016, January 15). NDP: Plasma clinics that pay donors should be banned by federal government, *Huffington Post*. http://www.huffingtonpost .ca/2016/01/15/ndp-wants-federal-ban-on-plasma-clinics-that-pay-donors-but -saskatchewan-oks-it_n_8992022.html.

25 Referring to Australia, Robert Slonim reports that "The National Blood Authority's 2016–2017 annual report indicates Australian imports of immunoglobulin, a plasma component, provide 44% of domestic demand. This costs A$120 million while the remaining 56% comes from domestic supply costing A$413 million. This implies the domestic supply of immunoglobulin costs over three times more per unit than what is imported, despite domestic donors not being compensated ... A competitive domestic market should successfully develop following the international market model, would provide new business opportunities and allow compensation to land in Australian rather than international donors' pockets." https://theconversation .com/how-australia-can-fix-the-market-for-plasma-and-save-millions-101609 (last accessed 27 February, 2021).

26 Lacetera, N., & Macis, M. (2018). *Moral NIMBY-ism? Understanding societal support for monetary compensation to plasma donors in Canada* (No. w24572). National Bureau of Economic Research.

27 Among the roughly 30% of Canadians who disapproved of plasma donor compensation, the majority cited moral concerns related to the exploitation of the poor and violation of human dignity, and safety concerns.

28 More recently, Al Roth and Stephanie Wang also found a disconnect between popular attitudes towards morally contested transactions (prostitution, gestational surrogacy, and global kidney exchange) and their legal and regulatory status. Roth and Wang note that "Because both markets and bans on markets require social support to work well, this sheds light on the prospects for effective regulation of controversial markets." Roth, A.E., & Wang, S.W. (2020). Popular repugnance contrasts with legal bans on controversial markets. *Proceedings of the National Academy of Sciences*, 117(33), 19792–8.

CHAPTER SEVENTEEN

Evidence-Based Interventions for Financial Well-Being

Daniel Fernandes

Money concerns are detrimental for well-being. A recent study found that about 40% of one's overall well-being is explained by financial well-being.[1] By social science conventions, variables that can explain more than 25% of the variance in an outcome are considered as having a large effect. This means that a large portion of the differences in overall well-being across people are explained by their differences in financial well-being. But to give a sense of how large the effect is, other important domains of life such as one's job, relationship, and health together explain about as much as financial well-being alone.

Most people suffer or will suffer because of money problems. Recent surveys suggest that about 60% of Americans now live paycheck to paycheck, and one in four have had problems paying their bills since the pandemic outbreak. Before the pandemic, only about half of Americans had the savings on hand to handle an emergency expense of $1,000 outside their budgets. Most people are very much aware of the importance of building emergency savings, but, despite all good intentions, fail to do so (a prime example of the intention-action gap).

For practitioners and organizations interested in improving the state of people's financial well-being, this chapter reviews the impact and effectiveness of four of the most commonly applied interventions: financial education, rules of thumb (heuristics), planning prompts, and peer influence.

FINANCIAL EDUCATION

How big is the effect of financial education interventions? A popular response to the lack of financial well-being is to try to improve financial literacy through, for example, a household finance course offering in high school or financial counseling. One reason to think this solution will help is that many people score low in financial literacy, and those who score high are typically better at saving for retirement and staying out of debt. It seems intuitive then that financial literacy would help people make better decisions. Unfortunately, a recent meta-analysis found that financial literacy educational interventions only have a small effect on improving financial behavior.[2] Their average effect size was about 0.064 standard deviations. Interventions with effect sizes of less than 0.1 standard deviations are considered as having a small effect by social science conventions. The study also found that interventions that are closer in time to the actual behavior that one is trying to improve produce stronger effects. A seminar or course at the workplace for new employees will not be present in their minds several years later when they are deciding what mortgage to take and whether to sign up for automatic savings transfers for retirement. The timing of interventions therefore matters.

A few of the education interventions in that meta-analysis were experiments, where instead of students self-selecting to receive financial education, participants were randomly assigned to either receive financial education or not. Those studies have more information value, as they provide the causal effect of financial education. Since then, a lot of new research has studied the effect of financial education using experiments. A more recent meta-analysis finds that the updated average effect size of experiments testing the effect of financial education is 0.065 standard deviations.[3] Therefore, the effect size in rigorous experiments is also small. Nevertheless, even small effects can have important consequences. For instance, considering that on average Americans have about 40k of non-retirement savings with the standard deviation of about 100k (numbers from 2019, before the pandemic),[4] if financial education increases savings by 0.1 standard deviations, this means a 10k increase, a substantial one.

When and how do financial education interventions work best?
Average effect sizes are informative but don't say much about when
financial literacy interventions work best. And indeed, some interventions are more effective than others. For instance, recent work
shows some positive effects of financial education when coupled
with a plan-setting intervention where people are asked to set concrete financial goals, such as opening a savings account, increasing
savings, reducing expenditure, or purchasing insurance, and do so
with a target date.[5] It has also been shown that financial education
and mathematical education in high school reduce the likelihood
of young adults having outstanding debt, but economics education
doesn't (most likely because economics students take more risks)
and the effects dissipate after a few years.[6] Yet another study finds
that teaching math in high school is better than teaching finance, as
it leads to greater participation in the financial market, investment
returns, and credit results.[7]

Financial education can also be more effective at changing particular financial behaviors. For instance, financial education interventions have been more effective at changing savings behavior (effect
size of 0.097 standard deviations) and budgeting behavior (effect
size of 0.147 standard deviations).[8] The latter suggests that financial
education for youth can produce spillover effects and improve non-
cognitive skills such as effort and initiative to be proactive at improving one's own financial habits. Recent research shows that indeed a
financial education intervention in high school also improved self-
control.[9] The intervention was divided into three phases in which
students learned about spending on needs versus wants and budgeting, financial products and services, and responsible consumer
practices and financial markets. Beyond self-control, the intervention improved shopping habits such as saving, comparing prices,
and bargaining.

Another financial education intervention among adolescents was
shown to reduce inconsistency in intertemporal choices four to 12
weeks after the intervention.[10] A typical pattern of inconsistency
in choices is that investors are present-biased in favoring sooner
smaller payments rather than later larger payments, especially
when the sooner smaller payments are immediate. The intervention

included a module on how and why to save and the tradeoffs between risk, return, and liquidity, and while it didn't increase savings, it decreased present-bias and increased the tendency of students to make choices consistent with the law of demand: to be more patient when the interest rate increases.[11] Smarter choices may have positive financial consequences. For instance, people who make choices more aligned with their own preferences are more likely to own a house in the Netherlands, which is most likely a good decision given tax benefits.[12] Financial education can therefore improve financial well-being by helping students to better evaluate the financial attractiveness of options, especially for more complicated decisions requiring a higher level of mathematical sophistication.

The aforementioned interventions suggest that financial education can improve financial decisions through two different processes: (1) by making young people better able to control their spending, understand the benefits of saving and restraint, and, as a result, increase their savings and self-control; (2) by driving students to better evaluate financial opportunities. While the former requires the understanding of the benefits of saving and restraint, the latter requires more knowledge of mathematics and economics.

Some specific features of interventions are also important. For instance, interventions that include the parents or spouses in the process are more effective.[13] Training multiple family members can create synergies of knowledge and financial decisions. In addition, enjoyment of financial education interventions may also play a role. Students who enjoy learning are more likely to continue studying and advance their knowledge in that domain. Enjoyment of financial education can make students more receptive of advice and more willing to change behavior. Financial education interventions that are more enjoyable may therefore produce stronger effects. For example, one study examined the effect of introducing messages on financial habits in a soap opera in South Africa in 2012 and found that, four months after, those who had watched the soap opera with financial messages were more likely to borrow from formal sources and less likely to gamble.[14]

Finally, providing the right incentives and education for teachers has been shown to matter. Education for teachers on how to teach may contribute to their engagement with the material. Teachers who are given pedagogical tools and who are more familiar with the content of the course may feel more accountable for the learning of students. Education for teachers may also serve to reduce any potential difference in the ability of teachers to transmit the knowledge, and it can be beneficial for teachers themselves. One study in particular examined the effect of financial education that included a teachers' guide on financial literacy and pedagogy and found that the program improved not only students' shopping habits but also teachers' savings and credit outcomes.[15]

Limitations of insights about financial education interventions. The chapters in the first part of this book outline how heterogeneity between different groups of people often matters when scaling experiments in the wild, yet it is less examined in smaller-scale, more controlled experiments. And indeed, most of the research on the impact of financial education fails to examine heterogeneous treatment effects. There are, however, a couple of noteworthy exceptions. One study found that a financial education intervention led to smaller increases in savings among those who already had savings at the start of the study.[16] Another study found that the benefit of financial education interventions is stronger among students of richer families (i.e., from households with a higher asset index).[17] But clearly there is a need for future research to pay more attention to heterogeneity in the effect of financial education.

RULES OF THUMB (HEURISTICS)

What are the rules of thumb that work? Another type of intervention to improve financial well-being is to provide rules of thumb, so-called heuristics, that can be easily used for difficult financial decisions. A recent study with a microfinance institution lending to individuals and small businesses in the Dominican Republic – mostly female business owners with no employees operating small retail shops, general stores ("colmados"), beauty salons, and food services for local markets – illustrates this nicely.[18] The microfinance institution either provided standard accounting training or introduced a rule of thumb of opening separate accounts for business and personal expenses to help manage the cash flow. The rule of thumb was meant to help with one of the most challenging tasks of a small business: Owners see the money coming in and feel tempted to use it for their personal benefit, particularly after a long day of work, when they may feel they deserve a reward. The decision not to overuse business returns is particularly difficult, because it involves not only a complex financial calculation but also the restraint of spending; two skills that humans are not very good at, namely, numeracy and self-control. And indeed, the group of individual and small business owners who learned about the rule of thumb to separate their business from their personal accounts outperformed the group with standard accounting training. Opening a separate business account allowed them to manage their revenue easily and perhaps helped them avoid overspending on their profits. Similarly, opening a separate savings account for retirement may help people to set aside money.

Pre-selected choices have a strong effect on the final choices of individuals. A recent meta-analysis shows that interventions where one option is the default make decision makers 0.68 standard deviations more likely to choose the default option.[19] Defaults work best when perceived by the decision maker as the recommended choice of a policymaker or the status quo. Researchers have found that different nudges such as providing defaults, sorting options, and reducing the number of options improve the quality of decisions, especially among consumers with low socioeconomic status, lower domain knowledge, and lower numerical ability.[20]

What are the rules of thumb that could work? Another easy-to-implement and useful rule of thumb that would improve financial outcomes is to pay the high-interest-rate debt first. Consumers tend to pay off first credit cards with the lowest balance rather than with the lowest interest rate[21] or split repayments to match the ratio of their card payments to the ratio of their card balances.[22] But neither of these prevalent strategies is optimal.

A related rule of thumb may aim to reduce the payday effect. More than half of the population increase their spending on paydays by over 25%.[23] People may avoid this bias by automatically saving part of their income on payday.[24] People can also restrain their expenses by using cash more often. The pain of paying helps consumers to avoid unnecessary spending. This pain is reduced when consumers use a credit card and other easy payment methods.

PLANNING PROMPTS

Plans as commitment devices. People often form intentions but fail to follow through on them. A lot of research shows that such intention-action gaps can be narrowed with prompts to make concrete plans about when, where, and how to act to achieve the intention. A recent study applied such a planning-prompt intervention to help consumers to follow through on paying their delinquent credit card dues.[25]

Long-term planning and pre-commitment also help. The Save More Tomorrow plan shows large savings effects by asking people to pre-commit to saving parts of future salary increases.[26] Future plans reduce the immediate pressure to act and allow for stronger commitments. Save More Tomorrow is a well-engineered plan that involves delaying a costly action to the future. People don't enjoy saving money now. But they are typically more in favor of costly actions if they expect them to happen in the future. The Save More Tomorrow program is built on the assumption that investors are more favorable towards a plan that delays a costly action to the near future and leaves the highly valued present undisturbed. Another important aspect for the success of the plan is that it links savings to a future pay rise and therefore keeps the take-home pay unchanged. Indeed, a recent study randomly assigned employees at a university to a choice between saving more in the future (two to six months later with no mention about saving following a pay rise) on the one hand, and the option of saving more now on the other, and found that offering the choice of saving more now or in the future does not lead more people to sign up to increase their savings.[27] The study also found that linking savings to a meaningful future event – "Save more after your next birthday" – is more effective at inducing savings. Perhaps a meaningful event (birthday, new year, new job) serves as a fresh start (see Chapter 8) for people to leave their past failures behind and do their best in their new beginning. Therefore, the "Save more after your next birthday" frame serves as inspiration for employees to increase savings, whereas the "Save more after a pay rise" in the Save More Tomorrow program makes it easy (and perhaps obvious) to save. People know they have self-control problems and are willing to tie their hands to increase saving in the future if they are provided inspiration or good conditions/reasons for it.

Plans as memory tools. Setting specific plans and intentions is even better, as it helps people achieve their goals by reminding them of their priorities. A lot of research in psychology shows that setting specific plans for what to do given certain contextual conditions is very effective at producing behavior change (the implementation intentions of making if-then statements). However, implementation intentions are not so beneficial in the context of multiple goals.[28] Therefore, people should focus on making specific plans for a few goals that are relevant to them.

Plans may also help investors see the big picture. Investors are sometimes stressed by short-term losses. By having long-term plans, they can look at their retirement accounts once a year to see whether the portfolio needs to be rebalanced. Recent research in psychology shows that plans reduce the intrusion of unfulfilled tasks in the mind (the Zeigarnik effect).[29] Making plans clears one's mind to focus on more urgent tasks. This may allow investors not to think about their day-to-day balances. In addition, by not constantly looking at their savings, investors avoid the temptation of using them. People can then set reminders to rebalance their portfolios from time to time. Smart reminders can help people remember their goals. Reminders can increase the likelihood of task completion if they occur at the right time for people to engage in action.[30] In addition, reminders work if they cut through the background noise by calling people's attention to a task.

One cautionary tale about financial goals is that people may end up being too committed to them. People become unwilling to touch savings put aside for a specific goal such as buying a car or paying for their children's education and instead take on expensive debt to cover new or unexpected expenses.[31]

PEER INFLUENCE

Peer influence can change behavior by providing the knowledge of what is the best thing to do as well as of what people should do (see Chapter 7 on norm nudging). In one study, for example, researchers randomly sent letters to employees of a large university asking them to participate in a fair about retirement plans. What they found was that their letter not only had a strong effect on the letter recipients signing up for retirement plans but also on other colleagues within the same department.[32] The attendance at the fair itself had no effect. In other words, the intervention had a peer effect. People may have started to talk about the plans within the departments in which one or more people received the letter, and it was these peer effects that ultimately influenced retirement plan participation.

Research in psychology shows that people don't like to receive formal advice.[33] This is in part because consumers oftentimes know what they need to do. Indeed, people seem to be averse to financial advice. Consumers actually don't seek and even avoid financial advice.[34] This may be also because misconduct and fraud are often observed among financial advisors.[35] In contrast, people are very much attuned to their peers. If someone receives information from the company HR department, others within the same department are likely to be interested and to learn more about it. It is very likely that the content of the letter will get spread and create awareness. In addition, people are more influenced by peers when they can observe their decisions.[36] As people don't usually talk about many of their financial decisions (such as how much to save for retirement), peers have more influence when their choices are readily observed.

However, people can learn from their peers. A recent study[37] asked participants to first answer a set of compound interest questions by themselves. Then, participants in one group proceeded to a face-to-face discussion about similar investments with a randomly assigned peer. Afterwards, participants again individually answered some compound interest questions. Participants who communicated with a peer subsequently performed better. Furthermore, pairs in which both parties knew little about finance benefitted the most from this communication as they learned together. If one partner knows better than the other, s/he is likely to take the lead in financial decisions.

Information about the behavior of others can also have adverse effects. One study found that providing information to employees who were not participating in a 401(k) retirement plan about peer participation rates reduced those employees' likelihood of joining.[38] Specifically, the peer information reduced the likelihood of joining the retirement plan among unionized employees who had a non-enrollment default (and were thus most in need of an intervention to enroll). This reduction was concentrated among low-income employees who perhaps perceived themselves as not being part of the group of employees that saves money for retirement. The important takeaway here is that information about what others are doing will not make one think that the same behavior should be pursued if one does not see oneself as being represented by the group.

People are also very attuned to the behavior and performance of others to assess and improve their social rank. People compare themselves to others to see where they stand. For instance, when tax records were made easily accessible online in Norway, and incomes became visible to everyone, the gap in happiness and life satisfaction increased between higher- and lower-income individuals, perhaps because they could easily compare their position in the social hierarchy.[39] In addition, in equal situations, people have a stronger desire to show off, as they can pass many others in the social rank,[40] and they fear being in the last-place position.[41]

We gather information from others to understand how we are doing, and what we should do.

CONCLUSION

This paper reviewed four types of interventions that were shown to improve financial decisions in previous research: financial education, rules of thumb, planning prompts, and peer influence. The most effective type of intervention for financial well-being may be rules of thumb, and defaults more specifically. Meta-analyses show that the effect size of defaults on decisions is about 10 times larger than the effect size of financial education on financial behavior.[42] However, financial education may help individuals to make more rational choices themselves. Planning prompts allow one to resolve to do something in the future when it is more convenient. Finally, people learn from others and especially from their peers. These interventions should be leveraged strategically by policymakers, employers, and individuals themselves to maximize their effects.

NOTES

1   Netemeyer, R.G., Warmath, D., Fernandes, D., & Lynch, J.G. (2018). How am I doing? Perceived financial well-being, its potential antecedents, and its relation to overall well-being. *Journal of Consumer Research, 45*(1), 68–89.
2   Fernandes, D., Lynch, J.G., & Netemeyer, R.G. (2014). Financial literacy, financial education and downstream financial behaviors. *Management Science, 60*(8), 1861–83.
3   Kaiser, T., Lusardi, A., Menkhoff, L., & Urban, C.J. (2020). Financial education affects financial knowledge and downstream behaviors. NBER Working Papers 27057, National Bureau of Economic Research.
4   Goda, G.S., Levy, M., Manchester, C.F., Sojourner, A., & Tasoff, J. (2019). Predicting retirement savings using survey measures of exponential-growth bias and present bias. *Economic Inquiry, 57*, 1636–58.
5   Carpena, F., Cole, S., Shapiro, J., & Zia, B. (2019). The ABCs of financial education: Experimental evidence on attitudes, behavior, and cognitive biases. *Management Science, 65*(1), 346–69.
6   Brown, M., Grigsby, J., Klaauw, W.V., Wen, J., & Zafar, B. (2016). Financial education and the debt behavior of the young. *Review of Financial Studies, 29*(9), 2490–2522.
7   Cole, S., Paulson, A., & Shastry, G.K. (2015). High school curriculum and financial outcomes: The impact of mandated personal finance and mathematics courses. *Journal of Human Resources, 51*(3), 656–98.
8   Kaiser et al. (2020).
9   Frisancho, V. (2018). The impact of school-based financial education on high school students and their teachers: Experimental evidence from Peru. Working Paper.
10 Luhrmann, M., Serra-Garcia, M., and Winter, J. (2018). The impact of financial education on adolescents' intertemporal choices. *American Economic Journal: Economic Policy, 1* (3), 309–32.
11 Meier, S., & Sprenger, C. (2012). Time discounting predicts creditworthiness. *Psychological Science, 23*(1), 56–8.
12 Choi, S., Kariv, S., Müller, W., & Silverman, D. (2014). Who is (more) rational? *American Economic Review, 104*(6), 1518–50.
13 See, for example, Bruhn, M., de Souza Leão, L., Legovini, A., Marchetti, R., & Zia, B. (2016). The impact of high school financial education: Evidence from a large-scale evaluation in Brazil. *American Economic Journal: Applied Economics, 8*(4), 256–95; and Doi, Y., McKenzie, D., & Zia, B. (2014). Who you train matters: Identifying combined effects of financial education on migrant households. *Journal of Development Economics, 109*, 39–55.

14 Berg, G., & Zia, B. (2017). Harnessing emotional connections to improve financial decisions: Evaluating the impact of financial education in mainstream media. *Journal of the European Economic Association, 15*(5), 1025–55.

15 Frisancho (2018).

16 Berry, J., Karlan, D., & Pradhan, M. (2018). The impact of financial education for youth in Ghana. *World Development, 102*, 71–89.

17 Frisancho, V. (2020). The impact of financial education for youth. *Economics of Education Review, 78*, 101918.

18 Drexler, A., Fischer G., & Schoar, A. (2014). Keeping it simple: Financial literacy and rules of thumb. *American Economic Journal: Applied Economics, 6*(2), 1–31.

19 Jachimowicz, J., Duncan, S., Weber, E., & Johnson, E. (2019). When and why defaults influence decisions: A meta-analysis of default effects. *Behavioural Public Policy, 3*(2), 159–86.

20 Mrkva, K., Posner, N.A., Reeck, C., & Johnson, E.J. (2021). Do nudges reduce disparities? Choice architecture compensates for low consumer knowledge. *Journal of Marketing*. In press.

21 See, for example, Amar, M., Ariely, D., Ayal, S., Cryder, C.E., & Rick, S.I. (2011). Winning the battle but losing the war: The psychology of debt management. *Journal of Marketing Research, 48*, 38–50; and Kettle, K.L., Trudel, R., Blanchard, S.J., & Häubl, G. (2016). Repayment concentration and consumer motivation to get out of debt. *Journal of Consumer Research, 43*(3), 460–77.

22 Gathergood, J., Mahoney, N., Stewart, N., & Weber, J. (2019). How do individuals repay their debt? The balance-matching heuristic. *American Economic Review, 109*(3), 844–75.

23 See, for example, Olafsson, A., & Pagel, M. (2018). The liquid hand-to-mouth: Evidence from personal finance management software. *Review of Financial Studies, 31*(11), 4398–4446; and Carvalho, L.S., Meier, S., & Wang, S.W. (2016). Poverty and economic decision-making: Evidence from changes in financial resources at payday. *American Economic Review, 106*(2), 260–84.

24 Carvalho, L.S., Prina, S., & Sydnor, J. (2016). The effect of saving on risk attitudes and intertemporal choices. *Journal of Development Economics, 120*, 41–52.

25 Mazar, N., Mochon, D., & Ariely, D. (2018). If you are going to pay within the next 24 hours, press 1: Automatic planning prompt reduces credit card delinquency. *Journal of Consumer Psychology, 28*, 466–76.

26 Thaler, R., & Benartzi, S. (2004). Save More Tomorrow™: Using behavioral economics to increase employee saving. *Journal of Political Economy, 112*(S1), 164–87.

27 Beshears, J., Dai, H., Milkman, K.L., & Benartzi, S. (2019). Save more later? The effect of the option to choose delayed savings rate increases on retirement wealth. *Wharton Pension Research Council*. Working Papers. 72.

28 Dalton, A.N., & Spiller, S.A. (2012). Too much of a good thing: The benefits of implementation intentions depend on the number of goals. *Journal of Consumer Research, 39*(3), 600–14.

29 Masicampo, E.J., & Baumeister, R.F. (2011). Consider it done! Plan making can eliminate the cognitive effects of unfulfilled goals. *Journal of Personality and Social Psychology, 101*(4), 667–83.

30 Rogers, T., & Milkman, K.L. (2016). Reminders through association. *Psychological Science, 27*(7), 973–986.

31 Sussman, A.B., and O'Brien, R.L. (2016). Knowing when to spend: Unintended financial consequences of earmarking to encourage savings. *Journal of Marketing Research, 53*(5), 790–803.

32 Duflo, E., & Emmanuel, S. (2003). The role of information and social interactions in retirement plan decisions: Evidence from a randomized experiment. *Quarterly Journal of Economics*, 118, 815–42.

33 Eskreis-Winkler, L., Fishbach, A., & Duckworth, A. (2018). Dear Abby: Should I give advice or receive it? *Psychological Science*, 29, 1797–1806.

34 Agarwal, S., Amromin, G., Ben-David, I., Chomsisengphet, S., & Evanoff, D.D. (2020). Financial education versus costly counseling: How to dissuade borrowers from choosing risky mortgages? *American Economic Journal: Economic Policy*, 12(1), 1–32.

35 Egan, M., Matvos, G., & Seru, A, (2019). The market for financial adviser misconduct. *Journal of Political Economy*, 127(1), 233–95.

36 Lieber, E.M.J., & Skimmyhorn, W. (2018). Peer effects in financial decision-making. *Journal of Public Economics*, 163, 37–59.

37 Ambuehl, S.B., Bernheim, D., Ersoy, F., & Harris, D. Peer advice on financial decisions: A case of the blind leading the blind? NBER Working Paper 25034.

38 Beshears, J., Choi, J.J., Laibson, D., Madrian, B.C., & Milkman, K.L. (2015). The effect of providing peer information on retirement savings decisions. *Journal of Finance*, 70, 1161–1201.

39 Perez-Truglia, R. (2020). The effects of income transparency on well-being: Evidence from a natural experiment. *American Economic Review*, 110, 1019–54.

40 Ordabayeva, N., & Chandon, P. (2011), Getting ahead of the Joneses: When equality increases conspicuous consumption among bottom-tier consumers. *Journal of Consumer Research*, 38(1), 27–41.

41 Kuziemko, I., Buell, R.W., Reich, T., & Norton, M.I. (2014). Last-place aversion: Evidence and redistributive implications. *Quarterly Journal of Economics*, 129(1), 105–49.

42 Kaiser et al. (2020); Fernandes, Lynch, & Netemeyer (2014); Jachimowicz et al. (2019).

CHAPTER EIGHTEEN

Financial Inclusion: Lab-Based Approaches for Consumer Protection Policymaking in the Wild

Rafe Mazer

Access to and use of formal financial services expanded rapidly in emerging markets over the past decade, with adult ownership of formal financial accounts increasing from 51% in 2011 to 69% in 2017.[1] Increased financial access has been linked to positive impact in the economic lives of households.[2] Part of this impact can be attributed to the rising use of digital financial services (DFS) in emerging markets, which can serve hard-to-reach or lower-income populations in ways not financially sustainable with traditional, branch-based financial service provision. The impact of DFS can be quite pronounced: A recent review of research on mobile money finds that it has contributed to reduced transaction costs, household consumption smoothing, women's empowerment, and poverty reduction.[3]

At the same time, formal financial services are not without risk, and history is replete with financial crises which have their roots in consumer finance.[4] In addition, there are new risks particular to DFS in emerging markets.[5] Markets where high-cost digital credit has proliferated[6] have shown that increased financial access of the wrong kind can have negative effects on individuals and households, such as selling assets or reducing food consumption to service debts or taking on additional debts to service the original loan.

Additional risks, such as phishing scams or overcharging by agents, have also emerged as challenges for consumers in DFS. Surveys of DFS consumers in Kenya and Uganda found that the majority had been contacted by third-party fraudsters seeking either account information or payments from the consumers' accounts.[7] In Nigeria and Uganda respectively, 33% and 31% of DFS consumers reported agents having charged them extra fees to complete a transaction.[8]

To remedy consumer risks in DFS requires proactive engagement by financial sector regulators such as central banks, microfinance authorities, and competition agencies. However, regulators are often seeking to address risks in DFS markets that are in a rapid state of innovation, which increases the difficulty of determining the most effective consumer protection policies for these new products and delivery channels. These regulators must also design policies that consider the potential differences in provider and consumer behaviors and risks due to the shift to digital delivery channels.

For regulators seeking to develop consumer protection policies that keep pace with the emerging risks related to DFS, behavioral research is an important tool that can be deployed in a relatively low-cost, short-term manner.[9] Globally, regulators like the United Kingdom's Financial Conduct Authority (FCA) have demonstrated the utility of integrating behavioral research methods into consumer protection and market conduct policy.[10]

However, financial sector regulators in lower- and middle-income countries (LMICs) may lack experience or familiarity with these research methods, owing to new and/or low-resourced consumer protection mandates and departments. The 2017 World Bank Global Financial Inclusion and Consumer Protection Survey found that 61% of specialized consumer protection units in financial sector regulators had been established since 2010, and 21% since 2013, demonstrating the relatively young nature of many consumer protection supervisory arrangements.[11]

Even with limited resources to conduct their own research, these consumer protection units need to be careful not to extrapolate behavioral research insights from highly different contexts in other countries to infer the correct policies for users of DFS in emerging markets. The nature of financial services, social and cultural norms, and other important factors vary greatly across countries. Financial sector regulators should not only learn from behavioral research, but, as has been emphasized in Part One of this book, also use a tailored approach and conduct their own research and in-situ testing in their markets. This is paramount, as the lives of consumers in LMICs – who often have high levels of informal sector employment, income variability, and reduced access to formal financial services – differ significantly compared to their "WEIRD" – Western, Educated, Industrialized, Rich, and Democratic – peers, who are the subjects of many classic behavioral experiments.[12]

For recently established consumer protection authorities, behavioral research methods like lab testing could be particularly appealing, as these experiments can be done with relatively small and incrementally increasing sample sizes. Newly established departments or authorities may have only limited budgets and small staff numbers dedicated to consumer protection, and may be under pressure to enact new policies or regulations in a relatively short timeframe. By using a mix of lab and lab-in-the-field methods – which involves running lab experiments in the locations where the population lives and works – these regulators can begin to integrate behavioral research into their policymaking processes in a relatively low-risk research setting with relatively small samples.

Lab and lab-in-the-field methods are also appealing because of the way they can limit political risk from consumer protection research. Consider, for example, a regulator who is developing a new standardized pre-contract Key Facts Document summarizing loan product terms. Live testing different versions of the Key Facts Document could create political risks. Were the regulator to randomly assign certain consumer segments with a version of a Key Facts Statement which was deemed to be less effective than another, there is the reputational risk that they had provided unequal protection to certain consumers under their mandate in a live market setting.

BEHAVIORAL RESEARCH IN CONSUMER PROTECTION

While behavioral research in consumer protection policymaking is still relatively underdeveloped in emerging markets, there is growing evidence of the potential these methods have to inform and improve consumer protection policies. To demonstrate the potential of these methods, I present three examples of lab and lab-in-the-field testing in the context of financial inclusion and innovative financial services:

1. Product transparency and disclosure of information
2. Product comparisons and shopping around
3. Consumer consent to use personal and financial information

Product Transparency and Disclosure of Information

Product transparency and disclosure of information is one of the most essential and least controversial consumer protection principles. It is hard to argue against the right of consumers to be informed of the terms and cost of the financial service they are acquiring. Pricing transparency also offers a useful starting point for regulators to familiarize themselves with behavioral research methods early on in the development of consumer protection policies, as transparency regulations or guidelines may be some of the first rules issued by a new consumer protection authority or unit.

In Mexico and Peru, researchers partnered with financial consumer protection authorities to lab test potential improvements to the ways in which loan and savings products were presented to consumers. In this lab setting, consumers were provided either existing product disclosure materials or new materials developed by the researchers, and asked to choose the best-value product amongst either five or 10 offers. The study found that the improved formats were particularly impactful for the selection of loan products.[13] For example, one of the innovations in the Mexico and Peru experiments was the presentation of costs of loans in monetary value (Mexican pesos or Peruvian soles) instead of percentage-based Total Annual Cost, as was the current regulatory requirement. Presenting the costs of a loan in monetary value improved ability to choose lower-cost loans by 8% and 4% in Mexico and Peru, respectively. Similar such findings were found in a lab experiment with digital lender Jumo in Kenya. In this study, consumers participated in a simulated borrowing scenario where they borrowed money to buy time to complete effort tasks which they were compensated for. The lab experiment found that when the finance charges of the loan were separated from the principal of the loan, consumers were able to make better decisions on how much time to purchase, with default rates of 20% instead of 29% for those where principal and finance were not separated.[14]

The Jumo study also sought to increase viewership of product terms and conditions. Prior analysis by Jumo had found that consumers who spent less time on the Terms and Conditions page were more likely not to repay their loan. To test how to improve Terms and Conditions viewership, the lab experiment tested a new screen which made skipping Terms and Conditions (T&C) an active, opt-out choice. This was done by moving "View T&Cs" from the bottom of the loan's main menu to its own screen where a borrower had to directly choose to skip T&Cs. This simple tweak increased viewership of Terms and Conditions in the lab setting from 9.5% to 23.8%.[15]

Beyond lab experiments, regulators can also consider partnering with individual providers to develop supplemental information interventions which further improve consumer understanding of product terms and their decision making. Because these interventions involve providing additional information beyond what is legally required, they also allow for experimentation in a live setting without the risk of appearing to be providing different consumer protection levels for different consumers. In the context of digital consumer lending, researchers partnered with a digital lender in Mexico to measure the impact of increasing the waiting time from when a consumer receives their online loan approval notice and when they receive the funds.[16] In their experiment, when waiting times to receive the funds were longer, repayment rates increased by 8% – representing a 21% decrease in default rates compared to those who did not face extra delays in loan disbursement. Given that digital credit surveys in Tanzania and Kenya have shown that these types of loans often go to household consumption needs,[17] this delay could be helping to reduce impulsive expenditures by consumers – although more research is needed to determine this. Further lab and field experiments which increase friction or borrower intentionality in high-cost digital credit should be a priority for regulators and providers, particularly in markets where these products are expanding rapidly and there is concern over consumer debt stress.

Product Comparisons and Switching

Improved product transparency is important not only for the ability to understand the terms of a product but also so that consumers can more easily compare, select, and switch to get the best financial services for their needs. However, behavioral issues like inertia can hinder consumers' propensity to shop around or switch providers, and lack of switching can lead to higher costs paid by consumers. One study in the Netherlands finds not only that inertia exists but also that this inertia is factored in banks' pricing strategies for long-standing customers.[18]

Policy efforts have been implemented in some jurisdictions to facilitate switching. This can be as simple as removing account closing fees – which create a financial deterrence for closing accounts – or more proactive measures such as mandatory account portability. In the United Kingdom, the Current Account Switch Service was launched in 2013 to make switching of current accounts easier by reducing days to switch, offering account number portability, and transferring automated debits, for example. As of 2019 this system had supported more than six million current account switches.

In Kenya, experiments were applied to understand the potential drivers and limitations on comparison shopping and account switching as part of the Competition Authority of Kenya's (CAK) "Competition and consumer protection in the Kenyan banking sector, Phase II" market inquiry.[19] Through a lab and lab-in-the-field experiment, CAK and the Busara Center for Behavioral Economics simulated early or late disclosure of product terms by lenders, finding that consumers who received cost disclosures earlier exerted 26% more search effort, on average, than those who received this information later in the shopping exercise. The experiment also found a 34% increase in ability to choose the cheaper deposit product across banks when information was presented in similar formats. Both

these findings provide evidence to support policy reforms emphasizing disclosure of terms early in the sales process, and standardized disclosure of terms across similar products and providers. The
market inquiry also tested these concepts in a real-world setting, by
sending text messages to participants sharing information on how
much they would save by switching accounts. However, these messages did not have a significant effect on self-reported use of new
providers by the participants, which shows that impacting switching behavior may require more aggressive policy interventions such
as making the actual process to switch easier, as was done in the
United Kingdom, versus simply providing information on the cost
savings switching may provide.

These findings have important implications for regulators seeking
to encourage greater switching behavior and comparison shopping
in financial services. Many jurisdictions have developed product
comparison websites where consumers can look at different offers
from providers and compare the prices. However, these price comparison websites are typically not linked to live product offers,
which creates a barrier between comparing a product and receiving
an actual product offer on the terms presented through the comparison website. By contrast, private sector services such as Lending Tree in the United States or Destacame in Chile and Mexico link
consumers directly to product offers from multiple financial service
providers. For regulators seeking to improve consumer choice and
switching behavior, provision of information may not be sufficient,
and additional behavioral research should be conducted to seek to
address the intention-action gaps that CAK and Busara's research in
Kenya identified.

Consumer Consent to Use Personal and Financial Information

As financial services have digitized, the volume of information
available on individuals has increased substantially. This data has
been used to expand access to financial services through improved
credit scoring via alternative data such as airtime top-ups on pre-
pay mobile phones or mobile money payments data.[20] At the same

time, emerging market governments are enacting a wide range of new data protection and data privacy laws to protect consumers from abuse and misuse of their personal data.[21]

These two developments – increased use cases of consumer data and increased calls for consumer privacy – create a tension for policymakers seeking to balance financial inclusion and data protection concerns. There is also evidence that the traditional "informed consent" model is likely insufficient to protect consumers' data in DFS, in part because of the information asymmetries between those providing the consent and those using their data.[22]

In recognition of these limitations, there have been increasing calls for providing consumers with direct access to and control over their digital information, and how it can be used and monetized. In the financial sector there are a diverse range of emerging models that seek to facilitate better consumer control and use of their data.[23]

However, making consumers truly empowered custodians of their data could be challenging in practice, particularly in markets where the concept of digital data is relatively new and devices may be limited in their interfaces to properly disclose and articulate choices consumers have regarding their data. Qualitative research with a digital credit scoring firm in Tanzania demonstrated both the challenges in explaining these "digital trails" to consumers and the potential of simple text messages to improve basic understanding of how consumers' mobile data is used for rural Tanzanians.[24] Another important factor is the availability of alternatives. Respondents in Tanzania remarked that even if they were concerned about how a lender was using their mobile phone data, if they needed the loan they would probably accept the terms anyway. In markets where financial access remains limited, and consumers' agency is reduced, encouraging more proactive data privacy behaviors may be harder than in other contexts where there is a "high privacy" alternative. Fortunately, there are relatively low cost, simple field experiments such as the two highlighted below which will allow regulators to identify how these trade-offs play out in their local market.

A lab-in-the-field study in the USA posits that "privacy valuations are extremely sensitive to contextual effects" and demonstrate this by identifying significant differences in consumers' willingness to allow their transactions on a VISA gift card to be linked to their name depending on whether allowing this increased their gift card from $10 to $12, refusing to allow this decreased their gift card from $12 to $10, or they were given the ability to choose between the two options at the outset.[25] This study found 52.1% of those who began with the $10 anonymous card choosing to keep it to preserve their privacy, versus only 9.7% of those who began with the $12 card willing to sacrifice $2 to have more privacy. That is, the study found a strong endowment effect among its participants: Whatever option they started out with (more privacy/less value gift card versus less privacy/higher value gift card) ended up being their preferred option.

A similar conceptual study was conducted in emerging market contexts in India and Kenya with loan products, with very different findings.[26] In both India and Kenya, borrowers were presented with loans of differing interest rates, with the interest rate tied to the level of data the borrower would have to disclose – more disclosure of data linked to a lower interest rate. The research ran multiple versions of competing loan offers adhering to this pricing model, and in all cases across both markets found more consumers opting for the higher price/more privacy loan option. That is, unlike the participants in the US, those in India and Kenya displayed relatively strong and stable privacy valuations. The differences in consumer behavior in these two studies shows how important it is to test behavioral concepts in the context (i.e., in-situ) where policies will be developed to reflect local behavioral patterns.

TURNING RESEARCH INTO POLICY ACTION

Behavioral research methods like lab testing have demonstrated their potential to inform consumer protection policy in LMICs, and may be particularly useful for DFS, where the product delivery channel and content are more standardized and less subject to variations in the conduct of sales staff. Lab testing is particularly suited to consumer protection policies that relate to consumer choice and information comprehension, and is likely not as useful for addressing consumer protection issues such as complaints handling/redress, fair treatment, or discrimination, which are more difficult to simulate accurately in a lab setting.

There are also implementation concerns which are raised when lab findings are proposed as evidence to inform consumer protection policymaking. Two of the more common concerns in the context of LMICs include:

1. Perceptions of the solutions as too prescriptive to mandate on private-sector actors.
2. Varying capacity of financial institutions to implement experimental solutions in the diverse financial sectors common to emerging markets. In some jurisdictions, regulators are responsible for providers ranging from major commercial banks to small FinTech start-ups and traditional microfinance institutions. In these cases, some of the more sophisticated or technology-dependent solutions identified in lab settings may be challenging for all regulated providers to implement.

These limitations can be easily addressed through the rule-setting and policy implementation processes by factoring in product types and market capacity when setting standards based on results from lab experiments. This is not dissimilar to how regulators apply the principle of proportionality in other policy mandates such as know-your-customer rules for account opening or rules around investor protections, and so should not be an impediment to conducting lab and lab-in-the-field research to help formulate consumer protection policies. As financial services in LMICs become increasingly digital, the potential for such tailored experimentation to test and measure the effects of different ways to present consumers with financial information and choices will only increase. Through well-timed and well-designed experiments, policymakers will be able to develop new regulations and standards that are better informed by evidence on what works – and doesn't – for consumers in these markets.

NOTES

1 Demirguc-Kunt, A., Klapper, L., & Singer, D. (2017). *Financial inclusion and inclusive growth: A review of recent empirical evidence*. World Bank. https://doi.org/10.1596/1813-9450-8040.
2 Demirguc-Kunt, A., Klapper, L., Singer, D., Ansar, S., & Hess, J. (2018). *The Global Findex database 2017: Measuring financial inclusion and the Fintech revolution*. World Bank. https://doi.org/10.1596/978-1-4648-1259-0.
3 Tavneet, S. (2021). Mobile money. *VoxDevLit, 2*(1). https://voxdev.org/sites/default/files/Mobile_Money_Issue_1.pdf.
4 Reinhart, C.M., & Rogoff, K.S. (2009). *This time is different: Eight centuries of financial folly*. Princeton University Press.
5 Garz, S., Giné, X., Karlan, D., Mazer, R., Sanford, C., & Zinman, J. (2020). *Consumer protection for financial inclusion in low and middle income countries: Bridging regulator and academic perspectives* (No. w28262). National Bureau of Economic Research. https://doi.org/10.3386/w28262.
6 *Inclusive finance? Headline findings from FinAccess 2019*. (2019). Financial Sector Deepening Kenya (FSD Kenya). https://www.fsdkenya.org/research-and-publications/inclusive-finance/.
7 See Mazer, R., Longman K., & Bird, M. (2021). *Consumer protection survey of digital finance users: Uganda* [Data set]. Harvard Dataverse. https://doi.org/10.7910/DVN/ROLCU4; and Blackmon, W., Mazer, R., & Warren, S. (2021). *Kenya consumer protection in digital financial services consumer survey*. Innovations for Poverty Action.
8 See Mazer, Longman, & Bird (2021); and Blackmon, W., Mazer R., & Warren, S. (2021). *Nigeria consumer protection in digital financial services consumer survey*. Innovations for Poverty Action.
9 Mazer, R., McKee, K., & Fiorillo, A. (2014). Applying behavioral insights in consumer protection policy (No. 90955, pp. 1–24). World Bank.
10 Dambe, K., Hunt, S., Iscenko, Z., & Brambley, W. (2013). *Applying behavioural economics at the Financial Conduct Authority* (SSRN Scholarly Paper ID 2930007). Social Science Research Network. https://papers.ssrn.com/abstract=2930007.
11 World Bank Group. (2017). *Global financial inclusion and consumer protection survey, 2017 report*. World Bank Group. https://doi.org/10.1596/28998.
12 Henrich, J., Heine, S.J., & Norenzayan, A. (2010). Beyond WEIRD: Towards a broad-based behavioral science. *Behavioral and Brain Sciences, 33*(2–3), 111–35. http://dx.doi.org/10.1017/S0140525X10000725.
13 Giné, X., Cuellar, C.M., & Mazer, R.K. (2017). *Information disclosure and demand elasticity of financial products: Evidence from a multi-country study*. World Bank. https://doi.org/10.1596/1813-9450-8210.
14 Mazer, R., & McKee, K. (2017). *Consumer protection in digital credit* (No. 119214, pp. 1–24). World Bank.
15 Ibid.
16 Burlando, A., Kuhn, M., & Prina, S. (2021). *Digital credit delivery speed and repayment rates*. Presented February 1, 2021. https://cega.berkeley.edu/event/digital-credit-speed-and-repayment-rates-in-mexico/.
17 Kaffenberger, M., Totolo, E., & Soursourian, M. (2018). A digital credit revolution: Insights from borrowers in Kenya and Tanzania. CGAP-FSD Working Paper, October, Consultative Group to Assist the Poor, Washington, DC.
18 Deuflhard, F. (2018). *Quantifying inertia in retail deposit markets* (SSRN Scholarly Paper ID 3237355). Social Science Research Network. https://doi.org/10.2139/ssrn.3237355.

19 Competition Authority of Kenya. (2017). *Competition and consumer protection in the Kenyan banking sector: Phase II.* Competition Authority of Kenya.

20 Björkegren, D., & Grissen, D. (2018). The potential of digital credit to bank the poor. *AEA Papers and Proceedings, 108*, 68–71. https://doi.org/10.1257/pandp.20181032

21 *Data Protection and Privacy Legislation Worldwide.* (n.d.). UNCTAD. Retrieved March 12, 2021 from https://unctad.org/page/data-protection-and-privacy-legislation-worldwide.

22 See Murthy, G., & Medine, D. (n.d.). *Data protection and financial inclusion: Why consent is not enough.* Retrieved March 28, 2021, from https://www.cgap.org/blog/data-protection-and-financial-inclusion-why-consent-not-enough; and Ombija, S. (2017). *Review of DFS user agreements in Africa: A consumer protection perspective.* International Telecommunications Union.

23 Mazer, R. (2018). *Emerging data sharing models to promote financial service innovation: Global trends and their implications for emerging markets.* 57. FSD Kenya.

24 Mazer, R., Carta, J., & Kaffenberger, M. (2014). Informed consent: How do we make it work for mobile credit scoring. CGAP Blog, February 8, 2016.

25 Acquisti, A., John, L.K., & Loewenstein, G. (2013). What is privacy worth? *Journal of Legal Studies, 42*(2), 249–74. https://doi.org/10.1086/671754.

26 Fernandez Vidal, M., & Medine, D. (2019). *Focus note: Is data privacy good for business?* CGAP. https://www.cgap.org/sites/default/files/publications/2019_12_Focus_Note_Is_Data_Privacy_Good_for_Business.pdf.

PART FOUR

Tools and Techniques

Implementing Behavioral Science Insights with Low-Income Populations in the Global South

Chaning Jang, Neela A. Saldanha, Anisha Singh, and Jennifer Adhiambo

THE SCIENTIST AND THE BUTCHER

In 2013, the newly opened Busara Center for Behavioral Economics in Nairobi, Kenya ran its first experiment. Our research question was straightforward: "What is the effect of stress on economic decision making?" We used a well-cited intervention from psychology to induce mild stress called the Trier Social Stress Test (TSST), in which those assigned to the treatment group were given a mock job interview in front of a panel of "experts" while those assigned to the control group were simultaneously to give a speech about a friend. The paper we based our intervention on had been cited over 5,000 times.[1]

Our experiment did not work. The reliable TSST had failed to elevate stress levels among our participants.

We went back to our lab staff. Did we carry out the protocols as designed? Did we get the translations correctly? Did we program the survey correctly? We had indeed done all of those things. However, like some of the cautionary tales from Part One of this book, we had failed to contextualize our intervention to the local (Kenyan) context.

Anyone who has been in Kenya for any appreciable amount of time can tell you that glossophobia (fear of public speaking) isn't high on the list of fears for a Kenyan. From an early age, children are emotive and communicative, and both pastors and politicians alike are prized for their oratory skills. Thus, speaking under scrutiny was not stressful for our Kenyan participants. Second, one of our participants pointed out a hilarious and scathing critique of our intervention. They earnestly asked, *"Why are we being interviewed by butchers?"* In our panel interview, we had followed the Western convention of "white coats = scientists." In Kenya, however, white coats are associated more with butchers and less with scientists. Rather than elevating the sense of stakes (and stress), we likely only added confusion (and perhaps primed people to pick up some grilled meat or steak on the way home).

Stories like these are neither unique nor uncommon. Over the years, we have learned (and are still learning) about what works in implementing behavioral science. In this chapter, we hope to share three big lessons that we have learned from our experiences at Busara: (a) Bring(ing) Your Own Biases, (b) Work It, and (c) Invest in Talent.

BRING(ING) YOUR OWN BIASES

As researchers, we bring our own biases to the table. Many of us have learned the concepts of behavioral science in a WEIRD culture (Western, Educated, Industrialized, Rich, Democratic). As Joseph Henrich's seminal work has shown, however, there are many differences: from visual perception to fairness and cooperation to reasoning and morality perceptions among cultures.[2] Gender differences in competition differ by whether a society is patrilineal or matrilineal,[3] and even the language we speak can affect our perspective of, and our actions in, the future.[4] In fact, we've seen that the mere presence of a WEIRD researcher can change behavioral outcomes in experimental games.[5]

We, along with collaborators from Princeton University, Strathmore University in Kenya, and the Centre for Social and Behaviour

Change in India, have run cross-cultural experiments of the common biases and heuristics along high- and low-income populations in the US, Kenya, and India. We have found, in some cases, that the results are more consistent across socioeconomic lines than across cultural ones. At other times, people respond consistently, displaying a common bias, but only when the right stimulus is triggered. So, if a study does not have the expected result, we first need to ask ourselves: Was the stimulus accurately contextualized? Did our participants understand it? Did they understand our task?

For example, we tried to replicate the "Representativeness Heuristic" (Linda is a bank teller) in India. Our first attempt, a direct translation, only making the names more Indian and making slight adjustments, failed to trigger the heuristic. We excitedly thought – look! An example of where Indians are different from Americans. On closer examination, we realized we had not contextualized the stimulus (the description of Preeti, our Indian Linda) properly. Once we did that, Indian respondents behaved like American participants.[6]

What does this mean for research? Rather than simply using off-the-shelf solutions,[7] we recommend allowing for multiple rounds of prototyping and testing (our Linda problem had required two rounds with our local staff and participants). We suggest involving members of the local community, both as research participants and as members of the research team. Also, rather than making assumptions, we have learnt that prototyping as often as needed, getting copious feedback, and letting our initial ideas go is better than internal discussions in the boardroom.

WORK IT

The Global South often lacks infrastructure that we take for granted to run quick experiments. For example, sending people a letter about other people paying taxes would not be feasible in Kenya, given that people often don't have street addresses. Many houses share mobile phones, which may make surveying unreliable, and seasonal worker migration means that tracking individuals becomes an entire project in and of itself. Universities don't have the well-funded psychology or economics labs with research participant pools to run experiments. So, adapting our research processes to work with existing infrastructure while building testing infrastructure is key. We are often not just testing the intervention but also simultaneously testing a platform to run the intervention for the first time in this context.

Building testing infrastructure is an investment in time, money, and ingenuity. Our first lab in Kenya took about eight months to set up – building out the space was relatively simple, but figuring out how to recruit and verify low-income populations, how to pay them using mobile money, how to design session flows for a new environment, how to procure touchscreen and battery backups; all this took a long time. Similarly, our collaboration with the Centre for Social and Behaviour Change in India took about eight months to show results. Although we had worked out many of the logistics and systems from our years of experience in Kenya, there were differences in local infrastructure (electricity, no community halls) that meant that our data collection efforts moved from community centers to a mobile lab. It required outfitting a bus with desks and laptops to drive from village to village, with all the associated liabilities of such a mobile lab. We therefore recommend adding 50% to all budgets (time and money) when setting up experiments for the first time, and increasing the patience and ingenuity budget by 100% while doing so! This investment has returns to scale, however, and experimental time does go down – we can now run over 200 participants a day in our Kenyan lab.

Factor in real costs of a study. Newcomers often expect that costs of running an experiment in the Global South will be "cheap," given the relatively low labor costs. This is not often the case. In our experience, a 30-minute experiment in the US takes 1.5 hours in Kenya. Our participants have likely never been in experiments before; hence seemingly trivial tasks like verifying identities, collecting consent, getting comfortable with touchscreen computers, and debriefing and compensation take much longer. Additionally, unreliable transport, lost wages, childcare, or even the perception of their participation by others in the community all weigh on an individual's decision whether or not to participate in research. This also varies by gender, introducing an unintended sample bias. In qualitative research on our own participant pool, women were much more significantly burdened with childcare, household chores, and even obtaining permission from their husbands to attend, and this difference was greater in Nigeria than in Kenya.

Make sure the platform works before testing. In our haste to embrace digital data collection, we often take infrastructure for granted. In Kenya we worked with a new interbank money transfer system to design SMS nudges to encourage individuals to transact. Halfway through the massive SMS campaign, we learnt that the system itself had an extremely high rate of failure – many transactions outright failed, leaving confused and frustrated customers. Rather than relying on your partners' word, we learnt to always test their platform prior to running studies.

While we believe that the problems of the Global South can best be addressed with better data collection and testing, we also acknowledge that there will always be frictions in these activities. In particular, resources will continue to be scarce and the time to test will often be a luxury during the implementation of programs. Hence, we also call on academics to collaborate across the Global North and South in order to develop better theories of human behavior, as well as better libraries of datasets that applied behavioral scientists in the Global South can rely on.

INVEST IN TALENT

Good behavioral science in the Global South will need good behavioral scientists. Unfortunately, supply is highly constrained – universities are only beginning to offer behavioral science courses and the ones in the Global North are too expensive for people to access. As a result, a lot of learning has to happen on the job. Don't just invest in people to *support* you, invest in them to *replace* you. Because talent and aptitude are more evenly distributed than opportunity, you'll need to invest in the people you work with to give them opportunities to learn and grow.

We invest heavily in formal and hands-on training to make up for the dearth of institutional behavioral science programs. We need to ensure that local researchers are fully involved in the project and that they stay with the organization.

We must treat our local researchers as contributors to *both* the intellectual and logistical elements of the project. This means involving them in planning meetings, discussing the experimental design and stimulus with them, and being okay with them actually tearing apart the study. Local researchers can be reluctant to give feedback, as many of them are getting trained on the job. This, along with cultural norms and perceptions of power, may lead them to believe they don't have the right to criticize. Leaders have a translation role to play – ensuring that the local researchers have the sense of safety to critique Western researchers but also ensuring that Western researchers understand the importance of this. The aforementioned "Butcher" incident would never have happened if we had encouraged critique. Having conducted hundreds of academic and applied research projects, though many WEIRD investigators early on are skeptical of, or outright refuse to engage in, contextualization with our local staff, we have never heard anyone claim that it was not a worthwhile investment.

Among our current staff, our local staff tenure is nearly *twice* that of our non-locals, and we've seen that experience has non-linear returns to quality. Take one of our very first staff, Jennifer, who actually predates Busara as an organization. She started off with no previous knowledge of lab experiments or behavioral science. Today we would venture to say she's the *single most experienced lab manager in the world*, personally running hundreds of experimental sessions with tens of thousands of participants. Her experience pays dividends on every project we run, and she's become the expert internally on running research, training field officers and PhDs alike. In her own words:

> According to Bill and Melinda Gates, where you are born is the single biggest predictor of your future. What does that mean for a girl child born in a low-income country? For me, my journey to behavioral science is not one of those studying in an economics

class but from the opportunity I have had in the past seven years interacting with experts in this field. When I first joined Busara, little did I know that it would get me to where I am today; working with researchers across countries and disciplines advancing behavioral science in the Global South, conducting experiments traditionally performed with WEIRD participants and translating them to a language that can be understood by both researchers and participants from a developing world context. Because of this, the local voice such as mine is increasingly being heard when designing research to test solutions for poverty-related initiatives. It is through this research that unlimited opportunities can be guaranteed to future children born in these parts of the world. I am Jennifer Adhiambo, and I am a behavioral scientist.

NOTES

1 Kirschbaum, C., Pirke, K.-M., & Hellhammer, D.H. (1993). The "Trier Social Stress Test" – a tool for investigating psychobiological stress responses in a laboratory setting. *Neuropsychobiology, 28*(1–2), 76–81. https://doi.org/10.1159/000119004.
2 Henrich, J., Heine, S.J., & Norenzayan, A. (2010). The weirdest people in the world? *Behavioral and Brain Sciences, 33*(2–3), 61–83. https://doi.org/10.1017/S0140525X0999152X.
3 Gneezy, U., Leonard, K.L., & List, J.A. (2009). Gender differences in competition: Evidence from a matrilineal and a patriarchal society. *Econometrica, 77*(5), 1637–64. https://doi.org/10.3982/ECTA6690.
4 Chen, M.K. (2013). The effect of language on economic behavior: Evidence from savings rates, health behaviors, and retirement assets. *American Economic Review, 103*(2), 690–731. https://doi.org/10.1257/aer.103.2.690.
5 Cilliers, J., Dube, O., & Siddiqi, B. (2012, October 23). "White man's burden"? A field experiment on generosity and foreigner presence. 42. Berkeley Symposium on Economic Experiments in Developing Countries (SEEDEC).
6 Laumas, A., Owsley, N., & Haldea, P. (2020, July 2). *How Preeti was born*. Medium. https://medium.com/busara-center-blog/how-preeti-was-born-af4583208fc9.
7 Chapter 3, this volume.

CHAPTER TWENTY

If You Want People to Accept Your Intervention, Don't Be Creepy

Patricia de Jonge, Peeter Verlegh, and Marcel Zeelenberg

In the summer of 2019, the Dutch bank ING changed the terms and conditions of its payment account. They informed customers that they would start using payment data to offer personalized tips and suggestions for other ING products. If, for example, they noticed that a customer was receiving child benefits, they might show an ad promoting a children's savings account. Or if a customer withdrew cash in an airport, they could show an ad pointing to their travel insurance offering. The policy was opt-out; customers would receive targeted ads unless they chose not to. This resulted in a media uproar, questions in Parliament, and an official letter from the Dutch Data Protection Authority warning *all* Dutch banks against this type of direct marketing.

If you have made it this far in the book, it should come as no surprise that interventions do not always result in the hoped-for behavioral change. But, as the example above shows, interventions can also fail in more spectacular ways than just "not working": triggering dislike and outrage and damaging your brand and reputation. Obviously, this is something you would rather prevent.

In this chapter we clarify why people sometimes react in this way and – most importantly – what you can do to prevent it. Our main advice – adapting Google's old motto – is simple: don't be creepy. That is easier said than done; hence we present a practical, three-item list of things to consider before scaling up an intervention.

BOOMERANG EFFECTS

We use the term boomerang effect (also backfire effect)[1] to refer to a behavioral change that is opposite to what was intended by a message or intervention. Think, for example, of an intervention aimed at reducing alcohol consumption among college students. If this intervention works as intended, college students will drink less than they did before the intervention. The intervention may also not work as intended, and leave alcohol consumption unaffected. But – a practitioner's worst nightmare – it could also cause a boomerang effect, where, as a result of the interventions, students actually start drinking *more*.

Broadly speaking, there are two paths via which this type of boomerang effect can occur.[2] In the first path, the intervention is **processed by recipients in a way that was not intended by the designer**. Let us again use the fictional example of the college campaign against alcohol use.[3] In an attempt to shock students out of ordering another beer, the campaign communicated the copious amounts of alcohol consumed by some students. Unfortunately, the non-existent designers of our campaign were unaware of the fact that this type of descriptive norm nudging can easily backfire (see also Chapter 7).[4] The above-average drinkers who saw the campaign were unimpressed and did not change their behavior. But below-average drinkers concluded that they were consuming less than what is considered "normal," and consequently started drinking more.

In the second path, people process or interpret the goal of the message as intended. In our alcohol campaign example, the students correctly infer that the goal of the campaign is to make them drink less. And **a perceived attempt at influencing behavior can make people feel angry and manipulated**. This can then motivate people to do the exact opposite of what you were encouraging them to do (in this case, drink more). It can also lead them to derogate the sender of the message. This second path to boomerang effects is known as reactance.[5] It is what happened in the ING example above, and it is the focus of this chapter.

WHAT IS REACTANCE?

Reactance occurs because people believe they have certain freedoms – for example, the freedom to choose how much alcohol they drink, or the freedom to keep their payment data private. If people feel a valued freedom is threatened, they will attempt to regain a sense of control and restore the freedom.

For reactance to occur, two conditions have to be met:

First, people have to perceive that you are attempting to influence them. Take note that this does not require that you are actually restricting their freedom. A government mandate banning certain choices can obviously trigger reactant responses, but so can nudges, and even light-touch recommendations or commercials. In the ING example, the bank did not take away their customer's freedom to choose privacy – after all, clients could opt out of targeted ads. But customers still felt angry, threatened, and manipulated.

Second, people must value the behavior you are targeting with your intervention. Not everyone values every freedom equally.[6] When the Dutch government imposed a curfew during the COVID-19 pandemic, this objectively meant we lost our freedom to leave the house at night. But because having young children means we rarely do so anyway, we do not highly value the freedom to leave the house. Therefore, the curfew did not make us angry, and it did not elicit a sudden desire to go for clandestine late-night strolls. It most definitely did not make us angry enough to pick a fight with the riot police, loot stores, or destroy COVID-19 testing centers, as did rioters in many parts of the country who obviously value the freedom to leave their house at night *very* differently than we do.

HOW COMMON IS REACTANCE?

We do not (yet) really know. In communication research, and in particular in health communication, boomerang effects are considered fairly common.[7] But in the case of behavioral interventions applied in policy and business, the field is still young. Moreover, as we and others have noted elsewhere,[8] there has been surprisingly little attention to how the recipients of behavioral interventions actually perceive these interventions.

A recent overview documents numerous instances of behavioral interventions that fail, including boomerang effects.[9] As Part One of this book suggests, this might be an underestimation. In many cases it is not very tempting for practitioners, policymakers, or even academics to publish about interventions doing the opposite of what was intended. It also seems reasonable to expect that as the use of behavioral interventions increases, people will become better able to recognize these attempts at influencing their behavior (as has happened with advertising).[10]

Luckily, a growing number of studies reports on the acceptance of behavioral interventions. A much smaller, but also growing, number of studies investigates how this support varies when some aspects of an intervention (like the language used in the description) are changed. These insights have allowed us to compose a three-item list of things to consider before you scale up an intervention. To prevent yourself from being creepy, and avoid reactant responses, we recommend that practitioners pay attention to:

1. Goal
2. Agent
3. Instrument

Each of these three elements is related to the extent to which an intervention is perceived as being creepy, or, in other words, whether it takes away a valued freedom, without sufficient justification, or in a way that makes people feel deceived or powerless.

GOAL

Surveys on the acceptance of interventions generally show that acceptance of behavioral intentions is higher than acceptance for taxes and bans, but lower than for informational and educational interventions. There is a catch, however. Studies show that people often conflate support for policy instruments with support for policy goals.[11] And most studies so far have focused on the approval of interventions promoting non-controversial health goals, like smoking cessation and healthier food choices. In fact, approval of health goals is so high that it can lead people to support even very controversial interventions like subliminal advertising.[12] We would be hesitant to extrapolate these expected levels of support to contexts other than health. Moreover, even when general support is high, the people targeted by an intervention (for example, smokers in the case of an anti-smoking intervention) generally support the intervention less than people who are not targeted (non-smokers).[13]

So, when designing an intervention, we encourage practitioners to consider whether they are restricting people's valued freedom of choice; for example, a freedom to choose a particular option, or to *not* choose a particular option. It is also important to consider whether the best choice in the particular context is a matter of debate. An easy way to do this is to put the end goal in the following sentence and see if it makes sense: "Who doesn't want …?" Compare "Who doesn't want *a healthier diet*?" with "Who doesn't want *personalized ads*?" to see what we mean here.

We are not saying that one should never attempt to change behavior that is valued highly. Even if smokers highly value the freedom to smoke, many would agree that encouraging people to quit is still the right thing to do. But it could mean that changing behavior will be harder, and that you might need to take some extra precautions – for example, in terms of the agent and instrument you are using – to prevent boomerang effects.

AGENT

Studies show that people have more of a problem with being influenced by some agents compared to others, and that they will make inferences about the motives and intentions of the agent implementing interventions.[14] It seems that people particularly look for cues about whether it is fitting for a certain type of agent to be involved in behavior change. Although this line of research is still quite limited, it suggests that people in some parts of the world are more wary of interventions by governments than of those by companies or independent experts (and the opposite might be true in other parts of the world). Perhaps it is because they are quicker to perceive government interference as paternalistic.[15] Obviously, this should not be interpreted as a license for commercial companies to do whatever they want. A large part of the ING controversy focused on the fact that banks provide services that people require to live their daily lives, and that it is virtually impossible for people to choose not to use these services. This meant that tolerance for a bank suddenly acting as an ad agency or tech company was low.

Therefore, our second piece of advice is to consider if the intervention makes sense when seen from the perspective of the consumer. Will they expect it, or will they be surprised? And how do they interpret the motivations? Are there other possible agents that may meet less resistance?

INSTRUMENT

A final relevant insight is that people prefer non-intrusive interventions (like information campaigns and educational initiatives) over more intrusive ones (like default changes). Unsurprising perhaps, but nonetheless a complication for practitioners, as more intrusive interventions often have larger effects.[16]

This makes it worthwhile to consider if one is using the least intrusive instrument possible to achieve a goal. Could the practitioner, for example, replace a default change with an active choice intervention? Or is there a way to make the preferred choice option more attractive, instead of making non-preferred options less attractive?

TEST

We end this chapter with a refrain that is repeated ad nauseam by behavioral scientists, not just in this book but more generally: test, test, test. When it comes to answering the questions above, *please* do not trust your own intuitions. Why? First of all because it is a general fact of (behavioral) life that trusting your intuitions about human decision making is a bad idea. And that even experts get things wrong. But, also, because research shows that the details of how you present an intervention matter. Describing the same intervention in different words (for example, promoting healthy food choices as opposed to discouraging unhealthy food choices) can lead to different levels of approval.[17] Various forms of transparency about the intervention can lead to different responses.[18] So, ask people how they feel about your goal, about you as an agent, and about the instrument you are using. And use experiments to test how people respond if they experience the choice as you have designed it.[19] Because, painful as it may be, you would rather have people tell you that you are being creepy before you invest valuable resources into scaling up your intervention than after.

NOTES

1 A bit confusingly, the name "backfire effect" is also used in research on correcting misinformation. While incredibly interesting, that research is outside the scope of this chapter.

2 This is a simplification of the insightful and highly recommended paper by Byrne, S., & Hart, P.S. (2009). The boomerang effect: A synthesis of findings and a preliminary theoretical framework. *Annals of the International Communication Association*, *33*(1), 3–37. https://doi.org/10.1080/23808985.2009.11679083.

3 While this particular example is fictional, there have been various – mostly unsuccessful – attempts to reduce alcohol consumption by students using social norms. See Foxcroft, D.R., Moreira, M.T., Almeida Santimano, N.M.L., & Smith, L.A. (2015). Social norms information for alcohol misuse in university and college students. *Cochrane Database of Systematic Reviews*, *2015*(12). https://doi .org/10.1002/14651858.CD006748.pub4. For a similar boomerang effect in the context of energy consumption, see Schultz, P.W., Nolan, J.M., Cialdini, R.B., Goldstein, N.J., & Griskevicius, V. (2018). The constructive, destructive, and reconstructive power of social norms: Reprise. *Perspectives on Psychological Science*, *13*(2), 249–54. https://doi.org/10.1177/1745691617693325.

4 See Bicchieri, C., & Dimant, E. (2019). Nudging with care: The risks and benefits of social information. *Public Choice*. https://doi.org/10.1007/s11127-019-00684-6; and Schultz et al. (2018).

5 Psychological reactance was introduced in Brehm, J.W. (1966). *A theory of psychological reactance*. Academic Press. For an overview of reactance theory in consumer research, see Clee, M.A., & Wicklund, R.A. (1980). Consumer behavior and psychological reactance. *Journal of Consumer Research*, *6*(4), 389–405. For more recent overviews, see Steindl, C., Jonas, E., Sittenthaler, S., Traut-Mattausch, E., & Greenberg, J. (2015). Understanding psychological reactance: New developments and findings. *Zeitschrift für Psychologie*, *223*(4), 205–14. https:// doi.org/10.1027/2151-2604/a000222; Rosenberg, B.D., & Siegel, J.T. (2018). A 50-year review of psychological reactance theory: Do not read this article. *Motivation Science*, *4*(4), 281–300. https://doi.org/10.1037/mot0000091.

6 As with many other subjects, there has been far too little research on non-Western (non-WEIRD) populations. The available research seems to indicate that reactance is universal, but that there are significant cultural differences in what type of threat triggers a reactant response. See Jonas, E., Graupmann, V., Kayser, D.N., Zanna, M., Traut-Mattausch, E., & Frey, D. (2009). Culture, self, and the emergence of reactance: Is there a "universal" freedom? *Journal of Experimental Social Psychology*, *45*(5), 1068–80. https://doi.org/10.1016/j.jesp.2009.06.005.

7 Byrne & Hart (2009).

8 See De Jonge, P., Zeelenberg, M., & Verlegh, P.W.J. (2018). Putting the public back in behavioral public policy. *Behavioural Public Policy*, 1–9. https://doi.org/10.1017 /bpp.2018.23; and Krijnen, J.M.T., Tannenbaum, D., & Fox, C.R. (2017). Choice architecture 2.0: Behavioral policy as an implicit social interaction. *Behavioral Science & Policy*, *3*(2), 1–18. https://doi.org/10.1353/bsp.2017.0010

9 Osman, M., McLachlan, S., Fenton, N.E., Neil, M., & Meder, B. (2020). Learning from behavioural changes that fail. *Trends in Cognitive Science*, *24*(1)2, 969–80. https://doi .org/10.1016/j.tics.2020.09.009.

10 Boerman, S.C., Willemsen, L.M., & Van Der Aa, E.P. (2017). "This post is sponsored": Effects of sponsorship disclosure on persuasion knowledge and electronic word of mouth in the context of Facebook. *Journal of Interactive Marketing*, *38*, 82–92. https:// doi.org/10.1016/j.intmar.2016.12.002.

11 See, for example, Tannenbaum, D., Fox, C.R., & Rogers, T. (2017). On the misplaced politics of behavioural policy interventions. *Nature Human Behaviour*, *1*(7), 0130. https://doi.org/10.1038/s41562-017-0130; and Reisch, L.A., & Sunstein, C. (2016). Do Europeans like nudges ? *Judgment and Decision Making*, *11*(4), 310–25. https:// doi.org/10.1017/CBO9781107415324.004.

12 Reisch & Sunstein (2016).

13 Reynolds, J.P., Archer, S., Pilling, M., Kenny, M., Hollands, G.J., & Marteau, T.M. (2019). Public acceptability of nudging and taxing to reduce consumption of alcohol, tobacco, and food: A population-based survey experiment. *Social Science and Medicine*, *236*(March), 112395. https://doi.org/10.1016/j.socscimed.2019.112395

14 Krijnen et al. (2017); Bang, H.M., Shu, S.B., & Weber, E.U. (2020). The role of perceived effectiveness on the acceptability of choice architecture. *Behavioural Public Policy*, *4*(1), 50–70. https://doi.org/10.1017/bpp.2018.1.

15 Bos, C., Van Der Lans, I., Van Rijnsoever, F., & Van Trijp, H. (2015). Consumer acceptance of population-level intervention strategies for healthy food choices: The role of perceived effectiveness and perceived fairness. *Nutrients*, *7*(9), 7842–62. https://doi.org/10.3390/nu7095370.

16 Diepeveen, S., Ling, T., Suhrcke, M., Roland, M., & Marteau, T.M. (2013). Public acceptability of government intervention to change health-related behaviours: a systematic review and narrative synthesis. *BMC Public Health*, *13*(1), 756. https:// doi.org/10.1186/1471-2458-13-756. Note that this study, and others, also show that people's intuitions about the effectiveness of interventions are often wrong: people generally believe less intrusive interventions to be more effective than more intrusive interventions.

17 It seems that people prefer interventions encouraging something, rather than interventions discouraging something. A case of loss aversion, perhaps? Bos et al. (2015).

18 De Jonge, Zeelenberg, & Verlegh (2018).

19 As, for example, argued by Michaelsen, P., Nyström, L., Luke, T.J., Johansson, L., & Hedesström, M. (2020, December 22). Are default nudges deemed fairer when they are more transparent? People's judgments depend on the circumstances of the evaluation. https://doi.org/10.31234/osf.io/5knx4.

CHAPTER TWENTY-ONE

Digital Nudging: Using Technology to Nudge for Good

Michael Sobolev

NUDGING AND DIGITAL TECHNOLOGY

Choices and behaviors increasingly happen in the digital world. In the modern world, most of us work, shop, and communicate with the help of digital technologies like Amazon, Gmail, and Zoom. Even our other daily behaviors such as sleeping, eating, and exercising are performed with our constant companions – smartphones, wearables, and smart home devices. Most of these devices and applications are powered by algorithms and recommendation systems, designed to automate and augment choices in daily life. As a result, the digital world is transforming human behavior as we know it.

The early success of digital technologies motivated the idea of nudging in behavioral science. Technologies simplifying consumer choices such as the ability to search quickly for products and recommendation based on collaborative filtering have led to the idea of choice architecture.[1] In the original version of the book *Nudge*, technologies guiding decisions such as GPS and automatic spell checkers are used as quintessential nudging.[2] The concepts of choice architecture and nudges, however, rose before the iPhone era. The current landscape of modern information technologies, powered by the ubiquity of smart technologies, significantly changed the choice architecture people face in their daily life. Choice architecture is now more digital and intelligent than ever.

Nudging techniques are far more common in the digital economy. Social media websites, such as Facebook, design choice architecture for engagement by curating information based on observed user preferences and past behaviors. Online shopping retailers, such as Amazon, nudge individuals to consume by scaling up traditional marketing tools of choice architecture with the help of personalized recommendations.[3] Smartphone devices and applications, where people spend hours a day, are designed to reinforce mindless consumption and habitual checking. These nudging practices are rapidly evaluated and adjusted with the help of online experiments in the form of thousands of A/B field tests.[4] In the digital age, technologists use habit formation and behavior change techniques to design products that stick.[5]

DIGITAL NUDGING

Digital nudging uniquely leverages both emerging digital technologies and insights from behavioral science. Digital nudging applies the idea of choice architecture[6] (e.g., defaults, decision aids) in digital environments[7] by passively changing user interfaces to guide choices. It augments effective behavioral nudges (e.g., feedback, reminders, planning prompts) by designing and implementing them in novel technologies such as mobile apps and wearable devices. These applications are powered by data and computing with goals of scalability, personalization, and optimization. Digital nudging ultimately allows designers to select the right nudge, at the right time, for the right individual by learning to adapt to an individual's preferences, state, and context.

Applications of digital nudging build on advances in the fields of human-computer interaction (HCI) and artificial intelligence (AI). Design is important. Research in HCI extensively explored how to design technologies to be persuasive and support behavior change,[8] allowing for the emergence of common principles for good design (e.g., self-monitoring, simplification, personalization, and rewards).[9] Data is also important. Recommendation systems on Google, Amazon, and Facebook are the ultimate AI technologies that simplify and guide choice by learning preferences from data on past choices.[10] Current and future advancements in machine learning and AI (e.g., reinforcement learning) will allow digital nudging applications to be more effective and precise.

EXAMPLES OF DIGITAL NUDGES

Defaults are a powerful tool of choice architecture[11] and digital technology is full of them – including security and privacy settings, tipping defaults on Uber, product ranking on Amazon. Defaults can be more useful to individuals if designed to fit their preferences. In Uber rides, nearly 60% of people never tip, and only 1% of people always tip.[12] This observation warrants personalizing the default option and avoiding active choice in every single ride. Beyond personalization on the individual level, the characteristics of a specific ride can also be used to tailor the tipping suggestion for every single ride (e.g., late arrival causes less tip). Technology defaults can and should become smarter and work for individuals.

Almost every active nudge can be augmented with technology and data. For example, reminders can be personalized to an individual and optimized using timing.[13] Similarly, feedback can be smarter. A famous example is the fixed criterion of 10,000 steps a day, which serves as an imperfect reference point for optimal behavior. Digital nudging allows us to design personalized and adaptive goals based on an individual's baseline, their ability to achieve the goal, and their previous response to feedback. This example illustrates the design principles of digital nudging.

To highlight digital nudging applications in the wild, I focus on three main domains: consumer choices, health behavior, and daily productivity.

APPLICATION AREAS

Consumer Choices

Digital technologies are transforming the choice architecture of everyday consumer decisions.[14] Organizations use information

Table 21.1. Examples of digital nudges in consumer behavior, health behavior, and work

	Consumer behavior	Health behavior	Productivity and work
Smart feedback	Personalized spending limits based on budgeting	Personalized and adaptive feedback on step counts	Setting time limits on distracting mobile applications
Smart reminders	Reminders to shop healthy when opening a grocery shopping app	Reminders to engage in physical activity based on calendar events	Reminders about important unanswered emails
Technology defaults	Personalized default tipping on Uber	Walking as default in Google maps and not public transport	Opening productive software (e.g., writing) as opposed to email as default

technology to personalize user interfaces and deploy recommendation systems to enhance engagement, influence choice, and increase revenue. Digital nudging tools can also be just as effectively targeted to help consumers choose products, services, and activities that maximize their own preference and utility (i.e., that are healthy, sustainable, and cost-effective).

Changing the underlying choice architecture is the standard approach in influencing consumer choice. For example, search ranking of products can account for factors such as nutrition and cost. Another approach is to provide the consumer with tools to change the choice architecture in support of their consumption preferences. For example, recommendations can be designed to be more user-centric by introducing preference elicitation mechanisms for users. A third approach is to design third-party digital nudging applications that augment consumer choices across platforms, such as automatically providing price comparisons to other online retail stores. The opportunities and design choices in digital consumer environments are almost unlimited.

Health Behavior

Changing behavior to sustain health is considered one of the most important challenges in the world today (see also Chapter 15). Mobile technologies are often proposed as the solution, as evidenced by the proliferation and popularity of mobile apps designed to help people become more physically active, eat healthier, stop smoking and drinking, and reduce stress. While health apps and devices are full of digital nudges, they are rarely systematically tested in controlled settings. To drive change, it is necessary to leverage emerging health technologies while accounting for basic elements of human behavior and ever-developing findings in the science of health behavior.[15]

Studies and clinical trials have targeted daily health behaviors such as medication adherence, physical activity, and smoking with a variety of nudges. Digital nudging is an approach that bridges the gap between technology design and nudging in support of health behavior. For example, reminders can be tailored and optimized with information about a user's past behavior and current context.[16] Nudging can also be designed to drive engagement and reduce attrition with evidence-based clinical products – a major challenge of current health technology. Moreover, the role of data and machine learning is rapidly growing to realize the vision of personalized and precision health technology.

Productivity and Work

The current and future state of work relies on digital technology. This is especially true for information workers – engineers, designers, administrators, and many others – who perform almost all of their daily tasks with digital products and services. Work technologies like Zoom for videoconferencing and Slack for communication are familiar to most of us and can be redesigned to support goals such as increased productivity and reduced stress. Digital nudging tools can support these goals in the flow of daily work.

Some simple productivity advice can be supported with digital nudging. For example, individuals should start working on their most important projects at the start of the workday rather than check and answer emails. Here, the gap between intention and behavior is substantial but can be mitigated with reminders and planning prompts. Digital nudging tools can support this behavior even further by (1) delivering reminders at the start of the workday based on location data; (2) defaulting operating systems to open the software with the most important project first; and (3) providing rewarding feedback when an individual follows through, with reminders when they do not. This example illustrates the breadth of possible nudging solutions to support routine behaviors in the workplace.

One of the more novel and interesting applications of digital nudging involves the use of technology itself. Choice architects – armed with the tools of behavioral science – are often responsible for creating engaging, addictive, and distracting digital technologies ranging from smartphones to social media websites. Digital nudging can help individuals self-regulate and tackle their own habitual and mindless use of technology. Examples of such digital nudges include changing the color of the screen to be less engaging and creating personalized and adaptive goals for distracting social media apps.

DESIGN OF DIGITAL NUDGES

Based on the synthesis of current research and affordances of technology, I propose three guidelines for the design of digital nudging solutions. These guidelines can apply to the digitization of existing nudging practices and the development of novel applications.

Principle 1: Technology

Designers of digital nudging should exploit the advantages of information technology. Choosing technology depends on the proximity of technology to the targeted behavior and the unique features of this technology. For example, (1) Online shopping websites allow designers to easily track and nudge behavior at the point of purchase using choice architecture tools; (2) Smartphones are personal and almost ubiquitous and allow one to design and deliver a large set of digital nudges via mobile apps; and (3) Wearables allow for the collection of novel data (e.g., heart rate) and nudge individuals with novel feedback (e.g., haptic feedback).

Principle 2: Data

Designers of digital nudging should identify the necessary data to track behavior and other contextual variables to optimize nudging techniques. For example, (1) Reminders can be delivered to anyone via text message, but tailoring reminders with data about location requires mobile devices and applications; (2) Planning prompts will be more effective when tailored with data from calendar events about other activities of daily life; and (3) Adaptive feedback on physical activity requires sensors equipped to capture these activities, e.g., in mobile phones or wearables.

Principle 3: Digital Experimentation

Designers of digital nudging should leverage computing and digital experimentation to rapidly optimize and redesign nudges and choice architecture. Digital experimentation should allow (1) Evaluation of a large set of possible nudges, (2) Personalization of nudges based on individual preferences and adaptation to changing contexts of daily life, and (3) Deploying and evaluating the effects of digital nudges continuously.

Challenges

Digital technology is not a panacea. For some choice setting, design of choice architecture and nudges can remain offline and without personalization. In others, technology might add unnecessary complexity and limit scalability of nudging. The science of digital nudging is still nascent and warrants caution before it is applied ubiquitously in every choice environment. The digital divide is real, and not everyone can benefit from digital technology equally. Designers should be aware of these challenges when working with human behavior and technology in both the rich world and low-resource environments.

CONCLUSION

In the future, more and more choices will be made on or with digital technology. Digital nudging leverages behavioral science and information technology to provide a new set of tools for designers to change behavior and create habits. Research and practice of digital nudging can potentially transform our understanding of human behavior and the effect of nudges.

NOTES

1 Thaler, R.H., & Sunstein, C.R. (2008). *Nudge: Improving decisions about health, wealth and happiness.* Penguin Books.
2 Ibid.
3 Johnson, E.J., Shu, S.B., Dellaert, B.G., Fox, C., Goldstein, D.G., Häubl, G., ... Weber, E.U. (2012). Beyond nudges: Tools of a choice architecture. *Marketing Letters, 23*(2), 487–504. https://doi:10.1007/s11002-012-9186-1.
4 Kohavi, R., & Thomke, S. (2017) The surprising power of online experiments. *Harvard Business Review.* https://hbr.org/2017/09/the-surprising-power -of-online-experiments.
5 Eyal, N. (2014). *Hooked: How to build habit-forming products.* Penguin Books.
6 Johnson et al. (2012).
7 Schneider, C., Weinmann, M., & Brocke, J.V. (2018). Digital nudging. *Communications of the ACM, 61*(7), 67–73. https://doi:10.1145/3213765.
8 Okeke, F., Sobolev, M., & Estrin, D. (2018). Towards a framework for mobile behavior change research. *Proceedings of the Technology, Mind, and Society.* https://doi:10.1145/3183654.3183706.
9 See Oinas-Kukkonen, H., & Harjumaa, M. (2009). Persuasive systems design: Key issues, process model, and system features. *Communications of the Association for Information Systems, 24.* https://doi:10.17705/1cais.02428; and Consolvo, S., Mcdonald, D.W., & Landay, J.A. (2009). Theory-driven design strategies for technologies that support behavior change in everyday life. *Proceedings of the 27th International Conference on Human Factors in Computing Systems – CHI 09.* https://doi:10.1145/1518701.1518766.
10 Jesse, M., & Jannach, D. (2021). Digital nudging with recommender systems: Survey and future directions. *Computers in Human Behavior Reports, 3,* 100052. https://doi:10.1016/j.chbr.2020.100052.
11 See Chapter 6 of this volume.
12 Chandar, B., Gneezy, U., List, J., & Muir, I. (2019). The drivers of social preferences: Evidence from a nationwide tipping field experiment. Working Paper. https://doi:10.3386/w26380.
13 See Chapter 9 of this volume.
14 Melumad, S., Hadi, R., Hildebrand, C., & Ward, A. (2020). Technology-augmented choice: How digital innovations are transforming consumer decision processes. *Customer Needs and Solutions, 7.* https://doi:10.1007/s40547-020-00107-4.
15 See Patel, M.S., Asch, D.A., & Volpp, K.G. (2015). Wearable devices as facilitators, not drivers, of health behavior change. *JAMA, 313*(5), 459–60. https://doi:10.1001 /jama.2014.14781; and Nahum-Shani, I., Smith, S.N., Spring, B.J., Collins, L.M., Witkiewitz, K., Tewari, A., & Murphy, S.A. (2017). Just-in-Time Adaptive Interventions (JITAIs) in mobile health: Key components and design principles for ongoing health behavior support. *Annals of Behavioral Medicine, 52*(6), 446–62. https://doi:10.1007/s12160-016-9830-8.
16 Nahum-Shani et al. (2017).

CHAPTER TWENTY-TWO

To Apply and Scale Behavioral Insights Effectively, Practitioners Must Be Scientific

Nathaniel Barr, Michelle C. Hilscher, Ada Lê,
David R. Thomson, and Kelly Peters

The last decade has seen unprecedented growth in the application of behavioral insights, with policymakers and business leaders increasingly using what is known from research on human behavior and psychology to attain diverse objectives.[1] Over the same period, the broader psychological and behavioral sciences research community has been oriented towards addressing what has been variably called a "crisis," "revolution," or "renaissance" through the 2010s, depending on whom you ask.[2] Movements to attempt to replicate existing findings, as a means to apprehend the extent to which insights from the field are robust, have become widespread – and the news has not been good. Nosek and colleagues took stock of the cumulative success of these initiatives, and across 307 replications of key findings, featuring much larger samples than the original research, just 64% reported significant effects in the expected direction, and effect sizes were only 68% the size.[3]

Thus, while the rise in interest in nudging and behavioral insights is a positive development, not surprisingly – given the emerging evidence that many published effects don't replicate even in controlled environments – practitioners are grappling with the fact that applying and scaling insights from behavioral science is unwieldy.

In some cases, what worked before, either in labs or pilots, fails to achieve the desired result or even produces results counter to expectations. Even in instances when effects in the expected direction are detected, effect sizes are often much smaller than seen in previous research,[4] a phenomenon referred to as voltage drop.[5] Paralleling the review of Nosek et al. cited above,[6] the review of Hummel and Maedche found that nudges produced significant effects 62% of the time.[7] Thus, applying behavioral insights is not as easy as picking up your favorite behavioral economics book, as simple as drawing on the classics of loss aversion, social proof, or defaults, or as fast as diving quickly into the latest issues of journals describing other initiatives. In the language of Chapter 3, off-the-shelf solutions might simply not work. The complex nature of human behavior and the world makes it much more fraught with nuance.

Rather than delve deeply into the causes of these challenges, here, we offer prescriptive advice as to what practitioners can and should do to ensure the optimal application and scaling of behavioral insights in light of these realities. In our view, based on extensive experience in applying behavioral science in the field, it is critical for practitioners to embrace the scientific method. Behavioral insights are a necessary but insufficient part of being a behaviorally informed organization. Frameworks for using behavioral insights that are non-scientific can have an alluring "elegant simplicity," but such approaches have pitfalls, as the application of insights is often reduced to a heuristic, checklist-based approach, rather than a nuanced, contextually dependent process.[8]

THE BEWORKS METHOD

For over a decade, we and our colleagues at BEworks have engaged with clients in the private and public sectors on a vast array of challenges. Our behavior-change projects have focused on challenges such as increasing savings contributions, expediting debt repayment, reducing fare evasion, improving graduation rates, reducing food waste, and increasing compliance with time-of-use energy pricing, to name but a few. Over the course of this work,

Figure 22.1. The BEworks Method

RESEARCH		STRATEGY	IMPLEMENTATION	
Discovery	Behavioural Diagnostics	Ideation & Design Lab	Build & Experiment	Choice Architecture
Study the Challenge from a Scientific Perspective	Diagnosis of the Challenge using a Behavioural Lens	Development & Prioritization of BE Strategies	Intervention Tested with Experiments	Evidence-Based Strategy

we have developed, deployed, and refined The BEworks Method, an approach that allows for the application of best practices from the scientific method in practical efforts to drive behavior change (see Figure 22.1). Though specific biases and interventions are crucial, we emphasize that the scientific and methodological aspects of the process are critical aspects of the quest to change behavior for the better and the goal for organizations to become behaviorally informed. Unlike other acronym-type frameworks,[9] the need to be scientific and to understand the contextual determinants of behavior empirically is embedded in this framework, and is viewed as an essential aspect of effectively deploying behavioral insights. Here, we offer a brief overview of the method and highlight lessons for practitioners on the immediate and long-term benefits of such an approach.

Discovery. Before any discussion of potential interventions can reasonably take place, it is critical to establish mutually agreed-upon operational definitions for the behavioral target. Too often, a failure to establish measurable, observable behaviors can lead to strategy being formulated without all parties even aiming at the same target, decreasing the odds that behavioral interventions are effective. Consider the example of a large bank that sought our help in applying behavioral insights to increase consumers' trust in their institution after a high-profile incident involving a breach of trust.

When we asked the leadership to define what trust meant, they realized the difficulty in doing so and finding agreement. Further, when they were asked how they would measure trust, so they could see if strategies to increase trust were effective or not, it became clear that moving to consideration of behavioral insights on increasing trust was premature. Through clarification of the precise behaviors in question, subsequent attempts to change them through the application of insights are more likely to succeed. The question of "to what end?" matters; practitioners must push leaders to approach strategic initiatives with the precision of a scientist.

Behavioral diagnostics. Once armed with operational definitions, equipped with measurable, observable behaviors to target, we can begin analysis towards diagnosing the factors influencing behavior in the context under scrutiny. These factors span both external and internal domains, such as the beliefs and biases of consumers, the social influencers on a consumer journey,[10] or practical constraints stemming from the political or environmental context. For instance, in recent research from BEworks aimed at uncovering the factors influencing willingness to take a COVID-19 vaccine, we found that those higher in conspiratorial thinking and intuitive thinking (amongst other factors) are less likely to say they will get a vaccine. Armed with this diagnosis, subsequent insights will be more directly aligned with barriers, increasing the odds of effectiveness. Such diagnostic work in advance of pulling insights for possible interventions affords greater precision and customization of solutions that fit specific thinking styles and situations.[11] Before considering any solutions, practitioners must dive deeply into diagnosing the challenge.

Ideation and design lab. Knowing the barriers allows us to select the appropriate interventions that are hypothesized to change the desired behaviors. Interventions can be selected from a list of usual suspects, including nudges; and frameworks such as TIPPME can be used to check for selection comprehensiveness.[12] This selection process is aided by the steps we have taken previously: First establishing precision around measurable, observable behaviors, and diagnosing factors influencing decisions and behavior, allows us to formulate more precise, testable, and contextually appropriate hypotheses about what interventions may work, how creativity can be applied to adapt interventions from the literature, and where in the journey they should be applied. To optimize the process, we advocate generating many possible interventions and then prioritizing on key dimensions,[13] in line with best practices from the science of creative problem solving.[14]

Build and experiment. Armed with intervention ideas, practitioners must next build out and test their ideas. We believe that the pursuit of applying and scaling insights in the long run is in large part dependent on the sophistication of testing that practitioners adopt. We have catalogued a litany of reasons why organizational leaders resist behavioral science approaches broadly and rigorous experimentation specifically,[15] but a hugely important task for practitioners is championing the benefits of experimentation. Even if the application of insights does not go as hypothesized, valuable learnings always emerge for organizations. Sufficient sample sizes and appropriate measures should be included to allow for comprehension of the heterogeneity of effects across sub-groups, which allows subsequent scaling to stick.[16] Our work has included diverse testing methodologies, ranging from online surveys and conjoint analysis, eye-tracking methodologies, and in-field experiments within retail environments, to in-field randomized control trials with thousands of participants. Practitioner teams should be equipped with members who are versed in advanced experimental methodology.

Choice architecture. After running experiments, data analysis to determine impact follows, which in turn guides implementation and plans for scaling. Here is where the practitioner and organization can find out what worked, what didn't, and other critical information around the impact of interventions. The effectiveness of these efforts to scale are facilitated by the sophistication of the in-situ experimentation conducted, which can allow understanding of both contextual dependencies and heterogeneous effects.[17] Without experimentation in a given context, simply pulling and applying research findings from past studies with hopes that they scale can be construed as operating "on blind faith."[18] In situations where the application of insights was effective, practitioners can work with organizational leaders to scale appropriately, or, when it was not effective, can take those valuable learnings back to the strategy table, reassess, and begin the process anew.

Lessons for practitioners. Through years of engagement in the application of behavioral insights, we have observed first-hand the benefits that such commitment to science can hold. Absent theory-driven strategic hypotheses, behavioral mapping and diagnostics, and rigorous experimentation, the application of behavioral insights can lead to sub-optimal attainment of short-term behavior change goals, not afford behavioral science the opportunity to reach its full potential, and even disrupt the current growth trajectory of this burgeoning field. For scientific thinkers, and those who appreciate that contextual complexities can change effects, the challenges that the replication crisis poses in applied work are unsurprising. Indeed, as others have articulated in this volume, expectations that interventions from the research literature could be directly applied without adaptation would be unwise. We must let scientific evidence drive our hypothesis generation and ideation, and trust the scientific method to tell us what works when and for whom. Doing so will maximize impact and will help preserve trust in our field. In short, we advise practitioners to embrace a scientific approach to behavior change.

PRACTITIONERS' ROLE IN SCIENTIFIC, ORGANIZATIONAL, AND SOCIETAL INNOVATION

Though we believe that deployment of a more scientific process in the pursuit of initiatives led by behavioral insights will lead to gains in the efficacy of interventions and strategies in the short term, we implore practitioners to think about the bigger picture. While it is imperative that non-scientists participate in behavioral science, it is important that the principles of science and scientific thinking remain present in the growth of the practice. This will help build a better base of insights from which to draw and expand the success of the field at large.

Historically, the predominant directional flow when applying behavioral insights has been from laboratory to field, from theory to practice. Now, in the face of concerns around replicability across the behavioral sciences, we feel that practitioners have an important role in not just knowledge application but also knowledge generation – but their practice must be scientific to do so. Conducting research in the wild aligns with many of the central calls for research reform, including a move from explanation to prediction,[19] a focus on practical predictive utility,[20] and increased focus on external validity and connection to the real world.[21] Thus, in the short term, the adoption of more scientifically rooted frameworks will not only benefit the core business of behavior change but will also help in the longer term to build a more contextually nuanced and ecologically valid set of insights from which to draw, driving innovation in the scientific understanding of human behavior in both the theoretical and practical sense.

Practitioners also have the potential to drive expansion of the scope of behavioral insights beyond the somewhat limited sphere of influence it typically occupies today.[22] Behavioral insights can serve as an integral facet of a transformative, over-arching framework for organizational and societal innovation. Adoption of scientific approaches affords organizational risk taking, wherein new behaviorally informed strategies can be tested and scaled, then further refined through subsequent iterative or radical advance. Enabling this form of innovation in organizations potentiates aspirational mandates aimed at benefitting all stakeholders, not just shareholders, through continued exploration of what works best for the most people. Many organizational leaders, like most humans, "desire certainty, and science infrequently provides it."[23] To make the most of behavioral insights, our job as practitioners is not simply to draw knowledge from the behavioral sciences but to implore leaders to be a part of this scientific process.

In looking back upon the replicability movement, Nosek and colleagues sense that the moments of difficulty were "eclipsed by excitement, empowerment, and enlightenment" at the recognition that a positive movement was underway.[24] We share this sense of optimism, as the problems for practitioners are outweighed by the immense opportunities associated with scientifically applying and scaling behavioral insights.

NOTES

1 See Chapman, G., Milkman, K.L., Rand, D., Rogers, T., & Thaler, R.H. (2020). Nudges and choice architecture in organizations: New frontiers. *Organizational Behavior and Human Decision Processes;* and OECD (2017). *Behavioral insights and public policy: Lessons from around the world.* OECD Publishing.

2 Nosek, B.A., Hardwicke, T.E., Moshontz, H., Allard, A., Corker, K.S., Dreber, A., ... Vazire, S. (2021, February 9). Replicability, robustness, and reproducibility in psychological science. https://doi.org/10.31234/osf.io/ksfvq.

3 Ibid.

4 DellaVigna, S., & Linos, E. (2020). *Rcts to scale: Comprehensive evidence from two nudge units* (No. w27594). National Bureau of Economic Research. https://doi.org/10.3386/w27594.

5 Al-Ubaydli, O., List, J.A., & Suskind, D.L. (2017). What can we learn from experiments? Understanding the threats to the scalability of experimental results. *American Economic Review, 107*(5), 282–6. https://doi.org/10.1257/aer.p20171115.

6 Nosek et al. (2021, February 9).

7 Hummel, D., & Maedche, A. (2019). How effective is nudging? A quantitative review on the effect sizes and limits of empirical nudging studies. *Journal of Behavioral and Experimental Economics, 80,* 47–58. https://doi.org/10.1016/j.socec.2019.03.005.

8 Soman, D. (2017). The elegant simplicity (and potential pitfalls) of simple frameworks. In OPRE Report 2017–23, Nudging Change in Human Services, Office of Planning, Research and Evaluation, US Administration for Children and Families.

9 Ibid.

10 Hamilton, R., Ferraro, R., Haws, K.L., & Mukhopadhyay, A. Traveling with companions: The social customer journey. *Journal of Marketing, 85*(1). https://doi.org/10.1177/0022242920908227.

11 Soman, D., & Hossain, T. (2021). Successfully scaled solutions need not be homogenous. *Behavioral Public Policy, 5*(1), 80–9. https://doi.org/10.1017/bpp.2020.24.

12 Hollands, G.J., Bignardi, G., Johnston, M., Kelly, M.P., Ogilvie, D., Petticrew, M., Prestwich, A., Shemilt, I., Sutton, S., & Marteau, T.M. (2017). The TIPPME intervention typology for changing environments to change behavior. *Nature Human Behavior, 1*(8), 1–9. https://doi.org/10.1038/s41562-017-0140.

13 Peters, K. (Spring 2020). Behavioral science: The answer to innovation? *Rotman Management Magazine.*

14 Isaksen, S.G., & Treffinger, D.J. (2004). Celebrating 50 years of reflective practice: Versions of creative problem solving. *Journal of Creative Behavior, 38*(2), 75–101. https://doi.org/10.1002/j.2162-6057.2004.tb01234.x.

15 O'Malley, S., & Peters, K. (2021). Gut check: Why organizations that need to be behaviorally informed resist it. In D. Soman & C. Yeung (Eds.), *The behaviorally informed organization.* University of Toronto Press.

16 Soman & Hossain (2021).

17 Ibid.

18 Al-Ubaydli, List, & Suskind (2017).

19 Yarkoni, T., & Westfall, J. (2017). Choosing prediction over explanation in psychology: Lessons from machine learning. *Perspectives on Psychological Science, 12*(6), 1100–22. https://doi.org/10.1177%2F1745691617693393.

20 Yarkoni, T. (2019). The generalizability crisis. [Preprint]. *PsyArXiv*. https://doi
     .org/10.31234/osf. io/jqw35.
21 See, for example, Lin, H., Werner, K.M., & Inzlicht, M. (2021). Promises and perils of
     experimentation: The mutual internal validity problem. *Perspectives on Psychological
     Science*. https://doi.org/10.1177/1745691620974773.
22 Thaler, R. (2020). What's next for nudging and choice architecture? *Organizational
     Behavior and Human Decision Processes*. https://doi.org/10.1016/j.obhdp.2020.04.003.
23 Open Science Collaboration. (2015). Estimating the reproducibility of psychological
     science. *Science, 349*(6251). https://doi.org/10.1126/science.aac4716.
24 See page 27 of Nosek et al. (2021, February 9).

CHAPTER TWENTY-THREE

It's All about the SOUL! Why Sort, Order, and Use Labeling Results in Smart Scorecards

Claire Heard, Elena Reutskaja, and Barbara Fasolo

Patient autonomy is high on the healthcare agenda and any Shared Decision Making initiative. The National Health Service in the UK,[1] for example, is working hard to improve opportunities for patients to make choices about their care, including where to go for tests or treatment. However, it is hard for patients to make high-quality decisions in an environment where the data is sophisticated, complex, and abundant. So how can policymakers help patients choose the highest-quality hospital from an array of many without limiting their freedom of choice?

Your task as a policymaker is to develop an online resource where users can first learn about their options (e.g., hospitals) and then choose one that they think is the best. You think of offering information in the form of a matrix (called a "scorecard") with options to choose from (e.g., hospitals) presented in the columns and values on which these options differ (e.g., quality, safety, location) in the rows. Now it is time to complete this scorecard with relevant data and present it to patients. This is where we suggest *adding SOUL!*

In particular, we propose that you should know (a) whether to Sort the hospitals by, say, quality or distance; (b) whether to Order information with benefits or risks first, and (c) whether to simplify the Use of Labeling or provide as much detail as possible.

In addition to capturing information succinctly, SOUL can enhance your scorecard and help patients make better-quality choices.

INTRODUCTION

This chapter uses research conducted in both an artefactual field experiment and a lab experiment to show how to enhance scorecards by sorting, ordering, and using labeling. Starting from the healthcare vignette above, we present three cases that illustrate how these ideas can be applied to improve the use of relevant information when evaluating options and making choices.

For the hospital scorecards, we will draw from a qualitative study consisting of seven focus groups and a large-scale, two-phase artefactual field experiment that compared (amongst others) two scorecard versions: with the best hospital either in the *first* (options sorted by quality) or *hotspot* position (options sorted by distance). Both versions presented the choice among five hospitals on nine performance indicators (covering clinical quality, clinical safety, patient experience, and distance)[2] and the hospitals were presented always as "columns."

For the treatment scorecards, we will draw from two small-scale studies (including eye-tracking data) comparing the risks and benefits of a single option. In particular, this experiment manipulated whether information about a drug treatment was presented with benefits first or risks first, and the orientation of this information.[3]

While we investigate scorecards in a healthcare environment – an environment where scorecards are increasingly being used across the world (e.g., in the NHS)[4] – any organization that develops scorecards for their clients (or uses scorecards within their organization) should consider a scorecard's SOUL. As choice environments become increasingly digitized, we see scorecards appearing across many different domains – from policy choices (e.g., social distancing policy),[5] to banking choices (e.g., choosing a current account) or consumer/travel choices (e.g., hotels, laptops).

This is important because behavioral research increasingly suggests that subtle changes to the choice architecture, such as different locations of the same options (different ways to sort/order options), can have a significant impact on decisions about health.[6] Other research has suggested that the language or format and how much or how little information we use can make a difference to how well we understand information.[7]

This chapter probes further into three aspects of this architecture, exploring the issues of Sorting, Ordering, and Using Labels, and shows what these mean for practitioners seeking to optimize scorecard design. We will illustrate how seemingly arbitrary design choices should not be overlooked[8] and provide insights into (1) how to sort a scorecard so that the best option is picked more often, (2) in which order to place benefits and risks of an option, and (3) why creating a consistent labeling system and balancing information specificity and completeness is important.

CASE 1: SORTING – IT'S NOT NECESSARILY BEST TO BE FIRST[9]

The problem. You want the "best" option to be selected more often in your scorecard, but you don't feel that a default (i.e., preselecting an option) is appropriate. Your first thought is that you could make the best option be chosen more often by sorting by quality. Intuitively, this could work, because the best-quality option (for example, a hospital with higher ratings on both quality and safety measures) is the first option that people see (e.g., the first column in a scorecard). However, the evidence shows otherwise.

The evidence. In our field study[10] we manipulated sorting by quality or by distance. Although, in general, people were better than random at selecting the best option in the set, decision makers chose the best-quality hospital more often when it was placed roughly in the middle (hot-spot) of the scorecard than when it was placed first. This could occur because people are unconsciously attracted to the center and are more likely to look for the best options in the middle,[11] which feels like balancing the trade-offs rather than the edges. This shows an edge aversion, rather than the edge advantage that the intuitive design – sort by quality – would have suggested.

Our advice. When designing a scorecard for an online resource, avoid placing your best options at the edge and instead choose a sorting method that puts the best options in the perceptual hotspot – i.e., the middle right of a scorecard.

CASE 2: ORDER – BE WARY OF PRESENTING RISKS FIRST

The problem. You are tasked with creating a web resource to explain the risks and benefits of warfarin (an anticoagulant medication) for the treatment of a deep vein thrombosis. This explains what a deep vein thrombosis is and what warfarin does. You pass along the information to the web designers and they ask whether you want the information presented with the risks or the benefits first (i.e., in the top or left position of a table). You wonder whether it matters, since all information is presented simultaneously.

The evidence. In a lab study,[12] we identified that even when information is presented simultaneously (in a table), what you present first matters. This is because information at the top or left of the display tends to be read first. In particular, when benefits were presented on the left or top of the display, people spent 50% of the time on risks. In contrast, they spent more (around 60%) of the time on the risks when the risks were shown to the left or top of the table. Thus, the risk information grabs more attention when read first. People may therefore struggle to disengage from the risk information – perhaps reflecting a bias to attend more to negative information[13] – and consequently spend less time on the benefit information. Our results suggest that a negativity bias could occur if one presents risk information first.

Our advice. If the goal is to aid informed decision making (and promote an environment more conducive to balanced search and attention), then avoid placing the risks of a choice option as the first piece of information. To nudge people's attention towards the risks, do the opposite.

CASE 3: USE LABELING – AIM FOR SIMPLICITY AND COMPLETENESS

The problem. You have chosen the indicators that are important for the public to consider when choosing a high-quality hospital and gathered the relevant information on each. You notice that there is a lack of consistency in the metrics used for the indicators. Some of these are simple and intuitive, others more complex and highly numeric – and require links to additional explanations. You wonder whether this is a problem.

The evidence. In our focus groups,[14] participants found it confusing when the indicator scores were counter-intuitive. In particular, mortality rates – where lower scores indicate better hospital performance – were reported as difficult to interpret and often interpreted in an opposite way. Secondly, participants appeared to rely on their initial understanding of the indicators and gave limited attention to links to detailed descriptions. Third, having a mix of labeling formats across indicators (e.g., ratios, scales, percentages, symbols) made comparisons more difficult. Participants preferred a consistent metric across indicators. Yet, missing data generated negative reactions (such as suspicion), and some participants would ignore indicators which had missing data (or at least discount a hospital with missing data).

Our advice. We advise that scorecard designers (1) create a consistent labeling system across indicators and make use of symbolic (e.g., ticks) and/or evaluative labels (poor, good, excellent), especially if your target population includes those with low numeracy; and (2) tailor information to be as specific as possible but be wary when specificity leads to a high proportion of missing data.

SUMMARY AND CHECKLIST

To conclude, it is clear that the choice architecture of a scorecard or information resource can impact how people search, interpret, and make decisions, yet choosing how to present information is often

Table 23.1. Checklist for enhancing scorecard design: SOUL

Design element	Design questions
S-Sort	Does your sorting method put the "best" options at the edge? Is there an alternative sorting method that moves these options into the middle right "hotspot"?
O-Order	Is your goal to create a balanced environment or to nudge attention towards risk information? If balance is important, avoid placing risk information first and instead discuss benefits first. If making the risks salient is important, then do the opposite.
UL-Use of labeling	Simplify the labeling to create a consistent labeling system across indicators. Tailor the information so that it is more specific to the exact decision being made without causing missing data points.

something that is overlooked. It is therefore important that design teams – from content designers to digital production teams – work together to identify the optimal scorecard design. To help begin such discussion, in Table 23.1 we present a checklist of design questions to ask prior to developing a scorecard. In addition, consistent with Chapters 1 and 3, we recommend always *pre-testing the design*. While we provide answers on how to sort, order, and use labeling, test out your design to see what happens. Things that seem to make intuitive sense (such as sorting by quality) can backfire.

NOTES

1 NHS (2019). *Your choices in the NHS.* NHS. Available at: https://www.nhs.uk /using-the-nhs/about-the-nhs/your-choices-in-the-nhs/.

2 Boyce, T., Dixon, A., Fasolo, B., & Reutskaja, E. (2010). *Choosing a high-quality hospital: The role of nudges scorecard design and information.* The King's Fund. https://www .kingsfund.org.uk/sites/default/files/field/field_publication_file/Choosing-high -quality-hospital-role-report-Tammy-Boyce-Anna-Dixon-November2010.pdf; Fasolo, B., Reutskaja, E., Dixon, A., & Boyce, T. (2010). Helping patients choose: How to improve the design of comparative scorecards of hospital quality. *Patient Education and Counseling, 78*, 344–9.

3 Heard, C.L., Rakow, T., & Foulsham, T. (2018). Understanding the effect of information presentation order and orientation on information search and treatment evaluation. *Medical Decision Making, 38*(6), 646–57.

4 NHS (2019).

5 See, for example, https://www.ecdc.europa.eu/en/publications-data/guide -public-health-measures-reduce-impact-influenza-pandemics-europe-ecdc-menu.

6 Barnes, A., Karpman, M., Long, S., Hanoch, Y., & Rice, T. (2019). More intelligent designs: Comparing the effectiveness of choice architectures in US health insurance

marketplaces. *Organizational Behavior and Human Decision Processes*; Bar-Hillel, M. (2015). Position effects in choice from simultaneous displays. *Perspectives on Psychological Science, 10*(4), 419–33.

7 Peters, E., Dieckmann, N., Dixon, A., Hibbard, J., & Mertz, C. (2007). Less is more in presenting quality information to consumers. *Medical Care Research and Review, 64*(2), 169–90.

8 See also Chapter 3 in this volume.

9 Reutskaja, E., & Fasolo, B. (2013). It's not necessarily best to be first. *Harvard Business Review* (January–February). https://hbr.org/2013/01/its-not -necessarily-best-to-be-first.

10 See Boyce et al. (2010); and Fasolo et al. (2010).

11 Raghubir P., & Valenzuela, A. (2006). Center of inattention: Position biases in decision-making. *Organizational Behavior and Human Decision Processes, 99*(1), 66–80; Valenzuela, A., & Raghubir, P. (2009). Position-based beliefs: The center-stage effect. *Journal of Consumer Psychology, 19*(2), 185–96; Valenzuela, A., & Raghubir, P. (2015). Are consumers aware of top–bottom but not of left–right inferences? Implications for shelf space positions. *Journal of Experimental Psychology: Applied, 21*(3), 224–41.

12 Heard, Rakow, & Foulsham (2018).

13 Vaish, A., Grossmann, T., & Woodward, A. (2008). Not all emotions are created equal: The negativity bias in social-emotional development. *Psychological Bulletin, 134*(3), 383–403.

14 Boyce et al. (2010).

CHAPTER TWENTY-FOUR

Applying Behavioral Interventions in a New Context

Barnabas Szaszi, Krisztian Komandi, Nandor Hajdu, and Elizabeth Tipton

Esther worked as a middle manager in the customer service department of a large firm. As a behavioral science enthusiast, she was looking for opportunities for using nudges. One evening, she noticed a recent study showing that a small change in communication nudged customers' behavior towards using emails instead of phones when they contacted the customer service department of a multinational corporation. The article argued that adding "87% of our clients in your area prefer to handle their complaints through our website" into their monthly newsletter increased the number of customers using the online form by 17%. As the idea seemed easily applicable and could potentially save thousands of dollars each day for her company, she decided to pitch its implementation to her team the next day. Her manager loved the idea, and in less than a month, an A/B test was put into motion with the target customers. When the data came in, her initial curiosity and enthusiasm quickly changed into disappointment and confusion – it seemed that the intervention had no effect whatsoever on the customers' behavior. What did Esther do wrong? How could she have minimized the probability of this failure?

This puzzling situation is familiar to many who apply behavioral science in the wild (see also Chapters 1 and 3 for other such instances). Our goal is to provide some answers and highlight some rules of thumb and practices to consider when applying behavioral interventions in a new context.

EXPECT THE EFFECTIVENESS OF NUDGES
TO VARY ACROSS CONTEXTS

Although this advice seems obvious, when we see the results of experiments backed by data and scientific methods, we tend to believe not just that the results hold but also that they generalize to our specific context.[1] This belief often due to some wishful thinking and many books, articles, and keynote presentations where the applicability of nudges is presented without drawing attention to their limitations. Nudges, however, often have different effects across different contexts: populations, locations, cultures, and times matter.

Each individual has their own experience, desires, and skills. The same social norm can influence, say, the reader and a 75-year-old grandmother very differently. While the reader might be nudged by social norms to switch to using email instead of the phone when making complaints, the same message might have no effect at all on the grandmother. Perhaps her different perceptions about the norms in her local network are different, or she lacks familiarity with smartphones or computers.[2] Even the same individuals behave differently across different situations and times. Maybe in the morning, an individual is too stressed to process any new information and misses the newsletter, but is likely to open non-work-related emails during their evening commute.

Consider the following widely used example of social norms and nudging. In a study, researchers aimed to reduce the energy consumption of US households by providing descriptive information on social norms. In a series of randomized controlled experiments involving roughly 588,000 households, an energy management company (Opower) tested whether providing information about the neighbor's consumption – that is, descriptive norms – impacts energy usage.[3] It was estimated that, on average, the program decreased energy consumption by 2%, an equivalent effect to an 11–20% electricity price increase. Given that the effects were robust and tested on a huge sample, it was thought that the success could be easily reproduced when scaling up the study to new states and other households. However, in later evaluations, the interventions had practically no effect on energy consumption.[4] Although at first sight such failure might be shocking, careful consideration of the context can provide some answers. While both the context and the details of the nudge remained the same, the types of households included in the scaled-up evaluations were different from those in the original studies, and, as a result, their behavior was much harder to change. Later research revealed that less environmentally friendly attitudes, lower-income and thus smaller households, and beliefs about local support of the provided descriptive norm might have all mitigated the effect of this nudge. Therefore, even in a case where there is seemingly little difference between the original and the new settings, there can be important contextual factors which significantly influence, and even diminish, the effectiveness of an intervention.

When applying nudges, a practitioner usually has a benchmark example in which a behavioral intervention successfully triggered the desired effect. Sometimes, it is reasonable to assume that the nudge will work in our context without deeper consideration, but in most of the cases, we need to put considerable energy into figuring out what can go wrong and how the new context is different from the benchmark example we have in mind.

In one of our studies, we aimed to explore all the main factors that influence people's choice in a given situation – in our case, it was choosing between the stairs and the elevator.[5] Only using information on the context of the choice, we accurately predicted in 93.26% of the cases whether one chose the stairs or elevator. Although in this study we have not assessed how the context influenced the effectiveness of an intervention, it is reasonable to assume that if the contextual factors had such an influence on people's choice, they can have a similar influence on the effectiveness of behavioral interventions influencing those choices.

The understanding of the context is often the difference between the application of successful and failed nudges.[6] In a recent study, discussed in Chapter 2, researchers showed that interventions on average only produced a 1.4% increase on the desired outcomes, an effect much smaller than one would expect when reading the published studies and articles on the topic.[7] The average effect is relatively small, but it is clearly different from zero (nudges work!), and the list of nudges shows huge variance in their effectiveness – ranging from backfiring interventions to highly successful ones.

EXPLORE THE CONTEXTUAL FACTORS THAT MAY INFLUENCE THE EFFECTIVENESS OF YOUR INTERVENTION

It is useful to think about the process of context exploration as analogous to an anamnesis in a therapy setting. No therapist would start a therapy without trying to understand the specific context of the patient. Behavioral interventions should not be employed without thoughtful exploration of the contextual factors either. It can designate the directions of thinking and help you decide about the proper intervention. We explore additional factors that practitioners need to think about in exploring the context.

The influencing contextual factors can be of many kinds: physical attributes of the environment, non-physical factors such as social, cultural, or psychological attributes and preferences of the target population, and the timing of the choice you want to influence. Another type of influencing factor concerns the behavioral intervention itself; are there specific situations when the intervention is not supposed to work? While there is no easy way to find all the factors, our emphasis is more on the need for a structured way to understand the context of a given decision or behavior. In recent years, human-centered design (HCD) has become a popular inspiration for organizations that want to better explore and understand their target groups. Complemented with analyzing – ideally – behavioral data, HCD might help a decision maker explore how each of the important dimensions listed above can have an influence. In fact, the combination of behavioral science and HCD has resulted in the new, increasingly popular field of behavioral design.[8] Although this process is not a guarantee of success, it can definitely help identify the biggest holes in the plan. More resources coming from reviewing the literature and reading about similar interventions, as well as conducting interviews and qualitative surveys or even focus group discussions, can lead to a more thorough list of the influencing factors.

In Esther's case, a range of factors can play a role; age, socioeconomic status, place of living, general attitudes towards computers or emailing, or perceived difficulty of use. Esther could conclude that her listed contextual factors can be compressed into two main categories that she thinks matter: age and tech savviness. Those who are older and not very tech-savvy won't contact customer service by email whatever nudges she uses, while with the younger and more tech-savvy people she will have a much better chance. As she also has information about the customers of her company, this information, and the estimated cost of the intervention, could help her decide whether it's worth trying to apply the nudge in her context.

TEST THE EFFECT OF THE NUDGE WITH CONTEXTUAL DIVERSITY IN MIND

While thinking through the contextual factors can be useful, the intervention must be tested in a small sample in a context similar to the one in which it will be deployed (in the language of Chapter 3, in-situ testing). As there are many books detailing the advantages of randomized testing and describing how to do it, we are not discussing them here. Instead, we will focus on one important and again often ignored attribute of testing, which can define the success of the whole endeavor – testing on a diverse sample.

When testing, it is critically important to build on context exploration to anticipate how the effect of the nudge might vary across your population. For example, in Esther's firm, a test with customer groups that typically already use both email and phone might be effective. Yet, a test on a population that typically only uses the phone might yield no results. Once the practitioner has identified subgroups across which they expect results to vary, they can focus efforts on recruiting subgroups most similar to the population whose behavior you aim to change. That way you can ensure that your test results will be similar to the results of the scaled-up behavioral intervention. Recall that this was not the case in the Opower study, which resulted in quite different results in the early study from those found in the full population. Carefully considering this heterogeneity and accounting for it will likely be tedious and will make testing complex. On the flip side, it will provide a study that is more representative and predictive – and will alleviate downstream surprises like the one Esther experienced.

CONCLUSION: STAY SKEPTICAL UNTIL YOU HAVE PROOF

So what would we recommend to Esther? In the wild, we constantly run into new configurations of the factors that might have an impact both on a target behavior and on the effectiveness of a nudge. Assuming that the effectiveness of the behavioral intervention will vary and may even not work is possibly the best motivation for any behavioral scientist to keep exploring the context of a behavior. We should not get carried away with any testing opportunity but instead focus on systematically building a diverse test sample that ensures we will end up being able to tell successful and failed nudges apart. After all, when exploring the wild, preparing for surprises is the best strategy one can follow.

NOTES

1 Szaszi, B., Palinkas, A., Palfi, B., Szollosi, A., & Aczel, B. (2017). A systematic scoping review of the choice architecture movement: Toward understanding when and why nudges work. *Journal of Behavioral Decision Making, 31*(3), 355–66. https://doi:10.1002/bdm.2035.

2 See also Chapter 3 of this volume for a discussion on heterogeneity, and Yeung and Tham (2021) for a discussion on "the problem with problems" in Soman, D., & Yeung, C. (2021). *The behaviorally informed organization.* University of Toronto Press.

3 Allcott, H., & Rogers, T. (2012). The short-run and long-run effects of behavioral interventions: Experimental evidence from energy conservation. https://doi:10.3386/w18492.

4 Allcott, H. (2015). Site selection bias in program evaluation. *Quarterly Journal of Economics, 130*(3), 1117–65. https://doi:10.1093/qje/qjv015; and Jachimowicz, J.M., Hauser, O.P., O'Brien, J.D., Sherman, E., & Galinsky, A.D. (2018). The critical role of second-order normative beliefs in predicting energy conservation. *Nature Human Behaviour, 2*(10), 757–64. https://doi:10.1038/s41562-018-0434-0.

5 Hajdu, N., Szaszi, B., & Aczel, B. (2020). Extending the choice architecture toolbox: The choice context mapping. PsyArVix Preprints. https://doi:10.31234/osf.io/cbrwt.

6 Tipton, E., Bryan, C.J., & Yeager, D.S. (2020). To change the world, behavioral intervention research will need to get serious about heterogeneity. Accepted for publication in *Nature Human Behaviour*. https://statmodeling.stat.columbia.edu/wp-content/uploads/2020/07/Heterogeneity-1-23-20-NHB.pdf.

7 DellaVigna, S., & Linos, E. (2020). *RCTs to scale: comprehensive evidence from two nudge units*. (Working Paper No. 27594) National Bureau of Economic Research. https://doi:10.3386/w27594. See also Chapter 2 of this volume.

8 Tantia, P. (2017). The new science of designing for humans. *Stanford Social Innovation Review*, 15, 29–33. See also Chapter 4 of this volume.

Contributors

Jennifer Adhiambo is a labs manager at the Busara Center for Behavioral Economics, where she is responsible for client and project management, specifically working closely with academics across the world to design, contextualize, and implement behavioral studies. She also has extensive experience implementing lab experiments in countries across the Global South. She holds a bachelor's degree in Education from the University of Nairobi.

Grusha Agarwal is a PhD student in the Organizational Behavior and Human Resource Management department (OBHRM) at Rotman School of Management, University of Toronto. Her research interests revolve around investigating behavioral approaches to diversity, focusing on organizational initiatives or nudges that can challenge and disrupt existing gender/racial biases, and using a social perception framework to understand identity and inclusion. Particularly, she is interested in the strategies minorities use to fit into society and in finding solutions that rectify structural and systemic biases. In her spare time, Grusha enjoys spending time with family, indulging in self-care, and listening to true crime podcasts.

Nathaniel Barr is a scientific advisor at BEworks and a professor of Creativity and Creative Thinking at Sheridan College. He earned his PhD and held a postdoctoral fellowship at the University of Waterloo. Nathaniel has published on a variety of topics within the cognitive and behavioral sciences, including creativity, innovation, the intersection of thinking and technology, pseudo-profound bullshit, and the importance of behavioral science in the Anthropocene, and has been awarded a number of federal research grants that meld behavioral science and creative arts/design to solve practical challenges. At BEworks, he advises on strategy, growth, partnerships, research, and writing.

Cristina Bicchieri is the S.J. Patterson Harvie Professor of Social Studies and Comparative Ethics at the University of Pennsylvania, where she is also director of the Philosophy, Politics, and Economics Program, the Behavioral Ethics Lab, The Penn Social Norms Group, and The Center for Social Norms and Behavioral Dynamics. The author of more than 100 articles and seven books, she is a world authority on the measurement of collective behaviors, and has consulted with the UNICEF Child Protection Section, the World Bank, the Ford Foundation, the Gates Foundation, BBC Media, and many other groups on behavioral measurement and change.

Romain Cadario is an assistant professor of Marketing at Erasmus University, Rotterdam School of Management. Before joining Erasmus University, Romain was senior academic researcher at the Susilo Institute for Ethics in the Global Economy, Boston University Questrom School of Business. His research develops and evaluates marketing interventions designed to stimulate societally desirable consumer behaviors.

Colin F. Camerer (PhD, Chicago) is a behavioral economist at Caltech. His research imports methods from psychology and neuroscience to improve economics. His science team is interested in a range of decisions, games, and markets and uses eye-tracking, lesion patients, EEG, fMRI, wearable sensors, machine learning, and animal behavior. Two major application areas are financial behavior and strategic thinking in games. Recent research includes studying visual salience in economic decisions, and novel neural autopilot and machine learning to understand habits. He has been a leader of academic societies, and served on many editorial boards. He was a MacArthur Fellow in 2013.

Pierre Chandon is the L'Oréal Chaired Professor of Marketing, Innovation and Creativity at INSEAD and the director of the INSEAD Sorbonne University Behavioral Lab. He was a faculty member or a visiting scholar at Harvard Business School, Wharton, Kellogg, and London Business School. He is an expert in food marketing and in the behavioral science of eating. His research shows how epicurean food marketing, by focusing on food as pleasure, not fuel, can help align health, business, and eating enjoyment.

Hengchen Dai (PhD, Wharton) is an assistant professor of Management and Organizations as well as a faculty member in the Behavioral Decision Making area at Anderson School of Management at UCLA. She studies when people are more or less likely to behave in line with their long-term best interests both inside and outside the workplace, and she applies insights from behavioral economics and psychology to steer people toward far-sighted decision making. She has worked with corporations, educational institutions, healthcare systems, and online platforms to conduct field studies that get to the heart of what motivates people.

Saugato Datta is a managing director at ideas42, where he works on the application of behavioral science in low- and middle-income countries in Asia and Africa with government agencies, multilateral organizations, and NGOs. His current work spans bureaucratic behavior, education, labor markets, agriculture, and social protection. He has also worked on public health and resource conservation. Before joining ideas42, Saugato was an economics correspondent at the *Economist*, and a researcher at the World Bank. Saugato has a PhD in economics from the Massachusetts Institute of Technology and undergraduate and Master's degrees from Cambridge University and the University of Delhi.

Patricia de Jonge is a PhD candidate in Marketing at the Vrije Universiteit Amsterdam and a behavioral science consultant. She studies the acceptability of (behavioral) interventions, particularly in financial decision making. Previously, she co-founded the Consumer Behaviour Expert team at the Dutch financial regulator AFM.

She is still figuring out how to improve her two daughters' acceptance of her parenting interventions. Spare time is spent hiking or sewing – but she hopes she will never have to sew a face mask again.

Barbara Fasolo (PhD, Boulder, Colorado) is an associate professor in Behavioral Science at the London School of Economics and Political Science. She co-founded and leads the LSE Behavioural Lab. Her research is on improving judgments and decision processes in the presence of risk and trade-offs, with a specific focus on strategic decisions, debiasing, and choice architecture. She has published in leading journals including *Nature*, the *Annual Review of Psychology*, and the *Proceedings of the National Academy of Sciences*. In her leisure time, Barbara enjoys travel, movies, cycling, and most of all espresso.

Daniel Fernandes serves as an associate professor of Marketing at Católica-Lisbon School of Business and Economics, Universidade Católica Portuguesa. In 2013, he obtained a PhD in Marketing at Erasmus University. Daniel's research interest centers on consumers' memory, financial literacy, decision making, and political ideology. He investigates the role of financial knowledge on financial decision making and the factors that explain this relationship, the conditions that facilitate consumers' memory, and how political ideology influences consumers' decisions and behaviors. He was a visiting research scholar at the University of Colorado–Boulder in 2010, and at MIT in 2016.

Alissa Fishbane is a managing director at ideas42, where she uses behavioral science to improve people's decisions and well-being. She has designed, tested, and scaled interventions to improve public safety and justice, financial stability, education, and public health, reaching over 20 million people globally. Her work has been published in *Science*, as well as featured in *NPR*, *Fast Company*, *Forbes*, and *Bloomberg*. She served on the World Economic Forum's Council for the Future of Behavioral Science. Previously, Alissa was managing director of Deworm the World, which she helped grow to reach 35 million children annually, and Latin America director for Innovations for Poverty Action.

Laura Goodyear is a PhD student at the Rotman School of Management, and a research coordinator with Behavioural Economics in Action at Rotman (BEAR). She has a Master of Science in Marketing from Concordia University, where her thesis examined how reminders of resource scarcity impact consumers' decision making. In her spare time, Laura enjoys cooking, learning about wine, and caring for her three pets.

Indranil Goswami is an assistant professor of Marketing at the University at Buffalo, where he teaches Marketing Research. Indranil researches prosocial motivation, incentives, consumer behavior, judgment, and decision making. In his past life, he was a computer science engineer. Indranil enjoys cooking, listening to music, and discussing politics.

Christina Gravert is an assistant professor of Economics at the University of Copenhagen, Denmark and the co-founder of Impactually, a behavioral science consultancy. Her research focuses on why good intentions do not translate into the desired actions and how to design policies that improve health and environmental sustainability. She brings behavioral science to the wild through conducting field experiments all over the world from the Nordics, the US, and South Africa to India.

Rishad Habib is an assistant professor in Marketing at the Ted Rogers School of Management, Ryerson University. She received her PhD in Marketing and Behavioral Science at the Sauder School of Business, University of British Columbia. Her research focuses on encouraging prosocial and sustainable decision making, particularly when such actions are rare. In her spare time, Rishad enjoys reading, painting, running, and hanging out with her cats.

Nandor Hajdu is a psychologist and currently a PhD student at Eotvos Lorant University. His research focuses on behavioral intervention design and the exploration of contextual influences in various intervention scenarios. He is also interested in meta-science and has participated in numerous large-scale replication studies.

David J. Hardisty (PhD, Columbia University) is an associate professor and chair of Marketing and Behavioral Science at University of British Columbia (UBC). He studies consumer decisions about the future, and how to nudge people to make more sustainable choices. He is the co-founder of the Decision Insights for Business and Society (DIBS) research cluster at UBC, and he co-launched the Advanced Professional Certificate in Behavioral Insights at UBC. In his time off, Dave enjoys hiking, gaming, and drinking Belgian-style beers.

Joyce C. He is a PhD candidate in Organizational Behavior and Human Resource Management at the Rotman School of Management, University of Toronto, and an incoming assistant professor of Management and Organizations at UCLA Anderson School of Management. Her research focuses on understanding mechanisms for the continued persistence of gender inequality in labor markets, and what organizations can do to disrupt them. Joyce's research has been published in *Nature Human Behavior*, *Academy of Management Journal*, and *Journal of Vocational Behavior*, and her work has been featured in *Scientific American* and *Harvard Business Review*. In her spare time, she enjoys running, hiking, bullet journaling, and baking an assortment of breads.

Claire Heard (PhD, King's College London) is a LSE Fellow at the London School of Economics and Political Science. Her research focuses on investigating how choice architecture (e.g., choice of format, language, and layout) and decision context can impact the decisions we make. A particular focus of her research in this area has investigated risk perception, risk communication, and decision making within the public health and emergency response domains. Beyond academia, Claire has a keen musical interest, having played the piano for 23 years.

Michelle C. Hilscher is a vice president at BEworks, heading the Discovery and Behavioural Diagnostics team and holding a leadership role in the BEworks Research Institute. She holds a PhD in psychology from the University of Toronto and previously worked as a research associate at Cortex, a governance consulting firm that provides advisory services to institutional investors. Michelle has experience and expertise spanning behavioral science and business, with interests in decision making, emotion, communications, consumer and user experience, board governance, group decision making, and strategic planning. At BEworks, Michelle leads projects in a number of sectors, with a strong interest in behavioral finance.

Tanjim Hossain (PhD, Princeton) is a professor of Marketing and Economics at the Department of Management–UTM and Rotman School of Management at the University of Toronto, where he serves as the chair of the Department of Management–UTM. He is also a chief scientist with Behavioural Economics in Action at Rotman (BEAR). His research interests are field and lab experiments, applied microeconomic theory, and auctions. His non-research interests are reading, reminiscing about traveling, and listening to traditional Irish and Western classical music.

Chaning Jang is Busara's chief executive officer. Dr. Jang has been a PI or co-PI on a number of field and lab experiments in Kenya, and multiple other geographies across Africa and Asia. His research explores how psychological and biological processes shape both human behavior and poverty alleviation efforts. Since Dr. Jang joined Busara in 2012, he completed a PhD in Economics at the University of Hawai'i at Manoa and postdoctoral research at Princeton University. Dr. Jang has a BS in Managerial Economics from UC Davis, and is a US Chartered Financial Analyst (CFA) level II charter holder.

Sonia K. Kang (PhD, University of Toronto) is the Canada Research Chair in Identity, Diversity, and Inclusion and an associate professor of Organizational Behavior and HR Management at the University of Toronto. She is a faculty research fellow at the Rotman School of Management's Institute for Gender and the Economy (GATE) and chief scientist, Organizations in Behavioural Economics in Action at Rotman (BEAR). Sonia's research explores the challenges and opportunities of identity, diversity, and inclusion and harnesses behavioral insights and organizational design to disrupt systems, processes, and structures that impede diversity, inclusion, and justice for individuals, organizations, and society.

Krisztian Komandi is a consultant and behavioral designer at Frontira Strategic Design. His background includes work at the Behavioural Insights Team in Manchester, regular consulting on behavioral science projects with startups, government organizations, NGOs, and businesses, as well as lecturing in applied behavioral science at Szechenyi Istvan College and Moholy-Nagy University of Art and Design.

Nicola Lacetera is a professor at the University of Toronto, chief scientist at the Behavioural Economics in Action at Rotman (BEAR) research center. He also serves as the PhD coordinator for the Strategic Management Area at Rotman. Among other affiliations, he is a research associate at the National Bureau of Economic Research and a faculty associate at the University of Toronto Centre for Ethics. His research concerns the ethical constraints and social support of markets, the motivations for altruistic behavior, and various topics in industrial and innovation economics.

Jessica Lasky-Fink is a PhD candidate at the University of California, Berkeley. Her research focuses on leveraging insights from behavioral science to improve government programs and services, especially for low-income populations. She holds a BA in Political Science and a MA in International Economics and Development. In her spare time, she enjoys traveling, hiking, and watching nature documentaries.

Ada Lê is a vice president at BEworks, leading the Ideation and Design Lab and innovative projects primarily in the healthcare, retail, and financial sectors. She earned a PhD in Cognitive Neuroscience from the University of Toronto and was a postdoctoral research fellow at York University. Her academic research, published in leading journals, examined how the human brain integrates complex dynamic information and impacts decision making and behavior. At BEworks, Ada applies this understanding towards issues across the business landscape, leveraging knowledge of how new information integrates with existing knowledge about the world to influence behavior to solve organizational challenges.

Elizabeth Linos is an assistant professor of Public Policy at UC Berkeley, and the co-director of The People Lab. Her research combines insights from behavioral science with theories of public management to support the people of government and the communities they serve. Prior to this role, Linos was the VP and head of research for the Behavioral Insights Team (BIT) in North America, where she worked with cities across the US to design and test improvements to service delivery. Linos holds a PhD in Public Policy from Harvard University and, as a parent of young children, has no interesting hobbies to share.

Mario Macis is a professor of Economics at the Johns Hopkins Carey Business School, affiliate faculty at the JHU Berman Institute of Bioethics, and research associate at the National Bureau of Economic Research. He studies the role of incentives and nudges in prosocial behavior, attitudes towards morally contentious exchanges, and other topics in health, development, labor, and organizational economics. He served as committee member or consultant for the World Bank, the National Marrow Donor Program, the United Nations Development Program, and the National Academies of Sciences. When not working, he enjoys hiking, soccer, the opera, and watching Quentin Tarantino movies.

Nina Mažar (Dr. rer. pol. University of Mainz) is a professor of Marketing at Boston University's Questrom School of Business, and co-founder of BEworks. With her focus on behavioral science, she examines ways to help individuals and organizations make better decisions and increase societal welfare. When not working, Nina enjoys randomly bursting into song and staging impromptu musicals with her daughter.

Rafe Mazer is a project director of the Consumer Protection Research Initiative at Innovations for Poverty Action. For more than a decade, Rafe has worked with governments, financial service providers, and researchers to leverage behavioral research to develop more effective financial consumer protection. Rafe's work has focused in particular on new financial technologies in emerging markets and the risks they raise for consumers. Rafe has worked with partners across Africa, Asia, and Latin America, resulting in numerous changes to consumer protection laws and product innovations that better protect users of digital financial services.

Katherine L. Milkman (PhD, Harvard) is the James G. Dinan Professor at The Wharton School of the University of Pennsylvania, host of Charles Schwab's behavioral economics podcast *Choiceology*, and former president of the international Society for Judgement and Decision Making. Katy is the co-founder and co-director of the Behavior Change for Good Initiative and author of *How to Change: The Science of Getting from Where You Are to Where You Want to Be*. She has worked with dozens of organizations on how to spur positive change, including Google, the US Department of Defense, the American Red Cross, and Morningstar.

Marc Mitchell is a father to four. He is also an assistant professor at Western University, where he specializes in chronic disease prevention and management. Mobile health interventions are his current research focus. As principal behavourial insights advisor at Carrot Insights Inc., makers of the Carrot Rewards app, he tested the impact of carefully designed financial health incentives in Canada. He is currently applying lessons learnt from this Canadian experience in the development of a new digital health initiative in the UK. His work has been featured in the *Globe & Mail*, the *Guardian*, CNN, and the CBC. Marc played professional football in the Canadian Football League for three years.

Kelly Peters is the CEO and co-founder of BEworks. After earning her MBA at Dalhousie and driving innovation in the dot-com industry for several years, Kelly transitioned to financial services and became a pioneer in the application of behavioral science, leading perhaps the world's first commercial applications of behavioral field experiments. Today, Kelly leads one of the world's largest behavioral science teams, solving challenges in diverse sectors around the globe, and, through her speaking and writing, shares her vision for the transformative impact of behavioral insights and scientific thinking for the economy and society to influential academic and industry audiences.

Elena Reutskaja is an associate professor of Marketing at IESE Business School (Spain). Elena's research interests lie at the intersection of behavioral decision making, marketing, and economics, with special focus on choice overload, choice architecture, and individual and group decision making, as well as neuro-marketing. Elena employs various methods in her research, including decision process tracing methods from mouse tracing and eye tracking to emotion recognition and brain imaging. Elena was also named one of the "40 Best Business Professors under 40" by *Poets & Quants*. She serves as a behavioral expert and advisor for a number of organizations in both the private and public sectors.

Jason Riis (PhD, University of Michigan) is the CEO and chief behavioral scientist at Behavioralize, a consultancy that he founded in 2018. His consulting work has helped Fortune 500 companies, startups, and non-profits develop and test initiatives inspired by behavioral science. Jason was a postdoctoral research fellow for Nobel laureate Daniel Kahneman and spent over a decade as a full-time faculty member at Harvard Business School and the Wharton School, where he remains an affiliate as a senior fellow at Wharton's Behavior Change for Good Initiative. Jason is passionate about behavior change related to health, wellness, and technology.

Carly D. Robinson (PhD, Harvard) is a postdoctoral research associate at the Annenberg Institute at Brown University. Her research interests sit at the intersection of education, psychology, and policy. In particular, she draws on insights from behavioral science and social psychology to design and experimentally test interventions that improve social support for students. Carly's current work focuses on improving teacher-student relationships, mobilizing family engagement, and increasing the accessibility and effectiveness of tutoring. In her free time, Carly enjoys reading fiction, outdoor activities, and rooting for New England sports teams.

Renante Rondina is a postdoc at Behavioural Economics in Action at Rotman (BEAR). He received his PhD at the University of Toronto, where he used eye tracking and MEG to study the cognitive neuroscience of memory and aging. Becoming interested in behavioral economics, he started a Mitacs Elevate postdoctoral fellowship at Western University, where he worked with Carrot Insights Inc. Currently, he is interested in applying behavioral insights to preventative health, with a focus on digital health and mental health. In his spare time, he and his wife like to cook, travel, and hang out with their dogs.

Jon Roozenbeek is a postdoctoral fellow at the Cambridge Social Decision-Making Lab at the University of Cambridge. His research focuses broadly on misinformation, conspiracy theories, online extremism, and vaccine hesitancy. As part of his work, he has developed several interventions that help reduce susceptibility to misinformation, including the online "fake news" game *Bad News*. Jon's doctoral dissertation (University of Cambridge, 2020) examined media discourse in conflict zones, particularly the "People's Republics" of Donetsk and Luhansk in eastern Ukraine. His work has received numerous distinctions, including the Frank Prize in Public Interest Communications and the Brouwer Trust in Science Award.

Neela A. Saldanha is an independent consultant, working at the intersection of behavioral science and development. She consults with non-profit organizations, has taught courses on behavioral science at Ashoka University–India, and writes on behavioral science, dignity, development, and the Global South. She was recognized by *Forbes* magazine as one of "Ten Behavioral Scientists You Should Know." Previously, Neela was the founding director of the Center for Social and Behavior Change at Ashoka University, which is funded by a grant from the Bill and Melinda Gates Foundation. In addition to her social sector experience, Neela has 15 years of private sector marketing, strategy, and consumer insights experience across multinationals in India and the US. She has an MBA from the Indian Institute of Management (IIM), Kolkata, and a PhD in Marketing (Consumer Behavior) from The Wharton School, University of Pennsylvania.

Anisha Singh is Busara's director for research and innovation. Her research focuses on the mechanisms and behaviors that contribute to gender differences and accurate measurement of key indicators. She leads the development and implementation of academically rigorous research and building of methodologically tested tools that enhance capacity to conduct quality research. Prior to joining Busara, Anisha managed a portfolio of field experiments with IFMR LEAD in India, expanding financial access, opportunities, and capabilities. Anisha holds an MSc in Social Cognition: Research and Applications from University College London, and a BSc in Economics from the Singapore Management University.

Michael Sobolev (PhD) is a behavioral scientist and technologist. Michael specializes in behavioral design of technology and behavioral data science. He completed his PhD in Behavioral Science from the Technion–Israel Institute of Technology in 2017. Over the last five years, he has continued his training and research as a postdoctoral fellow in Computer and Information Science at Cornell Tech in New York City. His current research focuses on behavior change technology, digital and mobile health, and recommender systems. Besides academic research, Michael leverages behavioral science and information technology to develop products that improve human productivity, health, and well-being.

Dilip Soman is a Canada Research Chair in Behavioural Science and Economics at the Rotman School of Management, University of Toronto, and the project director of the "Behaviorally Informed Organizations" initiative. He has degrees in behavioral science, management, and engineering, and is interested in the applications of behavioral science to welfare and policy. He is the author of *The Last Mile* (2015) and co-editor of *The Behaviorally Informed Organization* (2021), both for University of Toronto Press. His non-academic interests include procrastination, cricket, travel, and taking weekends seriously.

Barnabas Szaszi is an assistant professor at Eotvos Lorand University. His research mainly focuses on the methods and application of behavioral interventions improving the health, wealth, and happiness of vulnerable populations while he takes an interdisciplinary approach, leveraging theory from social psychology and behavioral economics. Barnabas also consults with companies, local governments, and NGOs to conduct behaviorally informed field experiments and has been awarded several research awards, including the Fulbright scholarship at Columbia University.

Piyush Tantia is chief innovation officer and a board member at ideas42, a social enterprise that uses insights from behavioral science to invent fresh solutions to tough social problems. As ideas42's founding executive director until 2018, he transitioned the organization from a research initiative at Harvard University to an independent 501(c)(3) non-profit. Prior to joining ideas42, Piyush was a partner at leading consulting firm Oliver Wyman. Piyush serves on the advisory board for the Master of Behavioral and Decision Science program at Penn, has been a visiting lecturer at the Princeton Woodrow Wilson School, and frequently lectures at other top universities.

Cassie Taylor is a vice president at ideas42, where she focuses on applying and scaling behavioral insights in postsecondary education. Prior to joining ideas42, Cassie managed the Behavioral Economics and Decision Research (BEDR) Policy lab at Carnegie Mellon with Professors George Loewenstein and Saurabh Bhargava. She also has experience working in consulting and startups. She holds an AB in Psychology from Princeton University and an MS in Education Technology and Applied Learning Science from Carnegie Mellon University. She enjoys backpacking, quilting, and board games.

David R. Thomson is a vice president at BEworks, leading the Experimentation and Choice Architecture team and projects in the financial and energy sectors. After earning his PhD in Experimental Cognitive Psychology from McMaster University, he was a postdoctoral fellow at the University of Waterloo, a Natural Sciences and Engineering Research Council of Canada Visiting Fellow at Defence Research & Development Canada, and a Canadian Institutes for Health Research Banting postdoctoral fellow at the University of Toronto. David's research on human memory, attention, and perception has been widely published in peer-reviewed journals.

Elizabeth Tipton is an associate professor of Statistics at Northwestern University, a faculty fellow at the Institute for Policy Research, and the co-director of the Statistics for Evidence-Based Policy and Practice Center. Her research focuses on the design and analysis of randomized trials, especially issues of generalizability and treatment effect heterogeneity, as well as methods for meta-analysis. Much of her work focuses on the fields of education and psychology, though she has also contributed to methods in economics and medicine.

Oleg Urminsky is a professor of Marketing at the University of Chicago Booth School of Business. He teaches courses on using experimental methods to improve decisions. Oleg does research on consumer decision making, including financial decisions, incentives, fundraising, and purchase behavior. Prior to becoming an academic, Oleg worked in political polling and advertising research. He enjoys snowboarding and bicycling.

Sander van der Linden, PhD, is a professor of Social Psychology in Society and Director of the Cambridge Social Decision-Making Lab at the University of Cambridge. He has won numerous awards for his research on human judgment and decision making, including the Rising Star Award from the Association for Psychological Science (APS) and the Sage Early Career Award from the Society for Personality and Social Psychology (SPSP). His research is regularly covered by popular outlets such as the *New York Times*, NPR, and the BBC. Before joining Cambridge, he held academic positions at Princeton, Yale, and the LSE.

Peeter Verlegh is a professor of Marketing at Vrije Universiteit Amsterdam. His research and teaching is focused on consumer behavior and marketing communication, with an emphasis on brands and social interactions among consumers (e.g., word of mouth, social media). His favorite brand is Van Moof, his favorite social interactions are bouldering and visiting local alternative music gigs, and his favorite consumers are his two daughters.

Katherine White is a professor of Marketing and Behavioral Science and senior associate dean, Equity and Diversity at the UBC Sauder School of Business. She holds a professorship in Consumer Insights, Prosocial Consumption, and Sustainability and is academic director of the Peter P. Dhillon Centre for Business Ethics. Kate's research focuses on how to encourage prosocial and sustainable consumer behaviors. Kate is the co-author of the *Elusive Green Consumer* in *Harvard Business Review* and over 50 published research articles. In her spare time, she hangs out with her husband, twin daughters, and exuberant husky, Roxy.

Marcel Zeelenberg is a professor of Behavioral Research in Marketing at the Vrije Universiteit in Amsterdam, and a professor of Economic Psychology at Tilburg University. He studies emotions in relation to decision making, the psychology of greed, and financial behavior. Marcel likes to think about how he could be a better and nicer person. During the coronavirus pandemic he grew a beard.

Jiaying Zhao is the Canada Research Chair in Behavioural Sustainability and an associate professor in the Department of Psychology and the Institute for Resources, Environment and Sustainability at the University of British Columbia. Dr. Zhao received her PhD in cognitive psychology from Princeton University. She uses psychological principles to design behavioral solutions to address financial and environmental sustainability challenges. Specifically, she designs effective behavioral interventions to alleviate poverty, promote individual actions to mitigate climate change, increase recycling and composting rates, and encourage biodiversity conservation actions.